An Introduction to Old Frisian

History, Grammar, Reader, Glossary

Rolf H. Bremmer, Jr.

University of Leiden

John Benjamins Publishing Company

Amsterdam / Philadelphia

TM The paper used in this publication meets the minimum requirements of
American National Standard for Information Sciences — Permanence of
Paper for Printed Library Materials, ANSI Z39.48-1984.

Library of Congress Cataloging-in-Publication Data

Bremmer, Rolf H. (Rolf Hendrik), 1950-
    An introduction to Old Frisian : history, grammar, reader, glossary / Rolf H. Bremmer, Jr.
        p. cm.
    Includes bibliographical references and index.
    1. Frisian language--To 1500--Grammar. 2. Frisian language--To 1500--History. 3. Frisian
        language--To 1550--Texts. I. Title.
    PF1421.B74   2009
    439'.2--dc22   2008045390
ISBN 978 90 272 3255 7 (Hb; alk. paper) / ISBN 978 90 272 3256 4 (Pb; alk. paper)
ISBN 978 90 272 9004 5 (Eb)

John Benjamins Publishing Co. · P.O. Box 36224 · 1020 ME Amsterdam · The Netherlands
John Benjamins North America · P.O. Box 27519 · Philadelphia PA 19118-0519 · USA

Table of contents

Preface   ix

CHAPTER I

History: The when, where and what of Old Frisian   1
> The Frisians. A short history (§§1–8); Texts and
> manuscripts (§§9–14); Language (§§15–18);
> The scope of Old Frisian studies (§§19–21)

CHAPTER II

Phonology: The sounds of Old Frisian   21

A. *Introductory remarks* (§§22–27): Spelling and
    pronunciation (§§22–23); Axioms and method (§§24–25);
    West Germanic vowel inventory (§26); A common
    West Germanic sound-change: gemination (§27)

B. *Ingvaeonic/North Sea Germanic sound-changes* (§§28–35):
    (1) Nasalization and rounding of long and short *a* before
    nasals (§§28–29); (2) Loss of nasal before voiceless fricative
    plus compensatory lengthenig (§§30–32); (3) Fronting of
    WGmc *ā* (§§33–35)

C. *Proto-Frisian sound-changes* (§§36–71): (4) Development of the
    West Germanic diphthongs *au, *ai and *eu (§§36–38);
    (5) Fronting of WGmc *a > PFris *æ (§§39–41); (6) Palatalization
    and assibilation of velar plosives (§§42–44);
    (7) *I*-mutation (§§ 45–47); (8) Breaking (§§48–50); (9) Labio-velar
    mutation (§§51–53); (10) Loss of intervocalic -*h*- and
    contraction (§§54–57); (11) Loss of unstressed prefix *ga-/*gi-
    (§§58–59); (12–13) Grimm's Law and Verner's Law (§§60–64);
    (14) Metathesis of *r* (§§65–67); (15) Loss of final -*n* (§§68–70);
    End of Proto-Frisian changes (§71)

D. *Overview of the origin of Old Frisian phonemes* (§§72–78):
    Short vowels (§§72–73); Long vowels and diphthongs (§§74–76);
    Consonants (§§77–78)

CHAPTER III

Morphology: The inflections of Old Frisian   53
    Word-classes, case and number, gender, verbs (§§79–82)
A.   *Pronouns*: Definite article and demonstrative
      pronouns (§§83–86); Personal pronouns (§§87–91);
      Possessive pronouns (§92); Interrogative pronouns (§§93–94);
      Relative pronouns (§95); Indefinite and impersonal
      pronouns (§96)
B.   *Nouns*: Classification (§§97–98); Weak nouns (§99);
      Strong nouns: masculine (§§100–102), neuter (§§103–104),
      feminine (§§105–07); the *i*-declension (§108);
      the *u*-declension (§109); Minor declensions
      (athematic and other) (§§110–113)
C.   *Adjectives*: Declination (§114); Strong declension (§115);
      Weak declension (§116); Comparison of adjectives (§§117–118);
      Irregular degrees of comparison (§§119–20); Comparison of
      adverbs (§121)
D.   *Numerals*: Inflection (§§122–123); Cardinals and ordinals (§124);
      Miscellaneous numerals (§125)
E.   *Verbs*: Types and features (§§126–127); Strong verbs (§§128–130);
      Class I (§131); Class II (§132); Class III (§133); Class IV (§134);
      Class V (§135); Class VI (§136); Class VII (§137);
      Weak verbs, two classes (§138); Class 1 (§139–140);
      Class 2 (§141); Preterite-present verbs (§§142–148);
      Anomalous verbs (§149)
F.   *Summary and Paradigms*: Verbal inflections: infinitives (§150);
      Various inflections (§151); Strong verbs (§152);
      Weak verbs: Class 1 and 'to have' (§153); Class 2 (§154);
      General remarks (§155)

CHAPTER IV

Lexicology: Word formation and loan words in Old Frisian   87
A.   *Word formation and affixation* (§§156–157): Nouns:
      Agentive suffixes (§158); Abstract suffixes (§159);
      Concrete suffixes (§160); Adjectival suffixes (§161);
      Adverbial suffixes (§162); Prefixes (§163);
      Linking morphemes (§164)
B.   Compounding (§§165–168)
C.   *Loan words* (§169): Celtic (§170); Latin (§§171–173);
      Continental languages (§174); Loan translations (§175)

CHAPTER V

Syntax: The sentence elements of Old Frisian   97

A.   *Concord* (§§176–77)

B.   *Cases* (§178): nominative (§179); accusative (§180);
      genitive (§181); dative (§182); prepositions and their cases (§183)

C.   *Verbs*: Mood (§184): indicative (§185); subjunctive (§186);
      imperative (§187); infinitive (§188); Tense (§189):
      simple present (§190); simple preterite (§191);
      compound tenses (§192–195); Voice (§196)

D.   *Word Order* (§§197–198)

E.   *Various Constructions* (§199–203)

CHAPTER VI

Dialectology: The faces of Old Frisian   109

      Diversity and uniformity (§204): Old Weser Frisian (§205);
      Old Ems Frisian (§206); Old West Frisian (§207–211);
      Word-geography (§212); Methodology (§213)

CHAPTER VII

**Two Long-standing problems: The periodization of Frisian
and the Anglo-Frisian complex**   119

A.   How 'Old' is Old Frisian? (§§214–219)

B.   The Anglo-Frisian Complex (§§220–225)

Reader   129

Glossary   187

Glossary of names   220

Bibliography   221

Index of forms in chapters on grammar   229

Preface

The aim of this book is given in the title: it claims to be an introduction to Old Frisian. The need for such a book has long been due, especially one that is written in English since the last introduction to Old Frisian in that language appeared in the late nineteenth century. It is true, Thomas Markey's *Frisian* (1981), a general survey of the language with much attention for the medieval period, is still available, but it lacks, for example, texts and a glossary. All other introductory books on Old Frisian are in German. Bo Sjölin's concise survey *Einführung in das Friesische* (1969), which devotes a considerable part of its contents to Old Frisian, offers neither texts nor glossary and is out of print. Likewise out of print is Paolo Ramat's *Das Friesische. Eine sprachliche und kulturgeschichtliche Einführung* (1976), which is particularly helpful for the historical and linguistic background. Ramat also offers a few small texts with grammatical comments, but his book lacks a grammar and glossary. Finally, Walter Steller's *Abriß der altfriesischen Grammatik* (1928) is the only book that is to some extent comparable in outline to the present one, but again has been long out of print.

The reason for writing *An Introduction to Old Frisian* is clear: Old Frisian is an independent, if small, branch of Germanic. In this language has been preserved a relatively large and interesting corpus of legal texts of mainly Germanic customary law. In addition, a scattering of specimens of other genres has survived which helps fill in our knowledge of the cultural interest of the literate medieval Frisians. The Old Frisian language has especially been studied for its linguistic importance: its vocabulary is often archaic in comparison to that of the contemporary neighbouring languages, its phonology and morphology frequently present problems of relative chronology and reordering, problems which also regard the position of Old Frisian within the West Germanic context, especially its close relation to English. Moreover, from a sociolinguistic point of view, it is fascinating to see how the language (with greater or lesser success) tried to cope with the pressure exercised on its speakers and writers by Low German from the east and south, and by Dutch from the west.

The book has been arranged in such a way as to afford students who first come to the language sufficient information for reading the texts on their own and for gaining an adequate insight into the variety of text genres and shapes of Old Frisian. Having completed this book, the road is open to further independent reading and study. The grammatical chapters are intended first of all to supply the necessary knowledge for reading the texts. Moreover, an effort has been made to supply material that will be of use to the advanced student who is interested in the earliest period of the Frisian language and/or in comparative Germanic linguistics. This material usually appears in small print. Serving two masters is a dangerous endeavour: some may think that what is being offered here is too much, while others would have wished for more.

The structure of the book is as follows: a general historical introduction provides the necessary background information on the history of the medieval Frisians, their language, their literature and the relevance of Old Frisian studies (Chapter I). Chapter II begins with an outline of the most important Old Frisian sounds, and is followed by those sound changes which have given Old Frisian its individual shape from West Germanic to c.1200, the time from which the earliest manuscripts survive. Chapter III surveys the inflectional and conjugational system of Old Frisian. It is perhaps wisest for those who want to proceed to reading the texts quickly to begin with this chapter: §§83–85; §§87–93; §95; §§99–100; §§103–105; §§138–141; §§115–117; §§152–154. Cross-references in Chapter III to relevant sound changes explained in Chapter II will help to understand seemingly disturbing deviations from the 'normal' patterns. From here on, the student may proceed to the discussion of the strong and weak verbs, and so on. Chapter IV provides an insight into the various aspects of the Old Frisian vocabulary, while Chapter V presents those syntactic features of the language that are helpful in reading the texts. Chapter VI presents an overview of the most important dialectal features of Old Frisian. Chapter VII, finally, discusses two problems that have moved many pens: the periodization of Old Frisian and the relation between (Old) English and (Old) Frisian. The texts in the Reader are given in an ascending degree of difficulty. It has been my aim to provide texts from a wide variety of manuscripts and an equal variety in subject matter. For didactic purposes the language of the first texts has been regularized somewhat in order to speed up familiarization. The explanatory notes provide comments on language and contents. All forms occurring in the Reader have been included in the glossary, but no references have been made there to the specific texts in which they occur, for reasons of space. The bibliography, finally, speaks for itself. However, students who have become still more curious should consult my *A Bibliographical Guide to Old Frisian*, which offers a full analytical bibliography of Old Frisian studies up to 1992. For surveys and concise discussions of various important topics relating to Old Frisian, I have regularly referred to the encyclopaedic compendium by Horst H. Munske (ed.), *Handbuch des Friesischen/Handbook of Frisian Studies* (2001), with contributions in both German and English. *Altfriesisches Handwörterbuch*, the new concise dictionary of Old Frisian by Hofmann and Popkema (forthcoming 2008) will also prove to be of great profit to the discipline in comparison to Hofmann's make-shift revision of Holthausen (1925/1984).

An advantage of having written this *Introduction* is that it has given me the opportunity to look afresh at language and literature alike. Therefore, what is presented in this book is not merely a rehash of existing grammars and readers, but a digest of recent developments and interests. I believe that the book offers many new insights and data which will help the student to appreciate the intrinsic value of the Old Frisian language and literature.

I am greatly indebted to Patrick Stiles, who not only encouraged me, some fifteen years ago, to write this book, and indeed has helped me to conceptualize it, but who has also contributed substantially to Chapter II (Phonology) and commented on an almost final version of it. A first draft of the book was used at Harvard University when, as the Erasmus Lecturer in the History and Culture of the Netherlands, I was invited to teach a graduate course on Old Frisian during the Spring Semester of 1994. I would like to thank the participants in this course, in particular Joseph Harris, Daniel Donoghue, Charles Reiss and Jeff Bourns. Revised and enlarged versions have since then been used for Old Frisian courses taught by Philippus Breuker (Leiden), Michiel de Vaan (Leiden), Jarich Hoekstra (Kiel), Anne Popkema (Kiel), Han Nijdam (Amsterdam) and Oebele Vries (Groningen). Their suggestions for improvement have been gratefully included into the present version. My gratitude for advise, comments and help in various matters are also due to Dirk Boutkan (†), Kees Dekker, Daniel O'Donnell, Tette Hofstra, Tom Johnston, Stephen Laker, Henk Meijering, Martina Noteboom, Arjen Versloot, two referees, and, of course, the students of Old Frisian courses whom I have taught myself. I owe a special word of gratitude to Karling Rottschäfer who has obliged me with many points for improvement. It is needless to say that I myself remain responsible for the contents of the final product. The material side of the production was in the able hands of Kees Vaes and Pieter Lamers of John Benjamins Publishing Company.

The present book differs in outline and presentation from all its predecessors. Those familiar with Old English textbooks will detect similarities with such well-known primers and readers as *Sweet's Anglo-Saxon Primer* and *Sweet's Anglo-Saxon Reader*, Albert H. Marckwardt and James L. Rosier's, *Old English Language and Literature*, Bruce Mitchell and Fred C. Robinson's *Introduction to Old English*, Peter Baker's *Introduction to Old English* and Randolph Quirk and C. L. Wrenn's *An Old English Grammar*. Such similarities are not incidental, but stem from my long-time teaching experience with these books. Their inspiration is also gratefully acknowledged here.

Note to the reprint

This reprint has given me the opportunity to make a number of minor typographical corrections and some small stylistic improvements. I am particularly grateful to Tom Johnston, Patrick Stiles and Oeblele Vries for their helpful suggestions.

Rolf H. Bremmer Jr, Leiden

	West Germanic			
...–c.200 AD				
c.200–c.500	Ingvaeonic or North Sea Germanic			
c.500–c.700	Proto- or Common Frisian			
c.700–c.900	Proto-Old South-West Frisian		Proto-Old East Frisian	
c.900–c.1100	Proto-Old South Frisian	Proto-Old West Frisian	Proto-Old Ems Frisian	Proto-Old Weser Frisian
c.1100–c.1550	† (no written records)	Old West Frisian	Old Ems East Frisian	Old Weser East Frisian

Table 1. Periodization of Frisian from West Germanic down to its various branches of Old Frisian (adapted from Århammar 1995: 71). Years are by approximation. Proto-Old South Frisian represents the unrecorded languages as spoken in Holland between the Maas and the Vlie. Not in this table is North Frisian. Island North Frisian developed from Proto- or Common Frision due to emigration of groups of Frisians before 800 AD, while Mainland North Frisian developed from Proto-Old Ems Frisian, as the result of emigration of groups of Ems Frisian around 1000–1100 AD. No written evidence survives of the Old East Frisian branches after c.1450.

Chapter I

History

The when, where and what of Old Frisian

The Frisians. A short history

§1 Today, the Frisian language is used in certain areas along the North Sea coast. To be precise, in the Netherlands: in the province of Fryslân/Friesland (*c.*400,000 speakers, about 75% of its inhabitants). In Germany: in Saterland, immediately south of the present district of Ostfriesland, Niedersachsen (*c.*2,000 speakers), and in the districts of Nordfriesland (*c.*10,000 speakers) and of Pinneberg (Heligoland, *c.*300 speakers), both in Schleswig-Holstein. In both countries, the language has a limited status. In the Netherlands, nevertheless, Frisian is recognized by law as an official language beside Dutch. As a spoken language, it enjoys a relatively healthy existence, owing to a fair-sized number of speakers (comparable e.g., to the number of speakers of Icelandic). As a written medium for all domains of the language, however, its position is weak, threatened as it is by Dutch. For the varieties of Frisian spoken in Germany, the situation is much worse. The fact that it is the language there of mainly agrarian communities which lack the support of a sizeable, well-educated group of speakers and writers has brought about that, sociolinguistically speaking, Frisian functions on the level of a dialect.

§2 The distribution of varieties of Frisian today reflects the outcome of a long historical process. When the Frisians enter history through the works of Roman and Greek authors (notably Tacitus, *Germania*, *Annales* and *Historiae*; Ptolomy, *Geographia*), they appear to live north of the Rhine estuary, up to the River Ems. It was a region just outside the Roman Empire, but the Romans made their influence felt. A number of times the Frisians were forced to pay tribute as subfederates, and, more than once, they rebelled against these attempts to subject them to Roman rule. On the other hand, Frisians served as mercenaries in the Roman legions, witness, e.g., their tribal name on votive stones found in Britain. Archaeological finds from the *terpen* (artificial mounds built to protect the inhabitants from flooding) make clear that trade was intensive between the Frisians and the Romans throughout this period. Whether the Frisians already were a Germanic tribe at the time is a moot point. It has been suggested on account of onomastic indications that they spoke a non-Celtic and non-Germanic, but nonetheless Indo-European dialect, and were only Germanized gradually in the early centuries of the Christian era. However this may be, like English, Dutch and German (High and Low), Frisian is a branch of West Germanic.

§3 With the retreat of the Roman legions from the Low Countries in the early fifth century, documentary information on the Frisians discontinues for more than two centuries. When they reappear in historical sources, they seem to have extended their territory considerably, occupying or dominating the entire coastal districts from the Sincfal, a bay on the south bank of the Scheldt estuary (near Bruges) to the Weser estuary in the north. They were ruled by kings ('war lords'), and their economy was based on cattle-breeding and seafaring. The North Sea being sometimes called the 'Frisian Sea' (*Mare Frisicum*) by contemporary (non-Frisian) sources testifies to their importance as a maritime tribe. In the late seventh century, the Franks began to extend their territory towards the north and first conquered the coastal area between the Scheldt and the Rhine. It was in this part (*Frisia Citerior*) that Willibrord started preaching the Gospel in 690. Both Frankish and missionary activities were temporarily brought to a stand-still during the reign of King Redbad (d. 719), but were renewed soon afterwards. This resulted in Charles Martel ('The Hammer') defeating the Frisians in 734 and establishing Frankish rule as far as the Lauwers. Christianization was also resumed by, amongst others, Boniface (martyred at Dokkum in 754), Liudger and Willehad. The subjugation of the Frisians to the Franks was completed by Charlemagne as a result of his punitive campaign against the combined Frisian-Saxon uprising under the Saxon Widukind. From the reign of Charlemagne dates the earliest Frisian legal codification, the so-called *Lex Frisionum*, drafted in Latin shortly before 800. This (draft) capitulary divides the Frisian territory into three regions: from the Sincfal (in the Scheldt estuary) to the Vlie (today a passage to the North Sea between the islands of Vlieland and Terschelling), from the Vlie to the Lauwers, and from the Lauwers to the lower reaches of the Weser. Of these three, the second region is the Frisian heartland. The late ninth and early tenth centuries saw recurrent Viking invasions in the Frisian lands. The Franco-Frisian port of Dorestad was sacked and plundered several times, and Viking leaders even were allowed by Frankish emperors to rule parts of Frisia, notably in the Rhine and Weser estuaries on the condition that they defended these areas against other Viking invaders. However, the Scandinavian presence never developed into something similar to the Danelaw or Normandy.

The loss of the Frisians' political independence prevented the development of an administrative centre in Frisia which might have provided a fertile ground for literary products. Also, as their conversion had been orchestrated from three different centres, the Frisian territory became divided ecclesiastically among the bishops of Utrecht, Münster and Bremen. These two facts – loss of independence as well as the absence of important secular and religious cultural centres within the Frisian territories itself – will have frustrated the development of a multi-faceted vernacular literature.

§4 With the division of the Carolingian empire at the Treaty of Verdun (843), Frisia was allotted in its entirety to Lotharingia (the Middle Empire), but the Lotharingian kings gradually lost their grip on the region. After the Treaty of Meerssen (870), Frisia was allotted first to West Francia but soon afterwards to East Francia. Owing to the fact they had switched quite frequently between the various Frankish kingdoms within a fairly short period of time, the Frisians succeeded in regaining some degree of independence within the Holy Roman Empire. Their natural habitat was to their advantage in this effort, secluded as it was from the inland regions by extensive marshes and peat-moors. To all intents and purposes, theirs was the only region within the Frankish sphere of influence to have escaped the full implications of the feudal system. Frisia between the Vlie and the Ems during the eleventh century owed allegiance to the counts of the (Saxon) Brunonian house, while in the twelfth century Frisia west of the Lauwers was nominally ruled by the counts of Holland. With decreasing success, both countships tried to maintain their authority over the Frisian lands (*terrae*). For some time, too, Frisia west of the Lauwers was jointly ruled by the counts of Holland and the bishops of Utrecht, the so-called Condominium (1165–1256). By the close of the thirteenth century, the counts of Holland had conquered Frisia west of the Vlie, a conquest begun around 1100. The clearest textual witness to the supremacy of the count of Holland over Frisia between the Vlie and the Lauwers is presented by the opening section of the *Skeltanariocht*, which describes in detail on what conditions the count should come to Frisia on his yearly itinerary. In East Frisian texts, the *greva*, or 'count', never figures as a political reality in the administration of the lands east of the Lauwers. In 1345, Count William IV of Holland was defeated and killed at the Battle of Staveren (frequently referred to as the Battle of Warns) in a dramatic attempt to reestablish his power in Frisia west of the Lauwers. East of the Lauwers, the political picture after 1100 is less clear, but they were mainly Saxon counts who tried to establish their rule in the East Frisian regions, if in vain. Hence, the Saxons often appear in Old East Frisian texts as the arch-enemies of the Frisians.

§5 After the turn of the millennium, the construction of dikes and the reclamation of land from sea gradually made the earlier way of living on *terpen* redundant because the population became less dependent on the tides of the sea. Moreover, the inland marshes and moors were being artificially drained and developed into arable land. These new water engineering techniques required a high degree of social and political organization. In the course of the twelfth century, the structure of power in the Frisian lands became based on a loose federacy or league of the so-called Seven Sealands. Its members convened annually at the *Upstalsbam* (Du. *Opstalsboom*), a natural elevation in the landscape and traditionally the place of general meetings in Brokmerland, not far from present-day Aurich. There is little evidence of the league having produced legal documents before 1300. The *Superior Statutes* ('*Urkera*') could be one such document (see §13, no. 6). The league was given a renewed and more formal shape by the *Statutes of the Upstalsbam* (1323), drafted in Latin. The renewed federacy, however, was short-lived. Significantly, there is no sign of these statutes having been translated into Old East Frisian. The Old West Frisian versions suggest that more importance was attached to these statutes there than in the East Frisian lands. Much more than sharing the same language, or partaking in the same political union, the Frisians distinguished themselves from neighbouring tribes by a shared legal tradition.

Frisian society in the High Middle Ages was socially stratified into three estates: *bellatores, oratores* and *laboratores*. However, unlike in much of Europe, the Frisian aristocracy was not made up of a feudal nobility, but consisted both of allodial landowners (called *nobiles, potentes* or *divites* in contemporary Latin sources and *ethela* or *rika* in Old Frisian) who lived off the income of their landed properties and of freeholding peasants who farmed their own, hereditary lands (called *einervad* lit. 'own inherited', so not in lease or in feudal tenure). Both groups considered themselves not subject to any feudal overlord but owing allegiance only to the king (i.e., the emperor of the Holy Roman Empire). Hence they called themselves 'Free Frisians' implying that they were exempt from feudal obligations. They administered the Frisian lands according to a communal system that was inspired by that of the emerging cities outside Frisia. Instead of a single ruler exercising authority, judicial decisions were taken at periodical meetings (called *thing* or *werf*) in which each free man had a vote. Judges were chosen from among their ranks and rotated annually. The absence of a monopoly of power, where it continued until the end of the Middle Ages (see §6), implied a continuation of the early medieval vengeance culture. When all attempts at reaching a reconciliation in court had failed, vendetta remained the only option to regain injured honour for a party. This situation explains the abundance of regulations concerning the organization of feuding expeditions and the long lists of compensations for physical and immaterial injuries (on the latter, cf. Bremmer 1998) in relation to a person's *wergeld* ('man compensation'), i.e., the value of someone's life expressed in money in relation to his position in society (e.g., Text VII).

The church in Frisia, too, had its own legal courts (*sineth* or *send* 'synod') in which especially matters of immoral conduct, such as adultery, abortion, neglect of Sunday observance, sacrilege or offences against clergymen were judged. The church was the channel through which a new stream of rules and decrees ('canons') joined the native tradition. In absence of the bishop, the *send* was presided by the dean, who, west of the Lauwers, had to be 'free and Frisian', fully consecrated and the son of a layman born in wedlock. East of the Lauwers – and this was unique – the dean (or 'provost' as he was called) was a layman and his office was often passed down from father to son. Again unique was the right of laymen to found a church on their land without first asking the bishop's permission, as long as they donated sufficient land to maintain a priest and a church. From 1150 onwards, members of the Frisian elite also actively participated in the founding of monasteries.

Finally, to the third estate belonged the half-free (*letar*) and unfree (*unein*), lease-holders (*hereman*), farmhands (*heine*, PL), maids *to ku and querna* 'for cow and quern', skippers, pedlars and, towards the end of the Middle Ages, most inhabitants of the emerging towns. For all of the three estates, then, we find legal provisions in proportion to the importance credited to them.

§6 Some noble families, however, gradually extended their influence and assumed the title of *haudling* (*capitanus, -eus* 'captain' or 'chieftain'). In the fifteenth century, the Cirksena dynasty consolidated their power in the lands between the Ems and the western border of the Bremen diocese and in 1464 Ulrik Cirkesena was created the hereditary count of East Frisia. With the by then Low German-speaking port of Emden as their capital, the Frisian language was abandoned there in administrative matters in favour of Low German. As a consequence, the Frisian laws were translated into Low German and partly maintained their force in that region in an adapted form until the introduction of the Napoleonic code in 1809.

Rüstringen, Astringen and Wangerland ceded their communal rights to the *haudling* Edo Wiemken and his descendants, while the last of this line, Maria of Jever, bequeathed her rights to the (Saxon) Counts of Oldenburg in 1575.

From about 1400 onwards, the Low German speaking Hanseatic city of Groningen extended its economic sphere of influence to the Frisian lands surrounding it (the 'Ommelanden'), between the Lauwers and the Ems. Their lack of any central political body worked against the highly individual Frisian lands, so that Groningen also imposed its political will through a policy of 'divide and rule' at the expense of the Frisian independence. As a result, the Frisian language ceased to be used for any kind of writing in the Ommelanden by the middle of the fifteenth century. Translated into Low German, the ancient laws remained in force in this region until c.1600 (Johnston 2001b).

§7 West of the Lauwers, internal strife amongst the Frisians likewise led to political disintegration. From the early fifteenth century onwards, a decades long and violent struggle between two factions resulted in virtual anarchy. Often, these factions – known as *Skier* 'Grey' and *Fet* 'Fat'; the former, according to tradition, grouped around the Cistercian monasteries whose monks wore grey habits, the latter around influential chieftains who prided themselves in their 'fat' cattle – asked non-Frisian powers, such as the city of Groningen, to support their position. Eventually, in 1498, Duke Albrecht of Saxony was invoked to establish order. As a result, the last of the Frisian lands lost its independence. In 1504, the traditional laws, which had already largely given way to Roman and canon law, were declared invalid and replaced by Saxon regulations. In a fairly short time, Frisian as the administrative language was replaced by Dutch mixed with Low German, first by the Saxon Chancery language, because the Duke of Saxony appointed administrators from Dresden to manage his affairs in Leeuwarden. After the Habsburg ruler Charles V had acquired both Frisia west of the Lauwers and the city of Groningen with its Ommelanden (as well as the rest of the Low Countries) around 1525, the administrative language became a southernly coloured Dutch, as from then on (until the revolt of 1568) the central government of the Low Countries resided in Brussels.

§8 The fate of the North Frisians was somewhat different. What is North Frisia now had not yet been inhabited by Frisians in the Roman period, but was colonized by them later in two successive waves. Frisians traders and farmers first settled the islands of Heligoland, Sylt, Föhr and Amrum and some other ones that have since been swallowed by the sea, probably following the trade route to Scandinavia (Haithabu and Ribe), some time in the late seventh or early eighth century. From where in Frisia they came is a moot point; in any case, their origin cannot be established linguistically. The assumption therefore is that at the time of the departure of what became the Island North Frisians, Proto-Frisian had not yet developed into its various distinctive dialects (cf. Århammar 2001a).

The marshy lands of mainland North Frisia were reclaimed much later – after 1000 (because of the diking technique), but before *c*.1200 (when they are mentioned by the Danish author Saxo Grammaticus). On account of certain dialect features these settlers hailed from the region where Old Ems Frisian was spoken. They were probably invited by the Danish king, as their reputation as water engineers stretched all over the Low German Plain. For centuries onwards, North Frisia belonged partly to the Danish kingdom and partly to the Duchy of Schleswig.

Texts and manuscripts

§9 Apart from just under twenty runic inscriptions dating from about 500 to 800 A.D. (ed. Quak 1990; cf. Page 2001) as well as some stray words in Latin texts (Nielsen 1994), the earliest Frisian text to survive in manuscript dates from *c*.1200. It concerns a fragment of a Latin Psalter with interverbal Frisian glosses (ed. Langbroek 1990). On linguistic grounds, the glosses are thought to derive from Fivelgo (north-east of the city of Groningen). The oldest entire Frisian manuscripts to have come down to us are the First Brokmer Codex (B1),[1] written on internal textual evidence after 1276 but not later than 1300, and the First Rüstring Codex (R1), dated on paleographical grounds to *c*.1300. Whereas the former manuscript contains only one text, the latter is a miscellany of mainly legal texts. However, it cannot have been the first attempt at compiling an Old Frisian manuscript. Some of the texts contained in it are not original for more than one reason: the scribe must have had more than one exemplar before him when he compiled his anthology, as appears on one occasion from his including

---

1.   For a key to the sigils with which the Old Frisian manuscripts are referred to, see §14.

two different versions of the same text (*Prologue to the Seventeen Statutes and Twenty-four Land-laws*, Text IV). When, where in Frisia, and at whose instigation these law codes were written down is not (yet) certain. The fact that the vernacular was preferred over the Latin – the traditional administrative language – suggests a time when jurisdiction had become a local affair without too much interference from distant, non-Frisian rulers, perhaps not long after 1225. Indicative for a well-established canon of texts by 1300 is the inclusion in R1 of the most important of the 'pan-Frisian' legal documents: the *Seventeen Statutes* (Texts V, VIa, VIII), the *Twenty-four Land-laws* (Texts Id, VIb) and the *General Register of Compensations* (Text Ic, VII). Like R1, all other medieval Frisian manuscripts produced east of the Lauwers are collections of legal texts, the latest one being the Fivelgo Manuscript from *c.*1450. The only exception is the *Brocmonna Bref* (Text XI), a set of legal regulations drafted around 1276 by the colonists of a district newly reclaimed from marshland. It is clear, though, that the contents of the *Brocmonna Bref* are connected to and supplement the regulations of the Emsingo district, from where the reclamation activities had been organized.

§10 Law and language proved so closely connected that no other text genres in Frisian have survived in independent manuscripts from the Frisian districts east of the Lauwers, with the exception of the glossed psalter fragment mentioned in §9. What little evidence remains of the existence of non-legal genres is usually contained in the legal collections themselves and in one way or another such texts can usually be associated either with legal matters or with historiographical accounts related to the 'Matter of Frisia'. They comprise short items, such as *The Five Keys to Wisdom* (Text II), *The Fifteen Signs of Doomsday* (Text III), and *The Ten Commandments* (Text IV). Religious texts from this area, in as far as they have come down to us, are written in either Latin or Middle Low German/Middle Dutch. A few Frisian charters and administrative documents with an East Frisian provenance survive, but it seems that here the position of Frisian had become so marginal after 1400 that it never stood a fair chance when the language of charters changed from Latin to the vernacular: Low German had already gained a higher prestige or, perhaps more importantly, proved more accessible to a larger public. In the lands between the Lauwers and the Ems, we find no original Frisian texts written after *c.*1450. From the late fifteenth until the end of the sixteenth century, there was an explosive reproduction of Old Frisian material in Low German translation in this area. Compared to the extent of the survival of Old Frisian manuscripts, the Low German corpus of manuscripts is enormous. The impulse for this multiplication of Low German law texts was highly ideological: the (now Low German speaking) 'Frisian' Ommelanden demarcated their special, independent position in this way with respect to the 'Saxon' city of Groningen. Ideological texts were borrowed especially from west of the Lauwers, but most of these – except perhaps such texts as *Rechten ende Wilkoeren* ('Rights and Statutes') and the *Excerpta Legum* ('Extracts of the Laws') – were probably never in use in legal practice. On the other hand, law texts stemming originally from the Ommelanden themselves (Vredewold, Langewold, Humsterland, Hunsingo, Fivelgo and Oldambt) were still used (especially as reference works at the regional courts or *werven*) throughout the sixteenth century. The vast majority of these local texts have survived only in Low German but were certainly translated from Old Frisian exemplars now lost (e.g., Johnston 1998b). Notwithstanding the fact that Frisian was given up in these regions so many centuries ago, the Low German spoken there in modern times still displays many traces of Frisian, especially in place-names and personal names as well as in vocabulary and in syntax (E. Hoekstra 2001; Scheuermann 2001).

§11 For Frisia west of the Lauwers, the heartland of the Frisian territory, the diversity and quantity of texts is somewhat greater. Besides some major legal manuscripts, well over one thousand charters and other administrative documents survive in Frisian (Vries 2001b). Also in this part of Frisia only, it seems, a number of chronicles of various length were produced, as well as texts with legendary matter; they provide a welcome change in genre (Texts XVII, XIX). The poetry that survives is of a historiographic nature and devoted to the 'Matter of Frisia'. Examples are *Fon alra Fresena Fridome* (Text XVI; although surviving in an Old East Frisian form, the original was composed west of the Lauwers), *Hoe dae Fresen Roem Wonnen*, and the long verse narrative *Thet Freske Riim*. Some texts appear in prosimetrum (i.e., half prose, half poetry), such as the semi-historiographical, semi-legal *Book of Rudolf* or some of the wedding speeches that fortunately survive in a Basle manuscript and testify to vernacular preaching in Frisian during the later Middle Ages (Text XVIII). Bible translations, whether whole or partial (with the exclusion of the *Ten Commandments*, Text IV) are signally absent, as are liturgical and devotional monuments. One will also look in vain for lyrical poetry or romances.

After Dutch had become the written medium for the administrators appointed by the Duke of Saxony, shortly after 1500, Frisian ceased to be used for official documents and correspondence, in a movement from higher to lower bodies of administration. By 1540, the production of Frisian documents had virtually come to a halt. A charter from 1547 drafted in Frisian is a last gasp of the language as a public medium. Only in the early seventeenth century do we see a hesitant attempt in this area to find a place for written (and printed) Frisian again.

Frisia west of the Vlie, in the area now made up by the provinces of North- and South-Holland, gradually (from south to north) had to give way around 1100 to a new name: Holland, under the rule of the counts of Holland. By 1300, the counts had managed to subject all of the former Frisian territory up to the Vlie. However, until today the northernmost part of North-Holland is still called (somewhat confusingly) 'West-Friesland', a testimony to a different reality in the past.

§12 No Frisian vernacular documents survive from the erstwhile Frisian district between the Scheldt and the Flie. Whether and to what extent Frisian was spoken as far south as the Scheldt estuary remains a scholarly debate. Fact is that the Frankish conquest of the southernmost part of early medieval Frisia brought along a shift of language. Gradually, the area where Frisian was spoken was pushed back to the north, and it is to be assumed that south of the line between Haarlem and Amsterdam the inhabitants had given up speaking Frisian in favour of Low Franconian (Dutch) by 1000. Vestiges of Frisian in this area survive in isolated words, in certain syntactic phenomena and in place-names. A complicating factor is the moot question whether such remnants are really Frisian or should rather be seen as Ingvaeonic (or North Sea Germanic) traits that were shared by the coastal Frankish dialect (Bremmer 2008b). In the area to the north of the line Haarlem–Amsterdam, Frisian remained in use much longer, perhaps even up to 1600 in certain remote pockets. This is also evidenced by a strong Frisian substratum in its local dialects today (Versloot 2003). However, no written medieval Frisian from this area survives.

§13 Many Old Frisian texts are older than the manuscripts in which they survive. Although it is often hard to say with absolute certainty how old certain texts are, there is consensus that at least parts of some legal regulations (e.g., *Seventeen Statutes*) reach back into Carolingian times. Whether these older law texts were originally drafted in Latin or immediately in Frisian has been and still is a matter of much debate. In the lands neighbouring on Frisia, no vernacular law texts are known from before 1200.

Below follows a survey of the most important texts, listed according to their (estimated) relative age. The list is much indebted to Sjölin (1969: 9–15), Munske (1973: 98–105) and Johnston (2001a), but may deviate from these sources when these scholars put a date much before 1200. Most of these texts listed below appear in the collective editions of individual manuscripts in the dual language series *Altfriesische Rechtsquellen* by Buma and Ebel, and others (1963–1977) (see §14). Mention is therefore made here only of monograph editions of individual texts.

1.   The *Seventeen Statutes* and *Twenty-four Land-laws* (or *Customary Law Regulations*). These are the earliest and most widely distributed of the legal texts. Their respective numbers were fixed probably in the early decades of the thirteenth century, when they were written down in Frisian. Whether some or all of these statutes and land-laws were first drafted in Latin or immediately in the vernacular is a matter of debate. The *Land-laws* were collected somewhat later than the *Statutes*. The contents of some of the *Statutes* were drafted during the late eleventh century, the *Land-laws* sometime between the early twelfth and the mid-thirteenth centuries. The recensions of these texts differ considerably from manuscript to manuscript. A synoptic edition of the *Seventeen Statutes* with commentary, translation and glossary: Hoekstra 1940.

2.   *The Elder 'Skeltanariocht'.* Compilation of instructions for the legal administration of West Lauwers Frisia, particularly concerning the duties of the *skelta*, the most important legal magistrate. Drafted *c.*1200 with older elements. Editions: Steller 1926, with commentary and glossary; Fairbanks 1939, with commentary and English translation. Breuker 1996, a fourteenth-century Middle Dutch translation with commentary and background articles.

3.   *General Register of Compensations*, so called as opposed to the many local such registers. The *General Register* survives only in Old East Frisian texts, but on account of passages from it in local Old West Frisian registers it must also have been known in the lands west of the Lauwers. The register contains a listing and qualification of injuries and the concomitant compensations. Its money system is basically Carolingian. Late-nineteenth-century scholars dated the text to the eleventh century, but if so it must have been in Latin. In all likelihood, it was written down in Frisian in the (early?) thirteenth century. The *General Register* is unique for the Germanic *wergeld* system in its size and detail. Even more detailed are a number of regional registers of compensations. Edition: Nauta 1941 (excluding F), with commentary and glossary.

4.   The *West Lauwers 'Sendriocht'.* A collection of instructions for ecclesiastical jurisdiction (*send* = synod), compiled during the thirteenth (?) century, but in part containing much older, perhaps even ninth-century elements, in view of, for example, the unlimited application of ordeals and the mention of baptizing pagans. Edition: van Buijtenen 1953.

5.   The *Legend and Statutes of Magnus.* As these *Statutes* contain elements from other texts such as the *Elder 'Skeltanariocht'*, they probably date from the later thirteenth century. The legendary leader Magnus seems to have entered the Frisian scene early in the same century.

6.   *The Superior Statutes ('Urkera').* These statutes, ranging in number from five to seven, have usually been linked with the League of the Upstalsbam (§5), a political movement active east of the Lauwers from before 1200 until into the early fourteenth century. With varying degrees of success, this league aimed at creating greater coherence among the Frisian districts. The *Urkera*, so-called because they were supposed to prevail over any other Frisian law, probably date from the thirteenth century.

7.   *Exceptions ('Wendar') to the Seventeenth Statute.* Cases in which the defendant was not allowed to swear an oath of innocence. The extant versions differ markedly. Date of origin: early thirteenth century?

8.   *Exceptions to the Sixteenth Statute.* Cases in which the defendant was not entitled to compensate his crime with money. The extant versions differ markedly. Date of origin: early thirteenth century.

9.   *The Eight Dooms ('Decrees').* A short collection of jurisprudence on matrimony, minority, guardianship, leasing of property and succession. Perhaps early thirteenth century.

10.   The *Younger 'Skeltanariocht'*. Jurisprudential extension of the *Elder Skeltanariocht*. Late thirteenth century. Edition: Van Klaarbergen 1947, with commentary and glossary.

11.   *The Book of Rudolf*. An imaginative compilation in prose and poetry of historiographical narrative, native law and canon law, attributed to a (spurious) Emperor Rudolf, with an ideological agenda of propagating the 'Frisian Freedom'. Drafted thirteenth century. Edition: Bos-Van der Heide 1937, with grammar. Fragments: Gerbenzon 1961.

12.   *Fon Alra Fresena Fridome*. Poetic version of the (spurious) Latin *Privilege of Charlemagne*. Composed late thirteenth century. Edition: Sipma 1947, with commentary.

13.   *Prologue to the Seventeen Statutes and Twenty-four Land-laws*. A treatise on the divine and secular origins of law. Date: *c.*1250.

14.   The *Hunsingo Statutes* of 1252. Regulations concerning penal, procedural and civil law from the Hunsingo District. Edition: Simonides 1938, with commentary.

15.   The *Brocmonna Bref*. Detailed legal regulations for the newly reclaimed Brokmerland, surviving in two, slightly deviating versions. Drafted between *c.*1250 and 1300. Edition: Buma 1949a, with glossary.

16.   The *Emsingo Book of Compensations*. A collection of penal and civil law from the Emsingo District. Drafted thirteenth or early fourteenth century.

17.   *Haet is Riocht?* A catechism on the essence and purpose of law, influenced by Roman and canon law, of which exits a shorter and a longer version. Drafted thirteenth or early fourteenth century. Synoptic edition of shorter version: Buma/Gerbenzon 1963: 29–40.

18.   The *Statutes of the Upstalsbam*. Regulations intended for entire Frisia, drafted in Latin during a general assembly at the Upstalsbam in 1323. All Frisian versions originate from west of the Lauwers. Edition: Meijering 1974, with commentary and glossary.

19.   *Processus Judicii* or 'Procedure of Justice'. A guide for legal procedure based on Roman and canon law, translated from the *Summa 'Antequam'*. Drafted fourteenth century.

20.   *Autentica Riocht*. Regulations excerpted from mainly Roman and canon law. Date: *c.*1400. Edition: Brouwer 1941, with commentary and glossary.

21.   *Excerpta Legum*. A collection of Roman and canon law, extant in four recensions. The most complete of these is known as *Jurisprudentia Frisica*. Drafted fourteenth century. Edition: Buma/Gerbenzon 1993; commentary: Gerbenzon 1956.

22.   *Old Frisian Wedding Speeches*. Three short speeches, written *c.*1445. Edition: Buma 1957, with commentary and glossary.

23.   *Thet Freske Riim*. A historiographical narrative in verse on the early (legendary) history of the Frisians. Before 1490. The poem was also translated into Middle Dutch as *Tractatus Alvini*. Edition: Campbell 1952, with commentary and glossary.

24.   *Gesta Fresonum*. A fifteenth-century Frisian translation of the early (?) fourteenth-century *Historia Frisiae* in which the highlights of Frisian history are paralleled with those of the Old Testament. Edition: Buma/Gerbenzon/Tragter-Schubert 1993.

25.   *Snitser Recesboeken*. A collection of mainly 'police' records of petty crimes brought before the burgomasters and aldermen of Sneek (Frisian: Snits), running from 1490 to 1517. Edition: Oosterhout 1960. No commentary or glossary, only index of names (Oosterhout 1964).

26.   *Charters, Chronicles, Letters*, and other official and private documents mainly from West Lauwers Frisia. About 1300 such documents have survived, the bulk of which was written between 1450 and 1525. The earliest one dates from 1329, the latest from 1547. Editions: Sipma 1927–41; Vries 1977; Gerbenzon 1965, 1967; Meijering 1986.

§14 The majority of the texts listed above have come down to us in more than one manuscript, in versions that often differ markedly from one another. The manuscripts in which they are found are on the whole younger than the date at which the individual texts were (supposedly) drafted. In the complicated process of copying and adapting, the form of the language was usually updated. Most of the manuscripts have received modern editions. The first comprehensive edition, arranged according to texts rather than to manuscripts, is von Richthofen 1840a. His edition is very reliable by the standards of his time and still useful, although he did not include any texts from F, U, Ro, A, P, and Fs (on these sigils, see below). On the other hand, von Richthofen also included medieval Low German law texts that were current in the Frisian lands, and which are often translations of law texts originally written in Frisian. Still very useful, though in places outdated, of course, is his accompanying dictionary to the Frisian texts in his edition (von Richthofen 1840b). Individual manuscripts and charters were diplomatically edited in the series *Oudfries(ch)e Taal- en Rechtsbronnen*, in 14 volumes (discontinued), provided with extensive introductions and Old Frisian–Dutch glossaries (apart from vols. 1–3 and 14 which contain no glossaries, only indexes of names; vols. 4 and 6, which have only word indexes, and vols. 5 and 12–13, with Old Frisian–German glossaries). All Old East Frisian manuscripts as well as the Old West Frisian manuscript J have been edited with a facing German translation in the series *Altfriesische Rechtsquellen* (discontinued). Following the format of the *Altfriesische Rechtsquellen* is the edition of Codex Aysma (Buma/Gerbenzon/Tragter-Schubert 1993). A generous selection of Old Frisian legal texts, including a complete version of the *Brocmonna Bref*, with facing Dutch and Frisian translations and with magnificent illustrations is Vries (2007).

The number of surviving Old Frisian manuscripts is fairly limited and it possible therefore to present here a survey of the most important ones. In Old Frisian studies it has become customary to refer to these manuscripts with a sigil, rather than to the actual shelf mark of the libraries in which they are kept. Sjölin (1966, 1984) has pointed out that the titles given by Buma and Ebel to the individual volumes of their series *Altfriesische Rechtsquellen*, such as **Das Rüstringer Recht** or **Das Emsinger Recht**, are misleading (cf. §213). Only very few of the texts contained in these manuscripts had any explicit relevance for the district from which they stem. Practically all of the collections of legal texts in these manuscripts are of a supraregional nature, with the exception of the *Brocmonna Bref* (B1 and B2). Most importantly, the legal compilations are not to be seen as official laws issued by legislative authorities, but as private collections intended for practical purposes.

An important aspect supporting the collection and survival of the Old Frisian legal codices has been their ideological value (Johnston 1998a). Through such collections of legal texts, of which there must have been dozens of manuscripts, the Frisians as it were demonstrated their independent position within the German (Holy Roman) Empire.

The order in which the manuscripts are presented here is chronological.

B1: The First Brokmer Manuscript or *Brocmonna Bref*, after 1276 but before *c.*1300. Oldenburg, Niedersächsisches Staatsarchiv, Bestand 24–1, Ab. Nr. 3. Editions: Buma 1949a; Buma/Ebel 1965.

R1: The First Rüstring Manuscript, *c.*1300. Oldenburg, Niedersächsisches Staatsarchiv, Bestand 24–1, Ab. Nr. 1. Editions: Buma 1961; Buma/Ebel 1963.

B2: The Second Brokmer Manuscript, completed 1345. Contains the *Brocmonna Bref* in a slightly longer version than B1. Hanover, Niedersächsische Landesbibliothek, Sign. XXII, 1423. Editions: see B1.

R2: The Second Rüstring Manuscript, copied *c.*1780 by Gerhard Oelrichs from a now lost manuscript from 1327. Contents not identical with those of R1. Hanover, Niedersächsische Landesbibliothek, Sign. XXII, 1431. Editions: Buma 1954; Buma/Ebel 1963.

H1: The First Hunsingo Manuscript, *c.*1325–50. Leeuwarden, Tresoar, Hs R2 (R = collection von Richthofen). Editions: Hoekstra 1950; Buma/Ebel 1969.

H2: The Second Hunsingo Manuscript, *c.*1325–50. Its contents are identical with those of H1, but presented in a different order. Also contains Latin versions of several pan-Frisian laws. Leeuwarden, Tresoar, Hs R 3. Editions: see H1.

E1: The First Emsingo Manuscript, *c.*1400. Groningen, Universiteitsbibliotheek, P.E.J.P. Hs. 13. Editions: Sipma 1943; Buma/Ebel 1965.

E3: The Third Emsingo Manuscript, *c.*1450. Its contents are not identical with those of E1 or E2. Leeuwarden, Tresoar, Hs R 1. Editions: Fokkema 1959; Buma/Ebel 1965.

F: The Fivelgo Manuscript, between 1427 and *c.*1450. Also contains some Low German legal texts. Leeuwarden, Tresoar, Hs R 4. Editions: Sjölin 1970–75; Buma/Ebel 1972.

E2: The Second Emsingo Manuscript, after 1450 but not much later. Its contents are not identical with those of E1 or E3. Also contains Low German law texts. Groningen, Universiteitsbibliotheek, P.E.J.P. Hs. 14. Editions: Fokkema 1953; Buma/Ebel 1965.

E4: *Processus Judicii*, copied *c*.1780 by Gerhard Oehlrichs from a now lost manuscript from 1457. Hanover, Niedersächsische Landesbibliothek, Sign. XXII, 1431.
Edition: Buma/Ebel 1965: D.

J: *Jus Municipale Frisonum* (often referred to as 'Jus'), copied *c*.1530, partly from a now
lost manuscript from 1464. Leeuwarden, Tresoar, Hs R 5. Edition: Buma/Ebel 1977.

U: Codex Unia, preserved in transcripts and collations made by Franciscus Junius
c.1660 from a manuscript from 1477 now lost. Oxford, Bodleian Library,
MS Junius 49 (transcripts) and MS Junius 109 (collations in his copy of the
incunable D). Not yet edited as a whole, but individual texts have been edited in
scattered publications.

Ro: Codex Roorda, 1480–1485. Leeuwarden, Tresoar, Hs R 6. Edition (unreliable,
incomplete): De Haan Hettema 1834–35, with Dutch translation. Digital facsimile
edition: 〈http://images.tresoar.nl/wumkes/pdf/HettemaM_JurisprudentiaFrisica
FriescheRegtkennis_1.pdf 〉.

D: 'Druk' or *Freeska Landriucht*. Incunable print, *c*.1485. Nine copies have survived:
(1) Leeuwarden, Tresoar, RAF 2; (2–3) Leeuwarden, Tresoar, 1074 R and A III 31
(FG 2); (4) Utrecht, Universiteitsbibliotheek J. oct 1112; (5) The Hague, Koninklijke
Bibliotheek 150 C 36; (6) Paris, Bibliothèque Nationale, Ms. Néerlandais 45;
(7) London, British Library, Add. MS. 48,951; (8) Oxford, Bodleian Library,
MS Marshall 60; (9) Oxford, Bodleian Library, MS Junius 109. No recent integral
edition, but fairly complete in von Richthofen 1840a. Digital facsimile edition:
〈http://schatkamer.tresoar.nl/landriucht/index.html〉.

A: Codex Aysma, *c*.1500. Oxford, Bodleian Library, MS Junius 78. Also contains
Low German/Dutch texts. Edition (with German translation): Buma/Gerbenzon/
Tragter-Schubert 1993.

P: Codex Parisiensis, 1483–1500. A composite manuscript of four parts, one of which
contains Frisian and Low German legal texts as well as a copy of D (see D.6).
Edition: Gerbenzon 1954.

Fs: Codex Furmerius, *c*.1600. A collection of transcripts made by the Frisian historian
Bernard Furmerius of various documents now lost. Leeuwarden, Tresoar, Hs 1183.
Edition: Buma/Gerbenzon *et al.* 1963.

Texts are also becoming available in digital format. One such opportunity is given on
〈www.wumkes.nl〉, a site that puts digitized facsimile editions of books relevant for
Frisian history on the Internet. Courtesy of the *Deutsches Rechtswörterbuch*, all volumes of the series *Altfriesiche Rechtsquellen* are available at 〈http://www.rzuser.uni-
heidelberg.de/~cd2/drw/ta.htm#afr〉 (see Bibliography: Buma and Ebel 1963–1977).
At the Fryske Akademy, Leeuwarden, a database, which will include all Old Frisian
texts, is under construction and will eventually be made accessible through the Internet 〈www.fa.knaw.nl〉.

Table 1. Distribution chart of multiple version texts. The horizontal numbers in the first row refer to §13, the vertical sigils to §14.

Text no:

↓MS	1	2	3	4	5	6	7	8	9	10	11	12	13	14	15	16	17	18	19	20	21
B1,2															+						
H	+		+			+	+	+					+	+	+						
R1	+		+			+							+[1]								
E1	+		+	+	+	+							+			+					
E2																+					
E3																+					
F	+		+	+	+	+	+	+	+				+	+			+				
J	+	+		+	+		+			+	+	+	+				+[2]				
D	+	+		+	+		+			+	+	+	+				+[2]	+			
U	+	+		+	+		+			+[3]	+[3]	+	+				+[2]	+	+	+	
Ro		+[4]															+[2]	+	+[3]	+[3]	+
A																	+[3]		+[1]	+	+
P																					+[4]
Fs			+[4]								+[4]			+			+	+			

[1] Two redactions. [2] Longer (younger) version. [3] Scattered passages. [4] Only some stray sections. (After Sjölin 1969: 12)

Language

§15 As we have seen, the earliest manuscripts with Frisian texts to have been preserved date back to *c.*1300. Despite the fact that for the contemporaneous neighbouring languages we speak of Middle Dutch, Middle English, Middle Low German and Middle High German, medieval Frisian is traditionally referred to as Old Frisian. This terminology has partly come about through a loose use of the term 'old' in former times in the sense of 'Frisian as it once used to be' (much like 'Ye Olde Englishe Tea Shoppe') which fell together with the threefold temporal distinction in the history of languages ('old', 'middle', 'modern') as advocated by German linguists in the nineteenth century. The earliest Frisian manuscripts, however, show a language which in comparison to Middle Dutch and Middle Low German still displays a number of features, such as a conservative inflectional system and a frequently archaic vocabulary, that justifies the qualification of 'Old'. It should be borne in mind that for the Scandinavian languages of this period we speak likewise of Old Norse, Old Danish, and so on. The problem of periodization is dealt with in some detail in Chapter VII.

§16 Traditionally, Old Frisian is divided into two major dialect groups: East and West. The dialect boundary runs along the river Lauwers, the northernmost part of

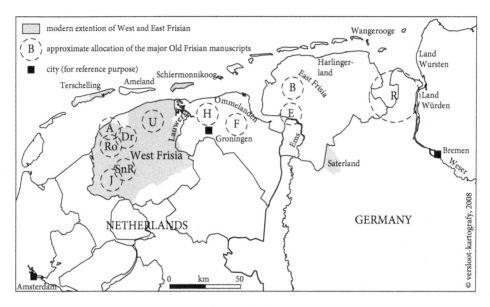

The distribution of the major Old Frisian manuscripts.

the present-day border between the Dutch provinces of Groningen and Friesland (no Old North Frisian texts having survived). According to this division the following manuscripts and fragments – not all of them mentioned in §14 – are written in Old East Frisian (from east to west): R1, R2, R3 (fragment, ed. Holthausen 1936), R4 (fragment, ed. Gerbenzon 1982), E1, E2, E3, E4, B1, B2, F, H1, H2, some four smaller documents from the Ommelanden (Blok 1896–99, nos. 748, 848 [also in Buma/Ebel 1969: B], 948; Alma/Vries 1990) as well as Ommeland fragments of the *Seventeen Statutes* (ed. Bremmer 1996) and of the Oldambt succession law (Alma 2000). A further refinement within Old East Frisian is that of Weser Frisian and Ems Frisian. The former is represented by the language of the Rüstring manuscripts (R1–4) (and its modern descendants, the dialects of Wangerooge, Wursten and Harlingerland, now all dead), the latter by the language of the remaining Old East Frisian manuscripts (and a few seventeenth-century texts from Emsingo, and the modern dialect of Saterland). The other Old Frisian manuscripts all have a provenance from west of the Lauwers, further to be called Old West Frisian. This branch is the ancestor of Modern West Frisian. For further details, see Chapter VI.

§17 The distinction of Old Frisian dialects is based on phonological, morphological and lexical (word-geographical) criteria. An important phonological criterion, for example, has been the development of Gmc *a* before nasal. In Old East Frisian this practically always appears as *o* (e.g., *mon* 'man'), whereas Old West Frisian favours *a* (e.g., *man* 'man').

In 1966, Bo Sjölin levelled serious criticism against this division. First of all, he argued that the traditional names for most of the manuscripts located east of the Lauwers (such as 'The First Emsingo Manuscript') were misleading, since they would rarely contain information to justify such a provenance. The inference philologists had made on the basis of such manuscript names, viz. that the language of such manuscripts consequently represented the regional dialect, Sjölin considered to be unwarranted. Secondly, according to Sjölin, the manuscripts traditionally designated as Old East Frisian were also the earliest manuscripts, whereas the Old West Frisian manuscripts were considerably younger, something which is also reflected in the vocabulary which tends to be more archaic in the East Frisian texts. Moreover, Sjölin demonstrated that in Old West Frisian texts, too, especially in early charters from Oostergo in West Lauwers Frisia (so the area closest to the Lauwers), *a* appeared as *o* before nasals, while some late East Frisian manuscripts, E3 and F, occasionally have *a* before nasal instead of *o*. Most importantly, Sjölin's approach was strictly synchronic, and above all based on a graphemic analysis of the texts, i.e., his conclusions were based on the written forms. Broadly speaking, the difference between what is traditionally known as Old West and Old East Frisian was a matter of different orthographical rather of phonological traditions. He therefore consciously wanted to exclude the possibility of establishing a dialect grouping of Old Frisian on the basis of modern Frisian dialects, which, by backward projection of reconstructed 'old' forms, could confirm what evidence there was of possible dialect features in Old Frisian. These considerations led Sjölin to abandon the dialectal distinction of East and West for the corpus of Old Frisian in favour of a chronological distinction between 'Classical' and 'Post-Classical' Old Frisian (in which the former more or less concurs with Old East Frisian and the latter with Old West Frisian). The language of the some 1000 charters, mainly stemming from Frisia west of the Lauwers, according to Sjölin, were a case in themselves and should therefore not be drawn into the discussion.

§18 Sjölin's far-reaching conclusions received a mixed response, especially from the side of Munske (1973), who demonstrated on word-geographical grounds that the traditional distinction between East and West was wholly warranted. Other scholars have stressed the usefulness of the modern dialects for determining earlier stages of language. In a retrospective article, Sjölin (1984) has clarified and maintained his theory although he also allowed for some mitigation to the extent that a major distinction between Old East and Old West Frisian seems justified to him after all.

However important it is to study the language of a manuscript in its entirety, it is likewise important to remember that most legal manuscripts are made up of individual texts of different dates and provenance. In a number of cases we are dealing with texts in manuscripts with an East Frisian provenance that demonstrably have an origin from west of the Lauwers (e.g., the poem *Fon Alra Fresena Fridome*, Reader Text XVI). For a full discussion of this problem, see Chapter VI.

The scope of Old Frisian studies

§19 Old Frisian has been studied for several reasons (Bremmer 2001; Feitsma 2001; de Haan 2001a: 32–34). In the seventeenth and eighteenth centuries, legal historians became interested in the ancient laws, while philologists such as the Dutchman Franciscus Junius (1591–1677) included Old and Modern Frisian in their comparative studies of Germanic. In particular, the claim from late medieval times onwards that Frisian was very similar to English increased its attraction, and this alleged proximity undoubtedly contributed to the Danish linguist Rasmus Rask (1787–1832) writing the first grammar of Old Frisian in 1825, after he had completed a similar one for Old English. When Jacob Grimm (1785–1863) devoted considerable attention to the Old Frisian language, literature, law and pagan religion in his series of books on aspects of the Germanic legacy (*Deutsche Grammatik, Deutsche Rechtsalterthümer, Deutsche Mythologie*, in which titles *Deutsch* signifies not 'German' but 'Germanic'), Frisian had secured a place in the philological curriculum. One of Grimm's students, Karl von Richthofen (1811–1888) published all of the Old Frisian legal texts available to him then, synoptically whenever possible. This volume was accompanied by a comprehensive dictionary which can still be consulted with profit. From then on, Old Frisian attracted the interest of many a famous Neogrammarian scholar, including the Germans Eduard Sievers, Hermann Paul (the latter invited Theodor Siebs to write the ground-breaking chapter on Frisian in *Grundriß der germanischen Philologie*), the Dutchman Willem L. van Helten, and even occasionally such American linguists as Leonard Bloomfield and Francis Wood. Frisian legal historians have studied the laws from the seventeenth century onwards as part of their own cultural tradition, but linguistic interests started in Frisia itself only in the early nineteenth century (Romantic period). In particular, the fact that especially in the Netherlands, Frisian scholars have preferred to publish the fruit of their work in either Frisian or Dutch, has made their work less accessible today to the international community of students.

§20 On the whole, the main scholarly interest seems to have been in the linguistic aspects of Old Frisian. Yet, the rich array of legal texts, of which the earlier ones display features dating back to the pre-Christian era, have repeatedly appealed to legal historians who, like scholars in related fields, were often looking for vestiges of Germanic paganism and way of life. The lure of the Germanic past has occasioned a relative neglect of later Old Frisian law texts which appear to be heavily influenced by Roman and canon law. Especially in the later Middle Ages, the reception of Roman law and canon law (i.e., decrees issued by ecclesiastical councils and authorities) in Frisia west of the Lauwers was enormous and unparalleled elsewhere in contemporary Western Europe. The change from the traditional, native legal concepts to the modern ones brought along a change in style. The terse, often alliterative and rhythmic prose (cf. Stanley 1984) was replaced by a stricter, more logical phraseology, and the native terminology was frequently abandoned in favour of a more Latinate one (Gerbenzon 1958).

§21   Old Frisian, then, though studied for such a long time, still remains a promising field of study. First of all, of course, as a precursor to the various Modern Frisian dialects. Though most Old Frisian texts have received a modern edition, a comprehensive dictionary of their vocabulary is still wanting, as is an up-to-date full grammatical description of the language. Other attractive problems of Old Frisian could be mentioned: what is the relation of Old Frisian to the other Germanic dialects, Old English in particular, and, one step further, how much Indo-European vocabulary has it preserved? In this respect, the etymological dictionary by Boutkan and Siebinga (2005), based, it is true, on the vocabulary of the First Rüstring Manuscript only, is a welcome start. A comprehensive study of the loanwords in Old Frisian, important for an insight into the cultural contacts of the Frisians through the Middle Ages, is bound to give fascinating results. From a sociolinguistic point of view Old Frisian is interesting, too. In all likelihood, most literate medieval Frisians were multilingual. Beside their native language they had a command (in varying degrees) of Low German, Dutch and Latin. How is this borne out by the texts that survive? What can the texts of mixed Old Frisian/Middle Low German/Middle Dutch tell us of the process of language shift? Vries (1993, 2001a) has well described and analyzed the external history of the disappearance of Frisian from the written scene for West Frisian, but the internal process still remains to be investigated. Syntax and style are much neglected aspects of Old Frisian language studies.

From the point of view of the contents of the laws, it can be said that today too little attention is paid to them in the world of Germanic and medieval studies. The only comprehensive study of, for example, penal law (His 1901) is badly in need of revision. Precisely because the Frisians had no feudal lords, their legal system and often complicated rituals, combined with the ideological discourse of the 'Matter of Frisia' which they construed to legitimize their exceptional position in relation to neighbouring peoples, remains a gratifying field of research.

Chapter II

Phonology
The sounds of Old Frisian

A. Introductory remarks

§22 Since we do not have any 'live' speakers of Old Frisian, its sounds ('phones') must be reconstructed. Such a reconstruction necessarily involves speculation, but on the whole the values of the Old Frisian sounds can be established with some degree of certainty. After all, the orthography of Old Frisian was based on that of Latin, the universal language of learning and writing in medieval Europe. Occasionally, however, scribes encountered difficulties when they were dealing with sounds that had no equivalent in the Latin alphabet, and here they had to be inventive.

§23 As sounds are the smallest components of a language, it is important to know what they are. We distinguish between sounds that change the meaning of a word, and those which do not. The former are called 'phonemes', the latter 'allophones'. Phonemes can be established by finding 'minimal pairs'.[1] For example, the difference between *feld* 'field' and *ield* 'money' depends on the initial sound. We therefore conclude that /f/ and /j/ are different phonemes in Old Frisian. On the other hand, a change in pronunciation does not always alter the meaning. For example, *f* (voiceless) in *hof* 'court' becomes *v* (voiced) when the word is inflected, e.g., *hove* (DAT. SG), without changing the basic meaning of the word. The alteration between *f* and *v* in this pair is therefore not phonemic but allophonic. Phonemes are given between slashes / /, allophones are not. Angular brackets ⟨ ⟩ are used to indicate spelling, while square brackets [ ] indicate pronunciation. We can distinguish between long and short vowels, and long and short consonants. In the notation of the International Phonetical Alphabet (IPA), length is indicated by the symbol ː. Traditionally, for the sake of convenience, length of vowels is indicated by a length-mark ('macron') placed over the vowel. Thus, *hof* 'hoof' in IPA notation is [hoːf], but in traditional notation, as used in this book, it is *hōf*. In 'Classical' Old Frisian, vowel length is not indicated in the manuscripts, but has to be established. Thus, a scribe made no distinction in his written language between *hof* 'court' and *hof* 'hoof (of a horse)'. That we are dealing with a

---

1. For a full survey of the Old Frisian phonemes of the Rüstring dialect established by means of minimal pairs, see Boutkan (1996: 19–20).

different pronunciation of the vowel, *hof* and *hōf*, we know either from our knowledge of the modern reflexes ('descendants') of these words (e.g., ModWFris *hôf* [hɔːf] and *hoef* [huf], respectively) or by comparing these words with cognate ('related') languages (e.g., G *Hof* and *Huf*, respectively). Sometimes, though, vowel length becomes clear because of a special feature in the language itself. This is the case in Old Weser Frisian, by means of its so-called 'vowel balance' (§205.1–2). In late Old Frisian, the length of vowel is often indicated by a following ⟨e⟩ or ⟨i⟩ e.g., *baem* [baːm] 'tree', *wiif* [wiːf] 'wife' (§207).

The situation is different for the consonants, which are usually written twice (doubled or 'geminated') to indicate length.

§24 *Axioms and method*
In much of the remainder of this chapter, attention will be given to the major soundchanges that occurred in the development of West Germanic, by way of Ingvaeonic/North Sea Germanic,[2] to Old Frisian. These changes gave Old Frisian its own, particular shape, distinguishing it from the other West Germanic languages. The period in which these changes took place is called Proto-Frisian (PFris). We do not know exactly at what time these changes took place, but it is possible to establish with a high degree of certainty when most of these changes took place in relation to one another. In other words, we cannot establish their absolute chronology, but their relative chronology can be reconstructed. In this chapter the relative chronology as outlined by Stiles (1995: 199–200; also see Fulk 1998; Nielsen 2001) is followed.

§25 The structure of items ideally include should the following items:
• Process of change (phonetically and phonologically), including implementation in the texts and dialectal differences[3]
• Instances: words affected
• Chronology, including changes which must succeed it
• Phonemicization

---

2.   Ingvaeonic, also known as North Sea Germanic, is a grouping within West Germanic from which Old English, Old Frisian, coastal Old Saxon and coastal Dutch are assumed to have developed. Ingvaeonic is generally seen as a dialect continuum stretching from Flanders along the coast to the German Bight, the varieties of which shared a number of conspicuous linguistic features.

3.   In addition to the various Old Frisian dialects, various modern dialect forms, especially from East and North Frisian, have often been adduced to illustrate certain changes. The following abbreviations for these dialects have been used: for West Frisian: Schierm. = Schiermonnikoog; for East Frisian: Saterl. = Saterland, Wang. = Wangerooge, Wurst. = Wursten; for North Frisian, Islands: Amr. = Amrum; Mainland: Ock. = Ockholm, Hall. = Halligen, Wied. = Wiedingharde, Mor. = Moring. NB. Ostfr. = Ostfriesisch, the Low German dialect spoken in the former Frisian districts there which still contains many Frisian substrate features.

- Research history: who first established the point
- Comments on developments in cognate languages
- Other details connected with the change
- References

Due to the introductory nature of this book, it has not been deemed desirable to have realized all of the above items here. Concerning the research history, for example, bibliographical references to studies published before 1992 have not abundantly been given on account of their being available in an analytical bibliography (Bremmer 1992). Also the appearance of Munske (2001) has made it possible to reduce the number of references. However, the more problematic a change is, the more items from the list above that are included in remarks in smaller print.

§26 *West Germanic vowel inventory*
Our starting point is the West Germanic vowel system in accented syllables:

> Short: *i, e, a, o, u*
> Long: *ī, ē$_2$, ā (< ē$_1$), ō, ū*
> Diphthongs: *eu, ai, au.*

A common West Germanic sound-change

Gemination

§27 An important change that took place still in the common West Germanic period, and hence was also shared by Proto-Frisian, is gemination.

> *Process*: Light-stemmed[4] syllables had their final consonant lengthened ('geminated' or 'doubled'), when it was followed by *j*. This *j* later caused *i*-mutation (§45) and was subsequently lost in all cases.

> *Instances*: e.g., *satjan > *sattjan (> OFris *setta* 'to set'). Only *r* was not geminated, e.g., *swarjan > OFris *swera* 'to swear'. Note that in final position geminates appear as single consonants, e.g., *kunja > OFris *ken* 'kindred', but are retained in inflected forms, e.g., *kenne* DAT.SG.

Remark
Unlike Old English or Old Saxon, Old Frisian also shed the *j* after light-stemmed syllables ending in -*r*: *swera* 'to swear' (OE, OS *swerian*), *nera* 'to save' (OE, OS *nerian*).

---

4.   A syllable is light (also: short) when it has a short vowel and ends in a single consonant.

B. Ingvaeonic/North Sea Germanic sound-changes

(1) Nasalization and rounding of West Germanic long and short *a* before nasal (*aN*)[5]

§28 *Process*
Long and short *a*, when followed by a nasal acquired a nasal timbre [ã(ː)] (as in French *blanc*), and were eventually rounded to [ɔ(ː)].

§29 *Instances*
The words containing *ā* that were affected are limited in number:[6]

kōmen 'they came'	vs MDu	*cwāmen*
mōna 'moon'		*māne*
mōnath 'month'		*mānd*
nōmen 'they took'		*nāmen*
ōne 'except'		*āno* (OS, OHG)
sōn 'soon'		*sān*

The *i*-mutation of WGmc **ā* (< PGmc **ē$_1$*) + N appears in OFris *wēna* 'to think, ween' (< **wōnjan* < **wānjan*), and *dēn* (past ptc. of *dwā* 'to do').

Words containing short *a* that were affected are far greater in number, e.g.:

komp 'field'	vs MDu	*kamp*
lom 'lame'		*lam*
hond 'hand'		*hand*
hona 'cock'		*hane*
long 'long'		*lang*
ongost 'fear'		*angst*
thwong 'force'		*dwang*

The change did not occur in unaccented syllables, but monosyllables in weak stress environments are affected, e.g., *fon* 'of' (< **fan*), *on* 'on' (< **an*).

---

5. Here and elsewhere, N = Nasal and C = Consonant.

6. Not attested for Old Frisian, but evident from modern dialects are: **spōn* 'chip, splinter', cf. ModWFris *spoen*, dial. *spoan*, ModLG [Ostfr.] *spōn(e)* (so a Frisian residue), IsNFris *spuun* [Sylt], MainlNFris *spoon* [Wied.], and **brōm* 'furze; broom' (ModEFris *brom* [Saterl.]).

REMARK
1. The change of *āN* > *ōN* was pan-Frisian as was *aN* > *oN*, but to a large extent in later OWFris *oN* changed back to *aN*, §208.1.
2. *Ondreus* 'St Andrew' (R2) evidences that loanwords could be subjected to this rule much later, since Rüstringen was converted to Christianity only around 800.

(2) Loss of Nasal before voiceless fricative plus compensatory lengthening

§30 *Process*
Before a nasal followed by a voiceless fricative (i.e., /f/, /χ/, /s/, /θ/), the preceding short vowel was nasalized (as, e.g., in French *vin* 'wine'). Afterwards, the nasal disappeared with compensatory lengthening of the preceding vowel.

§31 *Instances*
Here follows an inclusive list of the (Old) Frisian words that were the result of this process:

i + N:
- *fīf* 'five' (cf. G. *fünf*; ModWFris *fiif*)
- *Fīvel* 'river name' (Gmc **fimfla-*)[7]
- *hrīther* 'cattle' (cf. G. *Rind*; ModWFris *rier*)
- *sīth* 'companion' (cf. G. *Gesinde*)
- *stīth* 'strong' (Gmc **stenþia-*)
- *swīthe* 'very' (cf. G. *geschwind*)

o + N (< a + N):
- *bōs* 'cattle-shed, byre', attested as the first element in late OWFris *boes-doer* 'door of ~' (Gmc **band-sa-* 'stand in cattle-shed', related to 'to bind', with early loss of *-d-* in consonant cluster); cf. ModWFris *boas-doar*, ModLG (Ostfri.) *bûsdör*, MainlNFris *bousem*, DAT.PL. [Ock.]; ON *báss*, OE *bōsih*
- *bōste* 'marriage' (Gmc **band-sti-* 'bond', with early loss of *-d-* in consonant cluster)
- *brōchte* 'brought' (Gmc **branhta-*); later shortened to *brocht*
- **gōs* 'goose' (Gmc **gans-*); cf. ModWFris *goes*, MainlNFris *goos* [Wied.]
- *nōth* 'courage', e.g., in the name *Rēdnōth* (< Gmc **nanþa-*); cf. *nētha* below, and ModWFris *noed* 'care, responsibility'
- **ōs(e)* 'hole for a lace' (Gmc **ans-*); cf. ModWFris *oes*, MainlNFris *ous* [Ock.]

---

7. See Holthausen (1934), s.v. *fifel* 'giant, monster'.

- *ōther* 'other' (Gmc **anþera-*)
- *sōth* 'to which one is entitled' (Gmc **sanþa-*)
- *tōth* 'tooth' (Gmc **tanþa-*)
- *thōchte* 'thought' (Gmc **þanhta-*), later shortened to *thochte*

Affected by *i*-mutation (§45) are:
- *ev-ēst* 'envy' (Gmc *af-ansti)
- *hēla* 'heel' (Gmc **hanhila-*)
- *nētha* 'to risk' (Gmc *nanþjan)
- *sēft(e)* 'soft(ly)' (Gmc **sanfti-*)
- *tēi 'tough' (Gmc **tanhi-*); cf. ModWFris *taai*, MainlNFris *toi* [Ock.]
- the plurals *tēth* 'teeth' and *gēs* ⟨ghees⟩ 'geese' (cf. eModWFris *gies*, MainlNFris *gæis* [Ock.])

u + *N*:
- *dūst(slēk)* 'resounding blow' (Gmc **dunst-*)
- *kūth* 'publicly known' (Gmc **kunþa-*)
- *kūde* 'he knew' (< *kūthe < Gmc **kunþa-*)
- *mūth* 'mouth' (Gmc **munþa-*)
- *sūth* 'south' (Gmc **sunþa-*)
- *thūchte* 'seemed' (Gmc **þunht-*)
- *ūs* 'our' (Gmc **unsa-*)

Affected by *i*-mutation (§45):

- *kētha* 'to announce'

REMARK
Loss of nasal before fricatives *without* compensatory lengthening occurred in unaccented syllables, e.g., 3PL.PRES.IND verb endings, e.g., *helpath* < *helpanþ (without rounding of *a*), the ordinal *tegotha*, *tegetha* 'tithe (tenth)' < *tegunþon.

Loss of nasal plus compensatory lengthening resulted in the following contract verbs (§54):

- *hwā* 'to hang' < *hōhan < *honhan < *hanhan
- *fā* 'to catch' < *fuā < *fōhan < *fonhan < *fanhan

§32 *Chronology*
Nasalization took place before fronting of long and short *a* (§§33, 39), otherwise we would expect nasalized long and short *a* also to have been fronted in this position.

a. Some time after this change, the sequence of short vowel plus nasal plus voiceless fricative yields a long nasalized vowel plus voiceless fricative.

b. The development of the uniform present plural for verbs clearly follows (a), and is to be put early for reasons of linguistic geography, as it is also met with in Old English and Old Saxon, but not in Old Low Franconian/Old Dutch.

(3) Fronting of WGmc $\bar{a}$ (< PGmc $\bar{e}_1$)

§33 *Process*
WGmc $\bar{a}$ (< PGmc $\bar{e}_1$) was fronted (or raised) to [æ:], unless it was followed by a nasal in which case it had been rounded (§28).

§34 *Instances*
In Old Frisian, this sound appears in writing as ⟨e⟩, e.g., *skēp* 'sheep', *dēd* 'deed', *hēr* 'hair' (ModWFris *skiep, died, hier* as opposed to e.g., Du *schaap, daad, haar*, G *Schaf, Tat, Haar*). Also early Latin loans in West Germanic (cf. §171) containing $\bar{a}$ appear in Old Frisian with ⟨e⟩ (=$\bar{e}_1$), e.g., *strēte* 'street' (< L *strāta*; Du *straat*, G *Straße*). It seems that L *pālus* was borrowed twice: *pēl* 'pole' (only in B) shows the regular outcome, whereas more frequent *pāl* probably features a MLG/MDu loan form (wood being an import product).

§35 *Chronology*
Gmc **ai* was monophthongized to OFris $\bar{a}$ only after fronting had taken place, because the monophthongization product, i.e., $\bar{a}$, did not undergo fronting.[8]

C. Proto-Frisian sound-changes

(4) Development of the Germanic diphthongs **ai, *au* and **eu*

§36 *Process*
Gmc **au* monophthongizes without exception to OFris $\bar{a}$. On the other hand, Gmc **ai* has monophthongization reflexes in OFris spelled ⟨a⟩ and ⟨e⟩. The question why in some words **ai* developed to $\bar{a}$ and in other words to $\bar{e}$ (probably [æ:]) remains problematic and, in the end, unanswered (Hofmann 1995).[9]

---

8. Cf. Hofmann (1964/1989) on what may be regarded as Ingvaeonic/North Sea Germanic, as well as Århammar (1990: 11), esp. on morphological aspects.

9. Beside the literature mentioned in Bremmer (1992: 145), see van Helten (1890: §22) and Siebs (1901: §§54–59).

Probably at the same time, but not as part of the process, Gmc *eu* developed to a rising diphthong *iā*, unless followed by *i*, which led to *iū* (also found as *iō*).

§37 *Instances*

Gmc *au* > OFris *ā*: *āge* 'eye', *āk* 'also, eke', *bām* 'tree', *bāne* 'bean', *brād* 'bread', *kāp* 'purchase' (< L *caup*-), *lāf* 'leaf', *rād* 'red', *trāst* 'support, encouragement'.

The most frequent outcome of Gmc *ai* is OFris *ē*, e.g., *bēn* 'bone', *brēd* 'broad', *ēr* 'before', *ēre* 'honour', *hēl* 'whole', *hēlich* 'holy', *stēn* 'stone', *wēsa* 'orphan'.

Gmc *ai* > OFris *ā* is found in *āga* 'to have to', *āthum, -em* 'son-in-law', *fāch* 'outlawed', *fād* 'counterfeit', *frāse* 'danger', *gād* 'lack', *gāra* 'skirt, gore', **gāsem* 'armful' (cf. MainlNFris *goasen* 'double handful' [Wied.], *hār* 'honourable' (cf. OE *hār* 'grey'), *klāthar* (PL) 'clothes', *lāre* 'teaching, doctrine', *lāva* (PL) 'legacy, inheritance', *nā* 'no, never', *rāp* 'rope', *tāker* 'brother-in-law', *tāne* 'toe', *thā(m)* DAT.SG/PL of 'he, they', *thā* NOM/ACC.PL of 'the', *twā* 'two', *wāch* 'wall', *wāsande* 'windpipe, trachea', *wrāk* 'crooked'.

Finally, there is a restricted number of forms that show both *ā* and *ē*. They are: *ēfte* (rare) beside *āfte* 'lawful', *ēin* beside *āin* 'own', *(n)ēn* and *(n)ān* '(no) one', *ēnich/ēng* and *ānich/āng* 'any', *ēr(e)st* beside *ār(i)st* 'first', *gāst* 'ghost' beside *gēst* (rare, probably < LG/Du), *hēm* beside *hām* 'home', *klēth* beside *klāth* 'cloth, dress' (both SG), *lēsta* beside *lāsta* 'to perform', *sēver* beside *sāver* 'spittle, saliva'.

When (a) in weakly stressed position, or when (b) shortened before consonant clusters, the Old Frisian product of **ai* can be short *a*:

a. *skeltata* 'legal magistrate' (cf. OE *scyldhāta*, G *Schuldheiss*); *ănne* 'one' ACC.SG.MASC beside *ēnne*, *ărst* beside *ērst* 'first', *ăskia* 'to demand' (< **aiskōjan*), *aththa* 'juror, jury-man' (< **-aiþ-* 'oath'), *famne* 'girl, young woman' beside *fēmne* (cf. OE *fǣmne*), *fat* 'fat' (< Gmc **faita*), *flăsk* 'flesh',[10] *latte* 'led' (pret. of *lēda* 'to lead'), *măst* 'most', *măster(e)* 'master',[11] -*spătze* 'with spokes' beside -*spētze* (**-spaik-*).

b. When subject to *i*-mutation (§45), the monophthongization products of both **ai* and **au* merge as PFris **ǣ⁻* spelled ⟨e⟩. Examples: *hēla* 'to heal' (< **hailjan*), *lēda* 'to lead' (< **laidjan*) and *hēra* 'to hear' (< **WGmc haurjan*), *lēsa* 'to redeem' (< **lausjan*).

---

10.   The only attestation of OEFris *flesc* (H1,2) concerns an editorial emendation of ⟨flecsc⟩ to *flesc*. However, an emendation to *flasc* can be defended on paleographical grounds.

11.   Against an overwhelming majority of *măster(e)* in the Old Frisian corpus, there are only two instances in H (= Reader, Text II) with *mester*. Rather than attributing *măstere* to **maistar-* and *mēster* to **maistir-*, as van Helten (1890: §22γ) does, I suspect Low German influence for *mester*.

c. Gmc *eu (by way of WGmc *eo > *io > *ia >) > iā: e.g., biāda (< *beudan-), liāf (< *leuba-), thiāf (<*þeuba-), liācht 'light, not dark' (< *leuhta-). When followed by an i-mutation factor (§45), the result was iū (iō): liūde/liōde (< Gmc *leudi-), diūre/diōre (< Gmc *deurja-).

§38 *Chronology*
Monophthongization of *ai and *au follows fronting of ā, because the monophthongi-zation product ā does not undergo fronting. OFris ā < *au was also later than round-ing of WGmc ā before nasal, because they do not fall together. Monophthongization precedes i-mutation.

REMARK
The dual outcome of *ai as ā and ǣ is Proto-Frisian, since this outcome is also reflected in North Frisian, cf. Århammar (1990: 22), Hofmann (1995).

(5)   Fronting of WGmc *a > PFris *æ

§39 *Process*
Short a was fronted (or raised) to ⟨e⟩ /æ/ in both closed and open syllables, also when followed by a back vowel.

§40 *Instances*
For example: smel 'small' (< Gmc *smala-), stef 'staff' (<*staba-), thek '(thatched) roof' (<*þaka-), feder 'father' (<*fader), fere 'journey, expedition' (<*farō-), tele 'tale, reckon-ing' (<*talō-), dei 'day' (<*daga-), wein (<*wagna-, §43.c), weter 'water' (<*watar).

Before rC (without preceding w-), a also seems to have been fronted to e, cf. sterk (<*starka-), serk 'tomb' (<L sarcophagus; cf. OHG sarch), erm 'arm (SB); poor (ADJ)' (<*arma-), ers 'arse' (<*arsa-), merch 'marrow' (<*marga-). Problematic, however, are unfronted forms such as garda 'landed property', flarde '(individu-al) lung'.

N.B. Instances where *a was not fronted:

- before nasals in accented syllables, where a had become o (§28): e.g., lond 'land', song 'song'
- in the sequence (-)warC-, e.g., swart 'black', warm 'warm'
- before h(C), e.g., achta 'eight', nacht 'night', fax (< *fahsa-) 'hair', sax 'knife', wax 'wax', slā 'to kill' (< *slahan), tār 'tear' (< *tahru-)
- before lC, e.g., ald 'old', kald 'cold', half 'half', al(l) 'all', halt 'lame', salt 'salt'
- in some unaccented words, e.g., was (nas) 'was (was not)'

REMARK

In Old English, æ (the result of fronting) was retracted when followed by a back vowel, e.g., *stæf* 'staff' ~ *stafas* (PL). The absence of retraction from æ > *a* in Old Frisian is different from Old English. Compare OFris *slā* 'to strike' (Gmc *slahan*) and OE *slēan* (< *slæhan*), OFris *drega* 'to carry' (< *dragan*) and OE *dragan*.

§41 Chronology

On the assumption that breaking is a later change, which seems likely, then *æ, the fronting product of WGmc *a*, did not fall together with WGmc *e* until at least after breaking (§48).

(6)   Palatalization and assibilation of velar plosives

§42 Process

Palatalization involves the partial assimilation of the velar plosives *k* and *g* to adjacent front vowels (though not those front vowels deriving from *i*-mutaion) and /j/. Palatalization and subsequent assibilation took place in Proto-Frisian in accented syllables:

Initially, before front vowels *i and *e:

    a.   *g > j*
           k > k^j > t^j >> ts

In medial position, before *i or *j:

    b.   *-gg-* [gː] > *-gg^j-* > *-dd^j-* > *-dz-* before *j
          -ng- [ŋg] > *-ŋg^j-* > *-nd^j-* > *-ndz* before *j

Finally, after *e:

    c.   *-g > -j*

In order to explain the dual outcome of palatalized *g (i.e., *j* or *dz*), it is usually assumed that *g had two phonetic variants at the time of palatalization. Thus, *j* is thought derive from an earlier fricative [ɣ], and the assibilated variant *dz* from the plosive [g], which existed after *n* (i.e., *-ng-*) and in the geminate *-gg-* (Moulton 1972: 173):

a.   In initial position, the change takes place before front vowels as these existed after fronting of long and short *a* (§§33, 39) and the monophthongization of *ai* and *au* (§36).
b.   In medial position, variously before *i and *j (see above).
c.   In final position, only *g seems to have been affected, and only when following *e (whether original or the result of fronting). There is no palatalization of *g in final position after *i.

The combination *sk-*, whether initial, medial or final, was not affected, e.g., *skip* 'ship', *biskop* 'bishop', *Frēsisk* 'Frisian'.

§43 *Instances*

a.   Initial:

*kībō- > *tsīve* 'quarrel', **kinnu-* > *tsin* 'chin', **keuk-* > *tsiāk* 'cheek', **kerla-* > *tserl* 'man', **geutan* > **ǵiāta* > *iāta* 'to pour', **gelda-* > *ield* 'money', **gasta-* > **gæst* (fronting, §39) > *iest* 'guest';

b.   Medial:

*i: **(hama-)marki* > *hemmertse* 'village common' (once, against frequent *hemmerke*), **bruki-* > *bretse* 'breach, fine', **spræki* > *sprētse* 'speach', **langi-* > *lendze* 'length', **hugi-* > *hei* 'mind';
*j: **dīkjan* > *dītsa* 'to build dikes', **mangjan* > *mendza* 'to mingle, mix', **raikjan* > *rētsa* 'to reach, hand over', **saggjan* > *sedza* 'to say', **skankjan* > *skenza* 'to pour';

c.   Final:

*segla- > *seil* 'sail', **wagna-* > **wægn* (fronting, §39) > *wein* 'wain, cart', **daga-* > **dæg* (fronting) > *dei* 'day', **wega-* > *wei* 'way'.

§44 *Chronology*
Palatalization took place (cf. Stiles 1995: 195–96):

*   after fronting (§§33, 39) of both long and short *a* to *æ*, because palatalization takes place before and after these fronted vowels: **tsēse, tsīse* 'cheese' < **kæsi* < **kāsija-* (< L *cāseus*), *ts(i)etel* 'cauldron, iron pot' < **kætil* < **katila-* (< L *catillus*), **wagna-* > *wein* 'wain, cart'.
*   before monophthongization of **ai*, see Remark 1.
*   before *i*-mutation (§45), or at least before the unrounding of *i*-mutation products to *e*, because no palatalized products are found before mutated vowels: *kening* 'king', not **tsening* < **kuningaz*.

REMARK
1.   Palatalization clearly concerns separate changes in Old English and Old Frisian. Compare OE *ćēap* (with palatalization) and OFris *kāp* (without pal.) – both from Lat. *caupo* – which demonstrates that palatalization took place in each language after changes which are unique to each. Palatalization in Old Frisian is clearly absent before the monophthongization product of **ai* – and must therefore be earlier, as the following inventory of (Old) Frisian words shows:

     gād 'lack' (< **gaidwa-*)
     gāra 'skirt, gore' (< **gairan-*)
     gēr 'spear' (< **gaira-*)

MainlNFris *goasem* 'double handful' [Wied.] (< **gaisma-*)
gāst 'ghost' (< **gaista-*)
gēia 'to transgress; pay compensation' (< **gaigan*, cf. OE *forgǣġan*)
kēi 'key' (< **kaigi-/*kajjo-*)

Moreover, the conditioning factors for palatalization are not entirely the same in Old Frisian and Old English. They seem to differ medially (Århammar 1984: 139), e.g., OFris *tser(e)ke* 'church', *dīk* m. 'ditch', *rīke* 'powerful, rich', beside OE *ċiriċe, dīċ, rīċe*.
2.   Occasionally we find competing palatalized and unpalatalized forms, for example: *rītse* ⟨rize⟩ n. 'riches, property' (< **rīkja-*), beside *rīke, bretse* 'breach; infringement; fine' (< **bruki-*) beside *breke* (cf. OE *bryċe*). Some of these variants find parallels in old English dialects and can be explained as resulting from a process of analogy due to earlier palatalized and non-palatalized forms contrasting with the same nominal (Laker 2007: 182–83). Such forms contrast with the following which never show variation in Old Frisian, such as *lētsa* 'physician' (< **lǣkija-*, cf. OE *lǣċe*), *tiānspatse* 'with ten spokes' (< **-spaikija-*), *bereskintse* -⟨skinze⟩ 'bare-legged' (< **-skunkia-*), adjectival formations like *ētsen* 'oaken, made of oak' (< **aikīna-*) and *letsen* 'made of cloth' (< **lakīna-*), and past participles of strong verbs with the suffix *-ina-*, typical for Old Frisian, e.g., *letsen* 'closed' from *lūka* (Class II), *bretsen* 'broken' from *breka* (Class IV/V). Medial **k* is especially palatalized in weak verbs class 1: *bletsa* 'to denude' (cf. G *blecken*), *dītsa* 'to build dikes' (< WGmc **dīkjan*), *rētsa* 'to reach' (< **raikjan*), *lītsa* 'to equalize, level' (< **līkjan*), **thretsa, thritsa* 'to press' (< **þrukjan*; cf. OE *þryċċan*), *upwretsa* 'to tear up' (<*-wrakjan*).

(7)   I-mutation

§45 *Process*
If followed by *i* or *j* in the following syllable, back vowels were fronted and front vowels were raised. The mutation factor (*i/j*) subsequently disappeared or is retained as unstressed *e*.

- **æ* (the result of *a*-fronting, §39) > *e*
- unfronted *a* > *æ* (both long and short)
- furthermore, *o* > *œ*, *u* > *y* (both long and short)

Sometime by the end of the Proto-Frisian period, the mutation products of *u, o* and *a* were unrounded, which resulted in all the mutated vowels ending up as *e* (both long and short).

§46 *Instances*
The vowels in the left-hand column represent the West Germanic stage.

a.   Short vowels:
   a   **saljan* > **salljan* (gemination, §27) > **sælljan* (fronting, §39) > *sella* 'to sell'. So too: **satjan* > *setta* 'to set'; **badja-* > *bed(d)* 'bed'
   æ   **framjan* > **frammjan* > **fræmma(n)* > *fremma* 'to perform; give'

o   *ele* 'oil' (< L *oleum*)

u   **upin-* > **ypen* > *epen* 'open'; **kussjan* > **kyssa(n)* > *kessa* 'to kiss'; **kuri-* > **kyre* > *kere* 'choice'

The vowels in the left-hand column represent the Old Frisian stage.

b.   Long vowels:

ā   (< Gmc **ai*): **hailjan* > **hāljan* (monophthongization) > **hǣla(n)* > *hēla* 'to heal'. So too: **dailjan* > *dēla* 'to share'

  (< Gmc **au*): **haurjan* > **hārjan* (monoph.) > **hǣra(n)* > *hēra* 'to hear'

ō   (< Gmc **ō*): **blōdjan* > **blǣdjan* > *blēda* 'to bleed'

  (< Gmc **aNC*): **sanfti-* > **sōfti* > **sǣfte* > *sēfte* 'softly'

  (< WGmc **ā*): **wānjan* > **wōnjan* > **wǣna(n)* > *wēna* 'to think'

ū   (< Gmc **ū*): **brūdi-* > **brȳde* > **brēde* > *brēd* 'bride', **fūsti-* > **fȳst* > *fěst* 'fist'

  (< WGmc **uNC*): **kūþjan* > **kȳtha(n)* > *kētha* 'to announce'

c.   Diphthong:

Gmc **eu*:   **beudiþ* > WGmc **biudiþ* > *biu(d)th* 'he offers' (cf. *biāda* 'to offer')

  *leudī- (PL) > WGmc **leudi* > **liudi* > *liūde* 'people'

§47 *Chronology*

Apparently, palatalization of initial velar stops before front vowels preceded *i*-mutation, because palatalization is absent before front vowels that are the result of *i*-mutation. For example, no such forms exist as **tsening* 'king', we only find *kening* (< **kuning-*).

REMARK

As for the products of unrounded *i*-mutated long and short *u*, the exception is Island North Frisian where mutated *u* appears as *i*, e.g., *bridj* 'bride', *fist* 'fist' [Föhr-Amr.]. This is an indication that unrounding (§45) was not yet wholly completed when groups of Frisians left their original homelands to settle on the North Frisian islands (early eighth century).

(8)   Breaking

§48 *Process*

When short *e* or *i* occurred before the velar consonant clusters /χχ/, /χs/ and /χt/, a back glide developed. The outcome is a rising diphthong, usually written ⟨iu⟩, alongside ⟨io⟩.

REMARK

The development can be posited as follows: **i*> *iu* and **e*> **eu*> *iu*. The stage *eu* may well be a virtual one: presumably, WGmc **eu* had already developed to *iā*, so there was no /eu/-phoneme, and [eu] immediately merged with /iu/ of whatever sources.

§49 *Instances*

The following list is comprehensive:

- *tiuche* 'team; parcel of land' (< *tehhō-*), cf. Hofmann (1972–73/1989)
- **miuhs/*miux* 'dung' (< *mehsa-*); ModWFris *mjoks*, ModEFris *mjux* [Saterl.], IsNFris *njoks* [Föhr]
- *tyoxsele* late OWFris DAT.SG 'cleaver, adze' (< **þehsalōn* = G 'Dechsel'); ModWFris *tsjoksel*, ModEFris *thiuksel* [Wang.], MainlNFris *tjuksele* [Mor.] (cf. OE *þeox* 'spear')
- *Briocht* 'bright', only as personal name; ModWFris *Br(j)ucht* personal name (= 'bright' < **breht* < **berhta-*), cf. Miedema (1977). As an adjective it had lost currency before Old Frisian texts were recorded
- *fiuchta* 'to fight' (< **fehtan*)
- *kniucht* 'servant' (< **knehta-*)
- **pliucht*; ModWFris *pjocht* 'fore/aft of deck' [Schierm., 19th c.] (cf. Du *plecht*, G *Pflicht* < **plehta-* < L *plecta* 'wickerwork', and OE *plett* 'hurdle', OE *plihtere* 'lookout man at the prow')
- *riucht* 'right' SB./ADJ. (< **rehta-*) and derivatives
- *siochte* 'disease, illness' (< **suhti-*); ModWFris *sjocht(e)* 'illness', IsNFris *sjocht* 'flu' [Amr.]
- *siuchst, siucht* 'you, he see(s)' 2/3SG.PRES.IND (e.g., < **siht(h)* < **sihiþ* < **sehiþ*); also *siuch!* 'see' IMP.SG (but could be analogical)
- *sliucht* 'equal; slight' (< **slihta-*)
- **spiucht*; ModWFris *spjucht* 'woodpecker' (< **spihta-*)

REMARK

1. Some early grammars claimed that breaking affected only short *i* (van Helten 1890: §§39–40; Siebs 1901: §§23, 28; Steller 1928: §9.3). However, Heuser (1903: §24) suggested '*e* (*?i*)', van Helten (1907: 204–05, s.v. *kniucht*) later changed his mind, and Gosses (1928: 76–77) argued that both *e* and *i* werse broken. Löfstedt (1931: 139) and Campbell (1939: 105) both accepted breaking of *e* and *i*. Cf. also Århammar (1960: 285). The evidence of *thriuch* < **þerh*, which figures in older discussions, is questioned by Hoekstra (2000).

2. Note that old -*ti*-stem abstract nouns like *plicht* 'duty' (< **pleh-ti-*), *wicht* 'weight' (< **weh-ti-*) lack breaking because the consonantism was not velar on account of the following *-i*. This will also explain why amply attested *secht* 'illness' (< **suh-ti*) failed to undergo breaking. However, on *secht*, see also §50, Remark 2.

3. The big exception is 'unbroken' *sex* 'six' (Gmc **sehs*), perhaps on analogy with *sexta* 'sixth' and *sextich* 'sixty', or perhaps because of two *s*'s. Less likely, *sex* is a borrowing from Low German. Note that breaking does occur in OFris **miux* 'dung' (< Gmc **mehsa-*).

4. Does *tsiurke* 'church' show breaking? In all likelihood not (Stiles 1995: 213–14), because breaking is absent in such words as *merk* 'mark', *sterk* 'strong', *werk* 'work', and *serk* 'tombstone' (< **sark* < ML **sarcus* < L *sarcophagus*). The word *tsiurke* presents the only -*rk* environment, therefore, where breaking would have occurred (Steller 1928: §9.1 Anm. 2). The form *tsiurke* is found only in Old Ems

Frisian (and from there in Mainland North Frisian): OWFris *tserke* and Old Weser Frisian *sthereke* both have forms with *e*. The distribution of the various forms of 'church' is suggestive from the point of view of dialect geography: relic forms with monophthongs are found in marginal areas, so that *tsiurke* would be the innovation.

The following is an inventory of all surviving Frisian forms of 'church': ModWFris *tsjerke*, early ModEFris *zierck* [Emsingo], *serk* [Saterl.], *sjiriik* [Wang.], *schiräck* [Wurst., 18th c.]; MainlNFris *schörk* [Wied.], IsNFris *seerk* [Sylt], *sark* [Föhr-Amr.].

5.   The form *liucht* 'light, easy', as given by van Helten (1890: §39, from E1) and circulating in subsequent discussions, is spurious, cf. Sipma's edition (1941) of E1.

§50   *Chronology*

Breaking certainly seems to be Proto-Frisian on the basis of the distribution argument: it is found in all Frisian dialects, cf. Århammar (1990: 22). It must also be later than *i*-mutation, on account of *siucht* 'he sees' (see Remark 1, below). Moreover, breaking must have occurred before weakening of intervocalic -*χ*- to -*h*, again because of *siucht* < **sih(i)th*. Finally, it must have followed metathesis of WGmc **berht* > **breht*.

REMARK
1.   In the relative chronology of Old English sound-changes, palatalization is demonstrably later than breaking as a phonemic change. Breaking might therefore be regarded as the first unambiguously English sound-change. In Frisian, on the other hand, breaking is conventionally dated later than *i*-mutation (Stiles 1995: 194–95).

The form *siucht* 'he sees' (from earlier **sihiþ*) only has conditions for breaking as a result of apocope of the second *i*. It is hard to see how it could be analogical to infinitive *siā* 'to see' (from **se-an*, earlier **sehan*) – in fact, the latter form shows that it is unlikely that breaking predates loss of medial -*h*- because **siuhan* is unlikely to yield *siā*. Besides, the infinitive lacks the conditions for breaking, which took place in a closed syllable, cf. *tiān* '10' (OS *tehan*). NB. IMP.SG *siuch* 'see!' should have regularly developed breaking.

2.   Breaking could be a change that was active a long time in Frisian, cf. the occasional spelling in OWFris *triuchtich* '30' and OWFris *siuchte, siochte* 'disease' (ModWFris *sjocht[e]* and IsNFris *sjocht*) beside earlier attested *secht* (< **suh-ti-*). The occurrence of IsNFris *sjocht* [Amr.], *sjucht* [Sylt] would argue for an early and exceptional instance of breaking in an old -*ti*-stem abstract noun (§49, Remark 2). However, it has been suggested that OWFris *siuchte* and the modern forms would be the result of contamination of *secht* and *siūkte*, a change which must then have taken place independently in West Frisian and Island North Frisian (Århammar 2004: 111–12).

(9)   Labio-velar mutation

§51   *Process*

If followed by *u* or *w* in the next syllable, *i* was diphthongized to *iu* (rising diphthong). The *u/w* was subsequently lost.

§52 *Instances*

The following list is comprehensive:

- *diunk(er)* 'dark' (**dinkwa-*); cf. ModEFris *djunk* [Wang.], MainlNFris *jonk* [Ock.]
- **Iunga*, *Jonge* personal name (< **Ingwa-*)
- **iunk(er)* 'you two', oblique 2nd dual personal pronoun forms (< **inkw-*); IsNFris *jonk* [Föhr], MainlNFris *junk* [Mor.]
- **iukel* 'icicle' (< **jekula-*); ModWFris *jûkel*, ModEFris *(iis-)juukel* [Wang.]
- **iugel* 'gable' (< **gibla-*); IsNFris *jügel* [Sylt], MainlNFris *jöögel* [Mor.], ModEFris *juugel* [Wang.]
- *niugen* '9' (< **nigun* < **newun*); ModWFris *njoggen*, ModEFris *niuugn* [Wang.]
- *siugun* '7' (< **sigun* < **sebun*); ModEFris *siuugn* [Wang.] (§205.9)
- *siunga, sionga* 'to sing' (< **singwan*); ModWFris *sjonge*, IsNFris *sjong* [Föhr-Amr.]
- **siuka* 'to run, trickle' (< **sikwan*); cf. ModLG (Ostfr.) *sjoekzaand* [Gron.], MainlNFris *sjoksand* [Ock.] 'quicksand' (cf. Löfstedt 1931: 139–40, fn. 6)
- **stiunka* 'to stink' (< **stinkwan*); ModWFris *stjonke*, ModEFris *stjúnk* [Wang.]
- *thiukke* 'length and breadth, (thickness)' (< Gmc **þeku-*); ModWFris *tsjok*, IsNFris *sjok* 'thick' [Amr.]

§53 *Chronology*

Labio-velar mutation must be Proto-Frisian because of the distribution pattern of its reflexes, which are found in all the surviving Frisian dialects, cf. Århammar (1990: 22).

REMARK

1.   Phonologized by loss of post-consonantal *w*, it seems, would make labio-velar mutation early, but according to the standard view, at the time of Old English palatalization postconsonantal *w* was retained (cf. Luick 1914–1940: §637 Anm. 4), so also on that basis it must be later than *i*-mutation.

2.   The form *siugun* 'seven' (cf. Gmc **sebun*) is found only in Old Weser Frisian (§205.9).

3.   EFris *sliunger* [Wang.] 'to roll (of a ship on the waves); to saunter, stroll' might be another instance of labio-velar mutation, cf. ON *slyngva* (< Gmc **slingwan*, with frequentative suffix -*er*- in Wang.), but then we must take OFris *slinge, slinger* 'strap; sling' as Low German loans, which also ousted the mutated forms in all other branches of Frisian.

4.   Breaking and labio-velar mutation are actually different changes, because in the former soundchange, the conditioning factor is tautosyllabic (i.e., within the same syllable), whereas in the latter it is heterosyllabic.

(10)   Loss of intervocalic -*h*- and contraction

§54 *Process*

Intervocalic **h* < Gmc **χ* was dropped, resulting by contraction of the preceding and following vowels in either a diphthong or a long monophthong. The outcome particularly led to a number of so-called contract verbs (consisting of one syllable only).

The following combinations were affected:

1. WGmc *-eha- > iā
2. WGmc *-ōha- > uā, as does *-ō-a-
3. WGmc *-aha- > ā

§55 *Instances*

1. *siā* 'to see' < *se-an* < *sehan*; *tiān* '10' < *te-an* < *tehan* [NB. retained final -*n* (§68)]
2. *fā* 'to catch' < *fwā* < *fōhan* < *fonhan* < *fanhan* (§31); *hwā* 'to hang' < *hōhan* < *honhan* < *hanhan* (§31); *dwā* 'to do' < *dō-an*
3. *slā* 'to strike, kill' < *slahan* (the pre-form apparently lacks fronting [§39] of *a*: *slahan* > ⁺*slæhan* would have yielded ***slehan* > ***slean* > ***sliā*); *ā-* 'water' (in compounds such as *āburch* 'water defence, dike') < *aha*; *āra* 'harvest, crop' (pl. of unattested **ār* 'ear of corn' < **ahar*), *tār* 'tear' < **tahar*.

§56 *Chronology*

Loss of intervocalic *h* and contraction must have been later than (a) the merger of PFris *ō* (the result of rounding before nasals, §28) and WGmc *ō*; and (b) the loss of -*i* in final syllables, because *siucht* 'he sees' shows that at that time the value was still [χ] intervocalically (cf. §49, Remark 2). However, the loss of -*h*- is not especially linked to breaking, as the latter change took place in closed syllables.

§57 Medial *h* after the consonant *l* or *r* was lost without compensation. The only two certain instances are *bifela* 'to order' (< **bifelhan*) and *thweres* 'transversely' (< **þwerhes*).

(11)   Loss of the unstressed prefix **ga-/*gi-*

§58 *Process*

Germanic had a prefix **ga-/*gi-*, which has two main functions. First, to signal a perfective meaning for verbs, used especially with past participles. Secondly, when prefixed before nouns and adjectives, it expressed collectiveness, abstractness or accompaniment, e.g., *nāt/nāta* 'companion' (< **gi-nauta(n)*, related to *nāt* 'cattle'). In Old Frisian, after the consonant had been palatalized to [j] (§42), the prefix appears, if at all, in a reduced form as either *e*- or *i*-.

§59 *Instances*

The prefix is not recorded with verbs other than with past participles, and then only infrequently: *edēn* 'done', *e-ifnad* 'levelled', *enēdgad* 'raped', *eskepin* 'created', *escriuen* 'written', *ifestnad* 'fastened'.

Covered positions tended to be favourable towards preserving the prefix: *unidēld*, *unedēld* 'undivided', *unebern* 'unborn' (PAST PTC/ADJ), *unewaxen* 'not fully grown, not yet adult', *ēinebern* 'born unfree, serf' (PAST PTC/ADJ), but instances without the prefix are more common, e.g., *unwald* 'powerlessness, impotence'.

Occasionally, the prefix appears before adjectives, overwhelmingly in covered position: *enōch* 'enough' beside *nōch, unewis* 'uncertain' beside *unwis, unefōch* 'indecent'. No nouns have been recorded with the prefix in uncovered position, e.g., *nāt* 'companion' (cf. OE *ġenēat*, OHG *ginōz*), *fadera* 'godfather' (cf. OE *ġefædera*, OHG *gifatera*).

Since the reduced prefix still occasionally is there in Old Frisian, its loss must have been late.

(12)   Grimm's Law

§60 Before continuing with the discussion of some significant Proto-Frisian consonant changes, attention must be paid to a change in consonants that effected the transition of Indo-European to Germanic. First formulated by the German scholar Jacob Grimm, the change is known as Grimm's Law. This law concerned the development of the stops (or plosives).

§61 *Process*
According to Grimm, (a) voiceless Indo-European stops became Germanic voiceless fricatives: IE *p* > Gmc *f*, IE *t* > Gmc *þ*, IE *k* > Gmc χ; (b) voiced IE stops became Gmc voiceless stops: IE *b* > Gmc *p*, IE *d* > Gmc *t*, IE *g* > Gmc *k*; and (c) IE aspirated voiced stops lost their aspiration in Gmc: IE *bʰ* > Gmc *b*, IE *dʰ* > Gmc *d*, IE *gʰ* > Gmc *g*.

§62 *Instances*
The following examples illustrate Grimm's law. For the sake of convenience most illustrations of the Indo-European stops will be taken from Latin, some from Sanskrit (Skt), because these two Indo-European languages retained most of the original stops.

    a.   L *piscis* 'fish'   OFris *fisk* 'fish'
          L *vertō* 'I turn'   OFris *wertha* 'to become'
          L *centum* 'hundred'   OFris *hund(red)* 'hundred'

    b.   L *trab-s* 'beam of wood' OFris *thorp* 'village'
          L *edō* 'I eat'   OFris *ita* 'to eat'
          L *augeō* 'I increase'   OFris *āka* 'to increase'

    c.   Skt *bhrātar* 'brother'   OFris *brōther* 'brother'
          Skt *rudhiras* 'blood'   OFris *rād* 'red'
          Skt *jangha* 'lower leg'   OFris *gunga* 'to go'

(13)   Verner's Law

§63 Although Grimm was able to establish the most important relationships between the Indo-European stops and their Germanic reflexes, there remained some problems that he could not solve. For example, why was it that Latin *pater, māter,* and *frāter* did not all show the same consonant in Germanic, as illustrated by the following Old Frisian words: *feder, mōder* and *brōther*? The Danish linguist Karl Verner discovered in 1875 that this had something to do with accent patterns in Indo-European. He established that accent was free in Indo-European, and not yet fixed on the stem as was the case in the Germanic languages. Thus, the accent-pattern in Skt *pi'tar* was on the second syllable, and, according to Verner, this must also have been the case in the original Indo-European word for 'father'. On this and similar instances, he formulated his law.

§64 *Process*
In Proto-Germanic, accent was still free. If the stress in a word followed a voiceless fricative, it became voiced. Afterwards, stress became fixed on the stem syllable. Consequently, in such a situation, *f* > *v*, *þ* > *ð*, *s* > *z*, and *χ* > *γ*. Later, in West Germanic, *z* > *r* (a change known as 'rhotacism') and *ð* > *d*.

   Verner's Law explains why, for example, we have OFris *feder* 'father' rather than **fether* (cf. L *pater*) as against OFris *brōther* (cf. L *frāter*). In particular, it shows why there are consonant alternations in some strong verbs, such as OFris *wesa* 'to be' and its past plural form *wēren*, or OFris *wertha* 'to become' and its past plural *wurden*. But it also explains the consonantal relation between, e.g., OFris *kiāsa* 'to choose' and *kere* 'choice'.

(14)   Metathesis of *r*

§65 *Process*
When *r* preceded or followed a short vowel, it often changed position. The move could be left to right, from immediately before a vowel to immediately after it, or right to left, from after a vowel to before it. Further cases of metathesis concern the backward movement by which *r, l* changed position with the preceding consonant.

§66 *Inventory*
Examples of left-to right movement: *gers* (cf. Goth *gras*), *berna* 'to burn' (cf. Goth *brannjan*), *ferst/first* 'period of time' (cf. OHG *frist*), *ferthe/ferde* 'peace' beside *frethe/ frede* (cf. OHG *fridu*), *forma* 'first' (cf. Goth *fruma*), *bersta* 'to burst' (cf. OHG *brestan*), *burst/borst* 'breast' (cf. Goth *brusts*), *fōtwirst* 'ankle' beside *wrist* 'wrist'(cf. OE *wrist*), *gerstel* 'cartilage, gristle' beside *grestel* (cf. OE *gristle*), *Kerst* 'Christ' and the adjective *kersten* 'Christian' beside *Crist* and *cristen*, *kersoma* 'chrism, unction' beside *krisma*.

Examples of right-to-left movement: *andren* 'window' beside *andern*, *bren* 'child' beside *bern* (cf. Goth *barn*), *thruch* 'through' (cf. OE *þurh*), *Briocht* 'Bright (as personal name)' (< **berhta-*), *wrichta* 'worker, craftsman' (from *werka* 'to work', with PAST PTC *wrocht*), *fruchte* 'fear, fright' beside *furchte* (cf. OE *fyrhto*), *threft* 'need, want' (cf. *thurva* 'to need').

Typically, Old Frisian has *r-s* metathesis, where *r* moves around the *s*. Examples are: *ūrse* beside *ūser* 'our', *kairs(like)* 'imperial' beside *kaiser* 'emperor', *īrsen* beside *īsern* 'iron', *Irsahelesca* beside *Israheliska* 'Israelite', *-hūrsa* beside *-hūsera* 'inhabitant of' in compounds such as *Dichursa* 'inhabitants of *Dichusum*', *wērs/wārs* 'springtime' (Gmc **wesar-*), and possibly **iersen* 'yesterday' (Gmc **gesar-*; cf. ModEFris *jäärsene* [Saterl.], *júrsen* [Wang.] and MainlNFris *(an-)jörsne* [Mor.]; cf. Hofmann 1969/1989).

The combination *wr-* was prone to metathesis, too, resulting in such forms as *ruald*, *rwald* beside *wrald* 'world', *ruist* beside *wrist* 'wrist' (cf. van Helten 1890: §§84, 96β), *ruēka* 'to reject (an accusation)' beside *wrēka*, *ruōgia* 'to charge' beside *wrōgia*. Occasionally, the combination *wl-* underwent metathesis: *luīte* beside *wlīte* 'face'. The instances of *wr-* and *wl-*metathesis are indicative of an originally bilabial realization of /w/.

Instances of consonants other than *r* involved in metathesis seem to be practically confined to *l*: *nēlde* 'needle' beside *nēdle* (cf. Goth *nēþla*), *bold* 'moveables, chattles' (related to *bōdel* 'moveables'), *buld* 'coin, shilling' beside *blud*, *tō-skeldeia* 'to shake heavily, concuss' (cf. OHG *scutilōn* 'schütteln'), *ielren* 'of alder' (cf. OE *ærlen*), *monle* beside *molne* 'mill' (< **molene*) and the suffix **-sla*: e.g., *blōdelsa* 'bloody wound', *lamelsa* 'lameness'. But note *hlērde* 'ladder' beside *hlēd(e)re*, *hledder/hladder-* (with shortening), *bernde* 'burden' beside *berdene*, and late metathesis in the abstract suffix **-ness(e)* (§159), e.g., *sēkense* 'sickness' beside *sēknisse*.

§67 Chronology

Metathesis appears to have been a change that could occur at various times in the history of Frisian, which makes it difficult to date all the individual cases.

Some instances must be Proto-Frisian, as they occur in all the modern Frisian dialects, e.g., *thruch* (cf. ModWFris *troch*, ModEFris *truch* [Saterl.], IsNFris *troch* [Sylt]). Likewise *gers* (cf. ModWFris *gers*, ModEFris *gäärs*, MainlNFris *geers* [Hall.]). Note that *gers* is attested with NOM/ACC.PL *gerso* (R1). As a monosyllabic noun with a heavy (long) syllable, *gers* should regularly have lost its NOM/ACC.PL ending **-u*, cf. §103). It follows, therefore, that *r*-metathesis postdates loss of **-u* after heavy-stemmed syllables. It must have preceded breaking in view of *Briocht* 'personal name' (< **berht*) (§49). However, the presence of both metathesized and unmethesized in quite a number of forms suggests that metathesis was a rather diffuse phonological process.

(15)   Loss of final -*n*

§68 *Process*
In infinitives, weak adjectives and weak nouns, adverbs, numerals, and some prepositions, final -*n* in the unstressed sequence *-an* was lost.

§69 *Instances*
Examples are:

- infinitives: *rīda* 'to ride' (cf. OE *rīdan*), *dwā* 'to do' (OE *dōn*)
- weak nouns (§99): *hona* 'cock, rooster', OBL.SG and NOM/ACC.PL *hona* (cf.
  OE *hanan*)
- weak adjectives (§116, all oblique cases except GEN.PL): *alda* 'old', and
- adverbs: *hwona* 'whence, from where' (cf. OE *hwanon*)
- numerals: *thrina* 'threefold' (cf. OE *þrinen*)
- prepositions: *binna* 'inside' (cf. OE *binnan*), *twiska* 'between' (cf. G *zwischen*).

However, final -*n* was retained in compounds of which the first element is a weak noun,
e.g., *sunnandei* 'Sunday' (§99, Remark 2), and in cardinals, e.g., *tiān* '10' (< WGmc
tehan).

On analogy with OWFris *stān* 'to stand' and *gān* 'to go' – OEFris only had *stonda*
and *gunga* – at some point in time, monosyllabic infinitives in Old West Frisian added
the final -*n*, e.g., *dwān* 'to do', *siān* 'to see', cf. Meijering (1990).

§70 *Chronology*
The loss of final -*n* must be Proto-Frisian.

§71 *End of Proto-Frisian changes*
To sum up, sound changes (4)–(11) and (14)–(15) together contributed to giving
Frisian its own, distinctive shape and place within the Ingvaeonic/North Sea Germanic
branch of the West Germanic languages (§24). It would seem that especially with sound-
change (9), 'labio-velar mutation', Frisian began to distinguish itself from the other
Ingvaeonic/North Sea Germanic dialects (Bremmer 2008b). When groups of Frisians
started to settle on the islands off the coast of present-day Schleswig-Holstein in the
course of the eighth century, these ten specific changes had all taken place, because they
also feature in Island North Frisian.

The remaining sections in this chapter present a full, if not exhaustive, overview
of the origin of the Old Frisian phonemes, mainly in stressed syllables, as they appear in the manuscripts. Attention is also drawn to certain peculiar orthographic phenomena.

D.   Overview of the origin of the Old Frisian phonemes

§72 *Short-vowel system*
The Old Frisian short vowels can be arranged as follows:

	front	central	back
high	i		u
mid		e	o
low		a	

The positions indicate the position where the vowels are articulated in the oral cavity ('mouth').

§73 *Short vowels*

i a. WGmc *i*, e.g., *fisk* 'fish', *sitta* 'to sit'.
   b. Only in R: *i*-mutation (§45) of WGmc *a*, e.g., *hiri* 'army' (cf. WGmc **harja-*.
   c. Only in R: *i*-mutation (§45) of WGmc *u*, e.g., *kining* 'king' (cf. OE *cyning*).
   d. In OWFris: often *e* > *i* before *lC*, *rC*, and before Nasal (+ C) (C= *d, t, k (ts), l, r*), e.g., *skild* 'shield', *stirt* 'tail', *tsirl* 'man', *thinka* 'to think'.

e a. WGmc *e*, e.g., *helpa* 'to help', *feld* 'field'.
   b. WGmc *a*, e.g., *stef* 'staff' (fronting, §39).
   c. *i*-mutation (§45) of WGmc *a*, e.g., *sella* 'to give' (cf. Goth *saljan*) (by way of fronting, §39).
   d   *i*-mutation (§45) of WGmc *u*, e.g., *kest* 'choice' (cf. OE *cyst*), *gelden* 'golden, of gold' (cf. OE *gylden*).
   e. lowering of OFris *i* > *e* in open syllable when followed by *a* in next syllable (only in R, see §205.5), e.g., *binetha* 'beneath', *letha* 'bodily parts' (GEN.PL), *nema* 'to take', *to wetande* 'to know' (INFL.INF) as opposed to non-R *binitha*, *litha*, *nima*, *to witane*.

a a. WGmc *a*, e.g., *nacht* 'night', *was* 'was' (§40 N.B.).
   b. In a number of instances, esp. *i*-mutation (§45) of *a* followed by *NC* or *lC* (*ll*), appears as *a*, e.g., *kampa* 'duellist', *falla* 'to fell', *(bi-)kanna* 'to confess'. However, mutated forms – in this case *kempa, fella, (bi-)kenna* – are equally common.
   c. occasionally < *ia* by absorption of *j* after liquids,[12] e.g., *brast* 'breast' beside *briast*.

o a. WGmc *o*, e.g., *dochter* 'daughter', *holt* 'wood'.

---

12. A liquid is *r* or *l*, see §77.

b. esp. in OEFris < WGmc *a* + Nasal, e.g., *mon* 'man', *komp* 'field; duel', *long* 'long' (§29).

c. < WGmc *ō*, before shortening cluster, e.g., *sochte* 'sought'.

d. mutation of OFris *u* > *o* in open syllable when followed by *a* in next syllable (only in R, §205.5), e.g., *koma* 'to come', *dora* 'doors' (GEN.PL), *opa* 'up' as opposed to non-R *kuma, dura, upa*.

e. esp. OWFris shows lowering of *u* before N, e.g., *sonne* 'sun' (OEFris *sunne*), but in OWFris there is still variation in, e.g., *wulf/wolf* 'wolf'.

f. in OWFris, *-we-* > *-o-*, e.g., *hwet* > *hot* 'what', *hweder* > *hoder* 'whether', *twelef* > *tolef* 'twelve'.

u a. WGmc *u* is generally preserved, esp. before nasals, e.g., *iung* 'young'.

b. < WGmc *ū*, before shortening cluster, e.g., *thuchte* 'seemed'.

c. occasionally < *iu* (rising diphthong) by absorption of *j* after liquids, e.g., *flucht* 'he flees', beside *fliucht(h)*.

d. Any short vowel could be the origin of this 'neutral' vowel, which is found in unstressed position, e.g., the second vowel in *helpe* 'he may help', the second and third in *Drochtenes* 'of the Lord', etc.

§74 *Long-vowel system*

The Old Frisian long vowels can be arranged as follows:

front	central	back
[iː]		[uː]
[eː]		[oː]
[ɛː]	[ɔː]	
	[aː]	

§75 *Long vowels*

ī a. WGmc *ī*, e.g., *rīda* 'to ride'.

b. WGmc *i* + N + voiceless fricative (§31), e.g., *fīf* 'five', *sīth* 'companion'.

c. < WGmc *-iwi*, e.g., *nī* 'new', *hlī* 'cover, protection' (< **hliwi*, instrumental case of **hlewa-*), *knī* 'knee' (cf. *hlī*).

d. < WGmc *-igi-*, e.g., *līth* 'he lies (down)' (< **ligith*, with palatalized medial consonant, §42).

e. OFris *-ei* (< WGmc **-ag, *-eg*, resp.) becomes *ī* in Rüstring, e.g., *dī* 'day', *wī* 'way'.

f. WGmc *ē₂* appears in native words as *ī* e.g., *hīr* 'here' (always), *Frīsa* 'Frisian'; in the Rüstring dialect: *hīt* 'ordered', *līt* 'let' (the other dialects have *hēt, lēt*).

g. WGmc *i* + *j*, e.g., *frī* 'free'.

h. in Latin loan words, e.g., *pīne* 'pain' (L *pēna*), *fīre* 'holiday' (L *fēria*).

ē[eː] a. < WGmc *ē₂*, e.g., *hēt* 'ordered', *lēt*, *Frēsa* 'Frisian'.

      b. < L *ē*, e.g., *rēma* 'oar' (L *rēmus*).

      c. < *i*-mutation (§45) of WGmc *ū*, e.g., *brēd* 'bride' (< **brūdi-*).

      d. < *i*-mutation (§45) of NSGmc *ū* + Fric < WGmc *u* + N + Fric, e.g., *kētha* 'to announce' (< **kunþjan-*).

      e. < *i*-mutation (§45) of WGmc *ō*, e.g., *blēda* 'to bleed' (< **blōdjan*).

      f. In late OFris, lengthening of *e* before -*ld*,-*nd*-, -*rn*, -*rd*, -*rth*: *fēld* 'field' (earlier *feld*), *ēnde* 'end' (*ende*), *bērn* 'child' (*bern*), *swērd* 'sword' (*swerd*), *ērthe* 'earth' (*erthe*).

æ[ɛː] a. < WGmc *ai*, e.g., *stēn* 'stone' (§37).

      b. < *i*-mutation (§45) of WGmc *au*, e.g., *dēpa* 'to baptize' (< **daupjan-*).

      c. < WGmc *ā* (< Gmc *ē₁*, §33), e.g., *rēd* 'counsel'.

      d. L *ā*, e.g., *strēte* 'street' (< *[via] strāta* 'paved road').

      e. < *i*-mutation (§45) of NSGmc *ō* + Fric < WGmc *a* + N + Fric (§31), e.g., *sēfte* 'softly' (< **sanfti-*).

      f. < *i*-mutation (§45) of WGmc *ai*, e.g., *dēla* 'to divide' (< **dailjan-*).

      g. contraction of WGmc *a* + *a*, e.g., *ē-* 'water' (in place- and river- names), alternatively *ā-* (see there).

ū a. < WGmc *ū*, e.g., *hūs* 'house', *brūka* 'to use'.

      b. < NSGmc *u* + N + Fric (§31), *e.g., kūth* 'known, public', *mūth* 'mouth'.

      c. occasionally < *iū* by absorption of *j* after liquids, e.g., *lūde* 'people' (beside common *liūde*), *frūdelf* 'lover' (beside *friūdelf*).

ō[oː] a. < WGmc *ō*, e.g., *bōte* 'compensation', *sōne* 'reconciliation'.

      b. < WGmc *a* + N + Fric (§31), e.g., *bōs* 'byre, cattle-shed'.

      c. in late Old West Frisian in open syllables (§209) *o* > *ō*, e.g., *hona* 'cock' > *hōne* ⟨hoyne⟩.

ō[ɔː] a. WGmc *ā* (< PGmc *ē₁*) + Nasal (§29), e.g., *mōna* 'moon', *ōne* 'except'.

      b. Before *ld, nd, rd, rth, rn*, short *o* tended to be lengthened to [ɔː]: *gold* > *gōld*, *lond* > *lōnd*, *orda* > *ōrda* 'order' (< L *ordo*), *north-* > *nōrth-*, *horn* > *hōrn*.

ā a. < Gmc *au*, e.g., *bām* 'tree'.

      b. < Gmc *ai*, e.g., *klāth* 'cloth'.

      c. contraction of Gmc *a* + *a*, e.g., *slā(n)* 'to strike' (< **slahan*), *ā-* 'water' in compounds (< **aha*, cf. OS *aha*; see also above under *ē*), e.g., *āburch* 'water defence, dike', *ālond* 'island', *āpāl* 'water pile (used to make pile-planking as a water defence)'.

      d. < L *au*, e.g., *kāp* 'purchase' (L *caup-*).

      e. in late Old West Frisian in open syllables (§209), *a* > *ā*, e.g., *gravia* > *grāvia* 'to dig'.

f.   < MLG *ā*, e.g., *jāmer(lik)* 'misery; miserable', *pāl* 'pole, pile' (beside native *pēl*, only in B, §34).

REMARK

1.   In later texts, *ī* is also spelled ⟨ii⟩, ⟨ij⟩ or ⟨y⟩, e.g., *wiif/wijf/wyf* 'woman' (§207).

2.   Note that Old Frisian did not have a special character to distinguish in spelling between /ɛː/ and /eː/, but used ⟨e⟩ instead for both sounds.

3.   Sometimes, it is difficult to say whether *ō* < *a* + Nasal developed to either [oː] or [ɔː]. ModFris shows reflexes of both, e.g., ModWFris *boas(doar)* < [bɔːs-], but ModLG (Ostfri.) *bûs* < [boːs], South-Holland *boes* [bus], the last one a Frisian substrate word. So, too: ModWFris *spoen/spoan* 'spoon'.

§76 *Diphthongs*

Old Frisian also had a number of short and long diphthongs, both rising (i.e., the stress was on the second element) and falling (with stress on the first element):

1.   Rising, long:

    iā   a.   < WGmc *eu*, e.g., *biāda* 'to offer'.

              b.   < WGmc *-eha*, e.g., *siā* 'to see', *tiān* '10'.

              c.   < WGmc *-ijo-*, e.g., *friōnd* 'friend'.

    iū/iō a.   < *i*-mutation (§45) of Gmc *eu*, e.g., *liūde/liōde* 'people', *biuth* 'he offers'.

              b.   < Gmc *eu* + *w*, e.g., *triūwe* 'true, reliable' (but R1 *trē(u)w-*).

              c.   in some loans as an approximation of [yː], e.g., *criūce/criōce* 'cross' (probably derived from OS *krüse* < L *cruc-em*), *biūsterlīk* 'confused, bad' (< MLG *büster-*), and perhaps *tsiurke* 'church', if from OE *ċyriċe*.

    iē   a.   < OFris *-ēld* < *-eld*, in OWFris, e.g., *fiēld* 'field', usually spelled ⟨iee⟩.

              b.   < OFris *iā*. This diphthong [ɪeː] is typical for late Old West Frisian, e.g., *biēda* 'to offer'.

2.   The following three triphthongs were the result of the same phonological process in late Old West Frisian, also known as 'Jorwert Breaking' (Dyk 2007). See also §208.3.

    juːw   The sequences *īw-*, whether < *(-)īv-* or < *(-)iv-* resulted in a rising triphthong, e.g., *liuwes* GEN.SG of *līf* 'life, body', *skrīva* 'to write' *skrīwa* > *skriouwa*; *livath* > *liuwath* 3SG.PRES of *libba* 'to live'.

    joːw   The sequence *-ewa-*, *ewe-*, long and short: *ieva* 'to give' > *iewa* > *iouwa*; *ēwelīk* 'eternal' > *iouwelīk*; *ēvend* 'evening' > *ēwend* > *ioun*. Also the cluster /fl/, in which /f/ was first voiced to /v/ and then became /w/, underwent this change, cf. OEFris *tefle* 'table' but OWFris *tiōle* 'id.'

jɔːw   The sequence -*ēwa*, -*ēwe*/ɛː/: *ēwe* 'law' > *iouwe*, *lēven* 'tin-plate' > *liouwen*.

3.   Rising, short

   iu/io   a.   breaking (§48) of WGmc *i* and *e*, e.g., *riucht* 'right', **miux* 'dung'.

   　　　　b.   labio-velar mutation (§51) of WGmc *i*, e.g., *niugen* 'nine', *siunga* 'to sing'.

4.   Falling, long

   īe   especially in late Old West Frisian: *dīen* 'done' (< *dēn*), *hīed(en)* 'had' (SG/PL)

   ou   In later Old West Frisian, the sequences -*āw*- (< -*āv*- < -*av*-) developed into *ou* [ɔːu], e.g., *stavia* > *stāvia* > *stouwia* 'to spell'; -*ūw*- (< -*ūv*-) developed into [ou], e.g., *skūva* 'to push, shove' > *skouwa* (ModWFris *skowe* [skoːwə].

   ei/ēi   a.   < OFris *e* (of various origins) + palatalized *g* (§42), e.g., *dei* 'day' (**daga*-), *wei* 'way' (**wega*-), *hei* 'mind' (**hugi*-), *ēin* 'own' (< *ēgen* < **aigina*-), *fleil* 'flail' (< L *flagellum*).

   　　　　b.   *ei* 'ewe, she-sheep' (Gmc **awi*-).

   　　　　c.   in German loanwords, e.g., *keisere* 'emperor'.

   　　　　d.   of various origin: *kēi* 'key' (< **kaigi*-/**kajjo*-); *nēi* 'after' (PREP./ADV.) (< **nēₗhwia*); *ei-lond* 'island' (< **agwijō*); *bēia* 'to bend' (< **baugjan*).

   　　　　e.   Both in later Old East and in Old West Frisian, *ē* (of various origin) tends to be diphthongized before alveolars and dentals (§206.2): e.g., *breid* 'bride' (< *brēd*), *einde* 'end' (< *ēnde* < *ende*), *heinde* 'near-by' (< *hēnde* < *hende*), *heila* 'heel' (beside *hēla*), *mein*- 'common' (beside *mēn*), *meide* 'reward; bribe' (beside *mēde*), *leith* 'loath' (beside *lēth*), *feithe* 'feud' beside *fēthe*.

   　　　　f.   < MLG *ei* in *reid* 'reed' (instead of OFris **hriād* < WGmc **hreud*), a loanword through trading.

   āu/au   a.   e.g., *āut* 'something, ought' and *nāut* 'nothing, nought, not' < *(n)āwet* < *(n)āhwet*.

   　　　　b.   *ā* before *w* (< **w* or -*v*-), e.g., *āuwa* 'to show' (beside *āwa*), *hāud* 'head' < *hāwed* < *hāved*, *hauwa* 'property' (< *hāwa* < *hawa/hava*).

   　　　　c.   in OWFris -*ald*- > -*āuld*-, e.g., *hāulda* 'to hold', *āuld* 'old'.

REMARK

1.   The following examples do not contain diphthongs; here the digraph is extended over the syllable boundary:

(a) *fiand* 'enemy' (< Gmc **fijǣnd-*); (b) *wīa* 'to consecrate' (< Gmc **weih-ija-*); *sīa* 'to seep, trick-le' (< Gmc **seihwa-*); (c) with elision of medial consonant (§§131.4, 208.11), e.g., *līa* 'to suffer' (< *lītha*), *mīa* 'to avoid' (< *mītha*), *snīa* 'to cut' (< *snītha*); (d) in inflected and verbal forms, e.g., *wīe* 'way (DAT.SG R)', *sīe* 'be' (SUBJ); (e) *īe* in French loans and loan-suffixes: *amīe* '(she-)lover', *soldīe* 'soldiery'.

2.   〈ei〉 tends to fluctuate with 〈ai, ay〉, esp. in later texts, e.g., *fleil/flail* 'flail', *ein/ain/ayn* 'own'.

3.   Until some very late stage in Proto-Frisian, the *i*-mutated forms (§45) of Proto-Germanic long and short *a*, *o*, and *u* were **æ*, **œ*, and **y*, after which they entered a process of unrounding (§47R) to become eventually long and short *e*. However, unrounding of **y*, both long and short, took a different course in Island North Frisian, where the mutated product of Gmc long and short **u* appears as *i*. This is one of the indications that the Island North Frisians must have left the Frisian heartland before unrounding of *y* to *e* had taken place (Århammar 2001a, 2001b).

§77   Consonant system

In this and the following table, '≠' indicates 'phonemically distinct from', while '~' indicates 'allophonically related to'.

a.   Old Frisian had the following short consonants:

	labial	dental	alveolar	palatal	velar
stops	p ≠ b		t ≠ d		k ≠ g
affricates			tˢ ≠ dᶻ		
fricatives	f ~ v	þ ~ ð	s ~ z		χ ~ h ~ ɣ
nasals	m		n		ŋ
liquids					l, r
semi-vowels	w			j	(w)

Most of these consonants will not produce any difficulty. However, the following may need some further explication: [χ] is the voiceless fricative as in German *ach* 'oh', or Scottish *loch*; [ɣ] is like [χ], but voiced, as in (Northern) German *sagen* 'to say' or initially in Dutch *van Gogh*; [θ] which is represented in the above table, as elsewhere in this book, by 'þ', is the sound as in English *thief*; [ð] is its voiced counterpart, as in English *there*; [ŋ] is pronounced as the final sound in English *song*.

b.   Old Frisian had the following long consonants:

	labial	dental	alveolar	velar
stops	pː ≠ bː		tː ≠ dː	kː ≠ gː
fricatives	fː	þː	sː	χː
nasals	mː		nː	
liquids			lː, rː	

Consonant length is usually indicated in spelling as a double consonant. Thus, for example, the /pː/ in *stoppia* 'to stop' was pronounced twice as long as the /p/ in *hopia* 'to hope'. In late Old Frisian, however, double consonants merely indicate that the preceding vowel is short (§209).

§78 *Remarks on some consonants*[13]

1.   Stops

p   Intrusive *p* is often found between *m* and a following consonant: *kempth* 'comes', *nimpth* 'takes', *sompnia* 'to assemble'.

d   of various origin (WGmc *d, in late Old Frisian also from **ð/þ*), e.g., *dād* 'dead' (< **dauda-*), *dū* 'you' (< *þū*). Final devoicing of *d* > *t* occasionally occurs in late texts, e.g., *goet* 'good'. However, it is questionable whether the spelling reflects an actual pronunciation or whether it should be attributed to Middle Dutch or Middle Low German orthographic influence.

REMARK

Intrusive consonants – see also at *p* above – are not Proto-Frisian, cf. Hofmann (1976/1989: 368). In fact, intrusive *d* (between *n* and *l/r*) seems to appear only in Old West Frisian. Examples include: OEFris *thuner* 'thunder' (> Wang. *thuuner*, Wurst. *tonyʹhr*, MainlNFris *tuner* [Mor.]) as opposed to late OWFris *thunder* (> ModWFris *tonger*); OWFris *spindel* 'spindle' (no OEFris form attested, but cf. ModEFris *spilne* [Saterl., with metathesis] and cf. OE *spinel*, OHG *spinila*); OWFris *alder* < *alra* GENPL of *al* 'all' (as opposed to e.g., Saterl. *aller-*).

k   *k* regularly appears in Old East Frisian as *ch* before *t* in verbal forms, e.g., *brecht* 'breaks' (3SG.PRES) < *breka*, *secht* 'seeks' < *sēka*, *skecht* 'abducts' < *skeka*. Rather than indicating a fricative, such forms reflect an orthographic peculiarity determined by this position in which *ch* was probably still pronounced as [k].

g   is a voiced stop in initial position before back vowels and mutated vowels, e.g., *God*, *gelden* 'golden'; a voiced fricative [ɣ] in intervocalic position and adjacent to voiced consonants, e.g., *fōged* 'guardian', *folgia* to follow'; *g* [ɣ] is devoiced in final position (so phonetic), e.g., *berch – berge* 'mountain'. The fricative is also spelled ⟨gh⟩, especially in later texts, under Low German/Dutch orthographic influence.

        Occasionally, intervocalic *v* appears as *g* [ɣ], e.g., *progost* 'provost' (beside *provest*), *prōgia* 'to prove' (beside *prōvia*), *pāgus* 'pope' (beside *pāwes, paus*), *siugun, sogen* 'seven'.

        Before a front vowel, unless this vowel is the result of *i*-mutation (§45), Gmc *g appears as /j/, spelled ⟨i⟩ (§42), but also sometimes spelled ⟨g⟩, e.g., *ierne/gerne* 'eagerly',

---

13.   On the distribution of the consonants, cf. Moulton (1972: 155–58: 'The Evidence of Old Frisian').

most likely because of Dutch/Low German scribal habits. Note such hypercorrect spellings as *gē* 'yes', *gēr* 'year', in which ⟨g⟩ represents WGmc **j*.

Also note such forms as *nīge* (inflected form of *nī* 'new') and *forsmāge* (3sg.pres.subj < *forsmāia* 'to despise'), in which ⟨g⟩ is [j], used as a hiatus filler.

ng is pronounced [ŋg] (as in Mod E *finger*), so with a final stop, both medially and finally.

In the cluster *-ng-* [ŋg], when originally followed by *i/j*, the stop was palatalized and assibilated (§42), e.g., *mendza* 'to mix' (< *maŋgjan), *genzen* 'gone' (< **gaŋgina-*).

In unstressed position *-ng* [ŋg] tended to be reduced to *-g* [ɣ], e.g., *panni(n)g* 'penny', *kini(n)g*, *keni(n)g* 'king', *Skilinge* > ModWFris *Skylge* 'Terschelling'.

2. Fricatives

Old Frisian had no initial voiced fricatives (nor does any of the Modern Frisian varieties today). However, when ⟨v⟩, ⟨z⟩, ⟨d⟩ (< [ð]) appear in manuscripts in initial position instead of their voiceless counterparts, this is an indication of Middle Dutch, Middle Low German or Latin orthographic influence, or even possibly an indication of phonetic influence.

v is an allophone of /f/ (which occurs initially and finally), and appears intervocalically and adjacent to a voiced consonant, e.g., *hof* 'court' – *hoves* (gen.sg), *skrīva* 'to write' – *skrēf* 'wrote (sg)', *delva* 'to delve' – *dalf* 'delved (sg)'. Note that in compounds there is no voicing either, e.g., *bifara* 'before'.

In the course of the thirteenth century, /v/ starts losing its fricative quality intervocalically and adjacent to voiced consonants. It acquired instead a semi-vocalic character [w], e.g., *ewangelia* 'Gospel' beside *evangelia*, *iewa* 'to give' beside *ieva*; *gref* nom.sg 'grave' beside *grewe* dat.sg.

In late Old West Frisian texts, ⟨v⟩ can also be written for *w*, e.g., *vinna* 'to win', *vaxet* 'grows'.

A typical feature of Old Frisian, both East and West, is the fairly regular loss of *v* (pronounced as [w]) after *l* and *r* when followed by a vowel. This resulted in such doublets as *sterva* ~ *stera* 'to die', *delva* ~ *dela* 'to dig', and in inflected forms such as *turve* ~ *ture* 'turf, sod'.

ch represents [χ] and occurs medially and finally, e.g., *tiuche* 'team; parcel of land', *crocha* '(cast-iron) coal-pan'; *hāch* 'high', *āch* 'he ows' (of *āga* vb.).

z is an allophone of /s/, and appears intervocalically, but remains written as ⟨s⟩, e.g., *hūs* 'house' – *hūses* (gen.sg). ⟨z⟩ is used in some Old Frisian manuscripts to indicate both [ts] (see below) and [dz], e.g., *brenza* 'to bring'.

When ⟨z⟩ appears initially in late Old West Frisian texts where Old East Frisian has ⟨s⟩, it is under orthographic influence of Middle Dutch, but the realization nonetheless remains voiceless.

/ts/ is the outcome of palatalized *k (§42) and had a variety of orthographic representations. In initial position, for example, in R1 we find ⟨sth⟩, in R2, B, H ⟨sz⟩, in E2, F and J ⟨tz⟩, in E1 ⟨z⟩, in E3 ⟨tz, zt⟩. In B, the word for 'church' has ⟨sz, ts, tsz⟩: szurke, tsyureke, tszurke. Also for /ts/ in medial position, we find much variation.

th   voiceless th, i.e., [θ], as a rule appears initially and finally.
      Final -th first (e.g., falt 3SG.PRES 'falls'), and initial th- later (e.g., tyennya 'to serve', cf. thiānia) tended to lose their friction and appear as t.

th   voiced, i.e., [ð], appears intervocalically and in conjunction with voiced consonants, e.g., fethere 'fether', wertha 'to become'.
      Despite the general rule of voiceless fricatives in initial position, [ð] came to appear initially in weakly stressed pronouns and adverbs, e.g., thet 'that', thēr 'there'. Voiced th in these restricted cases eventually became d in Old West Frisian, to begin with the pronouns, e.g., der 'who, which', and adverbs, e.g., dus 'thus'.
      Intervocalic th was voiced, and often dropped in late Old West Frisian (§208.11), e.g., brōr ⟨broer⟩ 'brother' < brōther, snē 'cut' < snethe. Note, however, the early occurrence of deletion of medial th in Rüstring ōr < ōther 'other'.

h   As in the other Germanic languages, Old Frisian had a combination of initial h plus r, n, l, and w, e.g., hrene 'smell', hlāpa 'to leap', hnekka 'neck', hwā 'who'. Towards the close of the Old Frisian period, such aspiration before these consonants started to be dropped (Nijdam 1999).
      Occasionally, unhistoric h appears before initial vowels, e.d. hws 'us', hec 'each', hiō 'you' (see glossary, s.v.).

g   See §78 (1g).

3.   Semi-vowels

w   already occasionally in Old East, but especially in Old West Frisian, appears intervocalically as an allophone of /v/, e.g., hōwes (GEN.SG of hōf 'hoof'), or adjacent to a voiced consonant: selwis (GEN.SG of self 'self').
      There was a tendency for initial w to be absorbed into a following o or u, e.g., ulle 'wool', undad 'wounded (PAST PTC)', urde 'would be(come)', olcnum DAT.PL 'clouds', ord 'word' (Århammar 1977). This change points to a bilabial articulation of /w/ (as in English). It is also lost in weakly stressed positions, especially in compounds, e.g., sā 'so' (cf. OE swā), onderk 'tool' (cf. OE andweorc), ondlete 'face' (cf. OE andwlita) beside wlite, ondser 'answer' (cf. OE andswaru), onderd 'presence' (cf. OE andweard) beside ondward.

For /w/ written as ⟨v⟩, see §78 (2v).

i [j] is the continuation of WGmc **j* as in *iung* 'young', *iēr* 'year'. More frequently, it is the result of palatalization of WGmc **g* (§42), e.g., *ield* 'money', *ierne* 'eagerly', *ieva* 'to give', *iest* 'guest', also spelled ⟨j⟩ in Old West Frisian texts, e.g., *jefte* 'gift', *jef* 'gave'.

Chapter III

Morphology
The inflections of Old Frisian

§79 *Word-classes*
For Old Frisian we distinguish in this primer nine word-classes or parts of speech: pronouns (including articles), nouns, adjectives, numerals, adverbs, verbs, prepositions, conjunctions, and interjections.

§80 *Case and number*
Like the other Germanic dialects, Old Frisian is capable of indicating number, case and gender in its nouns, pronouns, and adjectives as well as in some numerals. The numbers are singular and plural. The cases are nominative, accusative, genitive and dative. The instrumental case is no longer productive, but lives on in a limited number of petrified combinations. Occasionally, traces of a locative case are found. Moreover, adjectives and adverbs have three degrees of comparison. Prepositions, conjunctions and interjections are indeclinable, and are not dealt with in this chapter.

REMARK
The dual has not been recorded for Old Frisian, but it is interesting to note that the dual pronouns survived until well into the twentieth century in some North Frisian dialects (§89).

§81 *Gender*
There are three genders: masculine (MASC), feminine (FEM) and neuter (NEUT). Gender is grammatical: a word is assigned gender irrespective of the 'sex' of what the word refers to. If there is congruence between gender and sex, this is coincidence: *thī mon* 'the man' (MASC), *thiu frōwe* 'the lady' (FEM), but *thet wīf* 'the woman' (NEUT). Pronouns, though, may attract natural gender. Thus, *thet wīf* (NEUT) will usually be referred to with *hiu* 'she' (FEM).

REMARK
Modern West Frisian nouns only preserve the distinction neuter versus non-neuter, because masculine and feminine gender have fallen together (they are 'epicene'). Only the West Frisian dialect of the island of Schiermonnikoog has preserved the three-gender system. Modern East Frisian and Mainland North Frisian have on the whole retained the three-gender system. Unique for the Germanic languages, feminine and neuter merged to neuter in the Island North Frisian dialects of Amrum and Föhr (Hoekstra 1996).

§82 *Verbs*

For verbs, Old Frisian distinguishes between strong and weak verbs, anomalous verbs and preterite-present verbs. Verbs have:

- two tenses: present and preterite (or: past);
- three moods: indicative, subjunctive, and imperative;
- non-finite forms: infinitive (one without and one – inflected – with *tō*;
- two numbers: singular and plural;
- three persons: first, second and third person singular present and preterite indicative, but, typically for Ingvaeonic/North Sea Germanic (§24), a uniform ending for the plural, both indicative and subjunctive, both present and past (§32.b);
- one voice: the active (the passive being formed with an auxiliary).

For further discussion and for an outline of verbal paradigms, see §§151–55.

A. Pronouns

Four cases can be distinguished: nominative (NOM), accusative (ACC), genitive (GEN), and dative (DAT). On the syntactic use of the cases, see §§178–82.

§83 *Definite article and demonstrative pronouns*
The definite article rarely has the demonstrative force it can have in, e.g., Old English.

§84 *thī* 'the, that'

	MASC	FEM	NEUT	PLUR
NOM	thī	thiu	thet	thā
ACC	thene	thā	thet	thā
GEN	thes	thēre	thes	thēra
DAT	thā(m)	thēre	thā(m)	thā(m)

In Old West Frisian texts *d-* often appears instead of *th-*.

REMARK
1. Beside *thiu*, we regularly find *thio*.
2. The femine forms *thēre* and plural *thēra* tend to drop the final vowel in later texts.
3. Beside *thene*, we often find *thine*, especially in Old West Frisian.
4. Beside *thes*, the form *this* frequently occurs. For DAT.PL, *thām* is the more frequent form, for DAT.SG.MASC/NEUT this is *thā*.
5. After the prepositions *bi, efter, til* and *with*, petrified instrumental forms of the NEUT.SG may appear: *thiu*. These combinations serve as conjunctions and are lexicalized. See also §100R.2.

§85 *this* 'this'

	MASC	FEM	NEUT	PLUR
NOM	this	thius	thit	thisse, -a
ACC	thissen	thisse	thit	thisse, -a
GEN	thisses	thisser	thisses	thisser
DAT	thissem	thisser	thissem	thisse(m)

In Old West Frisian texts, *d-* often appears instead of *th-*.

REMARK
1. Occasionally, *-e-* appears instead of *-i-*. For Old East Frisian this applies exclusively to R.
2. For DAT.PL, forms without *-m* are more common than those with *-m*.
3. For NOM/ACC.PL, forms in *-a* are restricted to feminine forms, it would seem.

§86 Other demonstratives are *iena, thī-iena* 'that one', of which only the element *thī-* is declined.

§87 *Personal pronouns*
First person singular and plural: 'I' and 'we'

NOM	ik	wī
ACC	mī	ūs
GEN	*mīn	ūser
DAT	mī	ūs

§88 *Second person singular and plural: 'you (thou)' and 'you (ye)'*

NOM	thū	ī, jī, gī
ACC	thī	iu, io
GEN	thīn	iuwer
DAT	thī	iu, io

In Old West Frisian, a new form *iemma(n)* (< *jī* + *man* [PL]) 'you men', hence 'you (PL)', appears besides the other forms. This form remains the same in all cases. Likewise in OWFris, *jī* is also used for the polite address.

REMARK
1. Like Old English and Old Saxon, Old Frisian makes no distinction between the dative and accusative forms of the first and second persons singular and plural, unlike Old High German (*mir, dir, uns, iu* DAT, *mih, dih, unsih, iuwih* ACC).
2. In late Old West Frisian texts, the singular pronoun usually appears with *d-*: *dū*, etc.
3. In clitic forms, *thū* appears as *-tū*, e.g., *skaltū* 'shall/must you'.

§89 Dual personal pronouns: 'we two' and 'you two'. No forms of the dual have been recorded for Old Frisian (Vries 1998), probably because there was no occasion in the legal texts, but their existence is evidenced by such pronominal forms as have survived into the twentieth century, e.g., for Island and Mainland North Frisian: NOM *wat*, GEN *onkens*, DAT/ACC *onk* 'we two' and NOM *jat*, GEN *jonkens* DAT/ACC *jonk* 'you two' [Föhr]; for Mainland North Frisian: NOM *wat*, GEN/DAT/ACC *unk* and NOM *jat*, GEN/DAT/ACC *junk* [Mor.]. However, the use of the dual in North Frisian became obsolete in the first half of the twentieth century.

§90 *Third person singular and plural: 'he, she, it, they'*

	MASC	FEM	NEUT	PLUR
NOM	hī	hiu, hio	hit	hia
ACC	hine	hia	hit	hia
GEN	sīn	hi(a)re	*sīn	hi(a)ra
DAT	him	hi(a)re	him	him, himmen, hi(a)rem

There are no reflexive pronouns; instead, the accusative forms function as such.

REMARK

1.   Beside forms with -*i*-, we find forms with -*e*-: *hene, hem*.
2.   Beside *him* (DAT.PL), we find *hiam* in R (on analogy with NOM/ACC.PL) and, in OWFris, *hiaram, hiarem* (influenced by the GEN.PL), as well as the compound pronoun *himman* (also found in F, due to OWFris inference), *himmen* (*hemman, hemmen*).
3.   The genitive pronouns of the 1,2SG, the masc. and neut. 3SG and the 2PL have not been recorded, but will have been the same as their respective possessive pronouns (§92).
4.   In OWFris, we also find the PL.GEN *har(r)a*.
5.   *sīn*, an old reflexive, does not belong here, historically speaking, but replaces unrecorded **his*.

§91 *Enclitical and unstressed forms of third person pronouns*

	MASC	FEM	NEUT	PLUR
NOM	-er(e)	-s(e)	-it, -(e)t	-s(e)
ACC	-ne	-s(e)	-it, -(e)t	-s(e)
GEN	-(e)s	–	-(e)s	-ra
DAT	-(e)m			

Cliticization, i.e., pronouncing an unstressed pronoun as if it were part of the preceding word, is a marked feature of Old Frisian and often obscures the text, because host word and clitic are usually written together. In the glossary all cliticized forms occurring in the Reader have been included. Some frequent combinations are: *hī'ne* = *hī* + *hine, hī't* = *hī* + *hit, thet(t)'er* = *thet* + *er*. Cliticized forms in the Reader are signalled by an apostrophe, e.g., *bitigeth'er*.

§92 *Possessive pronouns*

They are: *mīn* 'my', *thīn* 'your, thy' *sīn* 'his, its', *ūse* 'our', *iūwe* 'your'. All these are declined like strong adjectives (§114–15). The feminine and plural possessives *hi(a)re*, *har(r)a* are indeclinable.

§93 *Interrogative pronouns*

	'who'	'what'	
	MASC/FEM	NEUT	PLUR
NOM	hwă	hwet	–
ACC	hwane	hwet	hwette
GEN	hwam(me)s	hwes	–
DAT	hwam	hwam	hwette

Note that the distinction is according to persons and things, but not to gender. Number is occasionally attested for the neuter form.

REMARK

1. The originally short vowel was lengthened in final position.
2. The MASC/FEM.GEN forms *hwams*, *hwammes* have apparently been influenced by the dative.
3. Beside MASC/FEM.ACC *hwane*, we sometimes find the forms *hwene*, perhaps analogous to *thene*.
4. Beside *hwet*, we sometimes find *hwete* (perhaps cf. Goth *ƕata*) or *h(w)āt*, *haet* (influenced by *hwā* 'who' and/or, possibly, MDu/LG *wat* 'what'), and, in OWFris texts, *hot* (*we-* > *o-*; §73: *o* f).

§94 The adjectival interrogative is *hwelik* 'which' (*hwelk*, *hwek*), beside which occur in OWFris *hulk*, *huk*, *hok*. These forms are either declined like strong adjectives (§115) or remain indeclined. Furthermore, there are the pronouns *hwether*, *hweder* (*hwedder*, *hoder*, *hōr*) 'which of two'.

REMARK

In *hok*, *hoder*, *hōr* we find *o* < *we-* (§73: *o* f), and in *hōr*, moreover, regular (late) elision of intervocalic *d* < *th* (§§78.2th, 208.11, 209), the long vowel being the result of the fusion of the two vowels *o* and *e*.

§95 *Relative pronouns*

In this function we find:

1. the demonstrative *thī*, *thiu*, *thet*;
2. the indeclinable particle *thēr* (< adv.);
3. the interrogatives *hwā*, *hwet*;

4. the indeclinable particle *thē* (< OS *thē*; 13x in R1, 1x in R2, 2x in E2, 1x in a Fivelgo charter).[1]

The relative *thī*, etc., is sometimes followed by *thēre* 'there' (cf. G *der da*).

§96 *Indefinite and impersonal pronouns*

Some common indefinite pronouns are: *hwelik* 'each, every' (with variants *hwelk*, *hok*), *elk* (with variants *ellic, ek*) 'anyone, any', *iāhwelik* 'anyone', *ammon* (with variants *emma(n), immen*) 'someone', *āhwedder (āuder)* 'someone, one of two'; *iāhweder (āider)* 'each (of two)', *ōther (ōr)* 'another', *al(le)* 'all', *ēn* '(some-)one', *ēnich (ēng, aeng, anch, ing)* 'anyone'; the pronoun *hwā* on its own can mean 'anyone', but it is more often reinforced by a following *sā* 'so': *hwāsā* (cf. ModE *whoso[ever]*), or by a preceding and following *sā*: *sā hwāsā* 'whoso(ever)'; *sum* 'one of ...' in combinations like *twelvasum* 'one of twelve, i.e., with eleven others' (cf. §125). All these pronouns are usually declined like the strong adjective. The pronoun *ma* 'one, they, people' (cf. OE *man*, G *man*, Du *men*) occurs only in the nominative.

B.   Nouns

§97 *Classification*

In Indo-European a noun is composed of a root, a stem element (i.e., a vowel or consonant, also called 'theme') or another suffix, and an inflectional ending. Based on these features, nouns can be subcategorized into three types:

Type I: consonant stems, i.e., nouns which in Indo-European had their case-endings appended to a stem consonant. For Germanic, the most important of these are the so-called *n*-stems, also known as **weak nouns**;

Type II: vowel stems, i.e., nouns which in Indo-European have their case-endings appended to a stem vowel ('thematic vowel'), also known as **strong nouns**;

Type III: minor declensions, including other consonant stems and athematic nouns, i.e., nouns which in Indo-European had their case endings appended immediately to the root.

§98 As the three genders are grammatical (§81), their most conspicuous features should be recognized and memorized. The easiest cues in a text are the demonstratives and articles. Also indicative of gender are word endings and suffixes (on these, cf. §§158–60), particularly in the NOM.SG. Here follow the most significant endings:

---

1. In all likelihood, *thē* is a Low German borrowing, cf. Bremmer (2008a: 198–99).

Type I (§99)

- Weak masculine: *-a* (these are often agent nouns, e.g., *boda* 'messenger' (= 'he who brings a message'), *kempa* 'champion, fighter', *āsega* 'law-speaker'. Also words with suffixes ending in *-a* are masculine: *-elsa*, *-ma*, *-tha* (*-ta*, *-da*).
- Weak feminine: *-e*.
- Weak neuter: *-e*, only found in *āre* 'ear' and *āge* 'eye'.

Type II (§§100–09)

- Strong masculine: *-dōm*; agent nouns in *-ere*; concrete nouns in *-ing* and *-ling*, abstract nouns in *-ath*, *-ad*.
- Strong feminine: mainly abstract nouns such as those ending in *-e*, *-ene*, *-unge* (*-inge*, *-enge*), *-nisse* (*-nes(s)e*, *-ens(e)*), *-hēd*.
- Strong neuter: *-skipi/-skip(e)* (but also fem.).

Type III (§§110–13)

- No easily recognizable endings, as well as some minor groups that do not belong to Types I and II

Type I. Consonant stems

§99 *Weak declension (n-stems)*

SG	MASC 'bailiff'	FEM 'tongue'	NEUT 'eye'
NOM	skelta	tunge, -a	āge
ACC	skelta	tunga	āge
GEN	skelta	tunga	āga
DAT	skelta	tunga	āga
PL			
NOM	skelta	tunga	āg(e)ne
ACC	skelta	tunga	āg(e)ne
GEN	skeltena, -ana	tungena, -ana	āgena, -ana
DAT	skeltum, -em	tungum, -em	āg(en)um, -em

The declension of the weak nouns comprises a large number of nouns, e.g., masculine: *kempa* 'champion', *rēdieva* 'judge' ('counsel-giver'), *āsega* 'legal official' ('law-speaker'), *boda* 'messenger', *skelta(ta)* (< **skeld-hāta* 'guilt-caller') 'legal official'. Such nouns, when based on a verb, are agent nouns; others are *grēva* 'count', *frāna* 'legal official (of the lord)', *spada* 'spade', *neva* 'cousin', *Frēsa* 'Frisian', *hona* 'cock', *galga* 'gallows', *noma* 'name'.

Feminine nouns include, e.g.: *tāne* 'toe', *erthe* 'earth', *sunne* 'sun', *wid(w)e* 'widow', *frōwe* 'woman', *famne* 'young woman, girl', *herte* 'heart'.

There are only two weak neuter nouns: *āge* 'eye' and *āre* 'ear'.

REMARK

1. To this paradigm also belong words which originally had a *-jan (MASC) ending, e.g., MASC *willa* (cf. Goth *wilja*, OE *willa*) 'wish, desire', *erva* (cf. Goth *arbja*, OE *ierfa*) 'heir', *ebba* (cf. OS *ebbia*) 'ebb-tide'. These nouns show gemination (§27) and *i*-mutation (§45), when applicable.

2. In some compounds the earlier *-an* ending of the oblique case has been preserved, e.g., *fiārdandēl* 'quarter', *sunnandei* 'Sunday', *mōnandei* 'Monday', *sunnansedel* 'sunset', *mōdiransunu* 'mother's sister's son', *fidiransunu* 'father's brother's son', *fethansunu* 'father's sister's sun' (cf. §69).

3. Original FEM *-jōn* and *-īn*-stems (§§106–07) have adopted the strong FEM declension.

4. Occasionally early, but especially in later OFris, the ending *-a* is often reduced to *-e*.

5. The two neuter nouns sometimes appear without *-e* in NOM/ACC.SG Plural forms of *āge* show wide variation: NOM/ACC *āgon* R (probably the most archaic form, cf. Goth *augōna*), *āg(e)ne*, DAT *āchnon* (R), *āgenum*, *āgnem*, on the analogy with the GEN.PL ending. However, *āre* 'ear' has NOM/ACC. PL *āra*, DAT.PL *ārum*.

Type II. Strong declensions (vowel stems)

§100 *Masculine nouns (a-stems)*

'tree'	SG	PL
NOM/ACC	**bām**	**bāmar** (-er, -a, -an)
GEN	**bāmes**	**bāma**
DAT	**bāme**	**bāmum** (-em, -im)

Many MASC nouns follow this pattern, e.g., monosyllables such as *ēth* 'oath', *erm* 'arm', *mund* 'guardian', *stēn* 'stone'; bisyllables *kening* 'king', *etgēr* 'spear', *witsing* 'pirate, "viking"', *penning* 'penny', *angel* 'angel', *finger* 'finger'; *mōnath* 'month' has NOM/ACC plural *-ar*, beside an original endingless form.

REMARK

1. The GEN.SG often appears as *-is*, in late OFris as *-s*.

2. The locative and instrumental have collapsed with the dative ending. Remnants of the locative ending *-i* are preserved in some forms, e.g., *thin(d)ze* DAT.SG.NEUT (besides *thinge*), and often in place-names, e.g., *Wetsens* (beside *Wetsinge*): the *-i* has caused palatalization of *-ng-* (§42).

3. Both in late Old East (E3, F) and in Old West Frisian, the DAT.SG ending is frequently dropped.

4. The NOM/ACC.PL ending *-ar* (< *-ōzes*) is a typically Frisian phenomenon among the West Germanic dialects. It is restricted to Old East Frisian only, more precisely to R1, B1,2, E1,2,3,4 and H1,2. It is absent in F and R2,3,4. In all likelihood, the occasional presence of *-ar* in R1 does not reflect genuine usage but is the result in this manuscript of copying texts that originated from outside Rüstringen (Bremmer 2007a). If this is right, its occurrence is confined to Ems Old Frisian. On the distribution of *-ar*, cf. Meijering (1989).

5. NOM/ACC.PL *-an* derives from the weak declension, and is especially found in OWFris and must be considered as a loan suffix from either MDu or MLG.

6. Bisyllables like *angel, finger* drop the medial vowel in the plural: *anglar, fingrar*, but analogy with the singular forms has often restored the vowel.

7. DAT.PL *-um* is often reduced to *-em*, *-im*, while R typically has *-on* (after long or heavy syllables) and *-un* (after short or light syllables; on 'vowel balance', see §205.1–2) (cf. OS *-on*, *-un*).

§101 *Certain nouns belonging to the strong* a*-stems show a deviant pattern.*

'day'	SG	PL
NOM/ACC	dei	degar (-a, -an)
GEN	deis	degana (-ena)
DAT	dei	degum (-em)

The paradigm of *dei* is disturbed because of phonological reasons. First, **dag* became **dæg* through fronting (§39), after which the final *g* was palatalized after a front vowel, resulting in the diphthong *ei* (§42). Like *dei* 'day', are *wei* 'way', *hei* 'mind'. Palatalization of **g* was prevented in the plural forms because of the following back-vowel. In Old Weser Frisian, this new diphthong *ei* developed to *ī* (§205.6), resulting in forms like *dī*, *wī*.

REMARK
1. *hei* 'mind' is attested in SG only; originally **-i-*stem, cf. OE *hyġe*.
2. The SG paradigm of *wei* shows a variety of analogous as well as phonologically reduced forms: GEN.SG *wiges*, *weies*, *weis*, *wīes*, DAT.SG *wige*, *weie*, *wei*, *wīe*, *wī*.

§102 *Masculine nouns (*ja*- and* wa*-stems)*
These nouns follow the pattern of the *a*-stems (§100), with the only difference that NOM.SG ends in *-e*. For the *ja*-stems we witness gemination (§27) and *i*-mutation (§45), where applicable, e.g., *here* (R *hiri*; §205.4) 'army', *skrīvere* 'court clerk'.

REMARK
Polysyllabic words tend to shed NOM/ACC.SG *-e*, e.g., *riuchter* 'judge', *morder* 'murderer', *ridder* 'knight', especially in later texts.

§103 *Neuter strong nouns (*a*-stems)*

SG	'word'	'ship'	PL	
NOM/ACC	word	skip	word	skipe (-o, -u R)
GEN	wordes	skipes	worda	skipa (-ena)
DAT	worde	skipe	wordum	skipum

Heavy-stemmed monosyllabic neuter nouns have phonologically dropped their NOM/ACC.PL ending *-u*.[2] Like *word* are, e.g., *bēn* 'leg', *brēf* 'letter, writ', *skēp* 'sheep', *thing*

---

2. A syllable is long or heavy when either the vowel is long or when the syllable ends in two consonants.

'thing; court', *riucht* 'right, law', *horn* 'horn'. Also bisyllables like *hāved* 'head', *bēken* 'beacon', *wēpen* 'weapon', *weter* 'water'. However, occasionally plural endings slip in, e.g., *hornar, hāvda* Light-stemmed syllables like *skip* 'ship', are e.g., *gers* (< *gres*, §66) 'grass, herb', *lith* 'member' (PL *lithe* E, H, F, etc., *lithi* R).

REMARK
The plural ending -*u*, -*o* is confined to R, owing to 'vowel balance' (§205.1–2).

§104 *Neuter* ja- *and* wa-*stems*
Their distinctive features lost, these nouns follow the pattern as in §103, but the *ja*-suffix has brought about gemination (§27) and *i*-mutation (§45), where applicable, e.g., *bedde* 'bed' (DAT.SG of *bed*, cf. OE *bedd* NOM.SG), *ken* 'kin' (cf. OE *cynn*), *erve* 'inheritance, heritage'. As the last form shows, the suffix has sometimes been preserved as -*e*. For wa- stems, e.g., *smere* 'grease; pus', *mele* 'flour, meal' (cf. OE *smeoru*, OBL *smeorw*-; *melu*, OBL *melw*-).

REMARK
1.   The geminated consonants are visible only in the inflected forms, e.g., *bedde, kennes*.
2.   The -*w*- may for some time have been preserved in oblique cases, as Modern West Frisian forms show *w*-mutation, e.g., *smoar, moal*.

§105 *Feminine strong nouns (ō-stems)*

SG	'gift'	'wound'	PL	
NOM	ieve	wund(e)	ieva (-e)	wunda (-e)
ACC	ieve	wunde	ieva	wunda (-e)
GEN	ieve	wunde	ieva (-ena)	wunda (-ena)
DAT	ieve	wunde	ievum (-em)	wundum (-em)

Phonologically, the NOM.SG *-u* dropped after heavy-stemmed nouns like *wunde* (Proto Fris *wundu*), and indeed occasionally such forms are found, e.g., *wund, hēr* 'hire, lease'. However, on the analogy of the ACC.SG, the -*e* slipped into the NOM.SG zero ending. Some light-stemmed nouns like *ieve* are e.g., *seke* '(law-)case', *tele* 'reckoning; tale', *sege* 'saying, verdict', *klage* 'complaint'. Heavy-stemmed nouns belonging to this declension are e.g., *bōte* 'compensation, fine', *sōne* 'reconciliation', *nēthe* 'mercy'.

REMARK
Typical for Old Frisian is its predilection for fronted vowels in the NOM.SG of feminine ō-stems, as opposed to Old English (Århammar 1990: 22 [II.1]), e.g., OE *sacu, talu, sagu* (there is no OE cognate for OFris *klage*).

§106 *Feminine* jō- *and* wō-*stems*
Nouns originally belonging to these groups merged with the feminine ō-stems (§105), and the NOM.SG *-wō* appears as -*e*. Whenever applicable, the -*jō*-suffix brought about

gemination (§27) and *i*-mutation (§45), e.g., *helle* (cf. Goth *halja*) 'hell', *bregge* (rather than ****bredze*, cf. OE *brycg*) 'bridge', *egge* beside *edze* 'edge', *sibbe* (cf. Goth *sibja*, OE *sibb*) 'kinship'. Original *wō*-stem nouns are, e.g., *mēde* 'meadow', *sine* 'sinew, muscle'. The latter word shows preservations of **-w-* as *-u-* in *sinuwerdene* 'muscle injury'.

§107 *Feminine abstract nouns in *-īn*
This group comprises abstract nouns formed from adjectives. In Gothic, this declension was weak, but in Old Frisian, as in Old English, it was remodelled after the feminine *ō*-stems. However, the suffix has brought about palatalization (§42) and *i*-mutation (§45), when applicable, e.g., *brēde* (cf. OHG *breiti*) 'breadth', *elde* (cf. OS *eldi*, OE *ieldo*) 'age', *grēte* 'largeness, size', *helde* (cf. OE *hyldo*) 'loyalty', *len(d)ze* (cf. OE *lengu*) 'length'.

§108 *The* i-*declension*
The endings of this declension have been drastically remodelled, the masculine and neuter nouns according to the strong *a*-declension, the feminine nouns according to the *ō*-declension. Whenever applicable, the suffix has brought about palatalization (§42) and *i*-mutation (§45). Irrespective of gender, the declension can be divided into two groups: the suffix has regularly dropped after long-stemmed syllabic nouns, but remained as *-e* after short-stemmed syllabic nouns. Long-stemmed, e.g., masculine: *dēl* 'part', *iest* 'guest'; feminine: *kest* 'choice; statute' (OE *cyst*), *dēd(e)* 'deed'; neuter: *tiūch* 'testimony', *lēn* 'loan'. Short-stemmed, e.g., masculine: *breke/bretse* 'breach; punishment' (cf. OE *bryċe*), *mete* 'food'; feminine: *kere* 'choice; statute' (OE *cyre*), *stede* 'place'; neuter: *spere* 'spear'.

§109 *The* u-*declension*
Through analogical levelling, the major characteristics of this minor declension have become blurred, and only some short-stemmed masculine nouns show their former features, especially in the earlier texts.

SG	'son'	PL	
NOM/ACC	sune (-a,-e; -u R)	suna (-ar,-an,-en)	
GEN	suna	suna (-ena)	
DAT	suna (-e)	sunum (-em)	

Like *sune* is *frethe* (*fretho* R) 'peace' (cf. OE *freoþu*). Heavy-stemmed nouns, through their regular loss of *-u*, have gone over to the strong *a*- (MASC) and *ō*-(FEM) declensions, for example, masc. *wald* 'forest'; fem. *hond* 'hand', *feld* 'field'. To this group also belongs *fiā* (< **fehu*; cf. OE *feoh*) 'cattle; property'. In this word, intervocalic *-h-* was regularly lost (§54), and the ending *-a* was adopted from the GEN/DAT/ACC form, which is also *fiā*. The alternative genitival form *fiās* shows adaptation to the strong masculine declension. Two light-stemmed feminine nouns originally belong to this class, *dure* 'door' (actually a *plurale tantum*) and *nose* 'nose'. The latter has moved to the *ō*-declension (§105).

Type III. Minor declensions (athematic and other)

§110 A small but important group is formed by kinship names in *-r* (*r*-stems): MASC *feder, brōther*; FEM *mōder, dochter, swester* (R)/*suster*.

	SG	PL
NOM/ACC	brōther	brōther (-a, -an)
GEN	brōther (-es, -s)	brōthera
DAT	brōther (-e)	brōth(e)rum (-em)

Beside this original paradigm, we also find analogical forms: the masculine nouns adopt endings from the strong *a*-declension (§100), the feminine nouns those from the *ō*-declension (§105). Dative forms with *i*-mutation (cf. OE *mēder, dehter*) have not been recorded for Old Frisian.

§111 *Nouns in* -nd *(present-participle stems)*

	SG	PL
NOM/ACC	friūnd	friūnd (-a, -an)
GEN	friūndes	friūnda (-ena)
DAT	friūnde	friūndum (-em)

All nouns that belong here are masculine. Like *friūnd* 'friend' are *fiand* 'enemy', *wīgand* 'warrior', *werand* 'guardian, representative'. They are petrified present participles and agent nouns, showing endingless NOM/ACC.PL forms. However, as in other declensions, analogy has crept in.

§112 *Neuter nouns with* -r- *plural (IE* -os/-es *declension)*
On the whole, nouns of this declension went over to the strong declensions, probably occasioned by their characteristic NOM/ACC.PL *-r*. The most frequent representative is *klēth/klāth* 'cloth, piece of clothing', with PL *klāthar, -er*. Also the Old High German loanword *kind* 'child' has *-r* plural endings. Curiously, Old Frisian attestations of 'calf, egg, lamb' do not seem to have been recorded, but post-medieval forms show that they belonged here, too.

§113 *Mutation plurals (root or athematic nouns)*
The majority of these nouns (all except *brōk*) are so-called root nouns which had *-iz* as a NOM/ACC plural marker in Germanic, causing *i*-mutation (§45). Only a few of these survive in Old Frisian:

> MASC *mon/man* 'man' – *men* (also with unchanged plural *mon/man*)
> *tōth* 'tooth' – *tēth*
> *fōt* 'foot' – *fēt*

FEM   *kū* 'cow' – *kī*
        brōk (only in compounds) – *brēk* 'breeches'
        *gōs 'goose' – *gēs*

REMARK

1.   *bōk* 'book' can be both feminine and neuter, and sometimes appears with unchanged plural *bōk*, beside *bōka*.
2.   As in Old English, the GEN.PL of *kū* is *kūna*.

Final remark

It will have become clear that, in many respects, it is difficult to present neat nominal paradigms that clearly exhibit the historically 'correct' forms. Analogy and levelling have done much to reduce the wide variety that once existed, such that the Old Frisian nominal system consists basically of two patterns, i.e., a strong and a weak declension.

C.   Adjectives

§114 *Adjectives are declined according to syntactic context:*

a.   If they appear as the nominal part of the predicate (or: subject complement), they remain indeclined, e.g., *thī dīk is hāch* 'the dike is high', *thā dīkar send hāch*. Adjectives are also declined strong, if no definite determiner (i.e., definite article, demonstrative pronoun or possessive pronoun) precedes the adjective when it occurs in attributive position, e.g., *(n)ēn hāch dīk* '(no/a) high dike'.
b.   If preceded by a determiner, however, the adjective is declined weak, e.g., *thī hāga dīk*. The comparative of the adjective is declined weak, but the superlative forms of the adjective can appear both strong and weak.

§115 *Strong declension*

	MASC	FEM	NEUT	PLUR
NOM	grāt	grāt(e)	grāt	grāte
ACC	grātene	grāte	grāt	grāte
GEN	grātes	grātere	grātes	grātera
DAT	grāte	grātere	grāte	grāte

The most conspicuous form is DAT.PL *-e*, instead of the expected *-um*. Syncopated forms (i.e., forms in which the unstressed medial vowel has dropped) regularly appear, e.g., *grātne, grātre*. Adjectives that end in *-ch* and *-f* have *-g-* and *-v-/-w-* when followed by an inflectional ending.

Adjectives that formerly had an *-i/j-* suffix show *-e* in NOM.SG, and gemination (§27), *i*-mutation (§45), and assibilation, when applicable, e.g., *sibbe* 'related, akin', *grēne* 'green', *swēte* 'sweet'. However, final *-e* in these adjectives has also frequently dropped.

REMARK
Adjectives which originally belonged to the *u*- and *wō*-declensions have lost their distinctive features.

§116 *Weak declension*

'great'	MASC	FEM	NEUT	PLUR
NOM	grāta	grāte (-a)	grāte	grāta
ACC	grāta	grāta	grāte	grāta
GEN	grāta	grāta	grāta	grāta
DAT	grāta	grāta	grāta	grāta

The paradigm is like that of the weak nouns, except that DAT.PL ends in *-a* instead of *-um*. However, when an adjective functions as a substantive, the DAT.PL ending is *-um*, e.g., *alder* 'parent' (lit. 'elder') – *aldrum*, *iunger* 'younger one, disciple' – *iungrum*.

REMARK
When preceded by *(n)ēn*, comparatives in NOM.SG.FEM and NOM/ACC.NEUT have *-a* instead of *-e*.

§117 *Comparison of adjectives*
The endings of the comparative and superlative degrees are usually *-(e)ra* and *-est* (*-ist*), e.g., *sibbe* – *sib(be)ra* – *sibbest* 'related – more closely related – most closely related'. In R, we usually find forms in *-or* and *-ost*. If the adjective ends in *-r*, the ending is *-ra*, e.g., *diurra* 'more expensive', *firra* 'further; right (dexter)', with shortening of the long vowel/diphthong before the resulting consonant cluster, i.e., *-rr-*.

§118 A number of adjectives originally had a mutation factor in their suffix (*-ir-*, *-ist-*), which has brought about *i*-mutation of the stem-vowel (§45). The most frequent ones are:

ald 'old'	eldra/aldra, -er	eldest
fīr/fēr 'far'	firra/ferra	fīr(e)st
long 'long'	lengra/langra, -er	lengest/langest
nēi 'near'	niār	nēst

REMARK
Occasionally, the analogical comparative *fīror* is found.

§119 *Irregular degrees of comparison*
Some adjectives have comparatives and superlatives that are not etymologically related to the positive degree. They are:

gōd 'good'	bet(te)ra	best
grāt 'big'	marra/māra	măst/mĕst
evel 'bad'	wirra/werra	wĭrst/wĕrst
lītik 'little'	{ lessa/les(se)ra	lĕst/lērest
	{ min(ne)ra	min(ne)st

REMARK

Occasionally, the analogical superlative *lītikest* is found.

§120 Some comparatives and superlatives of adjectives have no positive forms, but find their origin in adverbs or prepositions. Note, in view of the -*r*-, that the superlatives here are based on the comparative forms. They include, e.g.:

(ēr 'before')	erra/arra 'earlier'	ēr(o)st/ār(o)st 'earliest'
(inna 'in(side)')	in(ne)ra 'inner'	inrest 'inmost'
(ūte 'out(side)')	ūt(e)ra 'outer'	ūter(o)st 'outmost'
(sūth 'southwards')	sūther 'more southerly'	sūthrost 'most s.'

Like *sūth* are *āst* 'east', *north*, *west* (but for these three no superlative forms have been recorded).

§121 *Comparison of adverbs*

Adverbs take the comparative and superlative endings from the adjectives: -*er* (-*or* R) and -*est* (-*ost* R, -*ist*, -*st*). Irregular degrees of comparison are:

ēr 'before'	erra/arra	ērest (etc.)
forth 'forwards'	forther/further	–
longe 'long'	leng	lengest
wel 'well'	bet	best
nēi 'near'	niār	nēst
fora 'before'	ferra/firra	fer(e)st/fir(e)st
(– 'much')	mā(r)/mē(r)	măst/mĕst
(– 'little')	min	–
(– 'little')	lēs	–

D. Numerals

§122 The numerals 'one, two, three' inflect as follows:

'1'	MASC	FEM	NEUT
NOM	ēn/ān	ēne	ēn
ACC	ĕnne/ănne	ēne	ēn
GEN	ēnes	ēn(e)re	ēnes
DAT	ēne	ēn(e)re	ēne

'2'	MASC	FEM	NEUT
NOM	twēn(e), twēr	twā	twā
ACC	twēne	twā	twā
GEN	twēra, -ī-	twēra, -ī-	twēra, -ī-
DAT	twām	twām	twām

'3'	MASC	FEM	NEUT
NOM	thrē	thria	thriu (thria F)
ACC	thrē	thria	thriu (thria F)
GEN	thri(r)a	thri(r)a	thri(r)a
DAT	thri(u)m, threm	thri(u)m, threm	thri(u)m, threm

§123 The remaining numerals are usually uninflected. However, note such phrases as *thera fiowera ēn* 'one of the four', *thera sexa allerlīk* 'each of the six'. Decades can take an ending too, e.g., *mith fiortiga merkum* 'with forty marks'.

REMARK
1.   On inflected forms of 'four', cf. Stiles (1986: 11).
2.   Inflection of collocations with decades from twenty onwards is restricted to Old Frisian and Old English, see §223.

§124 *The cardinal and ordinal numerals are as follows:*

1	ēn/ān	forma; formest
		fer(e)st
		ēr(e)st, ār(e)st
2	twēn(e), m.; twā, f/n.	ōther
3	thrē, m.; thriā, f.; thriū, n.	thredda
4	fiower, fiuwer	fiarda
5	fīf	fīfta
6	sex	sexta
7	si(u)gun, sogen, sawen, sowen	si(u)gunda, sogenda, sawenda
8	acht(a), (-e)	achta; achtunda
9	niugen, -un	niugenda
10	tiān	tiānda, tiēnde
11	andlova/elleva	andlofta/al(le)fta/el(le)fta
12	twel(e)f/tolef	twilifta/twel(e)fta/tolefta
13	threttīne, -ēn(e)	threttinda/threttensta
20	twintich/tontich	twintig(e)sta
21	ēn and twintich	ēn and twintig(e)sta
30	thritich	thritig(e)sta

70	siuguntich, sogen-, (t)san-	(t)si(u)guntigsta
80	achta(n)tich/	achta(n)tigsta/
	(t)achtich	tachtigsta
90	(t)niogentich	(t)niogentigsta
100	hundred/hunderd	hunder(d)sta
1000	thūsend	thūsen(d)sta

REMARK

1. The ordinal *achtunda* is an analogous form based on '7th' and '9th', while the ending of *achta* has been influenced by the ending of '5th', '6th' and '12th' or alternatively is a reduced form of **acht-otha*.

2. The Ingvaeonic/North Sea Germanic form *tegotha* 'tenth' (§31 Rem.) survives only in its narrowed meaning of 'tithe', *tiānde/tiēnde* being analogical formations (Stiles 1986: 14).

3. Beside the ordinal suffixes for '13–19' *-tinde*, we find the superlative suffix (as e.g., in Old High German and Middle Dutch). This suffix is also found with the ordinals of the decades.

4. The decades '70–90' occasionally show traces of the prefix *and-* (cf. OE *hund-*) in a reduced form *t-*: *tsawentich, tachtich, tniogentich*. The reduced prefix was eventually lost in '70' and '90', because of assimilation with the following consonant. The *t*-less forms *achta(n)tich* and *achtich* were also influenced by the numeral *achta* '8', while *achtantich* was influenced by '70' and '90'.

5. The word *ōther* appears sometimes as an ordinal, sometimes as a pronoun. It is often inflected strong, even when preceded by a determiner, cf. van Helten (1890: §266).

6. On *twel(e)f/tolef* and *twintich/tontich*, see §208.7.

§125 *Miscellaneous numerals*

In addition to the numerals, the following words were available for counting: the distributives *twīna, -e* 'twofold', *thrina* 'threefold' (cf. OE *þrinen*); the multiplicatives *ēnfald, ēnfaldich* 'once, one time', *twīfald(-ich), twīdubel, twīa* (cf. OE *twiwa*) 'double'; *thrīfald, thria* (cf. OE *þriwa*) 'thrice'.

The question 'How often?' could be answered with *ēnes* 'once', and by adding the inflected form of *hwarf* 'turning', e.g., *achta hwarve* 'eight times' or even with *a twīra wegena* 'two times'.

Fractions are *twēde* 'two third' and the nouns *twēdnath* 'a two third'; *thrim(m)ine* 'a third' and *thrimenath* 'a third part'. Also collocations may express fractures, e.g., *thī achtunda dēl* 'the eighth part'. Based on the latter expression are the nouns *twādēl* and *thrimdēl*, resp. 'one half' and 'one third'. Note such phrases as *ōther half, thredda half* 'the other half, the third half, i.e., one and a half, two and a half'.

Particularly when conjurors are stipulated, compounds like *twīrasum, thrirasum, sexasum*, etc., 'with one other, with two, five others' (lit. 'one of two, of three, of six') are often found.

REMARK

In late OWFris *twin(e)* (< *twīna* 'twofold') and *t(h)rin* 'threefold' acquire the meaning of plain 'two' and 'three'.

E.   Verbs

§126   *Types and features*

Following the traditional approach, we distinguish four types of verbs for Old Frisian: strong verbs, weak verbs, preterite-present verbs, and anomalous verbs. Of these four groups, that of the weak verbs was the only productive one: practically all new verbs that entered the language almost automatically were weak. The principal feature of the weak verbs is that its preterites and past participles were formed by means of the so-called 'dental suffix', i.e., -*d*- or -*t*-. Strong verbs, on the other hand, formed their preterites and past participles by means of a change of the stem-vowel. Although much fewer in number than the weak verbs, they were used very frequently. The groups of preterite-present and anomalous verbs were very small indeed, but, again, ranked high as for their frequency.

§127   For verbs, the following features can be distinguished (see also §§184–96):

a.   two tenses: present and preterite (or: past);
b.   mood: indicative, subjunctive and imperative. Traditionally, the non-finite forms, viz. the infinitive (both plain, ending in -*a* [but see §150], and inflected, ending in -*ane*, -*ene*) and the participles (both present and past), belong here, too;
c.   two numbers: singular and plural;
d.   three persons, but only the present indicative singular has three distinctive forms. The preterite indicative singular has two forms, viz. the first and third person forms, and the second. The plural present and preterite indicative have uniform endings for all persons (as in Old English and Old Saxon). The subjunctive, both present and preterite, has uniform endings for all persons, singular and plural;
e.   one voice: active.

Strong verbs

§128   For strong verbs we distinguish four essential forms, known as *principal parts*: infinitive, 1/3singular preterite, plural preterite, and past participle. The alterations of vowels in each of these principle parts are variously known as vowel-gradation, *Ablaut*, or apophony. Vowel-gradation implies that a change in the stem-vowel signals a change in meaning.

REMARK
1.   Gradation can be qualitative, that is, when the quality of the vowel changes, e.g., *rīda* – *rēd* 'to ride – rode' (PRET.SG) or quantitative, that is, when it was a matter of difference in length, e.g., *brek* – *brēkon* 'broke' (PRET SG and PL). In the principal parts, then, we distinguish the following grades for classes I–V: full grade (present and preterite SG), lengthened grade (PRET.PL of classes IV/V) and zero or reduced grade (PRET.PL classes I–III and past participle classes I–V).

2. Beside operating in the strong verbs, vowel-gradation was also a factor in word formation. We can detect a gradation-relationship between particular words, such as *biāda* 'to command' and *boda* 'messenger' (full grade), *snītha* 'to cut' – *snethe* 'a cut' (full grade).

§129 Note that:
1. *i*-mutation (§45) operates where applicable in the second and third person singular present indicative, and that
2. long vowels in these two forms are regularly shortened before the endings *-st* and *-t(h)*.

§130 As with the other Germanic languages, we distinguish seven different gradation-series and hence seven classes of strong verbs. The Germanic basic pattern and its Old Frisian reflex can be represented as follows:

PRESENT	PRET.SG	PRET.PL	PAST PTC
I Gmc *ei* + C	*ai*	*i*	*i*
OFris **rīda**	**rēd**	**ridden**	**ridden**
II Gmc *eu* + C	*au*	*u*	*u*
OFris **biāda**	**bād**	**beden**	**beden**
III Gmc *e, i* + CC	*a*	*u*	*u*
OFris a) **helpa**	**halp**	**hulpen**	**hulpen**
b) **binda**	**band**	**bunden**	**bunden**
IV Gmc *e* + C	*a*	*ǣ*	*u*
OFris a) **nima**	**nam**	**nōmen**	**nimen**
b) **stela**	**stel**	**stēlen**	**stelen**
V Gmc *e*	*a*	*ǣ*	*e*
OFris **ieva**	**ief**	**iēven**	**ieven**
VI Gmc *a* + C	*ō*	*ō*	*a*
OFris **fara**	**fōr**	**fōren**	**faren**
VII see §137			

REMARK
In the Rüstring texts, the PRET.PL ending is *-on* (after long or heavy syllables) and *-un* (after short or light syllables; on 'vowel balance', see §205.1–2).

§131 *Class I*
The basic pattern for the infinitive is *ī* followed by a single consonant.

INF/PRES	(3SG.PRES)	PRET.SG	PRET.PL	PAST PTC
grīpa 'to seize'	gripth	**grēp**	**gripen**	**gripen**

To this class belong, e.g., *bīta* 'to bite', *blīka* 'to appear, be visible', *glīda* 'to slide, slip', *drīva* 'to drive', *skrīva* 'to write', *hnīga* 'to bend, be inclined', *ita* 'to eat', *lītha* 'to suffer', *mītha* 'to avoid', *rīsa* 'to rise', *skīta* 'to shit', *slīta* 'to tear; vitiate (an oath)', *smīta* 'to throw', *snītha* 'to cut', *wrīta* 'to write'. Here too belongs the rarely attested contract verb **sīa* 'to seep, ooze' with *sīth* (3sg.PRES) and *esīn* (PAST PTC).

The stem-vowel of the PRET.PL and PAST.PTC often shows *e* instead of *i*. Verbs which ended their stem in *v-* show a further development in late Old West Frisian, as they developed a glide between *ī* and *v* when the latter had been bilabialized to a *w* ('Jorwert Breaking', §76.2), e.g., *skri(o)uwa* 'to write':

INF/PRES	(3SG.PRES)	PRET.SG	PRET.PL	PAST PTC
skriuwa	skrifth	scrēf	scriouwen	scriouw(e)n

By analogy, the PRET.SG adopted the form of the PRET.PL: *scriou*. Like *skriuwa* are, e.g., *bliuwa* 'to remain' (< *b(i)līva*), *driuwa* 'to drive' (< *drīva*).

REMARK

1. The effect of Verner's Law (§63) has usually been levelled out in this class, so that, e.g., *snītha* appears with a PAST.PTC *snithen*, *rīsa* with *(e)risen*. No *s* ~ *r* alterations occur in this class (as in Old English).

2. *ita* 'to eat' (PRET.PL *iten*, PAST.PTC *iten*) originally belonged to Class V.

3. Some verbs which in other Germanic dialects belonged to Class I, are weak in Old Frisian, e.g., *liā* 'to lend', *līde*, *līd* (cf. OE *lēon*), *skīna* 'to shine' (cf. OE *scīnan*), and *thigia* 'to prosper' (cf. OE *þēon*).

4. In later Old West Frisian, verbs which ended their stem in *-d* or *-th* first fell together, as intervocalic *-th-* usually became *-d-*, and next they regularly lost *d* in intervocalic position (§§78.2th, 208.11). Thus they ended up in shape as contract verbs (§54), but unlike these, they carried the stress on the first element of the digraph, e.g., *līa* 'to suffer' (< *lītha*), *mīa* 'to avoid' (< *mītha*), *snīa* 'to cut' (< *snītha*); however, *rīda* was not thus affected.

5. Palatalization of the medial consonant (§42) in the PAST PTC appears in *stritsen* from *strīka* 'to stroke, move'.

§132 *Class II*

This class can be divided into two groups: (a) the stem vowel is *iā*, and (b) the stem vowel is *ū*.

Pattern (a) of *iā* plus one consonant is as follows:

INF/PRES	(3SG.PRES)	PRET.SG	PRET.PL	PAST PTC
biāda 'to offer'	biut(h)	bād	beden	beden

Like *biāda* are, e.g., *driāga* 'to deceive', *fliāta* 'to flow', *liāga* 'to lie', *niāta* 'to use, enjoy', *riāka* 'to smoke', *siātha* 'to seethe, boil', *skiāta* 'to shoot'. The 2,3sg.PRES regularly show the result of *i*-mutation (§45), e.g., **biutst*, *biut* (also with *io*) 'you, he offer(s)'. Perhaps influenced by this vowel is *br(i)ouwa* 'to brew' (or Class VII?). Attested are OWFris *brouwa* (inf.), *briouwen* (a substantivized infinitive), *brout* (3SG.PRES) and *brouwen* (PAST PTC).

The operation of Verner's Law (§63) is visible in:

kiāsa/tziāsa	kiost/tziost	**kās**	**keren**	**keren**
	'to choose'			
-liāsa 'to lose'	-liust	**-lās**	**-leren**	**-leren**

Contract verbs (§54) are *fliā* 'to fly' and *tiā* 'to draw':

tiā	tiucht	**tāch**	**tegen**	**tein**

Pattern (b) has *ā̃* in its preterite tense forms:

slūta 'to close'	slut	**slāt**	*sleten	sleten

Verbs of group (b) include *hrūta* 'to rattle (in one's throat), *krūpa* 'to creep', *lūka* 'to lock', *skūva* 'to shove', *sprūta* 'to sprout'.

A characteristic feature of Class II is the *i*-mutated vowel of the past participle. This is accounted for if we assume that the past participle suffix was **-ina-*, rather than **-ana-*. If the medial consonant was *k*, it was palatalized and assibilated in the past participle: *lūka* 'to lock' ~ *letsen*. Also, if the medial consonant was *g*, it was palatalized, resulting in a diphthong: **tegin-* > **tejin* > *tein* (§42).

Note that the mutated vowel of the past participle has analogically been extended to the PRET.PL in Class II, e.g., *beden* 'they offered' – *beden* 'offered'.

REMARK
1. Occasionally, we find doublets: *kriāpa* – *krūpa*.
2. Contract verbs are parallelled in Old English, e.g., *flēon* 'to flee', *tēon* 'to draw'.

§133 *Class III*
This class can be divided into two sub-groups: (a) *i + NC*, in which the first consonant is a nasal, and the second may or may not be a nasal; (b) *e + C_1C_2*, in which C_1 is *r, l* or *ch*.

a.	INF / PRES	(3SG.PRES)	PRET.SG	PRET.PL	PAST PTC
	winna 'to win'	wint(h)	**wan**	**wunnen**	**wunnen**

Like *winna* are, e.g., *binda* 'to bind', *finda* 'to find', *(bi)kringa* 'to obtain', *kwinka* 'to disappear', *klinna* 'to sound', *thwinga* 'to force'.

Some verbs of this group have a different vowel (*e* or *u*) in the infinitive and present: *bigunna* 'to begin' beside *bijenna*, *burna* 'to burn' beside *berna* (*barna*), *runna* 'to run' beside *renna*.

b.	**helpa** 'to help'	helpt(h)	**halp**	**hulpen**	**hulpen**

This pattern is followed by, e.g., *belga* 'to be angry', *bersta* 'to burst', *delva* 'to dig', *urderva* 'to ruin, corrupt', *kerva* 'to cut, carve', *sterva* 'to die', *werpa* 'to throw', *wertha* 'to become'.

Verner's Law (§63) operates in *wertha* 'to become'. However, we frequently find verb forms with -*d*- (from PRET.PL and PAST PTC) in the first two principal parts. Conversely, we also find verb forms with -*th*- (from the PRES and PRET.SG) in the last two principal parts. Both patterns are due to analogical levelling. The 'correct' pattern is:

| **wertha** | wert(h) | **warth** | **wurden** | **wurden** |

Some members of this group show slightly different forms, on account of phonological changes. Because of palatalization (§42), *ielda* 'to pay' (< **geldan*) has the following sequence:

| **ielda** | ielt(h) | **gald** | **gulden** | **gulden** |

Palatalization also accounts for the form *breida, brīda* R (< **bregdan*) 'to pull', as a consequence of which the stem ends in only one consonant (other attested forms: *breit(h)* 3SG.PRES, *brūden* PAST PTC). Breaking (§48) has given *fiuchta* (< **fehtan*).

REMARK
1.   The verb *siunga* shows labio-velar mutation (§51) of stem-vowel < **singwan*.
2.   The -*u*- in the infinitive of *bigunna*, etc., will have come from the pret. plural, cf. Class II, pattern (b). This verb also has a weak preterite in OWFris: *begunde*.
3.   *v* was regularly dropped after *l* and *r* (§78.2v), resulting in forms like *dela* beside *delva* 'to dig' (*delth* 'digs', *dollen* 'dug'), *kera* beside *kerva* 'to cut, carve', *stera* beside *sterva* 'to die', *for'dera* 'to perish' < *for'derva*, etc.
4.   *bersta* 'to burst', with three consonants, shows metathesis (< **bresta*) (§65).
5.   Negative contraction is found with some forms of *wertha*: *nerth* (3SG.PRES), *nerthe* (PRES.SUBJ).

§134   *Class IV*
As can be seen from the survey in §130, the gradation series for Classes IV and V are exactly the same for Old Frisian. The reason is that *i*-mutation (§45) caused by the **-ina*- suffix of the past participle has obscured the original **u* in Class IV. On comparative grounds, the following verbs can be assigned to Class IV: those whose stems end in *l*, *r* or *m*. The other verbs with this gradation series whose stems end in a single consonant which is not a nasal or a liquid should be assigned to Class V. However, a small group cannot be assigned to either main group, as in the related Germanic dialects they sometimes belong to Class IV and sometimes to Class V. They are the verbs whose stems end in a single consonant, but have the stem vowel preceded by *r* or, more rarely, by *l*. For the sake of convenience, they are grouped here with Class IV.

a.   *VN-:*

INF / PRES	(3SG.PRES)	PRET.SG	PRET.PL	PAST PTC
nima 'to take'	nimth	**nom**	**nōmen**	**nimen**
kuma 'to come'	kemth	**kom**	**kōmen**	**kemen**

b.   *VC-* (*C = l, r*):

bifela 'to order'	-felth	-**fel**	-**fēlen**	-**felen**

Like *bifela* are *hela* 'to conceal', *stela* 'to steal', *bera* 'to bear' (*ber(e)n* 'born'), *skera* 'to cut'.

REMARK

1.   *nema* and *koma* are found in R only, the result of Rüstring *a*-mutation (§205.5).
2.   *bifela* (< **bifelhan*) originally belonged to Class III.
3.   On the problem of grouping verbs of Classes IV and V, see van der Rhee (1974).

§135 *Class V*
This class has a stem ending in *VC*, in which *C* is other than a liquid or nasal:

a. INF/PRES	(3SG.PRES)	PRET.SG	PRET.PL	PAST PTC
lesa 'to read'	lest(h)	**les**	**lēsen**	**lessen**
ieva 'to give'	ieft(h)	**ief**	**iēven**	**ieven**

Note that the expected *i*-mutation in the 2,3SG.PRES is absent in this class. Like *lesa* are, for example, *quetha* 'to say', *meta* 'to measure', *forieta* 'to forget', *treda* 'to tread', *wega* 'to weigh'.

Verbs whose stems end in *k*, like *breka* 'to break', *reka* 'to cover with ash', *spreka* 'to speak', *steka* 'to stab', *wreka* 'to avenge', have palatalized consonants (§42) in their past participle, because of the suffix **-ina-*: *bretsen/britsen, ritsen, spritzen, stetsen/stitzen*, etc. (forms with *-i-* are OWFris).

Verner's Law (§63) operates in *wesa* 'to be':

wesa	(is)	**was**	**wēren**	**wesen, -in**

The present tense forms of *wesa* can be found in §149 (b).

b.   A few verbs have present forms of the type of weak verbs class 1 (§139) in this class have weak presents. They are *bidda* 'to pray, ask', *sitta* 'to sit' and *lidza* 'to lie'. Because of some regular sound-changes, *lidza* shows a few deviant forms:

lidza	leith/līth	**lei/lēg**	**lāijen/lēgen**	**lidzen/lein**

c.   In Old West Frisian, *ieva* 'to give' developed forms which are quite different from those in Old East Frisian. Some of these forms are due to regular sound-changes (especially 'Jorwert Breaking', §208.3), others seem to have been caused by analogy (the inf. *iā(n)* attracted preterite vowels of *stān* 'to stand' of Class VI), or appear, in the case of *iond*, to have attracted the *-d* of the weak past participle:

iowa/iā(n)   iowt   **iōf/iō/iōg/iōd(e)   iōwen/iōden   iouwen/iond**

To this class belong some contract verbs (§54): *iā(n)* 'to confess', *siā(n)* 'to see' (*siucht* 'sees') – *sach* – *sēgon* – *sēn* (OWFris *siōn, sioen*), *skīa(n)* 'to happen' (*sketh* 'happens' – *skē* – *(e)skēn*), and, with regular loss of medial *d* (< *th*; §§78.2th, 208.11), *quān* 'to say' (< *quetha*).

REMARK
1.   *lidza* < **ligjan; leith* < **ligith* with palatalization (§42); *līth* is the regular Rüstring form (§205.6); *lei* 'lay' < **lag* by way of fronting (§39) and palatalization; OWFris *lēg* ⟨leeg⟩ is analogical with the past plural, just as is *laijen* with the past singular form.
2.   In late Old West Frisian we find new preterites, e.g., *iōde* 'gave', *siōd* 'saw', which were partly influenced by the preterite of *stān* 'to stand', partly by the weak verb endings.
3.   In Old English, too, *sēon* 'to see' is a contract verb.

§136   *Class VI*
This fairly small class can be subdivided into three groups. Most verbs follow the pattern of *fara* 'to go, travel':

a.	INF/PRES	(3SG.PRES)	PRET.SG	PRET.PL	PAST PTC
	fara	fer(e)th/	**fōr**	**fōren**	**faren/ferin**
	'to go'	far(e)th			
	draga/drega	dreith	**drōch**	**drōgen**	**dregen/drein**
	'to carry'				
	grava/greva	greft(h)	***grōf**	**grōven**	**-grōwen**
	'to dig'				

As can be seen, both the infinitival and past participle forms have more than one realization. The *e* in the infinitive must be accounted for by the *i*-mutated 2,3SG.PRES form. On the other hand, *a* instead of *e* the 2,3SG.PRES appears on analogy with the stem vowel of the infinitive. The past participle suffix **-ina-* often caused *i*-mutation of the stem vowel and palatalization of stem-final *-g-* and *-k-* where applicable (§42), e.g., *slein* 'struck', *batzen* 'baked' beside *backen* (from unrecorded **baka*). In *bigrōwen* 'buried', the vowel of the preterite has been extended to the past ptc. OWFris *grouwa* 'to dig' (inf.), with analogous *growt* 3SG.PRES, is the result of 'Jorwert Breaking' (§208.3). Like *fara* are, e.g., *bisaka/-seka* 'to deny (in court)', *wada* 'to wade', *waxa* 'to grow', and perhaps *walla* 'to boil'. The last one originally belonged to Class VII. Slightly deviating from this pattern is *stonda/standa* 'to stand' with *-n-* infix, which caused rounding of WGmc **a* > *o* (§28), later restored in Old West Frisian:

stonda/standa   stont   **stōd**   **stōden**   **stenden**

In Old West Frisian, an alternative infinitive *stān* existed alongside with *standa*, with a past participle *stenzen/stinzen*, on the analogy of *fān – fenzen* 'to catch' and *hwān – hwenzen* 'to hang', in addition to a past particple *stēn* on the analogy of *dwān – dēn*.

b. Class VI also has some verbs with a weak present:

skeppa 'to create'   skeppeth   **skōp   skōpen   skepen**

Similarly, *heffa* 'to raise', *steppa* 'to step', *swera* 'to swear'.

c. Contract verb *slā(n)* 'to strike' (§54):

slā(n)   sleith/slaith,   **slōch   slōgen   slein/slain**
                          slacht (OWFris)

This verb shows Verner's Law (§63) as well as the effects of the *-ina*-suffix in the past participle.

§137 *Class VII*

a. Traditionally, this class comprises the 'reduplicating' verbs. For Old Frisian, no reduplicating preterites have been recorded (cf. Goth *haitan – haihait*; OE *hātan – heht* 'to call – called'). However, generally speaking, this class contains all the strong verbs that do not fit into Class I–VI. A Remarkable feature of this class is that the stem vowel of the infinitive is similar to that of the past participle. Preterite singular and plural likewise have the same stem vowel, *ē* (but in R, it is *ī*).

INF	(3SG.PRES)	PRET	PAST PTC
hēta 'to call'	het/hat	**hēt/hīt**	**hēten**
lēta 'to let'	lat/let	**lēt/līt**	**lēten**
slēpa 'to sleep'	slept	**slēp**	**slēpen**
stēta 'to hit''	stat/stet	–	**stēten**
rēda 'to advise'	reth	**rēd**	**rēden/rāden**
(h)lāpa 'to leap'	hlapt(h)/hlepth	**hlēp/hliōp**	**(h)lēpen**
āka 'to increase'	–	–	**āken**
hāwa 'to hew'	haut	–	**hāwen**
bonna 'to summon'	bennest (2SG)	**bēn**	**(e)bonnen**
halda 'to hold'	halth/helth	**hēld/hīld**	**halden**
walda 'to rule'	–	**wīldon**	–
-flōka 'to curse'	–	–	**-flōkin**
wēpa 'to weep'	wēp(e)th	–	**wēpen**

Some verbs that traditionally belong to Class VII show preterite vowels of Class VI, and could therefore perhaps just as well be assigned to that class (although, characteristically, Class VI has a stem ending in only one consonant):

INF	3SG.PRES	PRET	PAST PTC
hrōpa 'to call'	hropth	**(h)rōp**	**hrēpen/hrōpen**
falla 'to fall'	falth	**fōl**	**fallen**

More complex is the verb 'to go':

(g)unga	gun(g)t(h)/gength/ gangt	**gēng/gīng/**	**gangen/gengen/**
		gong	**genzen/ginzen**

Beside *gunga* 'to go' (*unga*, with unexplained loss of initial *g*, is found only in B), Old West Frisian also has *gān*, cf. §149(c).

b.   Contract verbs:

fā(n) 'to catch'	fet(h)/fucht	**fēng/fīng**	**fangen/fengen/ fenzen**
hwā(n) 'to hang'	(hongath)	**hwēng**	**hwenzen/hwēn/ h(w)inzen**

The form *fucht* 'catches' occurs only in Old West Frisian.

c.   Also the following, scarcely attested verbs belong here: *bliā* 'to blow' (*blē* PRET. SG, *blēn* PAST PTC), *brēda* 'to burn (alive)', *miā* 'to mow' (*meth* 3SG.PRES), *(on)spīa* 'to spew, spit (at)' (*espīen* PAST PTC), *wīa* 'to blow' (*wē* PRET.SG), *grōia* 'to grow' (*groyt* 3SG.PRES, *grē* 3SG.PRES.SUBJ), *(be)skrīa* 'to cry (at)' (*skrit* 3SG.PRES, *(be)skrien* PAST PTC).

Weak verbs

§138 For Old Frisian only two classes of weak verbs can still be distinguished (as against four for Gothic, and three for Old Norse, Old High German, Old Saxon and Old English).

§139 *Weak verbs Class 1*
a.   Verbs of this class originally had their stems followed by the infinitival suffix **-jan*. This suffix often had a causative meaning when added to stems of strong verbs (the preterite singular form). Its meaning was factitive when added to nouns and adjectives, e.g., *sank* 'he sank' – **sankjan* 'to cause to sink, drown', *dōm* 'judgement' – **dōmjan* 'to make a judgement, to judge', *kūth* 'known' – **kūþjan* 'to make known, announce'. The *-j-* affected the preceding sounds as follows: (1) it caused gemination of the preceding consonant (except for *r*) if the stem was short in West Germanic (§27); (2) if the stem ended in a velar, i.e., *-g, -k, -(n)g*, these consonants became palatalized and assibilated

where applicable (§42); (3) it caused *i*-mutation of the stem-vowel, where applicable (§45). In all these cases, so also after *r*, the *-j-* that brought about the changes was lost.

Examples of change (1): (1): *sella* 'to sell' (< **saljan*); *setta* 'to set' (< **satjan*); *nera* 'to save' (< **narjan*).

Examples of change (2): *rētsa* 'to reach' (< **raikjan*), *sedza* 'to say' (< **sagjan*); *thendza/thantsa* 'to think' (< **þankjan*); *sendza/sandza* 'to make sink, drown' (< **sankjan*). However, forms without affrication also occur, e.g., *rēka*, *thenka* (*thanka*), *senka*. Note that because of palatalization of the stem-final consonant (§42), Class 1 verbs may look like Class 2 verbs, e.g.: *heia* 'to convene (a court or synod)' (< **hagjan*), *bēia* 'to bend' (< **baugjan*).

Examples of change (3): cf. *dōm* 'judgement' – *dēma* 'to judge'; *kūth* 'known' – *kētha* 'to announce'; *sēka* 'to seek' (< **sōkjan*).

b.   The preterite ending for Class 1 is *-de* after voiced, *-te* after voiceless consonants, irrespective of whether the stem is heavy or light, e.g.: *hērde* 'heard', *keste* 'kissed'. Verbs with a light stem ending in *-r* sometimes show *-ede* (as in Old English), but more often *-de*, e.g., *nerede* 'saved', *werde* 'defended'.

Geminated consonants are simplified in preterite and past participle, e.g., *sella* 'to sell' – *selde* 'sold' (PRET), *setta* 'to set' – *set* 'set' (PAST PTC). Stem-final *-d* or *-t*, together with the preterite ending, is often simplified to *-t-* in the preterite: *resta* 'to rest' – *reste* 'rested', *henda* 'to catch' – *hente* 'caught', *senda* 'to send' – *sente/sante* 'sent'.

Stem-final *-th*, *-d* and *-t* often appear in the preterite as *-tt-*, with regular shortening of the stem vowel if this was long: *kētha* 'to announce' – *kette* 'announced', *lēda* 'to lead' – *lette/latte* 'led', *grēta* 'to greet' – *grette* 'greeted', *mēta* 'to meet' – *mette* 'met', *strīda* 'to fight' – *stritte* 'fought' (late; originally strong Class I).

c.   The past participle more or less follows the pattern of the preterite. Both heavy- and light-stemmed verbs ending in a voiced consonant have their participles end in *-ed*: *hēred* 'heard', *rēmed* 'cleared', *lēned* 'borrowed', *nered* 'saved', *lemed* 'mutilated'. Stems ending in *-th*, *-t*, or even *-d*, may show *-th* or *-t*: *keth* 'announced' (*kētha*), *gret* 'greeted', *(e)went* 'went, turned', with shortening of vowel where applicable.

d.   The verbs *sedza* 'to say' and *ledza* 'to lay' have a preterite and past participle that deviates from their infinitival stems: *seide* – *seid* and *leide* – *leid*. The stem of, e.g., preterite **lag-de* first underwent fronting to **leg-ide* (§39) and then palatalization to *leide* (§42).

For a paradigm of Class 1, see §153.

§140   A small sub-group within Class 1 is constituted by verbs that had no *i*-mutation factor in their preterite and past participle forms. The common feature for Old Frisian is that their stems end in a velar consonant, which in the preterite and past participle forms turn out as -cht(e). Preceded by their Germanic stems, they are:

*werk-	wirtza, werka 'to work' – wrochte – (e)wrocht	
*þak-	thetsa 'to cover' – *thachte – thacht	
*þruk-	thritsa 'to press' – *thrachte – thracht	
*sōk-	sētsa, sēka 'to seek' – sŏchte – sŏcht	
*raik-	rēts(i)a, rēka 'to reach' – răchte – răcht	
*wrak-	wretsa 'to break, tear' (no past forms recorded)	
*þank-	thendza, thenka 'to think' – thŏchte – thŏcht	
*þunk-	thindz(i)a 'to seem' – t(h)ŭchte – *t(h)ŭcht	
*brang-	brenga, bringa, brendza 'to bring' – brŏchte – brŏcht	

REMARK
Long stem vowels tended to be shortened in past tense and past particple.

§141 *Weak verbs Class 2*
These verbs typically end their infinitives in -ia (< *-ōjan-). As can be seen from the Germanic form of the suffix, the ending could not bring about i-mutation of the stem vowel and/or gemination of the stem-final consonant (§27), as the thematic vowel -ō- preceding the -j- prevented this. The verbs *libba* 'to live', *hebba/habba* 'to have', *sedza* 'to say', which in an older phase belonged to Class 3 (§138), have merged with Classes 1 and 2 or show a mixture of forms, e.g., *lifde~livade* 'lived'.

The preterite and past particple endings are -ade and -ad:

makia – makade – makad 'to make – made – made'
folgia – folgade – folgad 'to follow – followed – followed'.

In later texts, the ending is -ede, -ed. In late Old West Frisian the -d- in the preterite and past participle of Class 2 starts to be dropped: *folge* '(he) followed', *make* '(he) made' (§210.4).

For a paradigm of Class 2, see §154.

Remarkably, Class 2 has remained very productive until the present day in Modern Frisian, the only branch of West Germanic to have preserved this class.

Preterite-present verbs

§142 This group of verbs has a strong preterite tense form with a present meaning. The new ('secondary') preterite tense form is weak, that is, it is formed with a dental suffix. The infinitives, too, inasfar as they have been recorded, are secondary formations. As the present forms actually exhibit the features of a strong preterite, they should show the regular vowel variation between singular and plural where appropriate, but analogical leveling has often simplified the picture. The endings, too, are those of the strong verbs. The origin of this group goes back to Proto-Germanic.

The semantic shift from preterite to present can perhaps best be illustrated with the verb *wita* 'to know', *wēt* 'I know', which is cognate with Latin *vidēre* 'to see', *vīdi* 'I saw/have seen'. What you have seen, you know. On the basis of the semantic shift: 'I have seen, therefore I know', the preterite forms of this class acquired present meanings. Formally speaking, e.g., *wēt* has the preterite vowel of Class I.

The verbs that belong to this category are often defective in their paradigms due to lack of attestations in the corpus of Old Frisian. Here follow the most important verbs, arranged according to the strong verb classes which they originally belonged to:

§143 *Class I*

        wita 'to know'

PRES.SG	**wēt**	PRET.IND	**wiste**
PL	**witen, -et(h)**	PRES.SUBJ	**wite**
PRES.PTC	**witande**	PAST PTC	**witen**

        āga 'to have; own; have to, ought to, must'

PRES.IND.SG	**āch**	PRET.IND	**āchte**
PL	**āgen**		

REMARK

1. R has *weta, wetande*, the result of typically Rüstring *a*-mutation (§205.5)
2. R shows unhistoric *h*-: *hāga, hāch*, etc.
3. In late Old West Frisian, the preterite of *āga* may appear as *ōchte*, influenced by Middle Low German/Middle Dutch.
4. Negative contraction is found in *nēt* 'knows not' and *nācht* 'ought not'.

§144 *Class II*

        duga 'to avail; be valid'

PRES.IND.SG	**dāch, dōch**
PL	**dāget(h), dāgen**
PRES.SUBJ	**dēge**
PRES.PTC	**dāgen(d)**

§145 *Class III*

Forms with -*o*- are late Old West Frisian.

        kunna, konna 'can'

PRES.IND.SG	**kan**	PRET	**kūde, kōde**
PL	**konnen**		**kunde, konde** (< MLG)
PRES.SUBJ	**kunne**		

        thur(v)a 'to need'

PRES.IND.SG	**thur(f), thor(f)**	PRET	**thorste**
2SG	**thurst**		
PL	**thur(v)-, thor(v)en**		
PRES.SUBJ	**thure, thore**		

On forms without -v-, see §78.2v.

*dura 'to dare; be able'

PRES.IND.SG	**dur, dor**	PRET **dorste**
PL	**duren, doren**	
PRES.SUBJ	**dure**	

§146 *Class IV*

skela, skila, sela 'must, shall'

PRES.IND.SG	1/3	**skel**	PRET.IND **skulde, skolde, solde**
	2	**skalt, skelt**	
PL		**skilen, skelen, -eth, sken**	
PRES.SUBJ.SG		**skele, skile**	

§147 *Class V*

muga 'to be able, may'

PRES.IND.SG	**mei**	PRET.IND.SG **machte, muchte,**
PL	**mugen, mogen**	**mochte**
PRES.SUBJ	**muge, moge**	

§148 *Class VI*

mōta 'to be allowed, may, must'

PRES.IND.SG	**mōt**
PL	**mōten**
PRET.IND	**mōste**
PRES.SUBJ	**mōte**

Anomalous verbs

§149 Three verbs are grouped together here, those that (a) are defective in their principal parts: *wella* 'to wish, want' lacks a past participle; (b) have forms in their principal parts that are etymologically unrelated: *wesa* 'to be'; or (c) have preterite forms that cannot be easily accounted for: *dwā* 'to do'. The verbs *stān* 'to stand' and *gān* 'to go' (only in Old West Frisian) are like *dwā(n)*, but take their preterites from *gunga* (VII) and *stonda* (VI).

a. **wella, willa** 'to wish, want to'

PRES.IND.SG	1	**wel, wil, wol**
	2	**welt, wilt**
	3	**wel(e), wil(i), wol**
PL		**wellat(h), willat(h), wollet(h)**
PRES.SUBJ.SG		**welle, wille, wolle**
PRET.IND.SG		**welde, wilde, wolde**
PL		**welden, etc.**
PRET.SUBJ.SG		**welde, etc.**
PL		**welden, etc.**

REMARK

The following contracted forms with *ne* 'not' occur: *nil, nel* (3SG.PRES), *nellat(h)* (PL.PRES), *nelle* (PRES.SUBJ), *nolde(n), nelde(n)* (PRET).

b. **wesa** 'to be'

PRES.IND.SG	1	**bim, bem** (OEFris), **bin, ben** (OWFris)
	2	**bist(e)**
	3	**is**
	PL	**sen(d), sin(d)**
PRET.IND.SG	1/3	**was**
	PL	**wēren**
PRES.SUBJ.SG/PL		**sē, sīe**
	PL	**wesse**
PRET.SUBJ.SG		**wēre**
	PL	**wēre(n)**
PAST PTC		**wes(s)en**

REMARK

1. Forms with *-ss-* are Old West Frisian (§209).
2. The following negative contractions occur: *nis* 'not is', *nas* 'not was', *nere* 'not were'.

c. **dwā(n)** 'to do'; **gān** 'to go', **stān** 'to stand'

PRES.IND.SG	1	**dwē**
	2	**dēst**
	3	**dēt(h)**
	PL	**dwāt(h), dwā**
PRET.IND.SG		**dēde**
	PL	**dēden**
PRES.SUBJ.SG/PL		**dwē, dwā**
PRET.SUBJ.SG		**dēde**
	PL	**dēden**
IMP.PL		**dwāt(h)**
PAST PTC		**(e)dēn, dīen**

The verbs *gān* and *stān* have the following notable forms for the present indicative: 3SG *gēt, g(h)eet, giet*; PL *gāt, gaet*; the PAST PTC is *(e)gēn*. Likewise: 3SG *stēt*; PL *stāt*; PAST PTC *stēn*. Analogical past participles occur: *ginzen/genzen* and *stenzen/stinzen*, cf. §136.

REMARK

The verbs *gān* and *stān* are typically Old West Frisian; *gunga* (*unga* for B) and *standa/stonda* are found in both West and East.

F.   Summary and paradigms

§150 *Verbal inflections: infinitives and present participles*
As a rule, infinitives end in *-a* or *-ia* (§68), except for OWFris *gān* 'to go' and *stān* 'to stand'. In Old West Frisian, a number of monosyllabic verbs (or 'contract verbs', §54) gradually adopted the *-n* of *gān* and *stān*, for instance: *dwān* 'to do', *tiān* 'to draw', *siān* 'to see'. For a discussion of this phenomenon and its dialectological implications, cf. Meijering (1990).

When preceded by *tō*, the infinitive is inflected and ends in *-ane*, *-ene*: *tō farane* 'to travel', *tō makiane* 'to make'.

The present participle ends in *-ande*, *-ende*: *farande* 'travelling', *makiande* 'making'. Especially in Weser Old Frisian, as represented by the Rüstring manuscripts, but also in the Ems Old Frisian dialect of Brokmerland, there is no distinction in form between the present participle and the inflected infinitive ('gerund'): both end in *-ande*, *-ende*, e.g., *tō metande* 'to measure'.

REMARK
Endings in *-ene* and *-ende* are typical for late Old Frisian.

§151 *Various inflections*
The 2nd and 3rd persons SG present of strong verbs show regular *i*-mutation (§45), though not infrequently the mutated vowel has been replaced by that of the 1SG/PL by analogy.

The 2SG.PRET.IND takes the vowel of the plural, though not many instances have been recorded. Unlike Old English, the 2SG.PRET.IND takes the *-(e)st* ending, adopted from the PRES.IND.

§152 *Strong verbs*
fara 'to go'

PRES.IND.SG 1	fare	PRET.IND.SG 1	fōr
2	fer(e)st	2	fōrest
3	feret(h), fart(h)	3	fōr
PL	farat(h), -et(h)	PL	fōren, -in
PRES.SUBJ.SG	fare, fara		
PL	fare(n)		
PRET.SUBJ	fōre(n)		
IMP.SG	far		
PL	farat(h), -et(h)		
PRES.PTC	farande, -ende	PAST PTC	faren
INFL.INF	farane, -ene		

§153 *Weak verbs Class 1:*

a. *dēla* 'to share'

PRES.IND.SG	1	**dēle**	PRET.IND	1	**dēlde**
	2	**dēl(e)st**		2	**dēldest**
	3	**dēlet(h), dēlt(h)**		3	**dēlde**
	PL	**dēlat(h), -et(h)**		PL	**dēlden**
PRES.SUBJ.SG		**dēle**			
	PL	**dēle(n)**			
PRET.SUBJ		**dēlde, dēlde(n)**			
IMP.SG		**dēle**			
	PL	**dēlat(h), -et(h)**			
PRES.PTC		**dēlande, -ende**	PAST PTC		**(e)dēl(e)d**
INFL.INF		**dēlane, -ene**			

b. The verb 'to have' (originally weak Class 3, cf. §138) appears as *hebba* in Old East Frisian, and usually as *habba* in Old West Frisian:

		OEFris	OWFris
PRES.IND.SG	1	**hebbe**	**hab(be)**
	2	**hest**	**hast**
	3	**het(h)**	**hat(h), hawet(h)**
	PL	**hebbath**	**habbet(h)**
PRET.IND.SG	1,3	**hēde**	1,3 **hēd(e), hāde**
	2	**hēdest**	2 **hēdest, hādest**
	PL	**hēden**	**hadden**
PRES.SUBJ.SG/PL		**hebbe**	**habbe, have**
PRES.PTC		**hebbande**	**habbande**
PAST.PTC		**heved**	**hawn**
INFL.INF		**hebbane, -ene**	**habban(e)**

REMARK

The verb 'to have' shows the following negative contractions: *nebbe, nest, neth, nath* (1,2,3 SG), *nabbeth* (PRES.PL), *nebbe, nabbe* (PRES.SUBJ), *nede* (PRET.SUBJ).

§154 *Weak verbs class 2: makia* 'to make'

PRES.IND.SG	1	**makie**	PRET.IND.SG	1	**makade**
	2	**makast, -est**		2	**makadest**
	3	**makat(h), -et(h)**		3	**makade**
	PL	**makiat(h), -et(h)**		PL	**makaden**
PRES.SUBJ.SG		**makie**	PRET.SUBJ		**makade(n)**
	PL	**makien**			
IMP.SG **maka**; PL		**makiat(h), -et(h)**			
PRES.PTC		**mak(i)ande, -ende**	PAST PTC		**(e)makad, -ed**
INFL.INF		**mak(i)ane, -ene**			

§155 *General remarks on the verb*

1.   In late texts, the infinitival ending *-(i)a* is often reduced to *-(i)e*.
2.   Verbal forms ending in *-e* may drop this vowel, if followed by the personal pronouns *ik, er, i,* indicated in this book by an apostrophe: *bonn'ic* 'I declare', *sprek'* *ik* 'I speak'. The 3SG.PRES.IND ending has often been reduced to *-t*; endings in *-eth* or *-ith* are rare. If the stem ends in *-k, -n(g), -f, -t,* or *-th,* we also find endingless forms such as *brek* 'breaks', *sweng* 'swings, throws', *delf* 'digs', *sterf* 'dies', *bet* 'pays a compensation', *keth* 'announces', *werth* 'becomes'.
3.   The 1,2PL forms of all tenses and moods may end in *-e* (*-u* in Rüstring texts), and endingless (zero) if the stem ends in a vowel, when the pronouns follow the verb: *hot āge wī tō dwāne?* 'what must we do?', *aldus skilu wī ... halda* 'thus we must preserve'; *fā jī up* 'raise (PL) up your hands', *ther brek'ī on thera liudfrethe* 'with it you (PL) broke the people's peace'.
4.   The present participle ending *-nd-* tends to drop its *-d-* in later Old West Frisian, e.g., *lidzen* 'lying'.
5.   The perfective prefix **ie-* (< **ga-, *gi*) has usually been reduced to *e-* or *i-* in Old East Frisian texts, or has disappeared altogether (§58). This process has proceeded even further in Old West Frisian, and all Modern Frisian varieties (West, East and North) have no such prefix before past participles any longer nor does it appear before any other inherited verbal form. However, under the influence of Middle Low German and Middle Dutch, the prefix is regularly found as *ge-* or *ghe-*.
6.   Occasionally, we find weak forms of strong verbs in late texts: *stritte* 'he fought' (Class I), *tsīezd* 'chosen' (Class II), *bande* 'he summoned', *houden* 'they hewed'; and the past participles *āket* 'increased', *bonned* 'summoned', *henged* 'hung', *lette* 'let', *ofret* 'dissuaded', *stet* 'hit' (all of these Class VII).

Chapter IV

Lexicology

Word formation
and loan words in Old Frisian

A. Word formation and affixation

§156
The bulk of the Old Frisian vocabulary was inherited from Germanic, many of which in turn stem from Indo-European. To this stock, words were added through (1) affixation, (2) compounding and (3) borrowing. Relatively little work has been done so far in this field of Old Frisian studies (Munske 2001a; cf. Bremmer 1992: §4.1). The following sections give a fairly broad survey of word formation and lexical borrowing but they do not aim at completeness.

Affixation (i.e., adding prefixes, infixes or suffixes to the stem of a word) was the most productive means of coining words in Indo-European. However, many Indo-European and even Germanic suffixes were no longer recognizable as such in Old Frisian times. In the following sections, the explicit (i.e., recognizable) suffixes and prefixes will receive particular attention.

As in the other Germanic languages, the stress in Old Frisian falls on the stem. The stress remains on the stem when suffixes are added, with the exception of suffixes borrowed from French, such as *-īe, -(e)rīe, -(e)ment*. Also when prefixes are added to the stem the stress remains the same, again with some exceptions. Where relevant, such instances have been noted.

§157 *Suffixes*
Suffixes can be added to nouns, verbs, adjectives and numerals. Such new formations are then known as 'denominal', 'deverbal' and 'deadjectival', respectively, or just 'derivational'.

Nouns

§158 *Agentive suffixes*
-*a*: used to form masculine agent nouns, usually added to a verbal stem: *kempa* 'champion', *boda* 'messenger', *āsega* 'law speaker, legal expert', *rēdieva* 'counsel-giver (i.e., judge)'.

-*and*: this present participle ending was used to form masculine agent nouns: *berand* 'bearer (i.e., guardian)', *werand* 'protector, guardian', *efterkumanda* PL 'aftercomers, posterity', *wīgand* 'fighter'.

-*ere*: this suffix (originally borrowed from Latin -*ārius*) replaced -*a* and -*and* in productivity to form both deverbal and denominal agent nouns, e.g.: *haldere* 'holder', *kāpere* 'buyer', *mekere* 'marriage broker (lit. maker)', *tapper(e)* 'publican'. Denominal, e.g.: *bogere* 'bowman', *hōdere* 'police officer (lit. hat bearer, as a symbol of his office)', *Rūmere* '1. Roman citizen; 2. pilgrim to Rome'. In late Old West Frisian, the suffix -*er* was extended with a preceding *k* for no obvious semantic purpose, e.g., *glesker* 'glass-maker', perhaps on analogy with *fisker* 'fisherman' and *flēsker* 'butcher'.

Some suffixes are used to make feminine agent nouns:

-*ster(e)*: used to make feminine agent nouns, e.g., *tapster* 'she publican, tapster', *baxter* 'she baker', *wulkemster* 'she wool comber'.

-*in(ne)*: used to make femal nouns, e.g., *afgodinne* 'idol'.

§159 *Abstract suffixes*
A wide range of suffixes were used to build abstract nouns (cf. Ahlsson 1960). Here follow some of the most frequent ones:

-*dōm*: usually added to an adjective to form deadjectival masculine abstract nouns, e.g.: *ētheldōm* 'nobility', *frīdōm* 'freedom', *wīsdōm* 'wisdom'.

-*skipi* (R), -*skip(e)*: usually added to nouns, which then became either feminine or neuter, e.g.: *āftskip* 'matrimony', *bodeskip* 'message', *fiandskip* 'enmity', *hērskipi* 'lordship', *witskipe* 'witness'.

-*ath*: to form masculine abstract nouns from weak verbs Class 2 as well as from nouns, e.g.: *somnath* 'gathering', *thingath* 'legal procedure', *thrim(e)nath* 'a third'.

-*ene*: to form deverbal feminine abstracts, e.g.: *blendene* 'blinding' (< *blenda*), *bōkene* 'conveyance by charter or deed' (< *bōkia* 'to bequeathe'), *heftene* 'fettering, captivity' (< *hefta* 'captivate'), *oliene* '(sacrament of) extreme unction', *stelene* 'theft' (< *stela* 'steal').

-*unge*/-*onge*, -*inge*/-*enge*, (the former two endings only in R): a very productive suffix, mainly to form deverbal feminine abstracts, e.g.: *wundunge* 'injury', *sellonge* 'sale', *barninge* 'fuel', *moninge* 'admonition'; denominal: *nettinge* 'net(work)'.

-*nisse*, -*nes(s)e*, -*ens(e)*: this suffix (the last form shows metathesis) builds both denominal and deverbal feminine abstract nouns, e.g., *īdelnisse* 'idleness', *stilnisse* 'menstruation (lit. stilness)', *thiūsternisse* 'darkness'; *heftnese* 'captivity', *setnese* 'decree', *sēknisse*/*sēkense* 'search', *untfengnesse* 'conception'. On the variant form -*ens(e)*, still productive in ModWFrisian, see §66.

-ithe (R), *-ethe, -de, -te*: the last two forms of this mainly deadjectival feminine abstract noun suffix are late. Examples are: *lamethe/lemethe* 'lameness, paralysis', *hirt-lemithe* 'paralysis of the shoulder', *thiūvethe* 'theft', *wīthe* 'relic; oath on the relics', *ermde* 'poverty', *diopte* 'depth'.

-elsa: this suffix (cf. §66) was used to form both abstract and concrete masculine nouns (both denominal and deverbal), e.g.: *lamelsa* 'paralysis', *blōdelsa* 'bloody wound', *sērelsa* 'injury', *wlemmelsa* 'injury', and, with 'contamination', *dreppelsa* 'threshold'.

-tha, -ta, -da: this suffix formed both abstract and concrete masculine nouns, e.g.: *ōsedroptha* 'eavesdrop', *tichta* 'accusation', *monda* 'intercourse (both social and sexual)'.

-ma: a suffix which in Proto-Germanic times formed both abstract and concrete masculine nouns. Only as an abstract noun suffix was it productive in Old Frisian (and later Frisian). Originally deverbal, in later Old Frisian it was also suffixed to adjectives and nouns. Examples of abstract nouns: *bōkma* 'legacy', *brekma* 'fine', *setma* 'decree', *bitichtma* 'accusation', *swētma* 'sweetness'.

-(h)ēd(e), -heid: this feminine suffix became productive especially in later Old Frisian, probably under influence of Low German and Dutch. Examples: *kirstenēde* 'Christianity', *wīshēd* 'wisdom'. With 'linking morpheme' *-ich-*: *onhaldicheid* 'abstinence', *ermicheid* 'poverty'.

Under the influence of Middle Dutch and Middle Low German, a number of French loan suffixes became very popular in late Old Frisian with which to coin new feminine abstracts. As in French, the stress fell on the suffix.

-īe [iːə]: Examples: *wōste'nīe* 'desert, wilderness', *sīmo'nīe* 'simony' (more likely straight loans), *tāve'rīe* 'witchcraft'.

-ēgie: *las'tēgie* 'loading- and discharging-berth for ships', *timme'rāgie* 'construction, building'

-(e)rīe: *forrēde'rīe* 'treason', *kalte'rīe* 'chat, gossip'.

-ment: this loan suffix (with final stress) served to form neuter nouns, as appears from the loan word *paye'ment* 'payment', but then became productive, e.g., *drēge'ment* 'threat' (or < MDu/MLG).

§160 *Concrete suffixes*

A number of suffixes were used to form concrete nouns, such as:

-ling: to form masculine nouns, (a) usually indicating a human: *etheling* 'nobleman', *frīling* 'free man', *ēgling* 'possessor', *hāvedling* (later *hādling*) 'leader', *iungeling* 'disciple', *-knīling* 'relative' (in a certain degree of kinship, called 'knee', e.g., *thredknīling* 'relative in the third degree'), *thredling* 'id', *sisterling* 'sister's son'. (b) With measures: *fiarling* 'a quarter (mark)', *halling* (< *halfling*) 'halfling, half a penny'. (c) As a diminutive: *ordling* 'rim' (< *ord* 'point'). Occasionaly found in adjectives: *sunderling* 'separate, special'.

-*ing*: this suffix is used to form masculine nouns, (a) referring to humans: *kening* 'king', *horning* 'illegitimate child', *hūsing* 'free farmer', *swiāring* 'son of brother-in-law', *wītsing* 'pirate, "viking"'. (b) Names of coins, e.g., *skilling* 'shilling', *penning* 'penny'. (c) Names of animals: *fering* 'young bull', *hēring* 'herring'. (d) Miscellaneous: *pralling* 'testicle'. (e) As GEN.PL, it was very productive as a patronymic formant, e.g., *Camminga*. It could also be used to denote an inhabitant of a certain land, e.g., *Riostring* 'inhabitant of Rüstringen' (cf. *alle Riostringa*, 'all inhabitants of Rüstringen', *Riostringa land* 'the land of the Rüstrings').

Adjectives

§161 *Adjectival suffixes*

For a full survey and discussion of adjectival suffixes, see Ahlsson (1991).

-*bēr*: this suffix usually has the same function as ModE '-able', e.g.: '*aubēr* 'showable, manifest, public', *ētbēr* 'eatable', *gungbēr* 'current (of money)', *unwandelbēr* 'not interchangable (of a piece of land)', *tilbēr* 'moveable' (deverbal); *ēr-, ārbēr* 'honourable', *skalkbēr* 'villainous' (denominal); *orbēr* 'useful, profitable', *epenbēr* 'public, manifest' (deadjectival).

-*ed, -ad*: this suffix was used for a pseudo-past participle construction, in which the stem is not ostensibly verbal but nominal and nevertheless assumes a weak past participle ending. Its meaning is 'provided with …' (Faltings 1996). Examples: *tolnad* 'with toll (of a market)'. With prefix: *bisibbed* 'related', *biwēsed* 'orphaned', *unbrōked* 'without trousers', *uniēriged* 'underage (of a child)'. In compounds: *blaulaid* '(covered) with blue roof slates', *einerved* 'with own, inherited land' (beside *einerve*), *epenuddrad* 'with dripping teats (of a cow)', *fiuwerfōted* 'four-footed' (beside *fiuwerfōte*), *fiuwerherned* 'four-cornered, square', *hasmūled* 'with a harelip', *tiānspetsed* 'with ten spokes' (beside *tiānspetse*), *tolufwintrad* 'twelve years old'.

-*en*: this suffix (< Gmc *-*īna*) was used to indicate the material (or sometimes the colour) it was made from. Where applicable it caused *i*-mutation and assibilation of a preceding velar plosive. Examples: *stēnen* 'of stone', *etsen* 'oaken' (cf. *ēk*), *gelden* 'golden', *wēden* 'blue (lit. of woad)'.

-*fest*: although originally meaning 'fixed, firm' as in *erthfest* 'firm in the earth', *bēnfest* 'grown onto the bone', the suffix also acquired a vaguer sense of 'provided with' as in *būkfest* 'marriagable, nubile (of grown-up girls)', *frethofest* 'requiring compensation (for peace)'.

-*ich/-ech* and -*och/-uch* (the latter only in R): the most productive adjectival suffix, denominal, deverbal and deadjectival, to indicate 'having the property of': *kreftich* 'powerful', *blōdich* 'bloody', *iēroch* 'of age, adult', *ūrhērich* 'inobedient', *underdēnoch* 'subject', *werthich* 'worth, worthy', *sōthech* 'true'.

-*līk*: the suffix forms deverbal, denominal and deadjectival adjectives. Examples: *godlīk* 'divine', *iērlīk* 'yearly', *untellīk* 'unspeakable', *biprōvelīk* 'demonstrable', *liāflīk* 'lovely', *netlīk* 'useful, profitable'.

-(i)sk, -(e)sk: to form adjectives from nouns indicating origin or association, e.g.: *mannisk* 'human', *Israhelisk* 'Israelite', *Engelsk, Anglisk* 'English', *Frīsesk* 'Frisian', *helsk* 'hellish', *wraldsk* 'worldly, secular'.

-lās: a deprivative suffix: *helplās* 'helpless', *hāvedlās* 'without a leader', *līflās* 'lifeless', *werlās* 'defenseless'. Originally an adjective, and still sometimes used as such (e.g., *and werth hi thenne lās* 'and if he then gets free').

-sum/-sim/-sam: this suffix was used to form adjectives denoting a characteristic, ability or inclination. Examples: *ērsam* 'honourable', *hārsum, -sam, -sim* 'obedient', *urietsam* 'forgetful'.

Adverbs

§162 *Adverbial suffixes*

Only a few suffixes were used to form adverbs. Adverbs could also be made by case endings (for genitive, see §181.3, for dative, see §182.5).

-e. This is one of the most frequent adverbial suffixes, e.g.: *īdle* 'vainly', *sēre* 'very, sorely', *sīde* 'amply, extensively', *riuchte* 'rightly'.

-līke. Actually, this is the adverbial extension of the adjectival suffix *-līk*, but it has virtually turned into an independent adverbial suffix. Note that some adjectives had two adverbial forms, sometimes with a slight semantic difference, e.g.: *sērelīke* 'carefully' (cf. *sēre* 'sorely'), *godilīke* 'divinely', *riuchtlīke* 'lawfully'.

-ling(e): with the sense of 'like, in the way of', e.g., *hondeling* 'like a dog'.

Miscellaneous

§163 *Prefixes*

Below follows a fairly complete survey of the prefixes that were common in Old Frisian.

a-: reduced (unstressed) form of *on-*, e.g., in adverbs like *atwā* 'in two', *abefta* 'behind', *awei* 'away', *atwiska* 'between', *abinna* 'inside', *abūta* 'moreover', *abuppa* 'above'.

ā-[1]: intensifying prefix, but often with no apparent change of meaning, e.g., *āsiā* 'to see', *āslā* 'to strike', *āspera* 'to perceive'. Not to be confused with

ā-[2]: 'eternal', a stressed prefix in adverbs and nouns, as in *ālang* 'everlasting', *ādēl* 'legacy, bequest', possibly also in *ābēl* 'lasting scar'.

and-/ond-: the original meaning 'against, opposite' is often preserved when prefixed (with primary stress) to verbs and nouns, e.g.: *ondward* 'present; answer', *ondwardia* 'to return; to answer', *ondlete* 'face' (cf. OE *andwlita*), *onderk* (< *ondwerk*) 'tool', *ondhāved* 'breakwater (kind of dam to brake waves)', *ondser* 'answer'.

be-/bi-: usually has an intensifying meaning (i.e., aiming at goal or object) when pre-fixed to verbs: *bibanna* 'to ban', *bidrīta* 'to soil (o.s.) with shit', *bifesta* 'to fasten'. It occurs in many compound prepositions and adverbs: *bifara* 'before', *binitha* 'beneath', and, with elision of the vowel, in *befta* 'behind', *binna* 'within', *buppa* 'above', *būta* 'outside'. The prefix carries stress in: *bīfang* 'court of law', *bīgerdel* 'girdle purse', *bi-iechte* 'confession'.

ē-: deprivative suffix in: *ēbēte* 'without compensation', *ēfelle* 'without skin', *ēfrethe* 'exempt from wergeld', *ēlīve* 'lifeless'.

ef-: deprivative suffix found in adjectives and nouns, as in: *eflīve* 'dead', *efsivene* 'drain-ing (of wound liquid)', *evēst* 'jealousy' (cf. OE *æfēst*).

fon-, fan-: usually found with verbs or with deverbal nouns, it expresses separation, as in *fondēla* 'to take a part from the kindred's property', *fongunga* 'to depart, go away'. With noun: *fonfere* 'departure'.

for-/ur-: unstressed, intensifying prefix, mainly found with verbs or deverbal nouns. It is often used with an overtone of destruction: *forbarna* 'to burn', *fordēma* 'to condemn', *forflōka* 'to curse', *urhela* 'to conceal, hide'. With nouns: *forrēd* 'treason', *urieft* 'forgiveness'.

fora-/fori-/fore-/fōr-: stressed prefix with various parts of speech, mainly indicating pre-eminence or precedence: *foribringa* 'to adduce', *fōrhāved* 'forehead', *foremund* 'guardian', *forespreka* 'advocate, spokesman', *fōrthocht* 'premeditated', *fōrmēls* 'in former times'.

forth-: stressed prefix with the sense of 'motion towards' or 'continuation': *forthfara* 'to move on', *forthfinda* 'to pronounce verdict', *forthgong* 'procedure', *forthsetta* 'to proceed, carry on'.

ful-/fol-: found with various parts of speech to express 'completeness': *fulbranga* 'to accomplish', *fulbrōther* 'brother-german, brother through both parents', *fulsibbe* 'wholly related', *fulwunia* 'to persist'.

mis-: used with various parts of speech to express 'wrongness': *misdēde* 'crime', *mislāvich* 'heretic', *mislīk* 'unequal, different', *misdītsa* 'to build dikes wrongly', *misskīa* 'to happen badly'.

of-: usually with primary stress, signifies separation and is found with verbs or dever-bal nouns: *ofbreka* 'to break off', *ofberna* 'to burn down', *ofdwā* 'to separate', *offlecht* 'tearing off', *ofgang* 'resignation (of office)', *ofsedel* 'dismounting (from a horse)'.

on-: with primary or secondary stress, indicates the beginning of an action, as in *onbidda* 'to worship', *onfalla* 'to contest', *onbreng* 'confirmation by oath of accusa-tion', or the being attached to something, as in *onfest* 'on the body (of a bodily part), whole', *onhebba* 'to have on', *onsīa* 'to sew on(to)'. In Old West Frisian, *on-* often appears as *a(e)n-*. To complicate matters, especially in later texts, *on-* is also a form of *un-* (see there).

to-, te-, ti-: found only with verbs, with a destructive meaning: *tobreka* 'to break apart', *torenda* 'to tear apart', *toslān* 'to break in pieces'.

tō-: this stressed prefix often has the same meaning as the preposition, and is found with verbs and deverbal nouns: *tōhlāpa* 'to walk towards, approach', *tōfere* 'arrival'. It is also used to make compound prepositions: *tōfara* 'before', *tōjenst* 'against'.

un-: negative prefix with adjectives and adverbs: *unbrōkad* 'without trousers', *unwis* 'uncertain', *unthingades* 'without accusation'; with nouns, it has a pejorative force and primary stress: *unweder* 'bad weather', *uniēr* 'bad year'; sometimes it has an intensifying meaning: *unskeld* 'great guilt', *unkost* 'great expenses', *unbōte* 'heavy compensation'. In OWFris, *un-* often appears as *on-*.

und-/unt-: prefixed to verbs or deverbal nouns which thereby usually acquire a deprivative or negative meaning: *undgunga* 'to go away, swear innocence', *undielda* 'to pay, pay damages', *undfā* 'to receive'. In later texts, it usually appears as *on-*.

ur-, or-: either means 'original, primary', as in *urdēl* 'judgement', with primary stress, or it signifies deprivation, i.e., 'without', as in *urwēna* 'hopeless'. It is also an unstressed form of 'for-', e.g., *urieta* 'to forget', *urbelga* 'to get angry', *formītha* 'to avoid'.

ūr-: contracted form of *over*: *ūrera* 'to plow beyond one's field', *ūrskera* 'to mow beyond one's field'.

wan-, won-: expressing negation, lack, privation, deficiency, e.g., *wanmēte* 'fraudulent measure', *wanwicht* 'fraudulent weight', *wanandert* 'failure to appear in court' ('lack of answer'), *wanhopa* 'despair', *wonsprēke* 'speech defect', *wanweder* 'bad weather'.

§164 Worthy of mention are a few 'linking morphemes' that had some frequency but apparently lacked any semantic function.

-el-: in a number of compound nouns, the first element was expanded with a linking morpheme *-el-*, for euphonic reasons it would seem (cf. Faltings 1987). The phenomenon is fairly late, and almost entirely restricted to Old West Frisian. Practically all the elements are verbal stems: *bedeldei* 'day of prayer', *festeldei* 'day of fasting', *itelmes* 'knife for eating'. Non-verbal first elements are found in, e.g., *weselkind* 'orphan', *commelduer* 'commander'. These last examples show the expansion of the morpheme.

-ig-/eg- Without exception, verbs augmented with this linking morpheme belong to weak verbs Class 2. The infix did not have any syntactic or semantic function but, it would seem, was entirely phonologically conditioned (cf. Hoekstra 1993b), and mainly appears after stems ending in a dental or alveolar (*-d, -t, -l, -s, -n, -r*), e.g., *endigia* 'to finish', *kriūsigia* 'to crucify', *āftigia* 'to marry'. Occasionally (by analogy), we find such verbs whose stems do not end in a dental, e.g., *lāvigia* 'to bequeath'.

-e- Occasionally, and late, *-e-* is found as a linking morpheme, e.g., *cronkebed* 'sickbed, death-bed', *palmebām* 'palm-tree', *gōdeweb* 'gold brocade'.

B. Compounding

An important creative source of new words was compounding two elements into one new word. Several combinations were possible:

§165 Nouns could be conjoined without a linking (genitival) morpheme to another noun: *bōklond* 'land bequeathed to the church by charter', *bronddolch* 'wound caused by burning', *fiskdam* 'fishweir'.

Relatively rare in Old Frisian, but more common in late Old Frisian, is the combination of a noun with a genitival ending which modifies a following noun, e.g., *brōthersbern* 'brother's child', *godeshūs* 'God's house, church', *dōmesdī* 'doomsday', *sumeresnacht* 'summernight'. No compounds are attested in which the -*s*- is added to feminine nouns.

Also combinations in which the first element of the compound features a weak ending are found: *mōnandei* 'Monday', *hēlgenamon* 'church warden', *bēnenaburch* 'womb' (cf. §99R.2).

§166 Nouns could be modified by a preceding adjective or adverb: *hāchtīd* 'liturgical feast', *sunderacht* 'consultation outside the law-court', *wil(d)diār* 'wild animal, beast'; *delgang* 'dismounting', *ērseke* 'old enmity'.

§167 Adjectives could be compounded by a preceding noun: *brondrād* 'burning red' (of gold), *nēdkald* 'bitterly cold', *strīkhalt* 'lame', *ūdertam* 'easy to milk (udder-tame)'.

§168 Adverbs could be formed by an adjective plus an inflected noun: *sunderlēpis* (to *hlāp* 'leap') 'special'.

C. Loan words

§169 Intercourse with speakers of other languages naturally resulted in the adoption of loan words. Borrowing often occurs when a new thing or concept is introduced or when speakers adopt words from a language which is held to be more prestigious. Many of these loans go back to the period before Frisian emerged as a separate language.

§170 From the Common Germanic or West Germanic period date the few Celtic loans *ombicht* 'office' and *rīke* 'kingdom, realm'.

§171 *Loans from Latin*
It is not always easy to establish the relative date of the Latin loans, especially since this aspect of the Old Frisian vocabulary has been little studied (cf. Wollmann 1990; for a preliminary inventory, but not yet exhaustive, see Dekker 2000). Contact between

the Germanic tribes and the Romans in the first centuries of our era resulted in such loans as *anker* 'anchor' (< *ancora*), *seine* 'drag net' (< *sagēna*), *tefle/tevle* 'writing tablet' (<*tabula*), *pet* 'pit' (<*puteus*), *komer* 'room' (<*camera*), *mentel* 'mantle, cloak' (<*mantellum*), *tsietel* 'kettle' (< *catillus*), *menote* 'mint; coin' (< *monēta*), *mūre* 'stone wall' (< *mūrus*), *tolene* 'toll' (< *tolōnium*), *tsīse* 'cheese' (< *cāseus*), *butere* 'butter' (< *buterum*), *ele* 'oil' (< *oleum*), *wīn* 'wine' (< *vīnum*), *piper* 'pepper' (< *piperum*), *fals* 'false' (<*falsus*), *sūter* 'tailor' (< *sutor)*, *ūre* 'hour' (< *hōra*).

REMARK
kiste 'chest' (<L *cista*) apparently is a MDu/MLG loan as it lacks initial palatalization (§42).

§172 The conversion to Christianity brought a new wave of Latin loans (which often were themselves loans from Greek). To the earliest of these words, dating back to perhaps even before the conversion, belong *biskop* 'bishop' (< *episcopus*), *diōvel* 'devil' (< *diabolus*), *kersten* 'Christian' (< *c(h)rīstiānus*). Other loans related to the conversion include *engel/angel* 'angel' (< *angelus*), *skrīva* 'to write' (< *scrībere*; the native word was *wrīta* 'to write'), *fīre* 'liturgical feast' (< *fēria*), *kersoma* 'chrism' (< *c(h)rīsma*), *degma/ dek(e)ma* 'tithe' (< *decima*), *seininge* 'blessing'(< L *signum* 'sign of the cross'), *papa* 'priest' (< L < Gr 'father'), *Pāska* 'Easter' (< L *Pāscha*), *spīse* 'food' (< ML *spēsa < expensa (pecūnia)* 'expenses for food'), *lēka*, *leia* 'lay(man)' (< *lāicus*).

§173 Because the Frisians were converted to Christianity by the Anglo-Saxons, it is quite likely for them to have adopted certain Old English words that related to the new religion. Yet, such words are hard to pin down. In all probability they include *trachtia* 'to yearn' (< OE *treahtian* 'to comment on, consider' < L *tractāre*), *(ur)diligia* 'to delete' (< OE *dīlegian* 'to blot out'; esp. 'erase what has been written' < L *delēre*), but these words may also have entered Frisian through German by way of Anglo-Saxon missionary centres in Germany, as did probably *sunnēvend* 'Sunday eve', in which the eve before a feast day was a loan adaptation of L *vigilia* 'vigil, devotional night watch'. Perhaps *tsiurke* 'church' (< OE *ćyrice*) is another Anglo-Saxon loan.

§174 *Loans from other Continental languages*
Old and Middle High German words usually arrived in Frisia via Low German. Some early examples of such loans are *keisere* (< OHG *kaisar* 'emperor'), *kind* 'child' (no initial palatalization!), *tins* 'tax' (< OS *tins* < OHG *zins* < L *census*; note that HG /ts/ has been replaced by Low German /t/). Later loans include *iunker* 'squire' and *iunkfrouwe* 'young woman, virgin'.

Old Saxon (or Old Low German) moderately and Middle Low German increasingly exercised their influence on the Old Frisian vocabulary, especially through commerce, to replace that language almost entirely east of the Lauwers by the end of the fifteenth century. Early such loans include *reid* 'reed' (Old Frisian should have been **hriād*), *thē* 'who, which' (indeclinable relative particle, §95.4), *swāger* 'brother-in-law', sometimes with vowel substitution, e.g., *reth* 'wheel' (< OS *rath*), *sletel* 'key' (< OS *slutil*) (cf. Bremmer 2008a).

French words also found their way to Old Frisian, in all likelihood through neighbouring languages. An early example, *c.*1200, is *paulūn* 'tent, tabernacle' (< OFr *pavilloun*). Other, often later examples include *payement* 'payment', *amīe* '(female) lover, concubine', *leverei* 'livery', *dz(i)upe* 'female dress', *kapōn* 'capon', *malātsk* 'leprous' (< *maladie*), the suffixes *-leie* 'kind of' (with GEN): *ēnerleie* 'of one kind', *-īe*, e.g., *soldīe* 'soldiery', *kalterīe* 'gossip, idle talk', *-agīe*: *timmeragīe* 'carpentry'.

From Slavic languages (presumably through Low German) the Frisians borrowed *prām* 'flat-bottomed vessel' and *cona* (*cone*?) 'fur', which was used in Rüstringen as a unit of currency.

§175 *Loan translations*

An interesting aspect of the conversion was the attempt to assimilate new concepts by translating them into Frisian. Quite a few such loan translations (or 'calques') also occur in other Old Germanic languages so that it is often impossible to say whether they were coined independently or were adopted from neighbouring languages. Specifically Christian calques from Latin include *himelkining* 'heavenly king' (< *rex coeli*), *himulrīke* 'heavenly kingdom' (< *regnum coeli*), *erthrīke* 'earthly kingdom' (< *regnum mundi*), *godeshūs* 'church' (< *domus Dei*), *dōmesdī* 'doomsday' (< *dies iudicii*), *elemechtich* 'almighty' (< *omnipotens*), *fadera* 'godfather' (< **gefadera* < L *compater*).

The names of the days of the week were translated during the Roman period: *sunnandei* (< *dies solis*), *mōnandei* (< *dies lūnae*), *tīesdei* (< *dies Martis*), *wednesdei* (< *dies Mercurii*), *thunresdei* (< *dies Iovis*), *frīadei* (< *dies Veneris*), *sāterdei* (< *dies Saturni*). Perhaps certain indications of time find their origin in Latin, too, such as *middei* 'midday' (< *meridies*), *evennacht* 'equinox' (< *equinox*).

Other loan formations, some of them very early, include *hertoga* 'army leader, duke' (< L/Gr *stratēgos*), *hāvedmon* 'leader, chieftain' (< *capitaneus*), *herestrēte* 'highroad, military road' (< *via militaris*), *federerve* 'patrimony' (< *patrimonium*; the native word is *ēthel*).

Chapter V

Syntax

The sentence elements of Old Frisian

In this chapter attention will be given especially to those syntactic phenomena that might present problems in reading an Old Frisian text. A detailed description of the syntax of Old Frisian, however desirable, is beyond the scope of this book. For a discussion of the study of Old Frisian syntax, see de Haan (2001b).

A. Concord

§176 As a rule there is concord in number, gender and case between nouns and their pronouns and determiners: **thi heliga biscop** 'the holy bishop', **allera kininga** *ieft* 'the gift of all kings', *Heinrik thi keyser* **thi** *was hertoga to Beygeron* 'Henry the Emperor, he (who) was Duke of Bavaria'.

Natural gender sometimes prevails over grammatical gender: *and ther en wif* (NEUT) *tohlapt and* **hiu** (FEM) *sa fir onefuchten werth thet ...* 'and if a woman approaches [viz. to a quarrel] and she is attacked to such an extent that ...', *thet hi ne muge bi* **sinre** (DAT.SG.FEM) **wive** (DAT.SG.NEUT) *wesa* 'that he is not able to be (i.e., have intercourse) with his wife' (cf. Rauch 2007).

Note that such neuter pronouns as *thet, hit, hwet* can be used with non-neuter predicates as well as with plural predicates, when serving as a provisional subject: **Thet** *send tha tian bodo* 'These are the Ten Commandments'; *Thin God* **thet** *is thi ena* 'Your God, he is the only one'.

§177 Even though a subject may consist of more than one element, the predicate can be singular when it precedes the conjoined subjects: *Under sine tidon* **warth** *Ruszlond and Polenera lond and Ungeron bikerd* 'In his days Russia and the land of the Poles and the Hungarians were converted', *sa* **wext** *thet merch and thiu hed* 'then the marrow and the skin grow'. This phenomenon is also quite common in Old English and indeed in other Old Germanic languages (Mitchell 1985: §30.2; Harbert 2007: 217–18).

Note the singular predicate, the multiple subject and the plural apposition in *Under sine tidon* **was** *Sancte Mertin and Sancte Ambrosius,* **tha haliga biscopar** 'During his days was (i.e., lived) St Martin and St Ambrose, the holy bishops'.

When a singular subject is followed by a collective noun as its complement, the predicate may switch from singular to plural: *Sinte Mauricius mit enen graet scaer ridderen* **ghinghe** *in dae lucht foer dae Friesen heer ende* **habbet** *al dae heydana wriaghet* 'St Maurice, with a large multitude of knights, went (sg) in the air before the army of the Frisians and (they) have put to flight all the pagans'.

B. Cases

§178 Old Frisian differs little in its usage of cases from any of the other Old Germanic dialects. For prepositions and the cases they govern, see §183.

§179 *Nominative*
The case (1) of the subject, e.g., *Thet sprec* **thi wisa Salemon** 'This said the wise Solomon'.
(2) of the subject complement (or: the nominal part of the predicate), e.g., *Thi fiarda was* **thi biscop Liudger** 'The fourth (missionary) was Bishop Liudger'.
(3) of address (vocative), e.g., **Asega**, *is't thingtid?* 'Asega, is it time for holding court?'

§180 *Accusative*
The case (1) of the direct object, *hit upriucht* **thene likkoma** 'it [the child] raises the body'.
(2) The accusative is also used to express time and extent of space, e.g., **niugen monath** 'nine months', *hi gunge* **tha niugen heta skera** 'he should walk the nine hot ploughshares'.

§181 *Genitive*
The case of (1) possession, e.g., **Adames** *liave* 'Adam's wife'.
(2) The subjective genitive, e.g., **thes kininges** *bon* 'the king's order', i.e., 'the king ordered'. The subjective genitive often appears with a pronoun: *sunder onspreke* **usis** 'without a claim of us, i.e., without us claiming … '; the objective genitive, e.g., *thruch* **Romera** *drede* 'for fear of the Romans' i.e., 'they fear the Romans', *wr anxte* **hara lywes** 'for fear of their lives'.
(3) The genitive is used adverbially, e.g., **thes otheres dis** '(on) the second day', *sa hi wither* **inlendes** *cume* 'if he returns in the land', **enis** 'once', **utwardis** 'outwards', **otheres** 'otherwise', **menis** 'falsely', **unthonkes** 'involuntarily', **unbethingades** 'uncontestedly'.
(4) The partitive genitive, e.g., **alra** *ek* 'each of all, i.e., everyone', **fiowera**sum 'with three others' (litt. 'one of four'), *sa hwersa ma ena monne enne top* **heres** *ofstat* 'whenever someone strikes off a tuft of hair of some other man', *fe* **husa** *ieftha fela*

husa 'few houses or many houses', *nebbe ic* **frionda** *enoch?* 'don't I have enough friends?'; likewise with the indefinite pronouns *nawet (naut, nat)* and *awet: dat hie des naet dwaen wolde* 'that he did not want to do anything of this', *nawet* **erges** 'nothing evil', *sa hwelik aldirmon sa* **thera wedda** *awet ovirte* ... 'whenever an alderman neglects anything of the compensations ...'. Sometimes a partitive genitive takes the form of a subject complement: *hia send* **kenenges mundes** 'they are (part) of the king's protection', *al thet* **Fresona** *wes* 'all who were (part) of the Frisians, i.e., everybody who was Frisian'.

Also measures are often expresssed by way of partitive genitive, e.g., *ur twene fiarderan* **biares** 'more than two quarters of beer', *en fiardandel* **ieldis** 'a quarter of the wergeld', *tha wi sigun hundred* **folkes** *santon* 'when we sent 700 (armed) men', *bi twa and thritega merkum* **hwites selveres** 'on pain of 32 marks of white silver'.

The partitive genitive also occurs with numbers: *thritich* **fota** *turves* 'thirty feet of turf', *thritich* **fethma** 'thirty fathoms'.

(5)   The genitive of respect: *and wrthe tha suthera kininge hanzoch and heroch* **alles riuchtes tinzes** 'and became subject and obedient to the southern (i.e., Frankish) king with respect to all legal tax'.

(6)   The genitive is governed by certain adjectives and verbs, e.g., *thet alter is* **thera erana** *wel werth* 'the altar is well worthy of the honours', **thes wiges** *plichtich wesa* 'to be responsible for the road', **sinere havedlesne** *skeldich* 'deserving of his head ransom'; *thet ma gerne fregie* **allera goda wenda** ... 'that a man should eagerly ask all good things ...', *ther* **thes** *wernde* 'who refused this', *God scel* **user** *walda* 'God shall rule us'. Some of these verbs have two objects, one in the dative (usually the person who is affected by the action of the verb) and one in the genitive describing in what respect this person is affected.

The genitival phrase can be the non-personal object in an impersonal verb construction (§203): *thet him* **sines godes** *se urbruden* 'that he (lit. him) be robbed of his property'.

(7)   The genitive may describe or define, e.g., *tha redieva* **thes erra ieres** 'the judges of the previous year'.

(8)   The noun *willa* 'will' in combination with the prepositions *thruch* 'through' and *um* governs the genitive, e.g., *thruch* **thes ethes** *willa* 'because of/on account of the oath', *thruch* **Godis** *willa* 'because of God', *um des willa* 'because of this'.

REMARK

1.   Adjectives that can take a genitival complement include *enoch* 'enough', *fe* 'few', *fule* 'many', *fri* 'free', *iech/iechtich/iechta* 'confessing, admitting', *las* 'without', *machtich* '(being) master of', *nette* 'useful', *ovirhere/-herich* 'disobedient, not willing to pay', *plichtich* 'responsible (for)', *sikur* 'not guilty', *(un)skeldich* '(not) deserving of', *urwene* 'without hope', *wenich* 'with hope', *(un)weldich* '(not) having control of', *werth* 'worthy of'.

2.   Verbs that can take a genitival object (G), sometimes accompanied by a dative object (D) in an impersonal construction, include: *bagia* 'to boast', *bersta* 'to lack', *bidda* 'to request', *biginna* 'to begin', *bi-ieria* 'to desire, wish', *bikanna* 'to confess', *biravia* 'to rob' (D G), *biseka* 'to deny, disavow', *bitigia* 'to accuse' (D G), *biwena* 'to think' (D G), *bruka* 'to use', *fregia* 'to ask', *missa* 'to lack', *monia* 'to exact payment', *niata* 'to enjoy' (and its compound *un(t)niata* 'to pay for, suffer for'), *un(d)gunga, un(d) riuchta, un(d)swera* all: 'to declare oneself innocent (by swearing an oath)', *urbrida* 'to rob' (D G), *wachtia* 'to be responsible for', *walda* 'to rule, have control over', *wardia* 'to take care of', *weigeria* 'to refuse', *werna* 'to refuse' (D G).

§182 *Dative*
(1)   The case of the indirect object used with a ditransitive verb, e.g., *hia urievon* **alle Frison** *frihalsa* 'they gave to all the Frisians freedom', *thet sin fiand* **him** *thene wi urstode* 'that his enemy blocked him the way'.
(2)   The dative is used as the object of verbs, e.g., *helpa* 'help': *sa mi ma ...helpa* **there wive** *of there nede* 'then one may help the woman out of her predicament'.
(3)   The dative may indicate interest, e.g., *thet* **him** *sin spise eta tuan enden ungunge* 'that his food would leave his two openings', *sa hwersa ma* **ena monne** *enne top heres ofstat* 'whenever someone strikes off a tuft of hair of some other man'.
(4)   The so-called benefactive dative (or dative of respect) is quite common, but best left untranslated, e.g., *God* **him** *reste* 'God rested (for himself)', *thi kining is* **him** *rike and weldich* 'the king is (by himself) strong and powerful'; *Tha hof* **him** *up Magnus an lofsang* 'Then Magnus raised a song of praise'.
(5)   The adverbial (instrumental) dative, e.g., *ief hwa* **nede** *nimth wida ieftha fomna* 'if anyone rapes (takes with force) a widow or a girl', *thet hi alsa* **sechte** *siak were* 'that he were so sick with sickness', *thet hit nahwedder* **froste** *ne* **hungere** *ne na* **nena unideva dathe** *ne urfari* 'that it [the child] would neither perish with frost nor with hunger nor ever with any other horrible death', **ovirbulgena mode** 'in/with an angry mood'.
(6)   Occasionally, the dative (of measure) appears with a comparative: **thrim wikem** *er* 'three weeks earlier'.
(7)   Many adjectives are used with the dative. They usually signify nearness or express an emotional relationship: *and* **alle liudem** *was't liaf* 'and to all people it was agreeable'. Adjectives compounded with *even-* 'equally' also govern the dative: *eider euenfir* **otherum** 'each equally much as the other one'.

Remark
1.   Adjectives governing the dative include: *tornig* 'angry', *wille* 'agreeable', *hanzoch* 'dependent', *harsum* 'obedient', *heroch* 'obedient, subject', *kuth* 'known, public', *lik* 'equal', *mene* 'familiar, in common', *swer* 'heavy', *swes* 'closely related', *underdenoch* 'obedient'.
2.   Ditransitive verbs governing the dative include: *folgia* 'to follow', *helpa* 'to help', *lera* 'to teach', *ofnima* 'to take away from; prevent', *sweria* 'to burden', *thankia* 'to thank', *tofara* 'to attack', *urbiada* 'to forbid'.

Prepositions

§183 The following is a fairly comprehensive list of the prepositions with the cases they govern.

ā + DAT	on, in, at; to, in(to) means of	mit(h) + DAT	with, through, by
afara + ACC	before, in front of with, after	nēi + DAT	in accordance
aiēn + DAT/ACC	against	of + DAT	out of, from
aling(a) + GEN	along during (cf. **en**)	on + DAT/ACC	in, to, on, at,
		ondling(a) + GEN	along (cf. **aling(a)**)
		ōne + DAT	without
alund (-ont) + GEN/ACC	until (cf. **und**)	ova (R) + DAT	on
an + DAT/ACC	in, on, at, through, against	over + DAT	over (cf. **ūr**)
anda, and, end + DAT/ACC	in, before, up to, until	sunder + DAT	without
an(n)a, -e + DAT/ACC	in, into, on	thruch + ACC	through, because of
antwiska + ACC	between	til + DAT/INS	to
		tō (*ti, te*) + DAT/ACC	to, up to, until,
bi + DAT	by, according to, with	tōfara + ACC	before, in front of
		tōiēnis, -ienst + ACC	against, opposite (cf. **iēn**)
binna + GEN/DAT	within, inside towards, at, in	twiska +ACC	between
bova (R) + DAT	above	um(be) + ACC	around, because of, concerning
buppa + DAT/ACC	above, over		
būta + GEN/DAT	outside, without	under + DAT	under, among
		up + DAT	up, upon
efter + GEN/DAT	after; throughout	uppa (*oppa*) + DAT/ACC	on, upon, at the risk of
en + DAT	on, at (cf. **on**)		
ēr + DAT	earlier; before	und (*ont*) + ACC	until
et + DAT	at, on, in, by	urmits + ACC	because of concerning, because of
fara + DAT/ACC	before (cf. **fori**)		
fon/fan + DAT	of, by, out of, from,	ūr + DAT/ACC	over, over and again (cf. **over**)
for + DAT	for		
fori (R) + ACC	for (cf. **fara**)	ūt + DAT	out, out of, from
		ūter + ACC	without
iēn(s), iēnst + ACC	against, opposite	with + ACC	against, towards
in + DAT/ACC	in, into		
in(n)a + DAT/ACC	in, into		
inōr, -ūr + ACC	to		

C. Verbs

§184 *Mood*

Traditionally, three moods are distinguished for verbs: (1) indicative, (2) subjunctive, (3) imperative, and (4) infinitive. The indicative is used to state fact, the subjunctive to state non-fact, the imperative to express a command. The infinitive gives the neutral, uninflected verb; when accompanied by 'to', the infinitive expresses purpose. The present participle expresses continuation, the past participle completion.

§185 *Indicative*

The indicative is mostly used to state a fact or an objective observation and is found mainly in independent statements: *Thit* **send** *tha siuguntine liodkesta* 'These are the seventeen statutes of the people'. In a relative clause: *thi prestere ther tha sigun wiena* **heth** ... 'the priest who has (received) the seven consecrations ...', *Rednath and Kawing, alsa* **hiton** *tha forma twene ther to Frislonde thene pannig* **slogon** 'R. and K., thus were called the first two (moneyers) who struck coins in Frisia'. In consecutive clauses, too, the indicative is found quite regularly: *Sa hwersa en mon sa fir onefuchten* **werth** *thet hi blodich* **stont** 'Whenever a man is (being) attacked, so that (as a result of which) he is bleeding'.

§186 *Subjunctive*

The subjunctive expresses subjectivity ('non-fact'), especially when it concerns volition, desire, conjecture or hypothesis. All the verbal forms in the following example are in the subjunctive: *To hwam sa ma en lond* **askie**, *sa* **onderte** *thi, ther eldest* **se**, *and* **spreke** ... 'Whenever someone should (legally) demand a piece of land from somebody else, then he should answer, who is oldest, and say ...'.

The subjunctive is often used in subordinate clauses, e.g., *Tha setten't tha tuelef apostola thet se hire brotherdel thermithe urleren* **hede** 'Then the twelve apostles decreed that in doing so she had lost her brother's part (of the wergeld)'.

However, both subjunctive and indicative forms may occur side by side, e.g.: *Hwersa ma anne thiaf* **feth** (IND) *and ma hine* **brenge** (SUBJ) *to ware and* **latt** (IND) '*ene umbe thene warf an hine* **biut** (IND) *ma to lesane* ... 'Whenever a thief has been seized and he be brought to the place of execution and he is lead around this place and he is offered to be ransomed ...'.

§187 *Imperative*

This mood is used to express a command: **Minna** *thinne God fore feder ende moder* 'Love your God before father and mother'.

§188 *Infinitive*

The plain infinitive (i.e., without 'to') is found with the following modal auxiliaries (mainly preterite-present verbs): *skela* 'shall', *muga* 'can, may', *thurva* 'to need', *kunna* 'can', *mōta* 'to be allowed, may, must', *wella* 'to wish, want to'. Occasionally, the plain infinitive is used with the verbs 'to sit, stand, lie, go': *hi ne **gunge** efter tha durun **stonda*** 'unless he goes and stands behind the door'. Also various other verbs can be followed by a plain infinitive, such as *tha thi Kening Karl **riuchta** bigunde* 'when Charlemagne began to administer justice'; *Hi **let** hit tha Fresum kundig **dwan*** 'He caused it to be made known to the Frisians', *and dwe alsa're him **dwa** hete* 'and let him do as he may order him to do'.

Verbs taking an inflected infinitive (or 'gerund', §150) include *āga* 'to have to' and *wita* 'to know', e.g., *sa ach ma sin haved of **to slane*** 'then one has to cut off his head' and *mi hit bikanna brother and swester, and **to nomande** wet sine nesta friond …* 'if it (the child) can recognize his brother and sister, and knows (i.e., is able) to name his closest relative …'. Of these two, the construction *āga tō (te, ti, til)* appears to have been in use up to the middle of the fourteenth century after which it was substituted by other verbs (Schilt 1990).

The infinitive is used especially in combination with 'to' (i.e., inflected infinitive) to express purpose, often with ellipsis of subject + finite verb, e.g., *Thera fif sinna werde iahwelikes bote sex end thritech scillenga, allarec [ach ma] mith ene ethe **te halene*** 'The compensation for the injury of each of the five senses (is) thirty-six shillings, each must be demanded with one oath', *[ach ma] thribete to betene* 'three times to be compensated'.

The infinitive is also found as a complement to an object (in so-called accusative plus infinitive-constructions), e.g., *tha segen hia anne thretundista **sitta*** 'then they saw sitting a thirteenth (man)'.

§189   *Tense*
Like the other Germanic languages, Old Frisian has only two tenses: (1) the simple present and (2) the simple preterite (or: past). Compound tenses, i.e., tenses constructed by means of one or more auxiliary verb, are not very frequent, but become more widely used in later texts.

§190   The simple present, besides expressing the factual 'now', is also used to express the future, usually with an adjunct of time. Compare: *Thet **is** thet thriu and twintigesta londriucht* 'This is the Twenty-third Land-law' with *Thes fifta dis **burnath** alle wetir* 'On the fifth day [before Judgement Day] all waters will burn'.

§191   The simple preterite is used to refer to an act completed in the past: *… tha tian bodo, ther God **urief** Moysese* '… the Ten Commandments which God gave to Moses'. It can express a continuing act in the past: *Tha **festade** Moyses twia fiuwertih dega and nachta* 'Then Moses was fasting for twice forty days and nights'. The pluperfect sense is also expressed by a simple preterite form: *Er **waren** se alle nakede Fresan, tha het se thi koning alle heran* 'Formerly they all had been naked Frisians, then the king called them all lords'.

§192   *Compound tenses*
The auxiliaries used to form compound tenses are *hebba/habba* 'have' (the former is found mainly in Old East Frisian, the latter only in Old West Frisian) and *wesa* 'be'. The

frequency of *hebba* as a full verb is much higher than that of the auxiliary. This latter function is clearly fairly young in Old Frisian. Compound tenses with *hebba* plus past participle are used to express the perfect tense: ... *thetti mon alles thes thenzie, ther hi* **gelesen hebbe** 'that a man should contemplate everything that he has read', *Credo and Pater Noster skil hi* **ilirnad hebba** 'He must have learned the Creed and the Lord's Prayer'. Occasionally, the pluperfect is formed by means of *hebba*: *Therefter ief God him tha twa stenena tefla, ther hi on* **eskrivin hede** *tha tian bodo* 'After that God gave him the two stone tables on which He had written the Ten Commandments', ... *an there selva skipnese ther se was, er se use Drochten* **eskepen hede** '... in the same shape in which it [the world] was before Our Lord had created it'. Note that the position of the auxiliary is final in these examples, as it often is in dependent clauses (cf. §195, 198), e.g., *Thit send tha fiftine tekna ther er domesdi koma skilun* 'These are the fifteen signs that shall come before doomsday'.

§193 Forms of *wesa* were used for the extended form. The progressive (or: continuative) form is rare in Old Frisian texts and when it occurs it is sometimes hard to decide whether a construction is really verbal or adjectival. However, the combination of *wesa* + present participle does not always seem to indicate a continuous act: *thi biscopisfrethe skel stonda alsa hi to Freslonde* **cumende is** *tian degar bifara sin keme* 'the bishop's peace must prevail when he [the bishop] is coming/comes to Frisia ten days before his arrival', *and hi* **hrutande se** 'and he be rattling (in his throat)', *gef hit* **is onsittande** 'if it [the eye] is sitting [viz. in the socket]', ... *and hiu naet* **fiuchtende is** '... and she is not fighting', *and him sin erm* **driapande se** *and lom* 'and his arm is drooping (or: limp) and lame'. In this last example the line between participle and adjective is vague.

A present participle can also be combined with such verbs as *wertha*, *kuma* or *sitta*: *Hwasa tha kininge* **werth foriwernande** ... 'whoever becomes rebellious against/starts resisting the king', *sa hwersa thi tegothere* **clagande kumth** 'when the tithe-gatherer comes complaining (i.e., makes a charge)', *sa hwersa* **cumth** *en erm mon to tha warue* **clagande** 'whenever a poor man comes and complains at the court-session', *hwersa en frowe nede nimen is end hiu* **sit wepanda** *and* **hropanda** 'when a woman has been raped and she sits weeping and crying'. Note that the auxiliary may precede or follow the participle or may even be separated from it.

§194 The verb *wesa* is also used as an auxiliary to express the perfect and pluperfect of intransitive verbs expressing change of state, particularly with verbs of motion: *thet hit nawet sa fir* **ekimin ne se** *thet hit hebbe her and nila* 'that it [the foetus] has not come (i.e., grown) so far that it has hair and nails'.

§195 Old Frisian expressed the perfect of *wesa* with 'have', but such periphrastic constructions are rare in early texts: *Thesse kinigar* **hebbath ewesin** *kinigar to Rume* 'These kings have been kings in Rome', ... *hit ne se thet him sin age binimen se ieftha lemed se ieftha* **bunden hebbe wesen** '... unless his eye has been taken or (he) has been crippled or (he) has been bound'. Tripartite constructions, as in the latter example, in which the auxiliary *wesa* itself is combined with *hebba*, are again extremely rare for Old East Frisian (Johnston 1993). Note the following two examples: *hit ne se thet tha wagar* **bewepin hebbe wesin** 'unless the walls [of the house] have been wept at [by a baby]'. This passage from E2 is found in another, slightly older manuscript (E3), where with some variation the construction is slightly different: *hit ne se thetta fiower herne* **bescrien se** 'unless the four corners [of the house] are (or: have been) cried at'. After 1450, the auxiliary 'to be' emerges side by side with 'to have' in Old West Frisian (Johnston 1994). In the same dialect, the tripartite construction with the past participle of *wesa* gains in frequency. Note that the auxiliary in the dependent clauses in the above examples wavers between final and penultimate position.

Other auxiliaries than *wesa* may be found in tripartite constructions, e.g., *ende (dat hiit) in Diin name* **begonnen moete wiirda** 'and that it may be begun in Your name'.

§196   *Voice*

There were two voices: (1) the active and (2) the passive voice.

The common verb to express the passive is *wertha* 'become' plus a past participle: *sa* **werth** *thet kind* **bilethad** 'then the child is shaped'. In combination with a past participle, *wesa* is used to form the perfective passive: *Alsa thi redieva* **biwernad is**, *sa ne mot ma naut sena* 'when the judge has been given security, one is not allowed to make reconciliations [i.e outside court]', *thermithi* **send***ti* **urbeden** *alle menetha* 'with this all false oaths have been forbidden to you'.

D.   Word order

§197   In declaritive main clauses, the order is SVO: *God scop* **thene eresta menneska** 'God created the first human being'. Frequently, however, the order is OVS in main clauses, often with a sense of emphasis (topicalization): **Thisse riucht** *keren alle Fresa* 'These rights all Frisians elected'; **thes greva bon** *bonne ic* 'I proclaim the count's proclamation'.

In interrogative sentences, the word order in main clauses is VSO, e.g., *Nebbe ic allera rikera frionda enoch?* 'Don't I have plenty of rich relatives (of all)?', *Wellath j thet lovia mitha hondum?* 'Do you want to promise that with your hands?'. Conditional clauses have the same order VSO: *Bitigeth er him thet …* 'If he accuses him of that …', *Is thet are fon there dede daf* 'If the ear is deaf because of that deed'; *skelma kempa, sa skelma thria kempa anda iera* 'if legal duels must be held, (then) they must be held three times a year'.

When a clause opens with an adverb or an adverbial adjunct, the verb also precedes the subject: *Therefter ief God him twa stenena tevla* 'After this God gave him two stone tablets', *Thes fifta dis burnath alle wetir* 'On the fifth day, all waters will burn'. This rule enables us to distinguish between *tha* 'then' (ADV) and *tha* 'when' (CONJ): *Tha Karl and Redbad in thet land komen, tha besette aider sine wei in Franekra ga* 'When Charlemagne and Redbad came into the land, (then) each took position in the district of Franeker'.

Generally speaking, in dependent clauses Old Frisian is a S(ubject) – O(bject) – V(erb) language, i.e., the object precedes the verb: *Hwersa ma* **wif** *nede nimth* 'When someone rapes a woman', *Thet is thiu sextendesta kest, thet alle Fresa* **hire feitha** *mith hira fia felle* 'This is the sixteenth statute, that all Frisians should redeem their feuds with their money'. However, as the following example shows – the same sentence taken from two different redactions of the text – variation was possible: *Ac tha Fresa ther skipbreckande* **hira gud** *urliasat/Ac tha Frese ther schipbrekende wrliaset* **hire goed** … 'But the Frisians who lose their goods (in) being shipwrecked …'.

The order is OSV in dependent conditional clauses with so-called Wh-words in the oblique case, whether or not compounded with *sa-* (Lühr 2007): **Hwamsa** *ma inna tha achne spie* 'Whomever is spat in the eye', **Hwene** *sa Northman nimath* 'Whomever the Northmen (Vikings) take captive'.

When the object is a personal pronoun, it may occur between V and S in such clauses as: *sa bislut* **hia** *God andere hille* 'then God will lock them up in hell'; *tha het* **se** *thi koning alle heran* 'then the king called them all lords' (cf. van der Meer 1990).

§198 Sometimes a 'heavy group', whether nominal or verbal, can be split and part of it appears in postposition: *mith brudena swerde* **and blodiga** 'with drawn and bloody sword', *efter thes bedon hit* **and bennon** *alle irthkiningar* 'after this all secular kings ordered and decreed it', *sa werthath tha sina ifestnad* **and tha eddra** 'then the sinews and veins are fixed', *thetter allera monna hwelic erie sinne mester* **and minnie** 'that each man should honour and love his teacher'.

A verb phrase can be split by a prepositional group: *Hwersa hir ene monne werth* **thruch sine macht** *undad* 'When here a man is wounded in his genitals', but it need not: *Hwersa ene mon stet werth* **truch thene maga** 'When a man is pierced through the stomach'. Note the different position of the auxiliary in these two examples (cf. §§192, 195).

E.   Various constructions

§199 Groups can be linked by means of coordinating conjunctions. These include 'cumulative' conjunctions, e.g., simple *and(e)/ende*: *Augustinus seith ande queth* 'Augustine says and remarks', *bētha … and: betha thes dis antes nachtes* 'both day and night'.

'Alternative' conjunctions like 'or', 'either … or' include: *fon falska* **tha** *fon fade* 'of counterfeited (money) **or** of degraded (money)', *nachtbrond* **ieftha** *morthdede* 'nightly arson **or** hidden crime', *sa* **hwether** *sa hi a warve se* **sa** *to ware kume* '**whether** he is at the law-assembly **or** comes to the law-assembly', **hoder** *jo liavera se thet ma jo alle* *haudie **than** j alle ain wirden* 'whether you rather be beheaded **or** become serfs', *mith cape sa mith wixle **sa** mith riuchte herwerum* '(either) with purchase **or** with exchange **or** with lawful leased properties'.

Involving negatives: *nauder golt ther selwer* '**neither** gold **nor** silver', *thet hit nen mon **ne** binere tha bitesze **ieftha** bitiune* 'that no man either hinders **or** takes possession of **or** claims it', *thettu **nebbe** thines bedda god stelen **ne** urhelen* 'that you have **neither** stolen **nor** concealed your spouse's property'.

REMARK
1.   As appears from the above examples, Old Frisian frequently features double or even multiple negation, which is nonetheless to be interpreted as simple negation, however. On the whole, the use of double negation tends to increase as the language becomes younger (Bor 1990).
2.   The form *nebbe* in the last example above is a contraction of *ne* + *hebbe* (SUBJ). Old Frisian has many instances of negative contracted verbs, see *wertha* (§133R.5), *wita* and *āga* (§143), *wella, willa* (§149.a), *wesa* (§149.b), *hebba, habba* (§153). Such negative contracted verbs often come with double negations.

§200   The definite article frequently appears where modern usage requires the indefinite article: *Hwersa en wif en morth clagath, and **thet** othere wif ... foribrangeth thet* 'Whenever a woman complains of a (violent) miscarriage, and another woman testifies to that', *sa falt **thi** sten wither **thene** sten* 'then one stone will fall against another', or 'then stone will fall against stone'.

§201   Pronouns are sometimes used to recapitulate a nominal group, e.g., *thi blata **thi** is lethost allera nata* 'the poor man (he) is most miserable of all companions', *Heinrik thi keyser **thi** was hertoga to Beygeron* 'Henry the Emperor, he (who) was Duke of Bavaria', *Thi Fresa fela sterka, **hi** for him and tha Saxinna merke* 'The Frisian, very strong, (he) went to the Saxon land', *Thet insigel **thet** was fan tha brondrada golde* 'The seal (it) was of fiery red gold'.

Likewise, pronominals can be recapitulated: *Bitigeth er him thet, **thet**ter hebbe misered* 'If he accuses him of that, that he [the defendant] has poorly ploughed'. In such cases, the former functions as a 'presumptive' pronoun, heralding the that-clause which functions as the actual object of the main clause.

§202   In object clauses following verbs of expression, the conjunction *thet* is sometimes dropped (as, e.g., in Modern English): *and queth aider [Ø] thet land were sin* 'and both of them said [Ø] that land was his', *Tha spreken se [Ø] hia ne kuden* 'Then they said [Ø] they were unable to'. On this phenomenon, see Hoekstra (1993a).

§203   *Impersonal verb constructions*
This construction involves predicates which lack a subject in the nominative, but have a pseudo-subject in the dative case instead. The predicate, as a rule, occurs in

the 3rd person singular, but is not restricted to a particular tense or mood (apart from the imperative). In Old Frisian, there are basically three types of syntactic structure in which the impersonal predicate can be found. They are: (a) *Ief* **him friunda** *berste* 'If he lacks relatives'; (b) *Ief* **tha scriuere** *thinze* **thet** … 'If it seems to the clerk of the court that …'; (c) *Indeen* **joe** *bylyaft dae penningen* … **op to lidzen** 'If it pleases you to pay the money'. In constructions of type (a), the predicate is complemented by an animate object in the dative which functions as the pseudo-subject. That is to say, in paraphrases or translations this constituent can be assigned the role of subject. As seen in the example of type (a), the predicate can also be accompanied by a complement in the genitive, in this case *friunda* (GEN.PL), usually expressing the cause or the occasion of the action denoted by the verb it qualifies, and is therefore conveniently termed the causative object. This causative object can also take the form of a prepositional phrase, e.g., *Nawet allena tha keninge* **and thisse bode** *nogade* 'The king was pleased not by this command alone'. Occasionally the verb 'to be' with an adjective appears in impersonal constructions, e.g., *is him hete, is him kalde* 'whether there is heat for him or cold'. On this topic in detail, see Bremmer (1986).

Chapter VI

Dialectology
The faces of Old Frisian

§204 *Diversity and uniformity*

Like Old High German or Middle English, Old Frisian is attested in a number of dialects. As noted in §§16–18, the basic division is into East (of the river Lauwers) and West (of the river Lauwers). The division is juridical – there were diverging institutions on either side of the divide – as well as linguistic (phonology, morphology and vocabulary). The division must also be very old: early eighth-century Frankish sources already mention a twofold division of Frisia west of the Lauwers as *Westrachia et Austrachia* 'Westergo and Oostergo'. Since Oostergo borders west on the Lauwers, the name implies that what lay beyond that river belonged to another cultural-geographical frame of mind. The diocesan division of Frisia concurs more or less with the dialectal division. It cannot therefore be entirely fortuitous that the eighth-century missionaries each targeted their own territory within Frisia Magna. If this assumption is right, it leads to the conclusion that the macro-dialectal difference must spring from an early intra-Frisian cultural diversity whose origins can no longer be fathomed but which must be very old. Old East Frisian can further be divided into Old Weser Frisian (diocese of Bremen) and Old Ems Frisian (diocese of Münster). For a detailed survey, see Versloot (2001a).

Old West Frisian (diocese of Utrecht) can be distinguished into South-Western (Westergo) and North-Eastern (Oostergo) areas. Westergo and Oostergo were originally divided by a sea arm, the Middle Sea, but when this water was gradually reclaimed from 1100 onwards, a transitional dialect area developed. North Frisian is not attested at all at the Old stage.

Notwithstanding the dialectal and cultural varieties within medieval Frisia, an overarching linguistic and ethnic identity prevailed. Focussing on the linguistic characteristics, (Old) Frisian shares the following (more remarkable) features (cf. Århammar 1990: 21–25):

a. Phonological:

- monophthongization of Gmc *au* > *ā* (e.g., *bām* 'tree', *rād* 'red') and of *ai* > *ā* and *ē* (§36), e.g., *fād* 'counterfeit', *mār(r)a* 'more', *rāp* 'rope', *wāch* 'wall' and *bēn* 'bone', *stēn* 'stone', with the same distribution of these lexemes for West, East and North Frisian

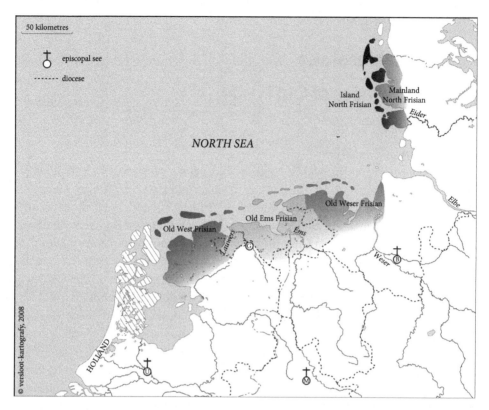

The geographical distribution of Frisian around 1300 in relation to the dioceses. U = Utrecht, M = Münster, B = Bremen. The Frisian archdeanery is separated from the rest of the Münster diocese by the diocese of Osnabrück. G = Groningen, added for orientation.

- fronting of Gmc *a* >*æ* (written *e*) (§39), e.g., *fet* 'vat, vessel' *stef* 'staff'
- breaking of *e* and *i* before *ch* + *C* (§48), e.g., *riucht* 'right', *tiuche* 'team; parcel of land'
- mutation of *i* when followed by *u* or *w* (§51), e.g., *niugen* 'nine', *siunga* 'to sing', *thiukke* 'length and breadth, thickness'
- loss of final -*n* (§68) in infinitives, e.g., *setta* 'to set', in endings of oblique forms of weak nouns and in endings of weak adjectives, e.g., *thes alda boda* 'of the old messenger', in some numerals, e.g., *thrina* 'three each', and in some prepositions, e.g., *binna* 'inside', *būta* 'outside'
- no initial voicing of fricatives (§78.2), unlike in Middle Dutch and Middle High/ Low German, e.g., *fisk* vs. MDu *visch*
- the adverb 'here' is *hīr* (< Gmc **hē₂r*), as opposed to OE, ODu, OS *hēr*.

b.   Morphonological:

- generalization of fronting (§39) in the singular of feminine *ō*-stemmed nouns (§105), e.g., *tele* 'reckoning; tale', *fere* 'journey' (cf. OE *talu*, *faru*)

- generalization of *-ina-suffix in past participles of strong verbs, especially Classes II, IV–VII, resulting in *i*-mutation of the stem vowel (§45), and, where applicable, palatalization of the final stem consonant (§42), e.g., *tein* 'drawn' (§132), *kemen* 'come' (§134), *bretsen* 'broken' (§135), *dregen/drein* 'carried' (§136), *fenzen* 'caught' (§137). Old Frisian is also the only West Germanic language to have the mutated form *epen* 'open'
- Gmc *fer- > PFris *fir(re) 'far' with vowel from comparative > OFris *fir* (cf. ModWFris *fier*, ModEFris *fiir* [Wang.], IsNFris *fiir* [Amr.]. All other West Germanic languages have -*e*-: OE *feor*, OHG *ferro*, OS *fer(ro)*.

c.   Morphological:

- NOM/ACC plural -*ar* in strong masculine nouns (§100): *bāmar* 'trees'
- personal pronouns *hiu* 'she' (NOM.SG) and *hia* 'they' (§90) begin with *h*- (with Old English) instead of *s*- (with Old Dutch, Old Saxon and Old High German)
- no separate reflexive pronoun (§90). (Old) Frisian did not adopt Old High German *sih*, unlike MDu (*sich*) and OS (*sik*)
- the use of the adverb *thēr* as a relative particle (§95) is not found in any of the neighbouring languages.

d.   Lexical:

A considerable number of words are typically Frisian (or sometimes Anglo-Frisian) as opposed to the other continental West Germanic dialects. They are either the result of typically Frisian innovations, whether in form or meaning, or are Ingvaeonic/North Sea Germanic relict words which were maintained, perhaps in an (un)conscious attempt, to differentiate Frisian from its surrounding languages. The following is a small selection of Old Frisian 'pass words' that still live on in two or three of the modern Frisian branches (West, East and North):

- *fēmne, famne* 'girl' (not 'woman' as in OE and OS), *kēi* 'key' (as opposed to Du *sleutel*, G *Schlüssel*), *tusk* 'tooth' (generic, not 'canine tooth'), *wēt* 'wet' (as opposed to Du *nat*, G *nass*), *bōgia* 'to live, dwell' (cf. OE *bōgian*, as opposed to Du *wonen*, G *wohnen*), *wērs/wārs* 'springtime', *hengst* 'horse' (generic, not 'stallion'; no traces of Du *paard*, LG *peerd*, G *Pferd* < MLat *paraveredus* 'courier horse'), *fule, -a* 'much, many' (< *fulu-) as opposed to OE *feala*, OHG, OS *filu* (< *felu-).

§205 *Old Weser Frisian: Rüstring*
Old Weser Frisian, the ancestor of the modern dialects of Wangerooge, Wursten and Harlingerland (now all three extinct), made up the Weser branch. It survives in two manuscripts (R1, R2) and in two fragments (R3, R4) (§16).

An important characteristic is the regular distribution of short vowels in unstressed final syllables ('vowel balance'; cf. Smith 2007):

1. *i, u* appear after short stem vowels in open syllables, e.g., *Godi* (DAT.SG) 'God', *skipu* (NOM.PL) 'ships', *sunu* 'son', *skilun* '(they) must'.
2. *e, o* appear after long or heavy stems or in syllables separated from the stem by another syllable, e.g., *liōde* 'people', *hēroch* 'obedient', *hunige* 'honey' (DAT.SG), *bēdon* '(they) ordered'. This principle of vowel balance enables us, for example, to distinguish the quantity of the stem vowel in such pairs as ⟨hove⟩, (DAT.SG) 'hoof' ~ ⟨hovi⟩, (DAT.SG) 'court(yard)' as long and short, respectively. This phenomenon was peculiar to Rüstringen and the stress pattern underlying it (i.e., division of stress over both syllables) is reflected in the descendant dialects of Wangerooge (Löfstedt 1932) and Wursten (e.g., Smith/van Leyden 2007).

Other peculiarities (cf. Buma 1961: 47–52; Boutkan 1996: 9–11) are:
3. *i* < Gmc **e* before *r* + dental: *hirte* 'heart', *irthe* 'earth';
4. *i* < *e* < Gmc **a* or < *u* + *i*-mutation: *hiri* 'army', *kining* 'king'.
5. *i* is lowered to *e* and *u* > *o* in open syllable, when followed by *a* in the next syllable ('Rüstring *a*-mutation'), e.g.:

    > *binetha* 'beneath' but non-R *binitha*,
    > *letha* GEN.PL 'bodily parts' but *lith* NOM.SG
    > *to wetande* 'to know' (INFL INF) but non-R *to witane*
    > *koma* 'to come' but non-R *kuma*
    > *dora* GEN.PL but *durun* DAT.PL (Löfstedt 1932: 14–21);

6. Gmc **-ag-*, after fronting (§39) and palatalization (§42) > *-ei*, and **-eg*, after palatalization > *-ei*, appear as *-ī*, e.g., *dī* 'day' (non-Rüstring *dei*), *brīn* 'brain' (non-R *brein*), *wī* 'way' (non-R *wei*), *brīda* 'to pull' (non-R *breida*), *līth* 'he lays' (non-R *leith*);
7. Gmc **ē₂* appears as *ī*, e.g., *Frīsa* 'Frisian', *hīt* 'was called', *līt* 'let (PRET)', *mīde* 'gift, present' (Hofmann 1964/1989);
8. the preterite-present verb *āga* 'to own; have to' appears almost always as *hāga*;
9. the numeral '7' appears as *siugun* or *sigun*, whereas in Old Ems Frisian this is *sogen*, and in Old West Frisian *saw(e)n, saun*;
10. The adjective/adverb for 'much, many' appears as *felo* (< OS *filu*) as opposed to *fule, -a* in all of the other Frisian dialects (Bremmer 2005).

The Rüstring dialect is furthermore characterized by a number of morphological innovations not found elsewhere in Old Frisian. These include:

11. the dative plural ending is typically *-on* after heavy (long) syllables, e.g., *ēthon* 'oaths', as against *ēthum, -em, -im*, or (late) *-in, -en* in the other dialects; and *-un*

after light (short) syllables, e.g., *durun* 'doors', *wikun* 'weeks'. Likewise, the past plural of verbs ends in either *-on* or *-un*, e.g., *slōgon* '(we) struck', *setton* '(they) placed, set' and *mugun* '(they) can', *skilun* '(they) must'.

12. the inflected infinitive (infinitive preceded by *to* or *te*) has adopted the same ending as that of the present participle: *-ande*; e.g., *to dēmande* 'to judge', *to hebbande* 'to have'.

13. the inflected infinitive of weak verbs Class 2 ends in *-ande* as opposed to *-iande* in the other dialects: e.g., *to clagande* 'to complain' (*clagia*), *to festande* 'to fast' (*festia*);

14. the superlative suffix appears as *-ost*, as against *-est*, *-ast* in the other dialects: *hāgosta* 'highest', *iungosta* 'youngest'.

15. DAT.PL of *hia* 'they' is *hiam*, as against *him* in the other dialects.

§206 Old Ems Frisian is recorded for two districts to the east of the Ems: Emsingo and Brokmerland, and for the so-called 'Ommelanden' (Oldambt, Fivelgo, Hunsingo, Humsterland, Langewold, Vredewold – the latter three in Low German guise [Johnston 1998b]) – west of the Ems.

The Ems branch is represented (from east to west) by the following manuscripts: E1, E2, E3, E4 (Buma/Ebel 1965: Text D, but an Emsingo text that was demonstrably copied from an Old West Frisian exemplar), B1, B2, H1, H2, F and by four Ommeland administrative documents dating to *c*.1400. Furthermore, a single leaf containing a variant text of the *Fia-eth* survives as do two early modern transcripts of now lost versions of the *Superior Statutes* and the *Bishop's Reconciliation of 1276*. Finally, snippets of text and isolated words are found in the *Psalter Fragment* (Bremmer 2007b), in a fragment of the *Seventeen Statutes* (Bremmer 1996), in a number of variant readings of the *Seventeen Statutes* and the *Twenty-four Land-laws* copied into the margins of E1 and H2 from manuscripts now lost, eighteen articles of succession law copied in the sixteenth century from a lost manuscript of the *Oldambt Landlaw* as well as in a number of Low German and Latin charters from east of the Lauwers with interspersed Frisian forms (Hofmann 1970/1989; Bremmer 2004: 75–78, 98). The modern dialect of Saterland is its sole survivor.

The following phonological criteria distinguish Old Ems Frisian from Old Weser Frisian:

1. absence of the features listed under §205.1–15;

2. before voiced alveolars (i.e., *d*, *l*, *n*), as well as occasionally before voiced *th*, *ē* tends to be diphthongized to *ei* (§76.4e), e.g., *breid* 'bride', *breid* 'broad', *meide* 'reward; bribe', *mein* 'common', *beil* 'boil', *heila* 'heel', *heilich* 'holy', *feithe* 'feud', *leith* 'hateful'.

3. intrusive *r* in unstressed *-en*, e.g., *wēpern* 'weapon' (beside *wēpen*), *lungern* 'lung' (beside *lungen*), *epern* 'open' (beside *epen*);

4. 'church' appears as *tsiurke* (with *-iu-*), as against Old Weser Frisian *sthereke* and Old West Frisian *ts(i)erke*;

5. peculiar to B1, B2 is *unga* 'to go', as against *gunga* elsewhere;
6. in late Old Ems Frisian, *ā* (either originally long or lengthened before certain consonant clusters) tends to be rounded to [ɔː], e.g., *ōftne* 'legitimate (ACC.SG.MASC)' (< *āft-*), *ōlsa* 'so' (*alsā*), *ōlle* 'all' (*alle*), *wōld* (*sket*) 'pigs' (< *wāld* < *wald* 'wasteland, forest').

§207 *Old West Frisian*

The major Old West Frisian manuscripts (J, U, D, A, Ro) are generally later (*c*.1450–1525) than the Old East Frisian ones (*c*.1300–1450), as mentioned in §14. Their texts therefore exhibit a language which chronologically speaking is not wholly congruent with Old East Frisian. Whereas the spelling in the Old East Frisian manuscripts is on the whole archaic (i.e., still rather 'phonetic', no indication of vowel length) and probably still based on Latin orthography, the Old West Frisian scribes have adopted certain Low German and Dutch orthographic conventions.

Vowel-length is rarely indicated in Old East Frisian, but this is frequently done in Old West Frisian for long vowels by adding ⟨e⟩: e.g., *baem* 'tree' (*bām*), *boek* 'book' (*bōk*), *hues* 'house' (*hūs*); or by doubling, e.g., *dwaan* 'to do' (*dwān*), *deel* 'part' (*dēl*), *wiif* 'woman' (*wīf*), also ⟨ij⟩ *sijn* 'his' (*sīn*) or ⟨y⟩ *lyf* 'wergeld' (*līf*), *sooth* 'truth' (*sōth*), and *huus*, *hws* 'house' (*hūs*). Occasionally, ⟨i, y⟩ is found as a length marker with other vowels, e.g., *teyken* 'sign' (*tēken*), *kuith* 'known, public' (*kūth*), or, with lengthening in open syllables (§209), *weisa* 'to be' (*wesa*), *hoyne* 'cock, rooster' (*hona*).

The fricative allophone of *g*, [ɣ], is often written ⟨gh⟩, e.g., *folghia* 'follow'. Also, /t/ is often written as ⟨th⟩ but still pronounced as [t], e.g., *thoe* [toː] 'to' (*tō*). The cluster [sk] usually appears as ⟨sch⟩, but is most likely still pronounced as [sk], e.g., *schetten* 'shot (PP)', *schip* 'ship'. Such spelling features almost immediately reveal a text's provenance from the area west of the Lauwers.

Not only did Middle Dutch and Low German spelling conventions influence Old West Frisian, the written language itself is marked by an increasing usage of loan words from these neighbouring languages.

§208 Significant phonological characteristics of Old West Frisian are (cf. J. Hoekstra 2001):

1. Gmc **a* underwent rounding before nasals (as appears, for example, from ModWFris *goes* 'goose' < **gōs* < Gmc **gans-*, §§28, 31), but was later restored, e.g., *man, hand, land, sang, lam*. It remained rounded in North-Eastern Old West Frisian before *-mb, -nn* (Sjölin 1966: 30–31; Spenter 1968: 14–15; Boutkan 1997).
2. intervocalic *v* > *w* (also in later Old East Frisian), e.g., *hove* > *howe* 'court (DAT.SG)', *hāved* > *hāwed* > *hāud* 'head'.
3. 'Jorwert Breaking' (§76.2). In symmetrical order, from high to low, long front vowels + /w/ became rising diphthongs:

/iːw/ > /juːw/

/eːw/ > /joːw/

/ɛːw/ > /jɔːw/

E.g., *skriouwa* (*skrīwa* < *skrīva*) 'to write', *iouwe* (*iēwe* < *ieve*) 'gift', *iouwe* 'law' (< *ēwa*); sometimes the initial /j/ is absorbed by a preceding *r*, e.g., *opgrouwa* 'to dig up' (*upgrēwa* [§209] < *upgreva*).

4. *e* (of various origin) before *r* + C and *l* + C often becomes *i*, e.g., *birch* 'mountain', *wirda* (< *wertha*) 'to become', *wirtza* 'to work', *wird* 'word', *wirtle* 'root'; *held* 'favour' > *hild*, *skeld* 'shield' > *schild*, *weld* 'power' > *wild*.

5. before *l* + C (*d, k, n, r*), *e* was lengthened, and afterwards diphthongized with stress first on the initial element (falling) and later on the second element ('late Old West Frisian Breaking'), e.g., *feld* > *fēld* > *fiēld* [fieːld] (rising); so too: *eldera* > *ēldera* (spelled ⟨eeldera⟩) > *ieldera* 'elder; parent', *ielkers* 'otherwise', *ielne* 'ell', *ielren* 'of alder wood'.

6. before *nd*, *e* tends to be diphthongized with stress on first element, e.g., *einda* 'to end', *seinda* 'to send', *beynd* 'bond, fetter'.

7. *-we-* > *-o-*: e.g., *hwet* 'what' becomes *hot* or *hat/haet*; *hwelk* 'which' becomes *hok*, *hwether* 'whether' becomes *hother*, *twelef* 'twelve' becomes *tolef*, *twintich* becomes *tontich*.

8. *iā* becomes *iē* [jɛː], e.g., *liāf* 'dear' > *liēf*, *thiāf* 'thief' > *tiēf*, *thiānia* 'to serve' > *tiēnie* (for *th* > *t*, see next item).

9. the last two examples also illustrate another phenomenon: voiceless initial *th* becomes *t*, while voiced initial and medial *th* become *d*, e.g., *det* 'that', *bēde* 'both'.

10. final voiced *d* tends to become unvoiced, e.g., *tīt* 'time', *goet* 'good', *antwert* 'answer', but in inflected forms *d* remains to be voiced, *tīden*, *go(e)de*, etc.

11. intervocalic *d* (also from *th* /ð/) tends to be deleted: *snede* > *snē*, *snei* 'cut', *snīa* 'to cut' (< *snītha*), *brōr* 'brother' (< *brōther*).

12. *u* + Nasal > *o*, e.g., *sond* 'sound, healthy', *stonde* 'time', *fonden* 'found (PP)', *on-* 'un-'.

13. the verb 'to have' appears as *habba* besides much less frequent *hebba*, as opposed to exclusively *hebba* in Old East Frisian.

§209 *Lengthening in open syllables*

As in most of the neighbouring Germanic languages of the later Middle Ages, including Danish, late Old Frisian saw lengthening of short vowels in stressed open syllables. For the purpose of this book, we confine ourselves here to late Old West Frisian. In fact, the process entailed three steps (cf. Versloot 2001b: 769–70):

- short vowels were lengthened in stressed open syllables;
- vowels in unstressed final syllables were reduced to [ə] and often dropped afterwards;
- geminated ('double') consonants became degeminated.

However, lengthening in open syllables was not carried through as completely as it was in the neighbouring languages: *i* and *u* were always lengthened, *a* and *o* frequently, while *e* remained short.

For Old West Frisian, words that originally ended in *-a* usually continued with *-e*, whereas words that originally ended in *-e* usually dropped the final vowel. This process also involved the realization of long consonants. In 'Classical' Old Frisian the following three forms were all phonemically distinct (i.e., their different pronunciations implied different meanings: *mete* '(I) measure' ≠ *mēte* '(I) meet' ≠ *mette* '(I) met'. The last form shows regular shortening of the originally long stem vowel (§139b).

Whereas in *mette* 'met', *-tt-* used to indicate that the pronunciation of the consonant was long, we see in late Old West Frisian a new orthographical phenomenon: a double consonant was now employed to indicate that the preceding vowel was short, e.g., *kerre* 'privilege' (< *kere*), *schetten* 'shot (PP)' (< *sketen)*, *wessa* [weza] 'to be' (< *wesa); fulle* 'much, many' (< *fule*).

§210   *Some typically Old West Frisian morphological criteria are:*
1.   the plurals (strong masculine) in *-a*, *-e* tend to be replaced by *-an*, *-en*.
2.   the presence of final *-n* in the infinitives of the monosyllabic verbs (e.g., *dwān* 'do', *siān* 'see') which is absent from such infinitives in Old East Frisian (Meijering 1990). Meijering also pointed out that the 'short forms' of the verbs 'stand' and 'go', *stān* and *gān*, were absent in Old East Frisian, which exhibits only the 'long forms' *stonda* and *gunga*. Old West Frisian texts, however, display both the long and the short forms.
3.   morphological innovations are also shown in the pronominal system: *iemma(n)*, *iemmen* 'you (PL: NOM, DAT, ACC)' and *hemma(n)*, *hemmen*, *himman* 'they (DAT, ACC)'. The form *himman* is also found in F (east of the Lauwers).
4.   the dental past tense marker in weak verbs of Class 2 is dropped, e.g., *wēpenia* 'to arm', *wēpen(a/e)de* (1,3SG.PRET), *wēpen(a/e)d* (PP) both become *wēpena/e* (Meijering 1980).
5.   later Old West Frisian shows an increasing collapse of the morphological system (also called 'syncretism'), in which the nominal and verbal ending *-a* is reduced to *-e*, e.g., *setta* (INF) > *sette* 'to set' and the plural endings *-an* (NOM/ACC), *-ena* (GEN.PL), and *-um*, *-em* (DAT.PL) become *-en*.
6.   final *-e* has often dropped, e.g., *here* 'army' > *hēre* (§209) > *hēr* ⟨heer⟩, *stede* 'place' > *stēde* (§209) > *stēd* ⟨steed⟩, *ik dēle* 'I share' > *ik dēl*; *restene* 'rest' > *resten*.

§211   *South-West versus North-East within Old West Frisian*
The fact that hundreds of dated and localized charters and other legal and administrative documents have survived from the area west of the Lauwers offers the possibility

to detect further dialectal distinctions within this area. To date, explorations in this respect have barely begun. An important isogloss was established by Miedema (1986), who demonstrated on the basis of authentic charters (i.e., not copies) that, especially before dental consonants (*d, t, l, n*) in closed syllables, OFris *e > o* in the south-west (roughly Westergo), while in the north-east (roughly Oostergo) *e > a*, e.g., *setta* 'to set', *sella* 'to sell' appear as SW *sotta, solla* and NE *satta, salla* (cf. Spenter 1968: 59–61), *wasa* 'to be' (Text XV) beside *wesa*. The middle region, however, retained *e*, thus SW *iold* 'money' as against 'regular' *ield*, SW *fiuld* 'field' as against elsewhere *field*. This divergent development can be dated to the fifteenth century.

§212 *Word-geography*
Beside phonological and morphological criteria, the Old Frisian lexis specially allows for a delicate subdivision between East and West, as Munske (1973: §§283–86) has convincingly demonstrated on the basis of the semantic field of 'crime', which is particularly well represented due to the Old Frisian text tradition. Munske's word-geographical approach offers promising perspectives, and deserves to be followed in other semantic fields.

Within the legal terminology, for example, it appears that Gmc *grōtjan* 'to address, greet' developed a specialized meaning in OWFris *grēta* 'to accuse'. This verb, with a number of derivations (e.g., *grētene* 'accusation', *grētwird* 'id.', *grētman* 'judge') is not found in Old East Frisian texts (apart from the *West Lauwers Synodal Laws* in F [see §213] and *How to Accuse a Thief* in H [Reader, Text IX]). Conversely, *rēdieva* (*rēdgeva, rēdia*) 'judge' is confined to Old East Frisian texts. The fortuitous survival of manuscripts might lead to unwarranted conclusions. For example, *kēthere* 'presider of the tribunal of *rēdieva*' is found only in B, suggesting that this office was confined to Brokmerland. However, the word has come to light in a number of Ommeland texts translated from Old Frisian into Low German (e.g., *Fivelgo Statutes, Humsterland Statutes, New Langewold Statutes of 1282*, cf. Johnston 1998b), which shows it to have had a wider distribution in East Frisian than just Brokmerland. This example counsels caution in drawing far-reaching conclusions from the limited material that has come down to us.

Other semantic fields seem to confirm that the Lauwers is a major language border within the Frisian area. It appears from the modern dialects that Frisian once must have had two verbs for 'to grind', **mala* and **grinda*. Old West Frisian retained **mala* > ModWFris *mealle*, which it shared with the other continental Germanic languages. Old East and Old North Frisian, on the other hand, selected **grinda*, as appears, for example, from IsNFris *grinj* [Föhr-Amr.], MainlNFris *grüne*, and EFris *griene* [Saterl.]. Interestingly, **grinda* is one of over 100 isoglosses which (Old) Frisian shares with (Old) English (Bremmer 1982).

§213 *Methodological remarks*

For historical linguists, the existence of dialects in older stages of a given language is undisputed. This existence was contested for Old Frisian by Sjölin (1966), however. Sjölin claimed, not entirely without reason, that the Old Frisian legal manuscripts often lacked external evidence as to their regional provenance (cf. §14). The manuscripts traditionally assigned to the districts east of the Lauwers clearly represent an older stage of the language than those from west of the Lauwers. Hence, Sjölin explained their linguistic differences as chronological rather than diatopical, and coined the term 'Classical Old Frisian' for the language represented by the majority of the Old East Frisian manuscripts, and Post-Classical for the other Old East Frisian manuscripts (E2, E3 and F) and for all of the Old West Frisian manuscripts. While Sjölin's observation of the diachronic differences between the two groups was in general conceded, his denial of there being any dialectal differences between Old Frisian at either side of the Lauwers has been demonstrated to be invalid by especially Hofmann (1971), Munske (1973: 184–88) and Meijering (1990). Some of the evidence is obscured by the fact that certain Old West Frisian texts were copied by East Frisian scribes and adapted to their own language system without completely obliterating all the Old West Frisian features. Such texts exhibit a *Mischsprache* that was never genuinely spoken, e.g., in texts from the Ommelanden, this 'mixed' dialect is found in the poem *Fon Alra Fresena Fridome* (H; Text XVI below), in the redactions of the *Legend and Statutes of Magnus* and the *West Lauwers Synodal Laws* as they appear in F; in a manuscript from Emsingo, we find Old West Frisian forms interspersed in the redaction of *Processus Judicii* (Bremmer 1996). Some Ems Old Frisian features have been isolated in texts from Rüstringen (Weser Old Frisian); they can only be explained by transmission through copying (Bremmer 2007a). Although Sjölin (1984) mitigated some of his earlier, far-reaching statements, he still maintained that the reconstruction of dialect areas within the zone from where the Old Frisian manuscripts originate should not be an object of Frisian linguistics, an opinion which the above has shown is untenable.

Chapter VII

Two long-standing problems

The periodization of Frisian and the Anglo-Frisian complex

From a comparative linguistic point of view, (Old) Frisian has been the subject of sometimes fierce scholarly debate. Two such controversial issues will be dealt with here at some length: the term 'Old Frisian' and the relation between (Old) Frisian and (Old) English.

How 'Old' is Old Frisian?

§214 Since the German scholar Jacob Grimm had subjected the German language, and with it all Germanic languages, to a tripartite period division of Old, Middle and Modern (*Deutsche Grammatik*, 3rd ed. 1831), it gradually became customary for historical linguists to adopt this model of periodization. Certainly, such a threefold division fulfills the scientific aims of classification and systematization. In addition, a neat division has its didactic advantages as any teacher will know. However, teachers will also be quick to add that time divisions are not as absolute as they seem and that certain features belonging to one period, e.g., 'Middle', may already be visible in the preceding one or, conversely, some features characteristic of the 'Old' period continue for a while into the 'Middle' period. After all, changes never happen overnight and not every change co-occurs at exactly the same time as another one. Furthermore, not all dialects act in unison. Quite understandably, the periodization of Frisian has also given rise to contention amongst scholars.

§215 The problem started in the early nineteenth century. Until then, medieval Frisian (to use a neutral term) had been called plainly 'Frisian'. Thus, for example, the Danish linguist Rasmus Rask entitled his grammar of medieval Frisian 'Frisian Grammar': *Frisisk Sproglære* (1825), which was then translated into Dutch as *Friesche Spraakleer* (1832) and into German as *Friesische Sprachlehre* (1834). On the other hand, the adjective 'old' was also used with respect to Frisian, even before Grimm's tripartite division, but merely with the meaning of 'venerable' or just 'very old' without any association with periodization, as appears, for example, from the title of Tilemann Wiarda's edition of the First Rüstring Manuscript: *Asega Buch. Ein altfriesisches Gesetzbuch der Rüstringer* (1805). The comprehensive dictionary of Old Frisian with which von Richthofen accompanied his impressive text edition of the Frisian laws in 1840 carried the title of *Altfriesisches Wörterbuch* (not **Wörterbuch der alten friesischen Sprache* or the like). Von Richthofen, a pupil of Jacob Grimm's, had apparently listened to his master's voice or maybe he had applied the title to his dictionary in imitation of Graff's *Althochdeutscher Sprachschatz* (1832–1846). In any case, *inside* his dictionary, in his preface, von Richthofen refers to the language only as 'Frisian', so always without the qualifying predicate of 'Old'.

§216 At the close of the nineteenth century, when the Neogrammarians with their strict rules dominated the linguistic world, scholars dealing with medieval Frisian were forced to defend themselves in applying the term 'Old' to medieval Frisian. Van Helten expressed his uneasiness with the terminology when he concluded his introduction to his *Altostfriesische Grammatik* (1890: XII):[1]

> For the age of these [Old East Frisian] dialects the age of the manuscript should probably serve as a rough benchmark, although the possibility cannot be entirely denied that some manuscripts represent a more or less older stage of the language in relation to the time when they were copied. Whether the greater or lesser conservatism to be observed here relates to the difference in age or should also partly count as an idiosyncrasy of the dialect in question cannot be determined, of course; (compare, e.g., in the Rüstring dialects, besides occasional antiquity in vocalism, the *-n* [as a dative plural marker, RHB] instead of the usual *-m* in the other dialects).

Van Helten realized that a language on the whole cannot be older than the manuscript in which it was written – certainly not, one could add, when it concerns 'living' legal texts with immediate relevance for everyday life. Nonetheless, van Helten left some room for the language of a text to be older than the manuscript itself. He also realized the peculiarity and seemingly contradictory features of the language of the Rüstring manuscripts – the vocalism of Rüstring Old Frisian seemed 'antiquated' (*altertümlich*) here and there, but the Rüstring dative plural ending *-n*, on the other hand, appeared to be younger than that in the other manuscripts. Van Helten was as yet ignorant of the fact that the peculiar vocalism of Rüstring Old Frisian was still present in his own lifetime in the modern descendants of this dialect (cf. §205.1–2).

---

1.   'Für das alter dieser mundarten ist wol das alter der mss. als ungefährer massstab anzunehmen, wenn gleich die möglichkeit nicht zu leugnen ist, dass die eine od. andre hs. eine im verhältnis zur zeit der schreibung mehr od. weniger ältere sprachstufe repräsentiere. Ob der hier zu beobachtende grössere od. geringere conservatismus mit dem verschiedenen alter in zusammenhang steht oder zum teil auch als eigentümlichkeit des betreffenden dial. zu gelten hat, ist natürlich nicht zu entscheiden; (vgl. z. b. im R dial. neben mancher altertümlichkeit des vocalismus das *-n*, f. durchgängiges *-m* in der andren mundarten).'

In his monumental description and grammatical analysis of all the Frisian dialects from all periods, Siebs (1901: 1168) voiced a similar embarrassment after his listing of the medieval East Frisian manuscripts:[2]

> Attempts have been made to deny the right to call the language of these sources Old Frisian; but although they [the sources] do indeed stem from a period where we designate the German language as *Middle* High German and [*Middle*] Low German, the phonological situation, however, is such that we have just as much right to speak of an Old Frisian language as we do of an Old Saxon or an Old High German language.

Both van Helten and Siebs justified their opinions with reference to the phonology, but refrained from presenting any systematically arranged evidence. They left it to the readers, it would seem, to gather such evidence for themselves from their lengthy and detailed grammars.

§217 One will realize that if a language can boast of an 'Old' period, its antiquity will add to its prestige. Particularly, because Frisian today is a minority language, both its speakers and many scholars who intimately study it have been concerned to secure an 'Old' period. On the other hand, time and again attempts have been made to deny an 'Old' period for Frisian and instead to make it step in line, chronologically at least, with the 'Middle' period of the neighbouring languages, such as Middle High and Middle Low German, Middle Dutch and Middle English. However, the discussion remains somewhat arbitrary, for 'that which we call a rose by any other name would smell as sweet' (Shakespeare).

One of the most significant criteria for establishing whether a language belonged to the 'Old' period since Grimm has been the quality of vowels in unstressed syllables. Whenever especially case endings still exhibited full vowels (/u/, /o/, /a/) in such syllables, these were taken to be indicative for the 'Old' period. However, Medieval Frisian on the whole does not display this feature to the same extent as do, for example, Old English or Old High German; hence it would not qualify for the predicate 'Old'. The only exception would seem the language of the Rüstring manuscripts, but here the presence of full vowels in unstressed syllables is a dialect feature – it was maintained in the 'Modern' dialects descending from it – and not an 'archaic', chronological trait (§206.1–2; Bremmer 2007a; Smith 2007; Smith and van Leyden 2007).

§218 The relative degree of arbitrariness of neat periodizations appears not only from establishing when one period ends and another one begins. For example, some

---

2. 'Man hat das Recht bestreiten wollen die Sprache dieser Quellen altfriesisch zu nennen; mögen sie aber auch aus einer Zeit stammen, deren deutsche Sprache wir als *mittel*hochdeutsch und -niederdeutsch bezeichnen, so sind doch die Lautverhältnisse derartig, dass wir mit dem gleichen Rechte von einer altfriesischen wie von einer altsächsischen oder althochdeutschen Sprache reden dürfen.'

scholars have Old English end at 1066 (the Norman Conquest of England), some at 1100 and still others at 1150. Traditionally, the dividing line between Old and Middle High German is drawn at around 1050, but it is realized that certain 'Old' texts already display some 'Middle' features and that twelfth-century texts can still look more 'Old' than 'Middle' German (Geuenich 1985: 983 [§1.2.2]). Important in this respect are the criteria that one selects in order to establish whether a language is 'Old', 'Middle', or 'Modern'. In a polemic, de Haan (2001c) and Versloot (2004), both of them Frisian linguists, revived the old debate. De Haan denied the predicate 'Old' for medieval Frisian and claimed that 'Middle' would be appropriate. Versloot, on the other hand, with some modification, argued in favour of the traditional terminology. Quite understandably, both scholars selected different criteria for their respective periodizations.

To de Haan, the following features are decisive (section numbers in this book are given here as a point of reference):

a.   the absence of full vowels in unstressed syllables (§39R.1);
b.   vowel lengthening [in open syllables] and consonantal degemination (§210);
c.   the absence of thematic vowels in the past tense of weak verb classes (§§139, 141);
d.   the absence of a subclassification in the *jan*-verbs (§141);
e.   syncretism in the system of verbal inflection (§§127d, 151);
f.   adoption of the -*(e)st* suffix for the 2SG preterite indicative (§151);
g.   the absence of 'old' nominal declensional classes (§§99R.1; 102, 104, 106–13);
h.   syncretism in the system of nominal flection (see previous);
i.   the presence of a relatively rich system of prepositions (§183);
j.   the deletion of Germanic /w/ and /j/ in certain environments (§27R; §§104, 106);
k.   the presence of 'contracted' verbs (§54);
l.   the properties of the system of negation [i.e., multiple negation] (§199R.1).

On the basis of his findings, de Haan arrives at a periodization in which there appears to be no place any longer for an 'Old' stage:

before *c.*1275   Ante-Middle Frisian
*c.*1275–1550   Middle Frisian
*c.*1550–present   Modern Frisian

The year *c.*1275 in this table refers to the date of the oldest vernacular Frisian law manuscript (§9); *c.*1550 marks the date of the last vernacular Frisian charter (§11). On the whole, de Haan focussed on phonological and morphological criteria, but he also considered certain syntactic phenomena (items [i] and [l]).

Versloot employed a much wider choice of criteria than had de Haan. Moreover, he paid closer attention to the distribution of these criteria in manuscripts and time. For example, Versloot detects no trace as yet of vowel-lengthening and consonant degemination in Old East Frisian (cf. de Haan's [b]). Weak verbs still have a thematic vowel, which however is -a- in Old Frisian (as in Old English) and not ō as in Old High German or o as in Old Saxon (cf. de Haan's [c]). New in Versloot's list of diagnostic criteria are, e.g., the longevity of the dental fricative th /ð, þ/ (§78.2 th), the retention of gender specific numerals (§122), the relatively late appearance of compounds of the type 'noun-Gen + noun' (§165), and, whether useful or not, the persistence of the indeclinable relative particle thēr (§§95, 204.c). The first two of these four features, the persistence of the dental fricative and gender of specific numerals, had (almost completely) been given up in Middle Dutch and Middle Low German, the particle thēr is unique for Old Frisian (OE used þe, Old Saxon thē). Versloot might also have added to his list the near absence of auxiliaries of tense until c.1450 (cf. §§192, 195) and the demise of the construction āga tō 'to have to' (§188) as indications of the relative age of a text. As a result of his analysis, Versloot arrives at a different, more detailed division:

before 1100	Runic Frisian
c.1200–c.1400	Old Frisian (including the language of R1, R2, R4, H1, H2, B1, B2 and E1, some texts in U and the Psalter fragment)
c.1400–1550	Middle Frisian: all the other texts hitherto called Old Frisian; the status of the oldest West Frisian charters (before c.1410) has yet to be studied in detail
1550–1800	early Modern Frisian
1800–now	Modern Frisian

Unlike de Haan, Versloot has the 'Old' stage begin at c.1200 which is based on the dating of the Old Frisian Psalter fragment (§9). Versloot's designation of 'Runic Frisian' for any form of Frisian before it turns up in manuscripts might be confusing, but what he means is that all we have of Frisian before 1200 is from Runic inscriptions; these inscriptions can be dated with some imprecision to between 500 and 800. For the scanty language material from the period before c.1200, Nielsen (1994) suggested to use the neutral term 'Ante-Old Frisian'.

Also from another angle, certain weaknesses in de Haan's analysis can be pointed out. When his list of criteria is applied to Old English, for example, it would appear that this stage of English hardly deserves the predicate 'Old', for by the year 900 (section numbers refer to this book):[3]

a. the full vowels in unstressed syllables had started to give way;
c. by 1000, Old English (West Saxon) had given up the thematic vowels in the past tense of weak verbs class 1, e.g., getrymde instead of earlier getrymede;
d. subclassification in -ōn/-ōian verbs had been given up;

3. The relevant Old English features can easily be found in Campbell (1959).

e. syncretism in the system of verbal inflection started as early as Ingvaeonic/North Sea Germanic with uniform endings for all plural persons, both present and past (§32.b);

f. the ending -*st* for the 2SG.PRET has been attested for Northumbrian Old English (analogous with the present tense -*st*);

g. a number of 'old' nominal declensions had already collapsed in the Old English period;

h. like Old Frisian, Old English (West Saxon) from its appearance in the ninth century onwards, shows no distinction between dative and accusative forms for the first and second persons singular and plural (§88) – but note the Old English (Anglian) accusative forms *mec* 'me' and *þec* 'thee, you' (cf. G *mich, dich*);

i. the Old English system of prepositions is richer than that of Old Frisian;

k. contract verbs abound in Old English (§131, Remark 2, §132, Remark 2, and compare such verbs as OE *slēan* 'to strike'; *fōn* 'to catch', *hwōn* 'to hang').

l. negative adverbs in combination with *ne* are 'frequently used' in Old English (Mitchell 1985: §1603).

Only de Haan's items (b) – lengthening in open syllables – and (j) – deletion of Gmc /w/ and /j/– are absent from this enumeration because they are not yet attested for the generally accepted Old English period. Consequently, one may question the suitability of de Haan's criteria in establishing whether Old Frisian is really 'Old' when they would demonstrate Old English not to be 'Old' at all.

§219 The same issue with respect to the tenability of the time-honoured threefold periodization for English has been tackled by Lass (2000). His selection of criteria is quite different from those of both de Haan and Versloot in that he pays less attention to detailed inflectional and conjugational endings. These are Lass's 'archaisms' (i.e., criteria that make a language 'Old'); section numbers refer to the present book:

a. Root-initial accent (§156);

b. At least three distinct qualities in weak inflectional syllables (e.g., §100);

c. A dual (§89);

d. Grammatical gender (§81);

e. Four vowel-grades in (certain) strong verbs (§128);

f. Distinctive dative in at least some nouns (e.g., §100);

g. Inflected definitive article (or proto-article) (§84);

h. Adjective inflection (§114);

i. Infinitive suffix (§127.b);

j. Person/number marking on the verb (§127.d).

Lass applied these criteria to a full range of Germanic languages, including Afrikaans, but excluding Danish, Swedish, Norwegian and Frisian. In the table I have adapted Lass's table by substituting Old Frisian for Afrikaans (M = Middle, N = New, i.e., Modern):

	Go	OE	ME	NE	OIc	NIc	OHG	MHG	NHG	MDu	NDu	OFris
a	+	+	−	−	+	+	+	−	−	−	−	+
b	+	+	−	−	+	+	+	−	−	−	−	+
c	+	+	−	−	+	+	−	−	−	−	−	(+)
d	+	+	−	−	+	+	+	+	+	+	+	+
e	+	+	−	−	+	+	+	+	−	−	−	+
f	+	+	+	−	+	+	+	+	+	+	−	+
g	+	+	+	−	+	+	+	+	+	+	−	+
h	+	+	+	−	+	+	+	+	+	+	+	+
i	+	+	+	−	+	+	+	+	+	+	+	+
j	+	+	+	−	+	+	+	+	+	+	+	+

As the table makes clear, application of Lass's criteria puts the oldest written stage of Frisian firmly into the 'Old' period. However, if we apply Lass's matrix to Frisian as it was written around 1500 west of the Lauwers (in the absence of written Frisian elsewhere), it appears that the language has moved towards the 'Middle' period: (b) there are no three distinct qualities in weak inflectional syllables any longer; (c) no trace of a dual is found; and (e) strong verbs tend to appear in three principal parts. Moreover, the three-gender system has begun to give way to one with two genders (MASC/FEM vs. NEUT).

   In conclusion, then, the way in which Frisian is divided into certain periods depends entirely on the criteria which one chooses in order to establish such periods. As long as scholars do not agree upon these criteria, periodization will remain a matter of debate. Each attempt to arrive at a periodization of a language will therefore be no more than a suggestion (Ernst 2005: 15). For this book, the conventional terminology 'Old Frisian' has been retained, but, whenever relevant, further distinction is made by using the term 'late Old Frisian' with reference to the late fifteenth and early sixteenth centuries. On the whole, this latter division concurs with the chronological distinction made by Sjölin (1966; 1969: 16–18) between 'Classical' and 'Post-Classical' Old Frisian (§§17, 213).

The Anglo-Frisian complex

§220 From the fourteenth century onwards there was a growing awareness that English and Frisian are very closely related languages (Bremmer 1989a). The explanation traditionally given for this observation was that Frisians presumably made up a large number of the Saxon tribes that conquered Britain in the fifth century. The evidence presented for the linguistic similarities was for a long time confined to lexical parallels. Only in the nineteenth century did scholars begin to underpin the century-old 'common place' with phonological and morphological data. A full survey and discussion of these Anglo-Frisian parallels is given by Nielsen who concluded that 'Old English is more closely linked to Old Frisian than any other Germanic language' (Nielsen 1985: 273; cf. Bremmer 1982).

§221 Some striking phonological parallels include: nasalization and rounding of *a*, both short and long, before nasals (§28); loss of nasal before voiceless fricative plus compensatory lengthening (§30); fronting of West Germanic *ā* > *ǣ* (§33); monophthongization of Gmc **ai* > *ā* (§36); fronting of *a* > *æ* (§37); palatalization and assibilation of **g* and **k* before front vowels (§42), and breaking of short *e* and *i* before certain velar consonant clusters (§48).

In addition to these parallels with 'common' Old English, we also find parallels between Old Frisian and certain Old English dialects. For example, unrounding of the *i*-mutation products to *e*, both short and long (§45), is also found in Kentish Old English, as is the phenomenon of rising diphthongs (§§36, 46c), and a 'vernerized' (§63) superlative form of 'little' (§119): OFris *lērest* ~ Kt *lǣresta* (once). With Northumbrian Old English, e.g., Old Frisian shares the loss of final *-n* in all kinds of endings, e.g., NhOE/OFris *ūta* (ADV.) 'outwards, to the outside', NhOE/OFris *fara* (INF.) 'to go' (§68).

For morphological parallels, the uniform verbal plural endings in Old English and Old Frisian (§82) are conspicuous; within Germanic, only Old English and Old Frisian share the comparative and superlative forms that come with 'little': OE *lǣssa*, *lǣst*/OFris *lēssa*, *lēst* 'less, least' (§119); neither Old English nor Old Frisian show gender distinction for the plural demonstrative and personal pronouns: OE *þā* 'those', *hīe* 'they' and OFris *thā* and *hiā* (§§84, 90); both Old English and Old Frisian preserved the *-i-* after the stem of weak verbs Class 2 (§141): OE *macian*/OFris *makia* 'to make'.

§222 Also on the level of the lexis, the relation between English and Frisian is remarkably close. An extensive investigation carried out by Löfstedt (1963–1969) brought to light some 120 exclusive Anglo-Frisian lexical parallels, as opposed to some 40 Friso-Scandinavian ones. The majority of the exclusively Anglo-Frisian shared words belong to the domain of agriculture, body/health and nature, e.g., OE *cǣġ*/OFris *kēi* 'key'; OE *bōgian*/OFris *bōgia* 'to dwell'; OE *fǣmne*/OFris *fomne* 'girl'; OE *lǣpewince*/ModWFris *ljip*, IsNFris *liap* 'lapwing, pewit'; OE *bræġen*/OFris *brein* 'brain' (also ME *brainepanne*/ OFris *breinponne* 'brain pan, cranium'), OE *wann* 'dark'/OFris *wonfelle* 'with bruised skin'. Even ModE *aye* 'yes' (first recorded 1576) has an exclusive parallel in late OFris *ay* (Bremmer 1989b).

A particular form of a lexical unit is the (more or less) fixed alliterative formula, of which Old English shares some 25 exclusive items with Old Frisian (Bremmer 1982),

such as OE *mærke and mǣre*/OFris *mār and mark* 'boundary and division' to establish boundaries between landed properties; OE *beornan and brecan*/OFris *breka ieftha
barna* 'to break and/or burn' with reference to a penal expedition. The exclusive parallel of OE *synn*/OFris *sinne* 'sin' is also preserved in a unique phrase: OE *synn and sacu*
'crime and lawsuit'/OFris *seka ni sinne* 'neither lawsuits nor crimes'. Even the game of
love was exclusively formulated, as shown by OE *cyssan and clyppan*/OFris *kleppa and
kessa* 'to embrace and kiss'.

§223 Exclusive parallels on the syntactic level are rare, whether because they are almost
absent or because the syntax of Old Frisian is an understudied chapter is difficult to
say. One parallel has been shown to exist in the syntactic behaviour of decades. In the
various Old Germanic languages, nouns preceded by a numeral below twenty were
inflected, e.g., *twelef skillingar, mith twelef skillingum* '(with) twelve shillings', while
nouns following decades from twenty onwards usually appear in the genitive plural,
e.g., *twintich skillinga* 'twenty shillings'. However, only in Old English and Old Frisian
do we find inflected nouns in such strings as OE *mid xxxgum cyningum* 'with thirty
kings'/OFris *mith lxxij scillingum* 'with seventy-two shillings' (Hofmann 1982/1989).

§224 It is clear from the above examples that English and Frisian share many exclusive parallels. The problem appears to be how to explain this close relationship
(Bremmer 1990). Contrary to what was generally believed in early modern times, there is
little evidence of Frisians having participated on any large scale in the settlement of Britain
in the fifth and sixth centuries. The scarce documentary sources from the early Middle
Ages are silent on the Frisians, apart from the Byzantine author Procopius *c*.500–*c*.565)
who mentions Frisians alongside Angles in Britain (he omits the Saxons). Archeolo-
gists today are more careful than in the past to identify early medieval objects and
designs found in England, as shown, e.g., by pots and combs, as being of Frisian origin. Unlike that of the Saxons and the Angles, the name of the Frisians was not given
to any large district in England. What place-name evidence betrays the presence of the
Frisians in Anglo-Saxon England, such as Friston or Frisby, is indicative of individual
settlements throughout the period until 1100.

On the other hand, the North Sea did not just divide, it also bridged England with
Frisia. An awareness of cultural similarity is evidenced by the fact that both in England and Frisia, the same runic characters were used to represent the new sounds that
had developed from Gmc **a*. In the original runic alphabet, *a* was represented by ᚠ.
In England and Frisia around 500 A.D., this rune came now to be used for æ, which
was the result of fronting (§33). Another development caused *a to* be rounded before
nasals to *o* (§28). For this new sound, whether long or short, a new runic character was
designed, ᚩ. Finally, for *a*, whether unchanged or the result of monophthongization of
*ai and (in Frisian) of **au* (§36), rune masters invented ᚪ. So instead of one, both the

Anglo-Saxons and the Frisians now had three variants of the same rune. Whether the innovations were made in Frisia or in England is not clear.

As skippers, Frisians played an important part in the transit trade between the Rhineland and England. Frisian slave-traders were active in London; the northern metropolis York even had a special quarter to accommodate the many Frisian traders there. Economic ties were evidently intense, so much so that around 700, the same silver coinage, *sceattas*, was struck both in England and in Frisia. Familiarity with the Frisians will have increased the wish of the Anglo-Saxons to convert the latter to Christianity, a project that was started in the last quarter of the seventh century.

§225   In the light of all this, how should we explain the close language parallels between English and Frisian? Rather than assuming that Frisians joined the Angles and Saxons in their occupation of Britain, it has been suggested that a considerably large number of Anglo-Saxons decided to stay in Frisia rather than to cross the North Sea. Especially, however, the general opinion today is that the Frisians were the last continental tribe to retain the many Ingvaeonic/North Sea Germanic features that once prevailed along the coast of the Low Countries and Germany and which the Anglo-Saxons had brought with them to Britain in the fifth century. When the Frisians were annexed by the Franks in the course of the eighth century, one of their ways of resistance would have been to withstand linguistic innovations that spread from the more central Frankish cultural centres. England remained outside this sphere of influence, because of its insular position. Secluded from the inland by vast marshes and oriented towards the sea, Frisian likewise escaped the fate of falling victim to Franconian; compared to the neighbouring Germanic languages, it has preserved many original Ingvaeonic features. When, many centuries after the migrations to England, the continental Saxons around 1000 began to extend their sphere of influence and started to threaten the Frisians, the latter, whether consciously or unconsciously, frequently chose those forms and words from a set of alternatives that were least like Saxon. Through this process of demarcating not only the territorial borders but also the linguistic ones, the Ingvaeonic/North Sea Germanic character of Frisian was even further accentuated (cf. Stiles 1995). In other words, the parallels are not purely the outcome of a shared origin in a hypothetical Anglo-Frisian mother dialect, as had commonly been assumed, but are also the result of cultural developments that reach back to before and after the migration of the Anglo-Saxons to Britain.

Reader

Contents

i	New Life:	130
	a. The Gestation of the Foetus (E1)	130
	b. Protecting Infants and the Unborn (F)	130
	c. Protecting Pregnant Women (R1)	131
	d. Another Protective Measure for Pregnant Women (E1)	132
	e. Adam's Creation (E1)	134
ii	The Five Keys to Wisdom (H)	134
iii	The Fifteen Signs of Doomsday (R1)	136
iv	The Ten Commandments (R1)	138
v	The Right to Pay Compensation and its Exceptions (F)	140
vi	The Right of Counter Action in Law (H)	143
vii	Compensations for Injuries (E2)	145
viii	Five Exceptions to the Right of Swearing Innocence (H)	148
ix	How to Accuse a Thief (H)	150
x	Miscellaneous Decrees:	151
	a. Mercy for a Thief (F)	151
	b. On Killing a Relative (R1)	152
	c. Permission to Break into a Church (R1)	152
	d. Abba's Hat (H)	153
xi	This is also Frisian Law (R1)	154
xii	New Land, New Laws (B)	158
xiii	The *Fia-eth* (E2)	160
xiv	*Asegariucht* (F)	163
xv	The Legend and Statutes of Magnus (U)	165
xvi	*Fon Alra Fresena Fridome* (H)	168
xvii	Charlemagne and Redbad (U)	174
xviii	A Wedding Speech (Ba)	177
xix	The Palm Knight (A)	181
xx	Hideous Crimes, Cruel Measures (J, Ro, F, SnR)	184

I. New Life

a.   The Gestation of the Foetus

Interspersed in the laws, we occasionally find texts that at first sight do not seem to belong there, like the following short account of the growth of the foetus, taken from E1. A similar text survives in Old English. Both versions ultimately derive from a late Roman gynaecological treatise by Vindicianus, which has here erroneously been attributed to St Augustine of Hippo. The purpose of the text in its Old Frisian context is to establish the age of the unborn child, if an abortion arises from a fight with a pregnant woman, in order to be able to establish the amount of compensation to be paid (Elsakkers 2004). A somewhat similar version of this text is found in E3.
      The text has been slightly normalized.

Augustinus seith ande queth thet thet kind an there modere bilethad werthe niugen monath. Anda tha eresta monathe, sa somnath thet blod efter there undfengnesse. Anda tha othere monathe, sa werth thi likhoma bilethad. Anda tha thredda monathe, sa werthath tha sina ifestnad and tha eddra, and werth thiu berd betein. Anda tha fiarda monathe, sa werth thet
5 kind bilethad. Anda tha fifta monathe, sa undfeth hit tha sele, and upriucht hit thene likhoma and undfeth thene om. Anda tha sexta monathe, sa wext thet merch and thiu hed. Anda tha sogenda monathe undfeth hit tha thermar. Anda tha achtenda monathe, sa wext thet her and tha neilar. Anda tha niugenda monathe, sa werthath se sketh and werth thet kind ebern.

Explanatory notes:

1   On the use and spread in Old Frisian of the verb *quetha* 'to say', see Krolis-Sytsema 1989; *kind* is a Low German loan (as shown by *k-* instead of *ts-*), competing with native *bern*; *niugen monath*: 'during nine months', accusative of time (§180.2); on the endingless plural of *mōnath*, see §100.

4   *ifestnad*: on the perfective prefix, see §155.5.

6   *wext thet merch and thiu hed*: note that the verb form is singular, whereas the subject ('merch and hed') is plural (§177).

8   *se*: 'they' (§91), that is, mother and child; *sketh*, see §139c.

b.   Protecting Infants and the Unborn

The following passage, taken from a large list of penal regulations in F, harks back to the description of the gestation of the foetus, preceded by a clause concerning infants and underaged children. The regulations are rubricated in the manuscript as *unierich kind*. In a somewhat different version they are also found in R1 (below Text Ic) and H. Such variations

of what probably started as one recension indicates how even such small texts were suscep-
tible to change.

The text has been slightly normalized.

Unierich Kind

Augustinus thi helga biscop seith: Alsa en unierich kind is in there bobbaburch – hwasa hit
bifiucht iefta biravath, thribete to betane iefta mith thrim riuchtum to riuchtane, alsa fir sa
thet ma clagia wel.

Thio berdwendene an tha forma monathe den: thet ield bi xii merkum iefta bi xii ethum.

5   And alle thre neste monath alsa.

Tha fiarda monathe den, en thrimen ield iefta mith fiowertega ethum to riuchtane. In
tha fifta monathe, sa hit lifheftich is, neilan and her heth, sa is't en twede lif.

An tha sexta ande sogenda monathe, sa mei't ful kuma – to ene fulla ield to ieldane.
Thruch tha morthkase ther den is binna tha benetaburch, thrimen further to betane. Ief ma

10   biseka welle, mith niogen skerem to sikriane thruch tha morthkase.

Explanatory notes:

1   The reference to St Augustine is found here because the author associates the contents
of these regulations with the text on the gestation of the foetus.

2   *thribete to betane*: elliptic for *ach ma thribete to betane* (§188).

3   *ma*: i.e., one of the parents.

6   *Tha fiarda monathe den*: add mentally 'Is thio berdwendene an … '.

7   *neilan and her*: whether or not a foetus had nails and hair was indicative of its capability
of living, cf. Text Ia, line 9.

8   *ful kuma*: it is not clear whether this should be read as one (compound) verb or an adjective and a verb. The meaning seems to be 'it [the seven-month baby] has potential to live
when it is born'.

9   *benetaburch*: one of the few 'poetic' compounds in Old Frisian. Literally 'fortress of the
bones', it is a 'kenning' for the womb; cf. *bobbaburch* in line 1 above.

10   *mith niogen skerem*: this is one of the eight types of ordeal in medieval Frisian legal
procedure. The defendant had to step on nine hot ploughshares, and the speed with which
his wounds recovered were interpreted as an indication of either his guilt or his innocence
(cf. Buma 1949b).

c.   Protecting Pregnant Women

In order to give an idea of how a description of the gestation of a foetus had actual value in
legal procedure, here follow three short stipulations as found in R1 from the *General Regis-*

ter of Compensations, in which the amounts for compensation are rated for various cases of miscarriages caused by violence. Similar passages occur in H (VII, 142–46) and F (above Text Ib) in which compensations are rated according to the age (in months) of the foetus harmed.

Hwersa en wif en morth clagath, and thet othere wif mith werde foribrangath thet hit nawet sa fir ekimin ne se thet hit hebbe her and nila, sa mot hi thes mith twilif hondon anda withon untswera.

Hwersa en wif morth clagath and hit alsa fir ekimin is thet hit ac hebbe her ande neilar, 5 sa skil ma thes mith niugun skeron untgunga.

Sa hwersa twene kedda fiuchtath and ther en wif tohlapt and hiu sa fir onefuchten werth thet hiu morth to mannon brange binna di and binna nachte, sa ne mi ma umbe thet morth nene witha biada.

Explanatory notes:

1   *morth*: '(secret) killing', here and in line 8: 'miscarriage, stillborn child'; *thet othere wif* 'another woman'. On the use of the DEF.ART, see §200.

2   *hit*: 'it', i.e., the unborn child; *hi*: 'he', i.e., the man accused of the deed, the defendant.

4   *neilar*: note this ACC.PL form with its untypical Old Weser Frisian stem vowel (§205.6) and plural ending *-ar* (§100R.4) competing with the regular form *nila* in line 2.

d.   Another Protective Measure for Pregnant Women

This regulation constitutes the twenty-third of the *Twenty-four Land-laws* (E1), but is also found in other manuscripts. Note how tone and style differ from Text Ib, although in principle the same crimes and the same punishments are involved: causing involuntary abortion, compensations and ordeals.

The text has been normalized and regularized.

Thet is thet thriu and twintigesta londriucht: Alther se en wif onefuchten and hiu se mith berde and hiu hire den nebbe blodelsa ni blodrennanda deda, dath ni dolch ni nena morthdeda, and hiu se sa fir urevelad and onefuchten inur tha benena burch thet'tet bern and thiu berd eflive wurden se – ief hi ie, sa ach hi't to fellane mith ielde and mith urielde 5 tha berd and tha grimma morthdeda. Thet ield and liuda wed alsa hage, sa liude loviath, and thet urield scel wesa twelef merk. Ac ief hiu eflive werthe, sa ach ma hia to ieldane mith sogen ieldem; and achta pund and achta enza and achta scillingar and achta pennengar: thet is hire riuchta witma. Ac ief hi biseke, sa sikerie hi'ne mith twelef monnem an tha

withem, iefta hi gunge tha niugen heta skere. Ac ief hi thira ordela nauder dwa nelle, sa
10 wisie're him enes bereskinzes kempa, binna thrim etmeldum to bifiuchtane, iefta ene sone
alsadene bi asega dome and bi skeltata bonne, thiu se nethelic and godelic.

Explanatory notes:

2   *hiu hire den nebbe*: *hire* is dative of respect 'as for herself' (§182.4).

3   *benena burch*: 'the fortress of the bones', cf. note on Text Ib, line 9; *thet bern and thiu berd*
'the unborn child', an example of the figure of speech called *hendiadys* (lit. 'the child and
the foetus').

4   *hi*: i.e., the defendant.

5   *Thet ield*: 'wergeld', viz. for the unborn child.

6   *hiu*: i.e., the pregnant woman.

6–7   There was no uniform monetary system in medieval Frisia. Currencies fluctuated both in
time and in region. However, the basic system was as follows: 1 pound = 12 ounces = 20 shillings =
240 pennies; 1 mark = 12 shillings = 144 pennies. A mark, therefore, amounted to 0.6 pound.

10   *bereskinzes kempa*: 'a bare-legged champion'. Plaintiffs and defendants were allowed
to employ professional fighters who would decide the case in a duel, which was seen as an
ordeal. The conditions under which a duel was fought were subject to strict rules.

11   *asega*: a major judiciary official whose name is best left untranslated, although 'legal
expert' comes close to it. However, he was not a judge in the modern sense of the word,
because his role in that respect was modest. In the early and high Middle Ages, a law suit
was purely accusatory, i.e., one party accused another one of some injustice (Text IX). It was
the task of the *asega* to see to it that the procedure from beginning to end was conducted
in the proper way. He knew the legal customs and laws inside out (Text XIV), and one of his
functions was to suggest to the assembled court what step next to take, including what
judicial sentence to pronounce (what 'doom to deal'). The *asega* also often played a role in
the argumentation and in the prosecution. In the law texts, the *asega* figures only in laws
that date back to the period in which counts were still active in Frisia; after 1200, the asega's
role was taken over by other officials. The word *a-sega* means 'law speaker'. In the nineteenth century, his role was compared to that of the Icelandic *lögsögumaðr*, who in a cycle
of three years, recited all the laws before the Allthing, the national legal assembly. However,
there is no evidence of the Frisan *asega* to have done so. Alternatively, *asega* can also be
taken as a loan translation of Latin *iu-dex* (from *ius* 'law' and *dicere* 'to speak'); the word has
cognates in Old High German *ēsago* and Old Saxon *ēosago*.

The *skelta* is an official whose duty it was apparently to 'name' a 'due' or 'debt'. In Frisian law
texts, the *skelta* is charged with the enforcement of the law. He summoned defendants to
court, and was present at the execution of a verdict. The *skelta* used to be appointed by the

count, but his office remained long after the counts had lost their authority in the Frisian lands. Compared to the *frana* (see Text V, line 11), the *skelta* was less important. Disregarding a *frana*'s ban was fined with two pounds, whereas ignoring the ban of a *skelta* could be paid off with two shillings. The title of *frana* defines his relation to the lord, that of the *skelta* defines his role in the legal procedures. Like the *frana*, the *skelta* was gardually replaced by other officials who were not appointed by a feudal lord, but chosen in turns from the ranks of the freeholding peasants (whose lands were *ein*, inherited from his parents or next of kin).

e. Adam's Creation

If the growth of a foetus is impressive, the creation of the first human being is spectacular. The account of Adam's creation was widely spread throughout medieval Europe, testifying to its popularity. The origin of this small representative of Christian imaginative literature in the corpus of Old Frisian texts goes back to early Judaeo-Christian traditions (Murdoch 1994). The line-division is guided by the capitalization of the manuscript (E1). The enumeration, enveloped in an opening and closing statement, has a certain rhythmic quality.

God scop thene eresta meneska – thet was Adam – fon achta wendem:

   thet benete fon tha stene,

   thet flask fon there erthe,

   thet blod fon tha wetere,

5 tha herta fon tha winde,

   thene thogta fon tha wolkem,

   thet swet fon tha dawe,

   tha lokkar fon tha gerse,

   tha agene fon there sunna,

10 and tha ble'r'em on thene helga om.

   And tha scop'er Eva fon sine ribbe, Adames liava.

II. The Five Keys to Wisdom

The Five Keys to Wisdom is one of a number of shorter texts dealing with 'imaginative' Christian topics, and which are found interspersed in the legal texts, even though it is not often clear what their immediate relevance is to the texts surrounding them. To facilitate memorizing, such texts were often structured on a numerical basis. The *Five Keys* finds its closest parallel in *Notulae Grammticales*, a thirteenth-century grammar of Latin, attributed to a certain Magister Cesar. The motif of the Five Keys, though, was wide-spread owing to its inclusion in *Facetus*, a didactic treatise presenting itself as a supplement to the popular *Distichs of Cato*. Versions of the *Facetus* exist in Middle Dutch, Middle Low German and Middle High German, amongst other ones. The Venerable Bede (or rather Pseudo-Bede) was also familiar with the topic and included it in his *Excerptiones Patrum*, though he still knew of only four keys. Yet, the Frisian version is unlike any other text, as far as we know. Contempt of wealth, for example, is found only in Bede. It seems, therefore, that the Frisian scribe combined at least two sources. The metaphor of the keys finds its origin in sentential admonitions which ultimately go back to Old Testament wisdom literature. For further information see Buma (1950: 29–34).

The text (H2) has been slightly normalized: ⟨v⟩ and ⟨w⟩ have been turned into ⟨u⟩ and ⟨v⟩ where appropriate. Occasionally, a nominal or verbal ending has been restored to its standard form. Corrections and emendations as suggested by Buma/Ebel have usually been silently adopted.

Quinque claves sapientiae

Thet sprec thi wisa Salomon, ther was allera ertheskera monna wisest, thet ma alle wished age te undslutane mith fif keiem. Thera fif keia heth allera ec sinne noma end ene sunderge wald.

Thi forma kei is *assiduitas legendi*: Nu ther alle wished is fon Gode iebeden ande risen and efter in tha bokem scriven, thet ma tha boc minnie ende tha gerne lese ande theron
5 thene wisdom. Hwande thit is thi forma kei there wishede. Ande hwasa thene orne wite, sa rede thi, ther kunne.

Thi other kei het *memoria retinendi:* Thet is thi thochta, thet'ti mon alle thes thenzie, ther hi gelesen hebbe. Ande thet hi riucht ieve and riucht nime.

Thi thredda kei is geheten *frequens interrogatio*: Thet ma gerne fregie allera godera
10 wenda, ther bethe tha live and there sele dege. End alsa thet en selich mon al befregad hebbe and efter gelernad, thetti gerne a riuchtlike thingum fulwunige.

Thi fiarda kei is geheten *contemptus diuitiarum*: Thet allera godera monna hwelic forsmage unriuchte rikedomar, thetti nene heva ni somnie fon rave ni fon thiufthem, fon nene meidem ni fon grate wokere. Wera fon Godes ievem and riuchtere tilathe scel ma
15 bethe lif ande sele nera, ande therunder riuct nima and riuct utieva.

Thi fifta kei is geheten *honor magistri*: thetter allera monna hwelic erie sinne mester ande minnie, ande therefter alle mesterskipe, ther him fon Godes halvem to geset se. Thet is ferest sin biscop and sin prester, hia se hwelikere meta sa se se. Hwande hia him crisma ande cristenede ieven hebbath and mith hira Godes wisdome alle liude ti himelrike skelen
20 leda. *Amen.*

Explanatory notes:

Assiduitas legendi 'constant reading'; *memoria retinendi* 'memorization'; *frequens interrogatio* 'frequent asking'; *contemptus divitiarum* 'contempt of riches'; *honor magistri* 'reverence for one's master'.

Not just the use of Latin in this text points to a literate clerical, perhaps even monastic audience. Also the mention of passing and accepting justice in the Fourth Key and the emphasis in the Fifth Key on respect for the clergy indicate that the legal manuscripts circulated in clerical circles. In medieval Frisia, priests often functioned as judges, an office which elsewhere was strictly forbidden to them.

1   *Salomon*: King Solomon is presented to us in the Bible as the wisest of men. To him are attributed several books from the Old Testament, such as *Proverbs, Ecclesiastes* and the *Song of Songs*, as well as the apocryphal *Ecclesiasticus*. In many medieval texts, Solomon figures as the champion of Christian wisdom.

2   *Thera … ec: ec* 'each' governs the genitive, so *allera ec* 'each of all', i.e., just 'each'. The genitival string *Thera fif keia* 'of the five keys' in turn depends on *allera*.

3   *iebeden*: note the preservation of the prefix **ge-* as *ie-*. Elsewhere in this text we find past participles either without any prefix, e.g., *risen* (3) and *ieven* (19) or with *ge-* as in *gelesen* (8), *geheten* (9), *gelernad* (11), *geset* (17). The prefix *ge-* points to Low German orthographic influence (§155.5). The same applies in all probability to *gerne* (9, 11) instead of *ierne*, and *mester* instead of *master* (§37.b, fn.).

13   On the medial *-g-* in *forsmage*, see §78.1g.

16–17   On the postposition of part of the verbal predicate in *thetter allera monna hwelic erie sinne mester and minnie*, see §198.

III. The Fifteen Signs of Doomsday

Where so many Old Frisian texts consist of purely legal matter, it is only fitting that attention should be given to the great cosmic event of the Final Judgment by God. Allusions to and statements about the signs preceding Doomsday found in the Bible and in early Christian imaginative writings resulted in a tradition in which the fifteen signs were enumerated. The most influential version of this text is that by the English Church Father, the Venerable Bede (673–735), with which text the Old Frisian version, found only in R1, shows the greatest affinity. For further reading, see Giliberto (2007).

The Rüstring variant of Old East Frisian shows some features which make it quite different from the other variants. For a brief survey, see §205.

In the following text ⟨u⟩ has been altered to ⟨v⟩ where appropriate.

Thit send tha fiftine tekna ther er domesdi koma skilun, ther Sancte Ieronimus fand escrivin an thera Iothana bokon.

Thes erosta dis sa stigath alle wetir fiuwertich fethma bova alle bergon and stondath to

likere wis and thiu mure, ther fon stene ewrocht is.

5   Thes otheres dis sa werthath se lik there selva skipnese, ther se bifara weron.

Thes thredda dis fallath se alsa side, thet se nen age bisia ne mi.

Thes fiarda dis sa somniath se alle fiskar, ther send an tha wetiron, tosemine and hropath

al to Godi, and tha stifne net nen manniska, buta God alena.

Thes fifta dis burnath alle wetir fon asta there wralde to westa there wralde.

10   Thes sexta dis sa send alle bamar and alle gerso mith ena blodiga dawe bifangen.

Thes siugunda dis sa fallath alle tha timber fon asta there wralde to westa there wralde

and werthath algadur tobreken.

Thes achtunda dis sa falt thi sten wither thene sten and tobrekth alsemin and tha berga

werthath e-ifnad.

15   Thes niugunda dis sa werth alsa grat irthbivinge, sa ther fon onbi-ienne there wralde

er nen saden nas.

Thes tianda dis werth thiu wrald e-ivenad an there selva skipnese, ther se was er se use

Drochten eskepin hede.

Thes andlofta dis sa gunth thi manniska with thene otherna and mi nen mon otheron

20   ondwardia fon there nede and fon tha ongosta, hwande thenne is iahwelik mon thes

sinnes biravad.

Thes twilifta dis sa werth egadurad alle thet benete efter there wralde anna ene stidi.

Thes thredtinda dis sa fallath alle tha stera fon tha himule.

Thes fiuwertinda dis sa stervath alle tha liode and skilun therefter upstonda mith

25   othera dathon.

Thes fiftinda dis sa burnth alle thiu wrald fon asta there wralde to westa there wralde

al to there hilleporta.

Therefter werth domesdi. Sa cumth use Hera mith alle sine anglon and mith alle sine

heligon. Sa bevath alle thiu wrald alsa thet espene laf, alsa se hini siath mith tha criose and

30   mith tha spiri and mith tha neylon and mith there thornena crona and mith tha fif wndon,

ther hi an tha criose tholade fori us and fori al mannesklik slachte.

Explanatory notes:

1 *Thit send*: the apparent lack of grammatical concord between a demonstrative pronoun
subject and the predicate is common in Old (and Modern) Frisian (§176); for the word order
koma skilun, see §192.

The attribution of this text to St Jerome is spurious, but is found even in Bede. The phrase
'Books of the Jews' refers to the Old Testament. Caie (1976: 235–40) lists all the allusions to

Judgment Day found in the Old and New Testaments as well as in Jewish and early Christian apocryphal works.

3 *Thes erosta dis*, etc.: adverbial genitive of time, see §181(3).

4 *wis*: the expected dative form should have been *wise* but the final, unstressed -*e* has dropped before the vowel of *and*; *and thiu mure*: 'like a wall'. For the use of the definite article here, cf. §200.

5 *skipnese*: abstract noun related to *skeppa* 'to create'. The vowel *i* might be accounted for by the palatal character of the preceding *k* and is also found in Middle Low German, cf. Ahlsson (1960: 122). Van Helten (1907: 248, s.v. *nette*) *suggested influence of skippere* 'creator'.

13 *falt*: the 'correct' verbal form should have been *falth*, but reduction to *t* is occasioned by the following *th-* of *thi*; *thi sten wither thene sten* 'one stone against another' (§200); similarly line 19: *thi manniska with thene otherna*.

15–16 *sa ther … nen saden nas*: on double negation, see §199R.

25 *dathon*: Richthofen read *clathon*, an understandable reading and one which makes sense. After all, the blessed in the hereafter will be dressed in snow-white robes. The Latin texts of, for example, Bede, Peter Comestor, and Thomas Aquinas all have *cum mortuis* 'with the dead', however.

29 *thiu wrald … alsa se hini siath*: note that the plural pronoun *se* 'they, i.e., the people of this world' refers back to singular *thiu wrald*.

IV. The Ten Commandments

The following Old Frisian version of the Ten Commandments – one of many in the corpus of Old Frisian – is taken from the *Prologue to the Seventeen Statutes and Twenty-four Land-laws* as found in the First Rüstring Manuscript. The *Seventeen Statutes* is probably the earliest Frisian vernacular legal text to survive. It is one of the supra-regional law codes, and versions of it, sometimes quite diverse, are extant in practically all major legal codices (R1, E1, H1,2, F, U, J and D). The *Statutes* themselves, at least in part, date back to the eleventh century, the introductory matter having been added perhaps a century and a half later for ideological purposes. In the *Prologue*, all law is said to derive, via the Roman kings and Moses, from God Himself (Murdoch 1998). It should be noted that the version of the Ten Commandments as presented here deviates in several points from those found in Exodus 20 and Deuteronomy 5.

Hir is eskrivin thet wi Frisa alsek londriuht hebbe and halde, sa God selva sette and ebad,

thet wi hilde alle afte thing and alle riuhte thing. Efter thes bedon hit ande bennon alle irthkiningar efter Romulo and Remo (thet weron twene brother ther Rume erost stifton), Iulius and Octavianus – alsa hiton tha forma fiuwer kiningar ther to Rume kiningar weron.

5   Thit riuht skref God selva use Hera, tha thet was, thet Moyses latte thet Israheliske folk thruch thene Rada Se and of there wilda wostene and se komon to tha berge, ther is eheten Synay. Tha festade Moyses twia fiuwertih dega and nachta; therefter ief God him twa stenena tefla, ther hi on eskrivin hede tha tian bodo; tha skolde hi lera tha Israheliska folke.

Thet was thet erost bod: *Deus tuus unus est.* Thin God thet is thi ena, ther skippere is
10   himulrikes and irthrikes, tham skaltu thiania.

Thet was thet other bod: *Non assumas nomen Dei tui in vanam.* Thu ne skalt thines Godis noma nawet idle untfa; thermithi send'ti urbeden alle menetha.

Thet was thet thredde bod: *Sanctifica diem sabbati.* Thu skalt firia thene helega sunnandi, hwante God him reste, tha hi eskipin hede himulrike and irthrike; therumbe skaltu ierne firia
15   thene helega sunnandi.

Thet was thet fiarde bod: *Honora patrem tuum et matrem tuam.* Thu skalt eria thinne feder and thine moder, thettu theste langor libbe.

Thet was thet fifte bod: *Non occides.* Thu ne skalt nenne monslaga dwa.

Thet was thet sexte bod: *Non mechaberis.* Thu ne skalt nen hor tha nen overhor dwa,
20   buta mith thinere afta wive skaltu godilike libba.

Thet was thet siugunde bod: *Non furtum facias.* Thu ne skalt nene thiuvethe dwa and ne skalt nawet ieria ova thines ivenkerstena hava, ther thi fon riuchta nawet wertha ne mugun.

Thet was thet achtunde bod: *Non falsum testimonium dices.* Thu ne skalt nen unriucht
25   tiuch dwa.

Thet was thet niugunde and thet tiande bod: *Diliges Dominum Deum tuum ex toto corde tuo et proximum tuum sicut te ipsum.* Thu skalt minnia God thinne skippere mith renere hirta and thinne ivinkerstena like thi selva. Thessa twa bodo beslutath alle tha othera bodo.

Thet send tha tian bodo, ther God urief Moysese and hi forth lerde tha Israheliska folke.
30   Thesse bodo hildon hia tha fiuwertich iera, tha se andere wostene weron. And lethogade hia fon monigere nede and latte se an thet lond, thet flat fon melokon and fon hunige, thet was thet helege lond, to Iherusalem. Alsa lat use Hera God alle tha to tha himulrike, ther tha riuchte folgiath. And alle tha, ther thet riuht ieftha enich riuht brekth – hit ne se thet ma hit thruch natha dwe, thruch thet tha natha send marra tha thet riuht – sa bislut hia God
35   andere hille, alsa Hi beslat tha Egypta liode anda Rada Se, tha se sine liodon skathia weldon, tha Israheliska folke.

Explanatory notes:

2   *alle afte thing and alle riuhte thing*: 'all things lawful and right'

3   *R. and R. (thet weron …)*: *thet* referring back to a plural subject is common in Old and Modern Frisian (as well as in ModDu and ModHG) (§176).

8   *Thi other kei*: on *other*, see §124.(5).

9   Actually, this is not the First Commandment but an admonition taken from Deuteronomy 6: 4.

11   In the medieval tradition, as in the Roman Catholic Church today, the Second and Third Commandments ('thou shalt not use the name of the Lord thy God in vain' and 'thou shalt not make a graven image') were taken as one, so that the Tenth had to be split into two in order to arrive at the total of ten. In the present version, the graven image is not even mentioned, while the Ninth and the Tenth Commandments ('Thou shalt not covet …') have been replaced by Christ's summary of the Law, cf. Matthew 22: 37–40.

19   *nen … tha nen:* 'neither … nor' (§199).

20   *mith thinere … wive*: note the incongruity in gender between pronoun (FEM) and noun (NEUT), and see §176.

22–23   *ther thi nawet wertha ne mugun*: *wertha* + DAT as full verb 'to befall to'.

30   *lethogade*: supply *hi*, i.e., Moses.

31   *melokon*: the occurrence of 'milk' in the plural in the phrase 'milk and honey' is parallelled in Old English, cf. Bosworth/Toller (1898), s.v. *meolc*, but is not commented on by Mitchell (1985: §1408ff.).

33–34   *hit ne se … thruch natha dwe*: 'unless it is done (viz. breaking the law) out of mercy'; *thruch thet* introduces a legal maxim.

34   *…, sa bislut hia…*: *hia* is the object of *beslut* and refers back to *alle tha, ther … brekth* after the author has lost track of his construction.

V. The Right to Pay Compensation and its Exceptions

The sixteenth of the *Seventeen Statutes*, here given in the recension of R1, states that the Frisians were entitled to buy off an imminent feud, occasioned by a serious crime, instead of having to suffer corporal punishment as had become the custom elsewhere in Europe in the same period. In the course of time the exceptions, already mentioned in the statute itself, were further elaborated upon. One such elaboration is given here according to E1, which contains five *wendar*. Such exceptions show that law was by no means a static thing,

but constantly subject to adaptation and alteration caused by the need of time and cir-
cumstance. Both passages are exemplary of ornamental, legal prose marked by alliteration
and rhythm.

The spelling of the texts has been slightly normalized, and emendations suggested by
previous editors have silently been adopted.

A. Thit is thiu sextinde liodkest and thes kininges Kerles ieft, thet alle Frisa mugun hiara feitha

mith tha fia capia. Thruch thet skilun hia wesa fri anna Saxsona merkon, uter stok and uter

stupa and uter skera and uter besma and uter alle othera pina. Ac wurthe're urwunnen and

urdeld anda liodthinge mith riuchtere tele and mith asega dome and bi lioda londriuchte,

5   bi skeltata bonne and bi keyseres orlovi ieftha sines weldiga boda, fon falske tha fon fade,

sa hach ma sine ferra hond opa tha thingstapule of to slande umbe tha twa deda. Ac hebbe

hi haveddeda eden, nachtbrond ieftha othera morthdeda, sa skil hi ielda mith sines selves

halse alle liodon to like thonke bi asega dome and bi lioda londriuchte, thet is, thet ma hini

skil opa en reth setta. Ac hebbe hi thiuvethe den bi Frisona kere, ief hi't an tha fia nebbe,

10   sa hach ma hini to hwande. Hwande alsa hi bi tha wie hongath, sa heth hi ivenes urgulden

liodon and frana. Morth mot ma mith morthe kela, til thiu thet ma tha ergon stiore.

B. Thet lest ma inna there sextendesta kest, thet alle Fresa mugen hira firna mitha fia fella,

ief hia't hebbath, bihalwa fif wendum:

Thi forma wend is thet: hwasa thet godeshus brecht and therbinna tha helega berant,

15   sa ach hi bi riuchte thet northhalde tre and thet niugenspatze fial and ne thor ma umbe

sinne ferech nanne fia biada.

Thi other wend is thet: hwersa hir en mon geng bi slepande monnem and bi unwisse

wakandum mith bernande bronde and mith riakande fiure to tha godeshuse and to tha

wathemhuse and therbinna bernt mon ieftha mar ieftha bethe twa, sa ach hi bi riuchte thet

20   northhalde tre and thet niugenspatze fial and ne thor ma umbe sin ferech nenne fia biada.

Thi thredda wend is thet: hwersa hir en mon inna anne wald fareth and ther liude

rawath and man morthath, sa ach ma him sin haved of to slane and ne thor ma umbe sin

ferech nanne fia biada.

Thi fiarda wend is thet: hwersa hir en scalk sinne afta hera urret ieftha morthat, sa ach

25   ma hine bi riuchte inna tsietele to siathane and ne thor ma umbe sin ferech nanne fia biada.

Thi fifta wend is thet: hwersa hir is en urredere and hi urreth lond and liude and hi

farth inur Saxenna merka and hi uthalath thene haga helm and thene rada skeld and thene

sareda riddere and hi binna Fresena merkum man sleith and burga barnt, sa ach ma hine

north inna thet hef to ferane and theron te sansane and ne thor ma umbe sin ferech nanne

30   fia biada.

Explanatory notes:

2 *anna Saxsona merkon*: throughout the Frisian laws, the Saxons figure as the Frisians' worst enemies. This statute claims that the Frisians also had the right of exemption of corporal punishment within Saxon territory. Note the enumerative style.

3 *wurthe're*: note the change from 'Frisians' in the plural to 'he', i.e., 'a Frisian' in the singular.

4–5 At a public court meeting, at least five conditions had to be met with before a man could be convicted of counterfeiting.

6 *sinne ferra hond* …: cutting off someone's right hand was a not uncommon measure in the Middle Ages for theft (as it still is in some Islamic countries). A maker of counterfeit was considered a thief, according to a stipulation in J, because *nen ierra tiaef nis dan di, deer stelt of helgum, herum ende dae lioedem*, there 'is no worse thief than he who steals from the saints (i.e., the church), the lords (i.e., secular authorities) and the people'.

11 *Morth mot ma mith morthe kela*: a legal proverb; *frana*: etymologically speaking, the word is a substantivized adjective to *frā* 'lord' (cf. OE *frēa*, OS *frōho*, OHG *frō* 'lord' and the Scandinavian god *Freyr* whose name means just 'Lord'), meaning 'belonging to the lord, representative of the lord'. Originally, the *frana* was the local representative of the count, and ultimately of the Frankish king. He was charged with presiding the court sessions and with collecting the fines on behalf of the count. When Frisia had eventually slipped out of the count's authority, the office remained for sometime as an independent position to disappear in the course of the thirteenth century.

12 *firna*: 'crimes'. The Rüstring recension has *feitha* 'feuds', which must be the more original word.

14 *tha helega*: 'the consecrated host'. Violation of the eucharistic host in effect resulted in the murder of Christ himself, cf. Galama (1990); *northhalde tre*: 'north-facing tree', a kenning for the gallows. In medieval times, both Germanic pagan and Christian alike associated the north with evil.

15 *niugenspatze fial*: 'the wheel with nine spokes', i.e., the wheel of torture upon which a criminal was tied and his bones shattered. For *fiāl* < *hwiāl*, cf. Århammar (1969). Århammar also points out that *reth* 'wheel', as used in Rüstring texts (cf. line 9), is a Low German loan with Frisian sound substitution (cf. §174). 'Wheel' is typically an Ingvaeonic word; *ferech* 'life' is an archaic word in Frisian texts and occurs almost only in combination with *fiā* 'money'. The same alliterative combination, here used as a kind of refrain, is also found in Old English and Old Norse, cf. Bremmer (1983).

22 *sin haved of to slane*: decapitation is rare in Frisian law, as is seething in a cauldron, and drowning in the sea, mentioned in the next two *wendar*. It would seem that these *wendar* enumerate the various ways of how to execute someone convicted for felony.

27 The 'high helmet' and 'red shield' signify the Saxon war gear.

Insolent Frisians

A brief passage in Ekkehard of Aura's *Chronicon universale* (written in Aura Abbey, Hessen, and completed 1125) reveals the indignation with which the nobility of the Holy Roman Empire considered the Frisians' increasing and successful attempts at consolidating their independent position. In the previous fifteen years they had killed Bishop Conrad of Utrecht, who had been enfeoffed with parts of Frisia, and they had slain Count Henry the Fat, 'the most powerful man of Saxony', upon his endeavour to enter Frisia with an armed force in order to (re)establish his authority. The Emperor's naval expedition likewise came to naught.

> In the same year [1114], the princes [of the Holy Roman Empire] swore to make an expedition against the Frisians in the second week after Pentecost, because they denied to expend the required (amount of money for their) subjection to the Emperor's lord [= the count] and the tribute which they had to pay annually by right. For swollen up by arrogance and protected by the natural fortification of their habitat, they rejected to subject themselves to any lord or to follow the command of anyone however powerful he might be. […] Next, the Emperor [Henry V] arranged with much eagerness a naval expedition against certain inhabitants of the marshy districts on the far side of the Frisians' islands.

VI. The Right of Counter Action in Law

The *Seventeen Statutes* belong to the earliest Frisian texts, and are thought at least in part to date back to the eleventh century, for example, on account of the mention of Viking raids. They precede the *Twenty-four Land-laws* in date as the *Statutes* are referred to in the other code. The seventeenth *Statute* (section A) states that all Frisians are entitled to a contradictory law-suit, i.e., the plaintiff and the defendant can state their case before the court, and the *asega* will then pronounce the verdict. Moreover, they can judge (*wita* 'know') their own deeds under oath. This must be the oldest part of the seventeenth *Statute*, since in what follows most versions differ sometimes dramatically. All kinds of restrictions (*Wendar*) were added to this statute, both within it and separately. The *Seventeen Statutes* end with an epilogue which follows here (B). Finally follows the conclusion to the *Twenty-four Land-laws* (C), as it shows how poetry sometimes ornamented the laws to enhance their special character. All three passages are taken from H1.

The texts have slightly been normalized: ⟨u⟩ to ⟨v⟩, and ⟨w⟩ to ⟨hw⟩, where appropriate.

A. Thet is thiu sogentendeste kest and thes Kenenges Kerles ieft, thet alle Fresa thingie bi twira tele and bi riuchtes asega dome; and allera monna hwelic wite't him selva anda withum, hwet hi geden hebbe. Mith thrim monnem mei ma alne tigtega bifella, buta dathe

and aubera dolge, bi scriveres worde and bi asega dome and bi liuda riuchte ieftha mith

5   sines selves sele te fellane, hit ne se thet hi en wed den hebbe anda urpena warve ieftha

anda heida thinge; sa ne mei hi thes weddes nene withe biada. Hwande en ierech mon mei

mith siner ferra hond urweddia and mith sinere tunga urmela al sin riucht.

B. Thit send tha sogentene kesta, ther Fresan mith hira fia capaden and hia fon riuchte

bruca scelen, alsa longe sa hia libbe, wither alle hera and alle husingar. Tha bad thi Kening

10   Kerl, thet hia alle afte thing and alle riuchte thing helde and lovade, alsa longe sa se lifde.

And hwasa hia thes riuchtes biravade, thet hi biravad urde fara Godes agnem and fara alle

Godes helgum a himelrike and erthrike to tha ewga liwe.

C.   Ut send tha riucht,

and ik bem self twera en godeskniucht.

15   Thisse riucht keren Fresa and bad him thi Keneng Kerl ti hebbane and te haldane to helpe

and to nethum alle Fresum.

Forth scele wi se halda,

and God scel user walda,

thes teddera and thes stitha,

20   and alle unriuchte thing scele wi formitha.

Explanatory notes:

1   *kest* and *ieft*: these two terms suggest the official status of a statute. The people have chosen (*kest* is derived from *kiāsa* 'to choose') a certain regulation, and the lord has granted it in return for which he received a remuneration (see line 8).

2   *bi twira tele*: by the account of two (parties), i.e., according to the principle of each free man having the right to make a declaration in court when he is accused of something.

2–3   The defendant has more right to deny under oath (i.e., to swear an oath of innocence) than the plaintiff has to accuse him, barring the exceptions mentioned. The oath was one of the most important proofs in the legal procedure; the Old Frisian terminology of swearing an oath is rich, cf. Popkema (2007).

5–6   *urpena warve ieftha heida thinge* 'a publicly summoned assembly or a ceremoniously opened court session'. On the absence of *w* in *urpena*, see §78.3w. Similarly *urde*, line 11.

5–8   A vow made at a solemn, public meeting (and confirmed by slap of hand) cannot later be overruled by oath, because an adult man realizes that he renounces his right to swear innocence when he makes such a vow.

17   On *scele wi*, see §155.3.

VII. Compensations for Injuries

One of the principles of Germanic law was that in general each crime could be redeemed by payment. In Frisia, the compensation for killing a man was called a *werield* 'a man's value', often shortened to *ield*, or simply *lif* 'life'. The compensations for all other crimes and inflicted injuries were fixed in relation to the full *werield*. Registers of compensations are known to us from many Germanic peoples, both in Latin and in the vernacular, but none of these is so detailed and elaborate as the Frisian registers, of which a variety of versions survive in East and West Frisian manuscripts.

The following tariffs are taken from the Emsingo Register (E2, with some adjustment from E1). They are illustrative of the detailed nature of such registers as well as of the variation in style.

The text has been slightly normalized.

De viribus

Hwersa hir ene monne werth thruch sine macht undad, thet hi nawit tia ne muge, niugen merk to bote fora tha niugen bern, ther hi tia machte.

Heth hi ac bern etein, sa nime ma't of tha berna and retse't tha unberna.

5   Heth hi thene winstera pralling behalden and thene ferra urlerin, thach mei hi kindar tia.

Heth hi thene winstere nawit, thach hi thene ferra hebba, sa is hi thes tuchtelas.

Thi blodrene fon tha machtem: fiower skillingar.

Enre frouwa hire macht torent: fiftene skillingar.

10   Is hiu ac alsa fir ewart, thet hiu hire mese nawit behalda ne muge: en thrimen lif.

Is hire en kere iefta blodelsa den: sex skillingar.

Basfeng

Thi basfeng buta clathim: thre skillingar.

Binna clathim: niugen skillingar.

15   Is't enra frouwa den, ther mith berne se, iefta enra frouwa, ther inna hira stilnese se: ene merc.

Ief ther ene frouwa ur ana bank wurpen werth, thet hiu benitha gerdle blike, thettet tha liude ursie: fiftene skillingar.

Enre frouwa hire thriu clathar thruchsnithin, thet hiu thruchskinich se – thet forma clath:

20 en and twintich penningar; thet inra: thritich enza; thet hemethe benithim: sogen skillingar.

De ventre

Thi wach thruchstet: ene merc.

Mith ene saxe den: thrimen forthera.

25   Hwersa ene mon stet werth thruch thene maga and hi thet muge bereda mittha letsa: thet send twa inwretsa dede.

Ief ther ene monne in sin briastem alsa fir werth befuchten, thet hi sine omme nawit behalda ne muge: en thrimen lif.

Enre frowa hire warte of tha briaste snithin: alwene skillingar.

30   En briast al of: en thrimen lif.

Thi lungirnsiama: en thrimen lif.

Thiu hageste buclamethe, thet hi ne muge a bethe ne a bedde, a widzie ne a weine, a wei ne a wetere, ne a glede ise ne a godishuse, bi fiure ne bi sinre wive wesa, sa hi er machte: en half lif.

35   Al ther ma ene monne smere ofkerft: thre skillingar.

De dorso [et] waldewaxa

Werth'er ac hwa undad inna sine bec iefta inna sine waldewaxa, thet him sin hnecka urbec and him sin heila up tie and hi a sine beke hine na umbekera ne muge, thet him tha sine sogin hwarlar alle wart se – thi forma, thet hi sa wel up kuma ne muge; thi other thet hi sa
40   wel to dele; thi thredda, thet hi sa wel anda ferra; thi fiarda, thet hi sa wel anda winstera; thi fifta, thet hi nawit sa wel forth; thi sexta, thet hi nawit sa wel urbec; thi soginde, thet hi sa wel trindumbe kuma ne muge. Thisse sogin hwarlar send alle en thrimen lif.

Hwasa otherem oppa thene buc hlapth thet him thet blod itta snabba rent: twa pund.

Rib tobretzen: fiftahalve skilling, thria to betene.

45   Hwersa thi mon undad werth inna thene bec, thet him al tha thriu welde ewert se, sa is thiu bote en half lif.

Explanatory notes:

The sub-headings in the manuscript are partly in Latin, partly in the vernacular, suggesting a learned (clerical) usership for the manuscript. *De viribus* 'About the genitals', *Basfeng* 'Indecent grabbing', *De ventre* 'About the stomach', *De dorso [et] waldewaxa* 'About the back and the spine'.

5–7   It was commonly believed in the Middle Ages that semen of the left testicle generated girls, and that of the right testicle boys, but I have been unable to trace any support for the idea of a man's generative power resting in his left testicle only.

11   *kere*: on the loss of *v*, see §78.2*v*.

27   *briastem*: unlike today, a man's breast was often referred to in the plural in Old Frisian as well as in other Old Germanic languages.

32–33   Note how this compilation of alliterative phrases catalogues a man's most important social functions. On *sinre wive* (35–36), see §176.

37   *undad*: on the absence of *w*, see §78.3*w*.

37–42   The text first mentions three possible handicaps caused by back or spine injury (*thet* [37] 'namely that'), to continue with the seven movements (*hwarlar* 'turnings' or 'rotations') that cannot be performed any longer (*thet* [39] 'so that'). The compensations for causing malfunction of each of these seven movements are then stipulated.

37   *urbec*, elliptic for *urbec tie*.

Dehydrated corpses as legal evidence

The reputation of Frisians amongst their neighbours was not always favourable and curious stories circulated about their customs. Thomas of Cantimpré (1201–1271) gives the following account of his journey to Frisia in his *Bonum universale de apibus* (Book II). Dodo was a former monk of Mariengaarde Abbey in Hallum, Oostergo, who had become a hermit.

> I have also seen another blessed man of the same order [of Premonstratensians], advanced to an extremely high age, called Dodo, a Frisian. He had served his Frisian people through dedicated preaching so that he greatly pacified them from their savageness. From very ancient times the Frisians had cherished a most horrible custom that when a man of one kindred had been killed by another kindred, the corpse of the killed man was not buried by his kinsmen but was preserved, suspended in a corner, and dehydrated in the house until the hostile kindred slaughtered many or at least one of the opposing kindred in revenge by way of compensatory death. And only then their victim was given a proper burial with great ceremony. The aforementioned brother removed from his people this most cruel and unheard of custom and advanced them to a gentler condition of life by frequent exhortation.

Some legal sources, notably the *Brocmonna Bref*, stipulate that kinsmen had the right to raise a complaint against the killer *uper bere and uper benke and uper epene grewe* ('over the bier and over the bench and over the open grave'). The purpose of this action, however, was to receive the *werield* due, precisely in order to prevent the kind of feuding described in Thomas's report. Nonetheless, even if Thomas's account is not 'historically' true – and this is what scholars believe – the anecdote is revealing of the Frisians' reputation abroad.

40   *to dele*: add: *kuma ne muge*; similarly in the following four points.

44   *thria to betene*: i.e., one must pay for up to three ribs; on the construction, see §188.

45   *tha thriu welde*: it is not entirely clear to which powers (or faculties) the text refers. 'Although the understanding is not a corporeal power, the operation of understanding cannot be accomplished in us without the operation of corporeal powers: that is, the imagination, the power of memory, and the cogitative power. … And as a result, if the operations of these powers are blocked by some indisposition of the body, the operation of the intellect is impeded, as is evident in demented and sleeping persons, and in others similarly affected' (Thomas Aquinas, *Summa contra Gentiles* III.84). If the text indeed refers to this common medieval opinion, it would bear witness of contemporary scholarly learned influence on the knowledge of anatomy. The compensation of half a *wergeld* for the back injury mentioned in any case is high enough for us to assume that some serious kind of debilitation is implied.

VIII. Five Exceptions to the Right of Swearing Innocence

The *Fif Wender* describe the conditions under which the perpetrator of a crime was not allowed to swear an oath of innocence. These are the exceptions to the general rule, as formulated in the last of the *Seventeen Statutes* (see Text VI above), which was that every Frisian had the right to swear to his own innocence upon the relics. The *Wender* are given here according to the recension of H2.

The text has been normalized skightly: ⟨u, v⟩ has been altered to ⟨v, w⟩ where appropriate; all verbal endings are rendered by *-th*, i.e., 3SG/PL.PRES, unless the stem ends in *-d, -t* or *-ch*.

Thit send fif wender ther nen witherield nis

Thi forma wend is: hwersa ma hemliachtes deis end bi scinandere sunna twene heran somnath end twene herefonan upriucht end ofledene weddath end tha twa folk mith case gaderlet end hwa thenna thena hlepth mith brudena swerde end mith blodiga, al thet thet
5 hi thenne fuchten heth an dolge enda daddele, sa scel hi't na scriveres worde a iechta alle beta end ne mei hi there dede nene withe biada.

Thi other wend is: hwersa en frowe nede nimen is end hiu sit wepande end ropande end hire foliath thi frana enta liuda end hiu en urpena warve end en heida thinge hire modwilla auth, thene friudelf urtiucht end to tha riuchta foremunda gength, sa ach hiu hire wergeld
10 and is't alla iechta tha liudum enta frana end ne thor ma umbe tha dede nene withe biada.

Thi thredda wend: hwersa ma on tha helga bonnena sinethe ieftha on tha heida thinge ieftha urpena warve en thing weddath ief enes thinges ieth, sa scel thet alle iechta wesa end ne mei hi thes thinges nene withe biada.

Thi fiarda wend: hwasa fereth nachtes be slepanda monnum end be unewissa
15 wakandum til otheres monnes huse end hove thruch thiaves lesta end brecht hole end herna end ma hine befereth ur sothe end ur sede end ur thet fatade bernde end ma him nimpth an honda tha blodega thiufthe, sa ne mei hi there dede nene withe biada end thenne ach hi bi riuchte thene swarta doc end thene northhalda bam. Alle liudem ielt'er te thonke thi ther hongath.

20   Thi fifta wend: hwersa ma tha menetara binna there kenenges meneta fad end falesc an honda begripth end hi tha kenenges meneta urtiucht end to there othere feth, sa is sin hals thera liuda, se't hia en lichtera londriucht sziasa welle, thet hi't mith sinre ferra hond fella mote. End ne thorf hi therumbe nene withe biada, hwande nen wirra thiaf nis than thi, ther stelth on helgum end herum end te like alle liudum.

Explanatory notes:

2 *hemliachtes deis*: adverbial genitive 'on a clear day, in broad daylight'; *bi skinandere sunne*: 'while the sun is shining'. Similar constructions of *bi/be* + PRES.PTC occur in lines 14–15.

3 *ofledene weddath*: 'and promises to take liability for the damage done during the raid'. The leader of a feuding expedition was held accountable for the damage done by the individual participants in his band; *hwa thenna thena hlepth*: 'whoever then attacks somebody else', note the use of DEM.PRON *thena* as INDEF.PRON referring to one of the two expedition leaders, cf. §200.

4–5 *... mith brudena swerde and mith blodiga*: 'with a drawn and bloody sword'. When two adjectives modify a noun, the second adjective regularly occurs in a post-modifying position (§198); *... al thet thet hi*: 'all that which he, i.e., all that he [a member of the band]'; *sa scel hi't ... beta* 'then he [the leader] must pay for it'.

5 *na scriveres word*. The form *na* is an early intrusion of Low German, which would have been *nei* in Old Frisian. The presence of the *scrivere* suggests these three words form a later addition.

8 *en urpena warve end en heida thinge*: 'at a publicly summoned assembly and a ceremoniously opened court session'.

9 *wergeld*. The spelling of the second element betrays Low German influence; the 'correct' form should have been *werield*.

13 *ne mei hi*: note the change in subject pronoun from INDEF *ma* to DEF *hi*.

14–15 *be unewisse wakandum*: 'when it was not certain that people kept watch'; *thruch thiaves lesta*: some discussion has been on whether *lest* here should be taken as meaning either 'trick, ruse', or 'desire', or 'track', 'footstep'. I have followed the last suggestion, in line with similar expressions in Old English (cf. Gerbenzon 1960).

20   *fad end falesc*: a stock alliterative phrase. Note the parasitic vowel in *falesc*.

21   *to there othere feth*: 'and adopts another (standard of currency)'. For the use of the DEF.ART here, see §200; *se't hia …*: 'unless they …'. Literally: 'be it (that) they', with deletion of CONJ *thet* before *hia* (§202).

IX. How to Accuse a Thief

Legal procedures tend to be complicated. One error of detail may make the case invalid. The text below is cast in direct speech, as if it were a form to be read out aloud. Rather than serving such a practical purpose, the author in all likelihood will have drafted this charge so lively as to be sure that all the procedural steps required would be included and none forgotten. The charge is pronounced by a representative of the victim of theft. The text, taken from H1, has occasionally been regularized.

'Ik spreke iu to fon tha liudum end fon tha frana end fon thisse selva monne ther i hir ursien end urhered hebbat on thisse liudwurpena warve, thet hi mi sine spreka befel and wel and min word ieth, thet i ewele deden end riuchte, thet i him toforen an thiaves lestum be slepandere thiade end be unwissa wakandum end breken sin hus uta in end therto sin

5   inreste helde end urstelen him sines godes alsa god sa fif end fiftich merka – thera merka ec bi achta enzum, thera enzena ec bi twintega penningum.

Ther brek'i on thera leida liudfrethe, ther biracht end bigripen was, mith wedde and mith worde, end thes frana allerhagesta bon end iuwe haudlesne. End biwene mi thes, thet i hiude te dei scelen tha thiuvethe witherweddia end there thiuvethe bote, alsa ik se iu

10   tosocht hebbe, pend end pennegad mith alsadena penningum sa ther end tha londe send ieve end genzie, ther ma cu and corn mithe ield. Tha scel'i on thera liuda wera brenzia end on thes frana end on thes clageres.

Ief i ac biseka wellath, sa skel'i hiudega te dei an stride withstonda, enne strideth swera end enne otherne hera. To tha mara stride hebbe ik iu begret end thes minnera ne bikenne

15   ik nowet. Enes eftes onderdes bidd'ic there gretene.'

Explanatory notes:

1   *iu*: the defendant is addressed with the plural pronoun for rhetorical and/or stylistic reasons. The intended effect is that of creating distance.

1 *thisse selva monne*: i.e., the plaintiff.

2 *and wel and*: the conjunction *and/end* 'and' can easily be confused with the preposition *and(a)/end(a)* 'in, on'; 'and well subscribes to my word (= accusation)'; *deden* as well as *toforen* (3), *breken* (4) and *urstelen* (5) all are preterite plural subjunctives, depending on *thet*.

3 *an thiaves lestum*: cf. note to Text VIII.14–15.

7 *brek'i*: contraction of *breke + i* (§155.2).

8 The former *end* is the preposition 'in, into', the latter *end* the conjunction 'and'; *bewene mi thes*: an impersonal verb construction (§203).

13 *scel'i*: contraction of *skele + i*; so, too, *skel'i* (13); *end on thes frana … clageres*, viz. were. On postposition, see §198.

14 The *mara strid* is the duel, the *minnera strid* is the kettle ordeal.

X. Miscellaneous Decrees

a. Mercy for a Thief

The custom of granting amnesty to a convicted criminal if a woman was willing to marry him was widespread in the Middle Ages. The following decree, found in F, is unique within the Frisian tradition, however.

Van ene thiaf

Thet is riucht: Hwersa ma anne thiaf feth and ma hine brenge to ware and latt'ene umbe thene warf an hine biut ma to lesane and nel ma hine nout lesa, sa urdelma hine sin hals. Therefter mei hine en mundlas meiden lesa, ief hio him to ena formund kiasa wele, ief en
5 meynwif mei hine lesa, dar ut'en bodelhus is, to afta. Sa mei hi sine hals bihalda.

Explanatory notes:

1 *van*: note this Low German form (instead of *fon*) in the title. On account of *van* and *dar* (5), Sjölin (1970: 52–53) assumed this short text to have been translated from a Low German source. Such an assumption is not necessary, however. These forms are rather indicative of the increasing pressure which Low German was exercising on Frisian.

2 *ware*: DAT.SG.M < *warf*; the voiced labial fricative *v* (> *w*) was regularly lost between a consonant (esp. *l* and *r*) and a vowel (§78.2v); *lat* 3SG.PRES.IND (in *latt'ene*): the vowel is actually that of the preterite, but has crept into the present (van Helten 1890: §289, Anm. 1). Apparently, the thief was led around in procession.

5   *dar*: a Low Germanized form of the typically Old Frisian relative particle *thēr*; *bodelhus* 'brothel' (< OFrench *bordel* + OFris *hūs*) shows occasional deletion of *r* before alveolar stop, a common rule in Modern Frisian.

b.   On Killing a Relative

This decree is unconnected to either the preceding or following text in R1 and is not found in any other Frisian legal collection. It prescribes in vivid terms how someone who has killed a close relative should be excluded from ordinary social intercourse. The only glimpse of hope for redemption is the outcast's participation in the Holy Eucharist, but in a way which underlines his isolated position in society.

Sa hwasa sinne feder ieftha sine moder, sine swester ieftha sinne brother ovirbulgena mode to dada sleith, sa ne mi him nen prestere skriva. Buta alsa longe sa're libbe, skil hi wondria and kriapa and festia ieftha hi skile alle there skena wralde ofstonda and gunga anna en claster and wertha tha abbete underdenoch and dwe, alsa're him dwa hete, and

5   nammermar ne mot hi anda godishuse wesa mith ore kerstene liodon, hi ne gunge efta tha durun stonda and bidde to sinere helde Godis uses Hera.

Explanatory notes:

1   *ovirbulgena mode*: i.e., as a result of the deadly sin of anger. Note the adverbial dative (§182.5).

2   *skriva*: 'to shrive, prescribe penance in confession'. In a legal context *skriva* ususally means 'to fix the compensation'. Beside this Latin loan word, Old Frisian also had the Germanic term *writa*.

4   On the plain infinitive with *hete*, see §188. Similarly with *gunge* (5).

5–6   *hi ne gunge … stonda*: 'unless he goes and stands …'.

6   *Godis uses Hera*: 'God our Lord', the genitive being dependent on *bidda* (cf. §181R.2). With 'God our Lord' the consecrated host of the Eucharist is meant, which through the mystery of transubstantiation had become Christ's body.

c.   Permission to Break into a Church

The church was one of the few sanctuaries in medieval Frisia (a king's residence being absent), and violation of its sanctity was severely punished. R1 lists the cases in which the church could be broken into with impunity.

Umbe thria havedneda mi ma thet godishus breka mith thes presteres orlovi, thet thi biscop ne mi nenne fretho theron bitella.

Thet forme is: sa hwersa en wif enedgad werth anda godishuse, sa mi ma thet godishus breka mith thes presteres orlovi and helpa there wive of there nede.

5   Thet other is: sa hwersa en mon anda ende leith and wili ologad wertha and thi oppermon nawet rede nis mith tha sletelon, sa hach ma thet godishus to brekande and Godi tha selva sele to winnande.

Thet thredde is: sa hwersa en iung kind to tha godishuse brocht werth, ther ma depa skil, and tha sletela unwisse send, sa breke ma thet godishus and depe thet kind.

Explanatory notes:

1   *thet thi biscop…*: 'so that the bishop…'.

6   *sletelon*: 'keys' (DAT.PL); a rare occurrence of this Low German loan (with Frisian sound-substitution, §174). The common word is *kei*, an Anglo-Frisian isogloss.

7   *tha selva sele*: lit. 'the selfsame soul', but *selva* rather reinforces DEF.ART *tha*: 'this soul'.

d.   Abba's Hat

Particularly in the thirteenth century and later, in the absence of counts, abbots could take on the role of 'ecclesiastical princes' and fulfilled the judicial tasks of secular lords in many respects: establishing peace between feuding factions, presiding boards of institutions that saw to the regulation of a district's water economy or advising assemblies that wanted to draw up statutes. As a sign of their dignity, they put on a special headgear. The following stipulation, taken from H2, was quite untypically concluded with a small and humorous poem.

Abba sin hod oferawad, tribete ti betane, allerec bi fiarda twede skillinge.

Nu is't al god,

nu heth abba sinne hod.

Thach'er'em nemmer nerthe,

5   thach scel't al god wertha.

Explanatory notes:

1   *Abba … oferawad*: an auxiliary like *is* must be thought before *Abba*; *thribete ti betane* (§188); *fiarda twede*: 'the fourth one two-thirds', that is three and two-thirds.

4   *thach'er'em*: 'though it (i.e., the hat) him (the abbot'; *nertha* (*ne* + *wertha*) is a full verb here, cf. Text IV.22–23, explanatory note. Translate: 'Though it may never befall him'.

XI. This Is Also Frisian Law

Many of the legal manuscripts contain regulations which seem to have been agreed upon as additional or improved provisions to the *Twenty-four Land-laws* and *Seventeen Statutes*. Such additional codes vary from district to district, and were probably drafted by a body of judges (whether clerical or secular) and approved of by a meeting of the freeholders ('the people'). The following is one of three such texts found in the Rüstring manuscripts. These texts have in common that most of the decrees begin with the formula *Thet is ac Frisesk riucht*. Owing to their additional nature there is little internal coherence to be detected in these collections, and they may well have been collected from non-Rüstring sources. The text given below, found in R1, proceeds from general legal principles to particular ones. Remarkable are the graphic descriptions of some of its regulations, indicative of the basically oral society in which they functioned. Well-known is the last section on dike maintenance which gets so lyrical about the dikes that it employs 'kennings' and metaphors to describe the new landscape. Both its deviating introductory formula ('Thet is ac londriucht') and its relative length mark it off from the rest. There is positive evidence that at least this section once formed an independent text originating from the area between the Lauwers and the Ems (cf. Johnston 1995).

In the following text ⟨u⟩ has been changed to ⟨v⟩, where applicable.

Thet is allera londa fere, thetter nen mon erga ne dwe.

Thet is ac Frisesk riucht: sa hwasa breke, thet hi bete, hit ne se thet hi forifongera winne.

Thet is ac Frisesk riucht: thetter alle sende sona stonda and thet ma alle weddeda wed elaste.

5   Thet is ac Frisesk riucht: sa hwasa ioldskipi infiuchte, sa skil hi twam monnon beta and thre fretha sella, allera erost thene ioldfretho, thet other thene liodfretho, thet thredde thene progostes fretho thruch thene meneth, ther hi esweren heth sina ieldebrotheron and ieldeswesteron.

Sa hwersa thi bon ena monne bitigath enere clagi and ther nen onspreke ne stont, sa mi're dwa hwedder sa're wili: ia tha biseka. Wili're biseka, sa skil hi thre withetha swera mith thrium monnon. Thene forma eth skil thi mon hera, thene otherne tha liode, thene thredda skil thi frana hera. Sa mi're mith thesse thrium ethon falla there lioda fretho and thes frana bon.

Thet is ac Frisesk riucht: sa hwersa thi blata enne hod stekth and sprekth: 'Ethelinga, folgiath mi! Nebbe ic allera rikera frionda enoch?' Alle tha, ther him folgiath and fiuchtath – thet stont opa hiara eina hava, thruch thet thi blata thi is lethast alra nata. Hi mi allera sinera frionda god ovirfiuchta, hi ne mi hit thach to nenere ofledene skiata.

Thet is ac Frisesk riucht: thet'ter ne hach nen husmon nenne hirifona on to bindande

20   and ana en or lond to tiande mith ena havedlasa hiri – thet is en havedlas hiri, sa hwersa

nen greva ni nen hertoga mithi nis. Sa brekth hi, the thene fona andere hond ferth, to allera

disthik thritich merk and alle tha, the him folgiath, en and twintich skillinga, thruch thet ther

ne hach nen husmon nenne hirifona on to bindande and ana en or lond to farande sunder

sines londes rede.

25   Thet is ac Frisesk riucht: sa hwasa oron en wetir betent and betimbrath tha inrosta

ieftha utrosta to skatha, sa brekth hi, thi thes werkes mastere is, allera distik en and twintich

skillinga and alle tha, the him folgiath, allerek fiardahalf wed thruch thet theter alle inwetir

stonda skilun, sa se God eskipin heth al there wralde to nathon.

Thet is ac Frisesk riucht: sa hwersa thi bon enne mon thria, niugun stunda, to tha thinge

30   lathat – neli hi thenne nawet a thing gunga and nen wed dwa, sa brekth hi thes forma dis

fiardahalf wede, thes otheres dis siugun skillinga wed, thes thredda dis tian reilmerk.

Thet is ac londriucht: thet wi Frisa hagon ene seburch to stiftande and to sterande,

enne geldene hop, ther umbe al Frislond lith. Ther skil on wesa allera ierdik ivinhar oron,

ther thi salta se betha thes dis antes nachtes to swilth. Ther skil thi utrosta anti inrosta thes

35   wiges plichtich wesa, tha strete thes wintres and thes sumures mith wegke and mith weine

to farande, thet thi wein tha oron meta mugi. Alsa thi inrosta to tha dike cumth, sa hag'ere

alsa gratene fretho opa tha dike, alsa're ova tha wilasa werpe and alsa're ova tha wieda

stherekhovi. Heth'ere thenne buta dike alsa felo heles londes and grenes turves thetter'ne

dikstathul mithi halda mugi, [sa halde hi'ne thermithi]. Ac neth'ere nauwet sa felo buta dike

40   heles londes and grenes turves thetter'ne dik mithi halda mugi, sa hag'ere binna dike thritich

fota turves and thritich fethma to gerse. Thet skel wesa alla fennon anda fili er Sante Vitesdi.

Uta skilu wi Frisa use lond halda mith thrium tauwon, mith tha spada and mith there bera

and mith there forke. Ac skilu wi use lond wera mith egge and mith orde and mith tha bruna

skelde with thena stapa helm and with thene rada skeld and with thet unriuchte herskipi.

45   Aldus skilu wi Frisa halda use lond fon ova to uta, ief us God helpa wili and Sante Peder.

Explanatory notes:

3   *sende sone ... weddade wed*: 'reconciled reconciliations ... pledged pledges': instances
of so-called *figurae etymologicae*. A *figura etymologica* is a rhetorical device in which two or
more different words that have the same root are used near to one another – in the same
sentence, often in the same clause. They must be different words and not just different
inflections of the same word. The presence of such classical rhetorical devices points to a
well educated author.

5–8   The decree seems concerned with violent entrance into a guildhall. What kind of guild is meant here is not specified, but it might refer to a parish guild. Such guilds were not centred on a craft, but gave the rich of an (urban) community the opportunity to get together for banquets, to organize yearly processions for the local patron saint and to pursue charity. Remarkably, brethren and sisters here are looked upon as equally important.

6   *thet other …, thet thredde*: 'secondly …, thirdly …'.

11   *… skil thi mon hera*: *thi mon*, i.e., the injured man.

14   *etheling*: freeholder, i.e., someone with three legitimate ancestors.

16   *thi blata thi*: note the use of the recapitulating relative (§201).

17   *hi ne mi … skiata*: 'yet he is not allowed to contribute it (i.e., the property) as a surety for the damage done during the raid'.

20   The definition of a *havedlas hiri* is apparently a 'gloss' (i.e., explanatory note) that was marginal in the exemplar but has ended up in the main text.

29   *thria*: 'three successive days', *niugun stunda* 'nine times', i.e., three times a day on three successive days'.

31   *reilmerk*: 'cloth-mark'. In the laws currency is often expressed in terms of cloth, so that *(h)reilmerk* actually means 'the value of one mark in weight of cloth'. In Rüstringen, for example, one *hreilmerk* equalled four *weda* or four *scillinga cona*. A *wede* literally means 'garment' (cf. OE *wǣde*), while *cona* is usually taken to be a Slavic loan meaning 'fur'.

32   *hagon*: see §143.2.

33   *allera ierdik ivinhar oron*: 'each yard equally high as the other one', i.e., the height of the dike must be measured with a uniform yard stick to make sure that it is sufficiently high where it stands on the sea.

34   *thi utrosta and thi inrosta*. The extremes of course include all those who live in between them, so that the phrase implies all the inhabitants of the land enclosed by the dike.

38   *heles londes, grenes turves*: the dikes were built and maintained with soil (clay) and sods. The tidal mudflats outside the dikes did not always provide sufficient material for the maintenance of the dikes. Therefore, freeholders who lived closest to the sea had to be given the right to cut sods in the lands behind the dikes, cf. lines 40–41: *sa hag'ere … thritich fota turves* 'he has the right to thirty (of) feet of turf'; *thritich fethma to gerse* 'thirty (of) fathoms for grass' (On the partitive genitive, see §181.4). After the dike has been brought up to height with earth (*lond*) and sods (*turf*), the still loose soil had to be fixed with (plaited) grass of a long species, e.g., bentgrass or (bul-)rush.

39   *[sa halde hi'ne thermithi]*: omitted in MS but restored conjecturally with the help of a Low German recension of this text.

41   *alla fennon anda fili*: a long-standing crux, solved by Hofmann (1998): *alla = alle a*, *anda = and a*; *fennon* is parallel to *thritich fota turves* and *fili* to *thritich fethma to gerse*. The word *fenne* is a technical term and indicates a pasture surrounded by ditches that drain the superfluous water; *fil(i)*, not recorded otherwise for Old Frisian, must be 'grass-land (in the wild, undrained)' and is related to OE *fileðe* (< *fil*- + suffix *-eðe*) 'grass-land, meadow'. Translate: 'This shall be (in force) universally on pastures and on grass-land before St. Vitus' Day'; *skilu wi*: on the verbal ending, see §155.3.

44   *thena stapa helm and … rada skeld*: the armour of the Saxon knights, the traditional enemies of the Frisians; cf. Text V.27.

45   *Sante Peder*: i.e., the Bishop of Rome, the Pope. According to legend, Frisian warriors had relieved Pope Leo III from a siege by his enemies in the days of Charlemagne, see 'The Legend and Statutes of Magnus' (Text XV). The form *Peder* rather than *Peter* betrays Low German influence.

An Englishman reports on the Frisians

Bartholomew the Englishman was a professor of theology at the University of Paris and joined the Franciscans in 1224. Later on in his life he moved to Magdeburg in Saxony. His most important work is *De proprietatibus rerum* ('On the Properties of Things'), the first true encyclopaedia (1240). It enjoyed tremendous popularity in the later Middle Ages and was translated into French, Dutch, Spanish and English. The following passage is a translation from the Middle English version. Bartholomew appears to be well informed on the geological and social conditions of Frisia. He knows of the Frisians' hairdo, of their typical weapon, the *kletsie* (a long spear that could also be used as a leaping-pole), and of their exceptional, non-feudal government. His idea of the Frisians' chastity, however, seems inspired by the wishful thinking of a clergyman.

Frisia is a province situated in the lower parts of Germany. It consists of a long strip of land along the sea coast, beginning at the mouth of the Rhine and ending at the Danish Sea. The Germans call the inhabitants of this province Frisians. They strongly distinguish themselves from the Germans in dress and customs. Almost all men have cut their hair all around. And the nobler they are, the more honour they reckon it the higher their hair is cut. The Frisians are tall of stature, strong of virtue, severe and sharp of spirit, quick and very agile of body. Instead of arrows they use iron spears.

The land is flat, with marshes, meadows and pastures with grass and herbs, but without trees and woods. They make fire with turfs full of bitumen and with dried cattle dung.

The men are free and not subject to the lordship of other nations. They risk their lives for the defence of their freedom and they are rather dead than subject to the yoke of slavery. They therefore reject the dignity of knighthood and do not tolerate that anyone amongst them should raise themselves and be more important under the title of knighthood. However, they are subject to judges whom they annually choose from amongst their midst. These [judges] administer and govern their community.

They greatly love chastity and punish all unchaste deeds very severely. And they keep their children chaste until they have come of full age. And for that reason, when they are married, they get manly and strong children.

XII. New Land, New Laws

The coastal districts were often surprised by floods, causing many casualties and loss of land. Such floods were named after the saint on whose day they occurred. One such flood, the St. Juliana Flood of 1167, may have given rise to the initiative of inhabitants of the Emsingo district to pack their bags and move land inwards to start a new life by reclaiming and colonizing a huge peat-moor that stretched all the way from the Ems to the Weser. This *palus Emsigoae* ('Emsingo marsh'), as it was called by Adam of Bremen (11th c.), was literally no man's land, and since the reclamation was a collective 'private enterprise', new governing institutions and new laws had to be drafted for the quickly growing community of settlers there. Therefore, the *Brocmonna bref* occupies a special position among the Old Frisian legal codes, since it contains none of the 'Pan-Frisian' texts, such as the *Seventeen Statutes* or the *Twenty-four Land-laws*. Although some parts of the 'Charter of the Brookmen' are dependent on, or elaborations of, legal provisions known to us from Emsingo, its structure and contents are in many ways novel and devised for a community that had no socio-political traditions. The Charter in its present form dates back to *c*.1275, though the two manuscripts in which it has come down are of slightly later date. Below follow a number of provisions that give us a glance of the position of women in 'Brookland'.

The sections below correspond to Buma and Ebel, *Das Brokmer Recht*, §§213 and 95–99, respectively.

Hwasa kerft of there wiue hire hocca.

Hwasa kerft of there wiue hire hocka, sa is'tet ful scondlic and nis naut skethelic. Sa resze ma

hire to bote en fiardandel hiris einis ieldes, and thi frethe alsa stor, ief thi redia thet onlet and

hiu thet biret mith tuam triuwe witem.

5   *Fon nedkestum.*

Alle nedkesta skel ma mith compe besla, hit ne se thet hi alsa blat se thet hi kampa naut

ne muge, and him nen holda tofarastonda nelle, sa skel hi unga to tha szetele. Is hiu alsa

blat thet hiu kempa nauwet ne muge, and hire nen holda tofarastonda nelle, sa lede hi sex

men of sine kenne, and efter swere hi mith fiuwer and twintege ethum, thet hi elle siker se.

10   *Fon urwald.*

Hwersa ma nimth ene frouwa mith wald and mith unwilla and breit hia inur dura and inur

dreppel, and hiu thet bihrope, and tha rediewa hia mith dome withedriwe, sa skel ma

hire resza en twede szeremonnes ield and tha liudem half sa stor, and tha rediem twene

skillengar. Kemth hiu thet alra hageste, sa skel hiu thet biweria mith fiower and twintege

15   ethum, and sa skel ma hia ielda mith ene szeremonnes ielde, and thet hus thera liuda, and

tha rediem ene hageste merc. Ac is't comp, sa hwile thet hus, and hire en szeremonnis ield,

and thi frethe half alsa stor; szetel and comp allen etta nedmonda.

Fon meke.

20 Hwersa ma ene founa of tha werem iefth ieftha spont, and hia makie ma mitha faderem unierich, sa resze ma hire to bote en twede szeremonnis ield and tha liudem half alsa stor and tha rediem ene merc. Is't en wilmec, and ma sziwe umbe thene boldbreng, sa skeppe thi redieva thene mekere, and therefter winne ma thene boldbreng mitha mekere and mith twam triuwe monnum ieftha wiwem, and thi redieva thet rede umbe thet mec. Thi thredda mot spreca fore thene alderlasa, fon eider sida binna thredda.

25 *Fon skekmeke.*

Hwersar en foune skecht, sa skeppe thet feder and brother, hu stor hia hire to boldbrenge resze.

Fon inlegum there wiwe.

Hwersar en wif fon tha grewe ingenth, sa skel hiu inlidza thene fiarda penning alle hires
30 godes buta lawem; ferth hiu fon tha grewe uta werem, sa ne mei se mith nanene thinge withecuma. Ac bitigiath ma hire dernfias, sa swere hiu ene fia-eth oppa tha dreppele; deth hiu en iechtech raf, sa skel thi redieva thet withedriwa.

Explanatory notes:

1   On the construction *there wiue hire hocca*, cf. §182.3.

2   *and na naut skethelic*: 'and (yet) not harmful (for her)'. The distinction being made is that between injured public honour and physical harm.

3   *and thi frethe alsa stor*: 'and the fine for breach of the peace (should be) just as large'. The *redia*, a shortened form of *redieva* (lit. 'counsel-giver') was the highest judicial official in Brokmerland. A college of sixteen *redieva*, chosen annually, governed this land.

6   *Alle nedkesta*: 'all (complaints for) nedkesta'. The precise meaning of *nedkest* is disputed. Literally, it means 'forced choice', but whether the forced choice implied only abduction, or, more dramatically, rape, is not easy to say. Since rape is explicitly mentioned further down ('thet alra hageste'), the word seems here to imply the former meaning; *hi*, i.e., the defendant; *kampa*: 'to fight a duel'. Judicial duels fought to settle a dispute were seen as an ordeal. The defendant was given the choice either to fight himself or to have a professional champion fight for him.

7   *szetele*, i.e., the 'kettle' ordeal. This implied that the defendant had to put his right hand into a cauldron filled with boiling water. Afterwards it was judged by the speed of the burns recovering, whether the defendant was guilty or not; *hiu*, i.e., the plaintiff.

8–9   *six men of sine kenne*: these had to act as witnesses.

12   *bihrope*: raising the alarm cry was seen as evidence for a crime taking place. If a woman was being raped and her cry not heard, she was assumed to have consented to the act. If she denied consent, the procedure for sueing the rapist was much more complicated.

14   *thet alra hageste*: the highest (i.e., the worst) of all (acts of violence), viz. rape.

16   *thet hus*: i.e., of the man found guilty. *Ac is't comp, sa* …: 'But if a duel is fought (and the defendant wins), then …'.

17   *szetel and comp allen* …: 'kettle ordeal and duel (are) equally (applicable) …'.

20   *ma*: i.e., the culprit.

23   The two reliable men or women had to act as witnesses; *and*: 'if'; *Thi thredda*: 'a relative in the third degree'.

26   *sa skeppe thet*: *thet* is the provisional subject, the full object being the clause introduced by *hu*.

29   *fon tha grewe ingeth*: re-enters from the grave (of her husband into the house and continues to manage the household); *fiarde penning*: the fourth part of the widow's own property was intended as the basis for her maintenance.

XIII. The *Fia-eth*

The 'property oath', mentioned in the previous text, is perhaps the most intriguing, and certainly the most complicated from the extensive corpus of Old Frisian oaths. The solemn 'So help you God …' is pronounced three times, followed by four extensive admonitions by the oath taker, a gruesome curse and concluded by, once more, the invocation of God's help. The text, as found in E2, is a fine specimen of the rhythmical and alliterative prose found elsewhere in Old Frisian laws as well as in Old High German and Old English (Stanley 1984). The concluding section explains who had to swear this oath and when. Parts of the admonitions and curses, especially the section beginning with *Nu hald thu* …, are reminiscent of the Old Irish *lorica*, a type of prayer which also makes use of the listing of bodily parts (Hill 1998). The general idea would then go back to the Anglo-Saxon missionaries, since they were much influenced by Irish learning. It is also possible that such enumerations are part of the Indo-European heritage, because similar enumerative curses are found in Sanskrit writings.

The text has been slightly normalized.

Alsa helpe thi God and sijn hilge modir, Sente Maria, alsa helpe thi God and Sente Michael and alle Godes anglar, alsa helpe dij God and Sente Iohannes Baptista, Godes depere, and alle patriarcha and alle propheta Godis, alsa helpe thi God and Sente Pedir and Sente Iohannes and alle tha tuelf apostela and tha fiower ewangelista, thet hia thi alsa wijse to're ferre hond uses Drochtenes to domesdeij, sa thu thinne eth elle riuchte swere and
5   naut menis.

Alsa helpe thi God and Sente Stephin, thi forma martir, and alle Godis martilar, alsa helpe thi God and thi trowa Sente Nijclaus and alle Godis biscopar, alsa helpe thi God and Sente Katherina and alle Godis megetha and alle sijne hilgha, ther send a himelrike and a erthrike, thet thu thinne eth elle riuchte swere and naut menis.

10   Thet thi God alsa hold and alsa helpande se – alsa bruc thu thines liwis and alre thine lithena, alsa bruc thu thines wittis and alle thines skettis, olsa bruc thu [thines] wedis and alle thines godis, [sa thu thinne eth elle riuchte swere and naut menis].

Ic witnie thi bij tha forma weda, ther ma thi ontach, tha thu anda tha ruald comest – thet is thet ereste wede, and thet leste, ther thu hebba scalt to domisdeij tofara tha
15   elemachtiande Godes ondleta and hit thenna thi alsa helpe tofara Gode, use Hera, and thu thet efter domisdeij alsa dreghe tha alonge ruald – tha thi tha fathera to thera tsiurca drogin and [thi] thi prester cristenede and crisma and tha helegha depinge onleijde, and bij tha liachtera, ther thi [thi prester] inna thine hond rachte, tha thi tha fadera to tha fonte drogin and thi thi prestere tha diowele bijnom and use Drochtene bifel; alsa thu kume tofara Godis
20   agenum and thu thenna nebba to iewena nauder golt ther selwer, wara tha thina erma sele, thet hiu tha diowele alsa undhverwe and use Drochtene alsa to dele werthe, sa thu thinne eth elle riuchte swere and nawit menis.

Nu witnie ick thi bi tha helga urleste and bi alle hilge scriftem, thet thi thi hilge urlest and tha hilga scrifta alsa to nethum werthe to domisdeij tofara tha ellemachtiande Gode bi
25   tha helgha *Corpus Domini*, bi tha Godis selwis lickoma, [and] bi there helga oliene. Nu bihald thu alsa tha oliene and thet ombecht and alle thisse wendar, ther ick thi tofara nomad hebbe, sa thu a thisse wordem nauwit liat se.

Nu witnie ick thi bi tha fia and bi tha federerwe, bi tha witha and bi tha forthskefte, bi tha fia, ther thu mitha ethe halst and welt behalda, thet thu ne thantse thine fia mith nene
30   falska te winnande.

Nu hald thu alsa wit and sketfia and alle thine forthrede, alsa thu thine eth elle riuchte swere and nawit menis.

Nu witnie ick thi buppa fon there pota al to're litteca tane, hit se a felle, hit se a flaske, hit se a edderum, hit se a sinum, hit se a herta, hit se a liwera, hit se a lithum, hit se a lithaletum,
35   hit se anda lessera, hit se anda marra, thet thu alla thina licoma alsa behalde tuisc il and sward fon farendum and fon fretma, fon beijlum and fon breinsechtum and fon tha letha fallenda ewele, sa thu thina eth al riuchte swere and nawit menis.

Urflokin and urmalediad wertha thi olle thine kata and olle thina lithmata, fliande werthe thi thin quick and alle thin woldsket, alsa fliande werthe thi tha riza sa thit wede

40   oppa [thina] liwe, and thetter fon thina liwa nen erwa ni sprute, [ief thu mith falleske swere], thet thu nebbe thinis bedda god stelen ne urhelen, sin ne wart, thin ne gret.

Thet thi God alsa helpe and alle sina helga, thet [thu] thina eth hebbe al riuchte sweren and nawit menis.

Qui debent iurare

45   Thine fia-eth aghen tha frouwa te swerene and therto achta withethar, alder ma him betighet dernfias, alsa hia oftne stol urtiath, and thet skel wesa bi achta markum thet lereste. Ac ach ma hine to swerane umbe alle tha lametha, ther uppa thet thrimene lif falleth, and therto niugen withethar. Kempth ac thiu bote uppa en half lif, sa send hit tuelf withethar to tha fia-eth. Kempth ack thiu bote uppa en tuede lif, sa send hit achtene withethar to tha fia-ethe.

Textual notes: 15 thines, MS *om.* 15–16 sa thu … menis, MS *om.* 21 thi, MS *om.* 23 thi prester, MS *om.* 32 and, MS *om.* 48 thina, MS *om.* 49 ief thu … swere, MS *om.* 51 thu, MS *om.*

Explanatory notes:

1   St Michael, archangel, whose task it is to guide souls to heaven.

6   St Stephen, proto-martyr (Acts 7).

7   St Nicholas, bishop of Myra, patron of young bachelors and students.

8   St Catherine of Alexandria, considered one of the fourteen most helpful saints in heaven, and patroness of virgins and female students (including nuns).

10   The clause beginning with *Thet thi God…* is left unfinished. With *alsa bruc* the construction is resumed as it was used in the first two paragraphs.

13   *ruald* for *wrald*: on metathesis, see §65; *Thet is thet ereste wede … ruald.* An explanatory remark, which was probably copied from the margin into the main text, for two reasons: Firstly, *forma* has not been repeated but replaced by the apparently more modern form *ereste.* Secondly, the second garment, to be worn on Judgement Day, does not really fit into the main text, but is introduced here for the sake of balance. Read: *and thet leste (is thet wede),* … .

16   *tha alonge ruald:* ACC. of time 'the everlasting world', i.e., 'world without end, for ever and ever' (L *in saeculum saecolorum*). In compounds, *a* often means 'permanent(ly), eternal(ly)' (Oosterhout 1969).

18   *thi thi*: the former is the dative of *thu.*

25   *Corpus Domini,* i.e., the consecrated host.

41   *sin ne wart, thin ne gret:* 'his [property] not decreased, yours not increased', the auxiliary to be mentally supplied is *nebbe* from the preceding clause.

46   *and thet skel wesa* … 'and that (i.e., the contested property) must be (worth) eight marks at the least'.

A plague upon you!

Some of the curses in the *Fia-eth* concern loss of cattle and a disease producing boils. In the thirteenth-century *Bloemhof Chronicle*, the two are closely associated. A new disaster followed upon a flood that had devastated the Wolds [a district] in the previous year:

> In the year of Our Lord 1250 the beginning of the summer, however, was much too dry, and a contagious disease spread among the cattle, and almost all the cattle that had remained alive after last year's flood, or that had been newly bought after the other cattle had perished, died. And in the heat of the summer the corpses of the animals started to rot and spread an unbearable stench which also infected people. Contaminated air, according to Galen, is much more harmful than is contaminated food.
>
> In the Wolds, a different kind of infectious disease spread among the people. A kind of poisonous blister developed between flesh and skin, initially as big as an acorn. People thought that it was caused by the bite of some insect or other, but those who more diligently examined this, said that a few days before it erupted, they could feel a distemper that seemed to pervade the entire body and was looking for some way out and most often would erupt near the neck above the shoulders. If the blister was immediately cut away from a person on the first day, and the spot was cauterized with iron, recovery was possible. If not, death would follow within seven days. Without surgical intervention hardly anyone stayed alive.

XIV. Asegariucht

This text, surviving only in the Fivelgo Manuscript, is one of the livelier pieces in the corpus of legal texts (cf. O'Donnell 1998). Drafted in the thirteenth century (possibly in Frisia west of the Lauwers), it records in dialogue form how the tasks are to be divided between the *asega* (A) and the legal executives. The latter are probably the *skeltas* (S), although they are not mentioned as such.

The text has been slightly normalized: ⟨w⟩ has been written ⟨u⟩ or ⟨v⟩, where appropriate; final devoicing of weak past participles has been 'restored'; some verbal and nominal endings have been standardized. Scribal errors have been silently corrected.

(S) 'Asega, is't thingtid?'

(A) 'Alsa hit is. Alsa forth deis, sa i bi londriuchte iuwe thing heia and halda ur alle iuwe

berieldan, alsa fir sa't him iuwe bonnere keth heth, sa ach i him to urbonnane thingslitene,

dernsone, sunderacht and unhlest, thetter en mon dwe bihalva iuwe orleve, sa hwether sa

5   hi hir nu a warve se sa hi forth to ware kume.

Thes greva bon bonne ic ur alle mine berieldan, alsaden to lastene, sa thi asega heth
to riuchte deled. And hebbe allera monna ek mene with sine sele, thet hi riuchte tichtan to
ware brenge and thet unthelande se, ther on tha liude falle and on thene frana.'

(S) 'Asega, hot age wi to dwane on thisse nie iera?'

10 (A) 'I agen frethe to bonnane tham erst, ther is allerharist: alle godishusum and alle
godismonnum and thes godeshuses erve thene alrahagista frethe, thet hit nen mon ne
binere tha biteszie iefta bitiune, bi-ere iefta biskere. Thet agen tha liude to loviane and i
agen iuwe bon theron to ledzane. Wellath i thet lovia mitha hondum?'

(S) 'Ge, God, wi.'

15 (A) 'Sa fa i up alle menlike. Sa biad ic iu thes greva bon alsadene to lastane, sa thi asega deled
heth and i lowad hebbath.'

(S) 'Asega, hwet agen wi forth to dwane?'

(A) 'I agen frethe to ledzane alle widum, alle wesclinem and walberum and unewaxena
kindum bi x liudmerkum and hira twifalde bote.'

20 (S) 'Hwet agen wi mar?'

(A) 'I agen frethe to ledzane alle riuchte husliudum, allera monna hwelikum binna durum bi
there haudlesene, buta durum bi x liudmerkum, and alsadena hevum and alsadena werum
to bisittane, sa'r biseten and bineten hede siker and sanlas, hwether sa'r thene on kemen
were mith cape sa mith wixle sa mith riuchta herwerum, hit ne se thetti hera scele thet lond

25 sella an cap iefta an wixle; sa is alle londa ec an kap frei. Bitigeth er him thet, thetter hebbe
misered, misskered, misdommad, misditsed iefta misgulden, sa scel hi'ne alhir onspreka. Sa
is hi thach niar thet to betriane and sines hera hild to winnane than eng mon him is of to
drivane, sa fir sa'r'et alle beteria welle; thet age i to dwane.'

(S) 'Hwet age wi mar to dwane?'

30 (A) 'Silan to hlidiane and thorpemaran to remane, herewegan and hemeswegan to stiftane,
dikan and domman and grundiete to slane, bi evennachte evenhach erthe, bi sumeresnacht
a fulla hrive hrivad and buta uppe litzed, bi middesumera an fulle wirke wrocht, hit ne se
thet tha liude er kiase. Sa is't thera liuda kera ther bifara thes asega dome. Thit agen tha
liude to loviane and i iuwe bon theron to ledzane.'

Explanatory notes:

1   The duty of the *asega* was to 'find justice'. He had stored the law in his memory, concluded what measure applied to a certain case and advised the court. He presided over the
sessions of the courts of law, and confirmed the verdicts of the jury. The *skelta* saw to it that
the law was enforced (cf. note to Text Id, line 11).

2   *thing heia and halda*: a stock phrase, which also occurs in Old English (cf. Stanley 1979).

5   *warve/ware*: the latter form shows regular loss of *v* after *r* (§78.2*v*).

6   *greva*: the count's presence in this text is an indication of its belonging to the first half of the thirteenth century; *alsaden to lastene*: the object 'it' is understood.

9   The occurrence of OWFris *hot* 'what' (§208.7) instead of OEFris *hwet* in this text betrays it to have been 'translated' from OWFris into OEFris (cf. §213); *age wi*: on the verbal ending, see §155.3.

18–19   … *alle widum … kindum*: widows, orphans, pilgrims and minor children were considered in canon law as *personae miserabiles*.

25   *Bitigeth er him*: 'If he (i.e., the landlord) accuses him (i.e., the leaseholder) …'.

30   Before *Silan*, '*I agen*' is understood by way of ellipsis: '*I agen silan to hlidiane*, etc.'. Similarly, *agen* has been omitted in line 34 after *i*. A *sīl* was a discharging-sluice or outlet, with a slight tilt, made of timber, enabling superfluous water from reclaimed land to run onto the mudflats beyond the sea-dike during ebb-tide. A flap-valve on the seaside of the sluice prevented the salt water from penetrating the polder. It was an ingenious system and worked without an operator. Several such medieval sluices have been excavated, cf. Reinders (1988).

31   … *bi evennacht evenhach erthe*: 'on 21 March the *grundiete*, i.e., pools that had remained behind a dike after a flood or break-through, should have been filled up as high as the surrounding level'; *erthe* here is dative, as adjectives compounded with *even-* govern the dative (cf. §180.7 and Bremmer 1984: 30–31).

32   *a fulle hrive hrivad* 'completely made even by raking', literally 'raked to the full rake', a *figura etymologica*; *litzed* 'levelled (viz. the embankment) by heaping up turfs'. *an fulla wirke wrocht* 'made according to the prescribed measures', literally 'worked to the full work', again a *figura etymologica*.

XV. The Legend and Statutes of Magnus

This text is one of many dealing with the theme of the 'Frisian Freedom'. Until the close of the Middle Ages, Frisia managed to maintain some kind of independence, and, at least in practice, escaped the feudal system. The Frisians claimed obeyance only to the Holy Roman Emperor. To undergird their freedom which, according to legend, they had received from Charlemagne himself, a wide variety of stories sprang up, celebrating the Frisian freedom. The *Statutes of Magnus* is a good example of such blending the legendary with the legislative genre, so popular among the medieval Frisian texts.

The text follows the recension of U, with some variants adopted from J. Additions in square brackets are based on the text as it occurs in D and J, to supply omissions made by Franciscus Junius (1591–1677) when he copied the text from MS Unia somewhere in the 1660s.

Qualiter Romani a Frisonibus sint victi

Wella J harkia and leta jo rathia fan tha arsta kerum ther tha Fresan kerrin tha hia an Rome
thine fristol bicrongen and that strid [up]ehewen ward tuischa thine Koning Karle and tha
Romera heran umbe this Pawis [Leo] agene. Tha brochte ma tha nakeda Fresan allis an fara,

5   hu se arst vrslain worde. Tha binetthen't tha Fresan mith tha live; efter thiu bifochten hia't
manlike mit[tha] handum, tha[t] hia Romera burg wonnen. An there thredda tid this deis,
tha [tha] Romera heran ower hara mos waren, tha brochte Magnus, ther Fresane fanare was,
sinne fana uppa tha hagista tore ther binna Rome eng was. Hu leith that tha Koninge Karle
was! Er waren se alle nakede Fresan, tha het se thi koning alle heran.

10   Tha bad ma tha herim gold and godeweb. Tha bad ma tha herim allerlikum sinne breida
scild mittha rada golde ti bislane. Tha bad ma tha herim allerekum ti settane ina en sundrich
rike, and ma [him] therof thach thianede as ma ene weldega koninge s[c]ulde. Alle tha jefta
ther thi koning bad, tha wit[h]sprec Magnus and kas en other, hale bettera, ande alle Fresan
an Magnus kere jen. And kas, that alle Fresan fri heran were, thi berna and thi onberna, also

15   lange so thi wind fan tha olcnum we, and thio wrald stode, and wellat wasa mith tha kere
thes koninges hacha herenatan.

Alderefter cas Magnus thine letera kere, and alle Fresan an sinne kerre jen, that ma tha
Fresum tha holtena wittha of tha halsa spande, and se emmermer wolde wesa fri heran, thi
berna and thi unberna, also lange so thi wind fan tha vlcnum we, and thio wrald stode, and

20   se mit tha kere wolde wasa thes koninges [hacha] herenatan.

Tha cas Magnus thine thredda kere, and alle Fresan an sine kere ien, thet se nene
koningscilda har ne golde than riochte huslada tha scelta, hit ne se thet alle dumme liude
anda bannum [har] vrberede, and hia's thanne wel moste unjelda.

Tha cas Magnus thine fiarda kere and alle Fresan an sine kere ien, and cas betera than

25   alle tha jefta ther thi koning bad, that se nene himelscilda har ne golde than riuchtne decma
tha prestere ther tha haudsto bisonge, hit ne were thet alle dumme liude an tha bannum
har urberde and hia's thanne untgolde.

Therefter cas Magnus thine fifta kerre and alle Fresan an sinne kerre ien, that se nene
hera fordera an here[ferd] ne volde folgia, than aster ti ther Wiser and wester ti ther Fle, up

30   mittha flode and wth mittha ebba, truch that se thine ower wariad deis and nachtis with
thine Nordkoning and thine wilda witzing and this ses flod mit tha fif wepnum: mit suerde,
mit scilde, mit spada, and mit forca, and mit etkeres orda.

Therefter cas Magnus thine sexta kere and alle Fresan and sine kere ien, that [se] hara
ain riucht halda wolde binna hara ain sawen selandum bi this pawis and this koningis jefte,

35   bi alle riochta bannim and bi asega domum, and bi alle riuchta papena ordelim, as hi hede

tuer lecan ti folgerum.

Alderefter cas Magnus thine sawenda kere and alle Fresan an sine kere ien, that him thi

Pawis Leo and thi Koning Karle wolde jowa en bref and en insigel ther hia moste on scriwa sawin

karan and xvii kesta and xxiv landriuchta and xxxvi sinithriuchta. That orlof jef him thi Pawis Leo

40   and thi Koning Karle mittha munde and efter weddaden hia't mittha handum. En helig biscop

set and scref hit mittha handum and Magnus sprack hit mittha munde vt'er teula ther God selva

hade geven Her Moysi up tha berge to Sinay. Tha thet bref allerarst birat was, hu fro tha manig

ethele Fresa was! Tha gengen hia alle [gather] tofara thine Pawis Leo and thine Koning Karle stan.

That bref him thi pawis jef. A, ho hi't him hage biplach! Hi het that tha Fresan that riucht also

45   feste helde, so hia thine Cristena nama habba wolde, and se tha suthirna here and riuchte herig

wolde wasa, hwand hia in that nordkoningrike herden, and alle hethen waren.

Allerarst tha him that breef an tha hand com, tha hof him up Magnus an lofleysasang

'Crist si unse nathe, kyrioleys', and [remden this Koningis Karlis hof and] alle Romera land.

Ac band're an sine skeft this koningis hereteken, hu hit alle tha folke trowe ware that alle

50   tha Fresan ware fri heran, thi berna and thi unberna, also lange so thi wind fan tha olcnum

woe, and thio wrald stode.

That bref and that insigel brochte Magnus inor Fresland; that les ma in Almenum in

Sente Michaelis dome, ther to thirre tid was mith holte and mith reile ramed. Ther nas in

Freslande eles naut manich. Ther les ma wt'a breve sawin karan, and xvii kesta, and xxiiii

55   landriuchta, and xxxvi sinithriuchta, alle Fresum [ti love and] ti erim.

Explanatory notes:

1   *Qualiter … victi*: 'How the Romans are conquered by the Frisians'. *Wella J harkia …*: The text clearly addresses an audience and purports to tell of the 'genesis' of Frisian law; *kerrin*: note that the double consonant is used here to indicate that the preceding vowel is short (§209).

4   *Pawis Leo*: Pope Leo III (ruled 795–816). He was the pope who conducted the ceremony during which Charlemagne crowned himself emperor in 800. An attempt was made to deprive him of his eyes and tongue in order to disqualify him for the pontificate, but his enemies were prevented from carrying out their evil plans. In Frisian legend, his opponents succeeded in their plans, but the Frisians released Leo, and his sight was miraculously restored to him. Leo's mutilation is also recorded in, e.g., the *Anglo-Saxon Chronicle*, for the years 796 (F) and 799 (D, E); *tha nakede Fresan*: i.e., not just without protective armour but also as a token of their 'barbarous' state. Until that time, the Frisians allegedly were still *ain* 'own(ed)', i.e., serfs, and as a sign of their servitude they had to wear a wooden collar (*withtha*). This curious symbol finds its origin in a misinterpretation of the word *frihals* 'freedom' (cf. OE *frēols*), which literally means 'free neck'.

7   *Magnus*: the legendary leader of the Frisian troops in Rome. He seems to derive his existence from St Magnus, who was worshipped in Bari, Italy, and whose cult was introduced to Frisia by Frisian crusaders. His cult spread from Frisia west of the Lauwers to the other Frisian districts, including North Frisia, before 1300. Instead of being rewarded with riches and wordly power, Magnus chose for freedom of feudal status and freedom of legislature for the Frisians. On the Magnus tradition, cf. Noomen (1989).

14–15   *also lange … stode*: a so-called 'eternity' formula. Usually such formulas were employed to conclude charters and wills, cf. Vries (1984). On the loss of *w* in *olcnum*, see §78.3*w*; *wasa*: on *wasa* instead of *wesa*, see §211.

30   *deis and nachtis*: 'day and night'. Adverbial genitive (§181.3), in which the feminine gender of *nacht* was adjusted to the masculine gender of *dei*.

30–31   *with thine Nordkoning and thine wilda witzing*: according to legend the Frisians formerly owed allegiance to the Danes. It is uncertain whether *witzing* here just means 'pirate', or more specifically 'Viking', cf. Fell (1986).

34   *sawen selandum*: the seven 'Sealands', or 'lands on the sea', a division of Frisia Magna which went back to at least the thirteenth century.

38–39   *sawin karan … sinithriuchta*: 'the (seven) *Statutes of Magnus*, *Seventeen Statutes*, *Twenty-four Land-laws*, and *Thirty-six Synodal Laws*'. These were apparently seen as the core of the Frisian legal monuments; *karan*: a typically north-eastern dialect feature, see §211.

47   *hof him up*: on the use of the dative pronoun, see §182.4.

48   *Crist si unse nathe*: the last two words are Middle Low German (instead of OFris *use nethe*), suggesting that the service in church, inasfar as it was conducted in the vernacular, was held in Low German rather than in Frisian.

53   *mith holte and mith reile*: 'with timber and with cloth'. It is somewhat surprising to see that St Michael's dome in Almenum (a parish near Harlingen in Westergo) was covered with cloth (canvas?). The redaction if this text in the Fivelgo Manuscript reads *mith hreide* 'with reed', and indeed, a thatched roof makes better sense. In any case, the fact that the church was said to be of timber and not of stone, and the roof thatched instead of slated or tiled, suggests a date before (tuff-)stone churches were introduced to Frisia (i.e., in the course of the twelfth century).

XVI. Fon Alra Fresena Fridome

This account of the martial deeds of the Frisians earning them Charlemagne's sympathy is an interesting element in the various forms in which the Frisians celebrated their freedom. In form, it is unique: the two episodes are recounted in stanzas of four lines, each concluded by a stanza of two lines. The metre and length of lines are sometimes quite irregular. The reason for this irregularity probably lies in the fact that the poem was written down as prose with no clear indication of line division, inviting a scribe to add a few words here and there as he saw fit. The fictional narrator steps forward in line 83, while the audience is addressed in both of the two-lined stanzas. The poem, found only in the two Hunsingo manuscripts, received a thorough edition from Sipma (1947). The major source for the poem is a (forged) Latin charter, dating to the close of the thirteenth century, in which Charlemagne grants freedom to all Frisians. The text of this Latin charter is also found in H (ed. Hoekstra 1950).

The preservation of the poem is fortuitous: there are clear indications in the language of the text in the Old East Frisian Hunsingo MSS that it was copied/adapted from an exemplar that originated from west of the Lauwers. This suggests that even in the thirteenth century West Lauwers Frisia played an important part in the development and proliferation of the notion of the Frisian Freedom.

Thit was to there stunde

tha thi Kening Kerl riuchta bigunde.

Tha was'ter ande there Saxinna merik

Liudingerus, en hera fele steric.

5   Hi welde him alsa waldlike

tha tegethan (ther hi fon riuchte scolde) bihalda tha Kening Kerlis kairslica rike.

Ac welde hi ma dwan:

Hi welde tha sterka Fresan under sinne tegetha tian.

Hi bibad'it efter alle sine rike

10   thet ma hine heta scolde koning waldelike.

Tha thi Kening Kerl thit understod,

tornig was him hirumbe sin mod.

Hi let hit tha Fresum tha kundig dwan,

hodir hia thene nia kening mith him mith stride welde bistan.

15   Tha Fresen gadere komin,

uppa thit bodiskip se anne god red genomin.

Thi Fresa fele sterka,

hi for'im tha and tha Saxinna merka.

Tha Sassiska heran thit fornomin,

20   up tha felda hia Fresum toionis komin.

Tha fugtin se alsa grimlike,

ofslog ma tha Saxum bethe thene erma and thene rika.

Thag to tha lesta

feng ma of tha Saxum heran and ridderan tha besta.

25 Iha band ma alsa sere

mith ene sterka mere.

Iha latten se tha waldelike

alder iha thene Kening Kerl urnomin ande sine rike.

Tho hi thet fornom

30 thet him thi Saxinna hera alle bundin kom,

wel was him ande sine hei.

Hi bad tha stulta Fresa godne dei.

Hi nom se tha ande palas sin,

hi scanct'im bethe mede ande win.

35 Tha Fresan forin utes koninges howe,

to iher londe iha weder komin mith halika lowe.

Aldus hebb'i ursten

hu't tha sterka Fresa is with thene Saxa tha forgen.

Thit sce therna to ener stunde,

40 thet tha Romera heran with thene Kening Kerl strida bigunden.

Stultlike

weldin hia thene tins bihalda tha keninglika rike.

Thi kening thit serlike

kundegeia let alle sine keningrike.

45 Iha komin alle tosamenc,

ther werin ande sine rike, sibbe and framede.

Tha Fresan thit mere fornomin,

to thes keninges howe unelathadis se ther komin.

Iha werin ther nette ande god,

50 hwand hia drogin enir stultere lauwa mod.

Iha sprekin ther tofara tha keningge wigandlike,

iha welde allena fiuchta with tha Romera heran fore thet kairslike rike.

Iha nomin tha scerpa swerd and hiera honda,
iha gengin tofara there burig stonda.

55 Tha heran binna there burig thit gesegin,
uppa thene feld ion tha Fresan to stride tha tegin.
En ordil warth ther upgehewin,
monig diore wigand warth nither tha there geslagin.

Tha to there stunde
60 thi Fresa hastelike on tha heran fiugta bigunde.
Serlike tha heran umbe tha segin,
alle balde se to there burg flegin.

Thi Fresa folgade mith untwivilika sinne,
hu hi tha burg kreftlike winne.
65 Thach uppa thet leste
wunnin iha tha burg and heran tha besta.

Tha porta gundtma bisluta,
thi Kening Kerl mith sine folke was'ter abuta.
Iha funden't and ihera rede,
70 iha welden tha Kening Kerl iowa bethe burg ande liude.

Thi kening thogte ande sine mode,
hu hi tha stulta Fresa thisse waldelika deda lania scolde mith eniga gode.
Hi iof him mitha allera arista
iefta tha masta.

75 Twintech merka fon brondrada golde,
ther thi Fresa iera hec tha kairscipe to tegetha iowa scolde.
Thiu iefte, ther hi hede tha Fresum gedan,
thiu moste emmer and emmermar ewelika stan.

Ther hi to bad kairslike,
80 thet se ne scolde nen hera thuwingga waldelike,
hit ne were thet iha bi ihera goda willa welde thet dua,
thet se anne hera wolde undfa.

Thag ne wen'ik ande mine sinne,

thet hia bi willa angne hera gewinne.

85   Nowet allena tha keningge and thisse bode nogade,

thes heliga Pawis Gregorius weld hi hirto fogade.

Hi bed hit ita pawis tha,

thet hi tha Fresan mitha gastelika riuchte welde bifa.

Hewelike alle hi to bonne se dede,

90   ther tha Fresum tobrogte enige nede.

Alder bibad hit thi Kening Kerl opinbere,

thet Fresan iera hec nige redian him kere.

Tha kairslika crona hi uppa ihera hawid sette,

alderumbe hi se scera lette.

95   Thag ief se thet ne welde nowet dua,

ut mostin se him ihera her leta frilike waxa,

thet hit alle liude magte tha sian,

thet hi se fri hede gedan.

Hi bebad hit him tha keninglike,

100   alle thi Fresa, ther were sterik and rike,

thet iha anne slag and ihera witta hals scolde him undfa,

therefter moste hi ridder biliwa.

Wepin scolde hi thereffter drega alle scone,

and sine scelde moste hi melia tha keninglika crone.

105   Thet hi thissa iefta tha Fresum hede evelike dan,

ther hi keningan and hertigan to witscipe up nom and ondris monege halike man.

Thach to lesta,

hu hit tha efterkumanda evelike wiste,

ande tha brewm hit ma biscref.

110   Fon tha ieftum ther abuta nowet urieten bilef.

Thet insigel thet was fon tha brondrada golde,

hu hit alle liude wiste, thet thius ief ewelike stonda scolde.

Thisse bref ma tha fri Fresa iof and sine hond,

mith dole and mith erum hi wider for and sine ain frilike lond.

115 Aldus mugin hit alle liude forstan,

thet thi Kening Kerl thene Fresa umbe thet kreftlike strid fri hewet gedan.

Textual notes: 6 tha tegethan MS tha gethan; 10 scolde MS scode; 12 sin MS si; 15 togadere MS gadere; 16 bodiskip MS bodisclskip; 29 fornom MS fornomen; 32 hi MS thi; 34 scanct'im MS scanctum; 36 komin MS kom; 37 hebb'i MS hebhi; 54 gengin MS gegin; 64 winne MS wnne; 70 welden MS welde; 76 hec MS het; 78 emmermar ewelika MS emmermare velika; 79 to MS ta; 81 ihera MS iera; 83 ne MS om.; 92 hec MS het; 104 keninglika MS kenlika; 106 keningan MS kenigan; 114 ma MS nia.

Explanatory notes:

4 *Liudingerus*: the Latin form of this name betrays the poet's use of the Latin charter when he composed his poem.

6 In the MS, after *tegethan* follow the words *ther hi fon riuchte scolde*, which cause intolerable hypermetricality and will therefore have been a gloss that slipped into the text some time during its transmission; *kairslica < kaiserlica*. Metathesis of *s* and *r* in this form is quite common, cf. line 76 *kairscip* (< *kaiserscip*) and see §66.

13 *kundig*: a Middle Dutch/Low German form, as 'proper' Old Frisian would have had *kuth*. Other such traces in this text include 4, 17: *fele* (instead of *fule*); 10, 35: *koning-* (instead of *kening-*); 19: *Sassiska* (instead of *Saxiska*); 29: *tho* (instead of *tha*); 39: *therna* instead of *thernei*; 44: *kundegia* (instead of *ketha*); 58: *geslagin* (instead of *-slein*); 91: *opinbere* (instead of *epinbere*); 98, 105, 117: *(ge)dan* 'done' (instead of *den*); 101: *slag* instead of *slek*; 103: *scone* (instead of *scene*); 106: *ondris* (instead of *othris*); 117: *hewet* (instead of *heth*), the frequent occurrence of the prefix *ge-*, and frequent spellings with ⟨g⟩ instead of ⟨ch⟩: *tornig* (12), *fugtin* (21), *fiugta* (60), *thāg* (83), *tōbrogte* (90), *magte* (97). So many loan forms and spellings, disproportionate in comparison to the other texts in H, suggest that the author was familiar with and consequently influenced by reading or hearing poetry from neighbouring cultural areas.

17 *Thi Fresa*: in the text 'the Frisian' (singular for the collective) is frequently used beside *tha Fresan* 'the Frisians'.

18 *for'im*: (*fōr him*) verbs of motion are frequently reflexive.

51 *Iha* 'they' for *hia*, *ihera* and *iera* 'their' for *hiera*, *hec* (76) 'each' for *ec* and *hewelike* (89) 'eternally' for *ewelike* shows the scribe (or rather, the scribe of his exemplar) to have had difficulties with his 'h's.

61   The second *tha* ('then') is weakly stressed as the stress falls on *umbe* and *segin*.

70   *iowa* 'to give', also in 76, is typically an Old West Frisian form as opposed to *ieva*; similarly, *iof* 'gave' (73) but OEFris *ief* (114), see §208.3. Other West Frisian forms include (-)*stan* (14, 78, 115) but OEFris *stonda* and infinitives ending in -*n*: *dwan* (7, 13) but OEFris *dwa, tian* (8) but *tia, sian* (97) but *sia*, see §210.2. Furthermore: *hodir* (14) but OEFris *hwether* (§208.7), *toionis* (20; otherwise only in OWFris); *tosamene* (45; otherwise only in OWFris; OEFris *tosemine* [R1]).

92   *nige*: on the *g* as a hiatus filler, see §78.1*g*.

113   *bref* ACC.PL 'charters', an endingless neuter plural (§103), cf. *brewm* in line 109, which is DAT.PL and not ACC.SG.MASC as Sipma claimed (followed by Buma/Ebel); *tha fri Fresa* 'to the free Frisian', free in the sense of 'without a feudal superior'.

114   *mit dole*: the meaning and etymology of *dole* is contested. Apparently a noun, it has been translated with 'pride' (perhaps with an eye to MLG *dōl* 'overbearing, proud, reckless').

XVII. Charlemagne and Redbad

One of the more interesting traditions in the legendary Matter of Frisia is the account of how Charlemagne duelled with King Redbad in order to gain suzerainty of Frisia. Following his victory, Charlemagne seeks to impose law amongst the Frisians. Time and again, the Frisians try to dodge his attempts, until finally Charlemagne has their representatives set out to sea in a rudderless boat. The remainder of the story, relating the divine origin of Frisian law and legal institutions, attains mythological dimensions. It contains indications that it may date back to pre-Christian times. Charming as the legend may be, the frequent use of paratactic constructions shows that the genre of narrative prose was rarely practised in medieval Frisia.

The text below, from U, has been slightly regularized.

Fan tha koningen Karle ande Redbad

Tha thi koning Karle and thi koning Redbad fan Danemerkum in thet land komen, tha
bisette aider sine wei ina Franekra ga mith ene hereskilde, and quath aider thet land were
sin. Tha wolden hit wise liude sena and tha heren wolden hit bifiuchta. Thach wisade ma
5   there sona also lange thet ma hit op tha twer koningen ief, hoder so otherne an stille stalle
urstode, thet hi wonnen hede. Tha brochte ma tha heren togathere; tha stoden se en etmel
al umbe. Tha let thi koning Karle sine handskoch falla; tha rachte'ne him thi koning Redbad.
Tha quath koning Karle: 'A ha, a ha! Thet land is min!', ande hlakkade – alderumbe hat sin

wurth 'Hachense'. 'Hwerum?', quath Redbad. Tha quath Karle: 'I sind min man worden'. Tha
10   quath Redbad: 'A wach!' – alderumbe hat sin wurth 'Wachense'.

Tha for thi koning Redbad uta lande ande thi koning Karle wolde thingia. Tha ne moste're,
hwand ther lethegis landis so fule naut ne was, ther hi uppa thingia machte. Tha sante're
boda in tha sawen Seland and het thet hia him wonnen ene fri sto, ther hi uppa thingia
machte. Tha kapeden se mith skette and mith skillinge Deldamanes. Ther thingade're uppa
15   and lathade tha Fresan tofara him and het thet se riucht keren, also hia't halda wolden. Tha
beden hia ferstes ti hara forespreka; tha ief hi him orlof. This ora deis het hi thet se fara thet
riucht komen. Tha komen se and keren foresprekan, tolif fan tha sawen Selandum. Tha het
hi thet se riucht keren. Tha ieraden se ferstis: this thredda deis het hi se koma. Tha tegen hia
nedskin. This fiarda deis also; this fifta also. Thit send tha twa ferst and tha thria nedskin, ther
20   thi fria Fresa mith riuchte mei habba.

This sexta deis het hi thet se riucht keren. Tha sprecken se hia ne kuden. Tha sprek thi
koning: 'Nu lidze ik io tofara thre keran: hoder io liavera se thet ma io alle haudie than i alle
ain wirde, than ma io en skip iowe also fest and also sterk, ther anne ebba ande anne flod
mei withstan and thet sunder aller handa rother and rema and towe'. Tha keren hia thet
25   skip, ende folen ut mitha ebbe also fir thet se nen aland ne muchten sian. Tha was him lethe
to mode.

Tha sprek thi ena ther fan Widekines slachte was, thi forma asega: 'Ik habbe herd thet
us Hera God, tha hi an erthrike was, tolif iungeran hede and hi selva threttundista were
and hi to himmen kome al bi sletena dorum and traste se and lerde se. Hu ne bidda wi
30   naut thet hi us anne threttundista sende, ther us riocht lere and ti lande wise?' Tha folen
hia alle an hara kne and beden inlike. Tha se tha bedinge heden eden, tha segen hia anne
threttundista an there stiorne sitta and ene goldene axe up siner axla, ther hi mithe to lande
wether stiurde with stram and with wind.

Tha se to lande komen, tha warp hi mith there axe up thet land and warp ene ture up.
35   Tha untsprang ther en burna – alderumbe hat thet 'ti Axenhove'. And et Eswei komen hia
to land and seten umbe tha burna. And hot so him thi threttundista lerde, thet nomen hia
to riuchte. Thach ne wiste't nemma under tha fulke, hot thi threttundista were ther to him
komen was, also lik was he allerekum. Tha hi him thet riucht wisid hede, tha neren ther mer
tolif. Alderumbe skelen in tha lande threttene asegan wesa and hara domen agen hia to
40   delane et Axenhove and et Eswei. And hwerso hia an twa sprekath, so agen tha sawen tha
sex in ti haliane.

Aldus is't landriucht alra Fresena.

Explanatory notes:

3   *and quath aider thet land* …: note that the object clause begins without the conjuction *thet*. Similarly line 25: *Tha spreken se hia ne kuden.* On this phenomenon, see §202.

5–6   *an stille stalle orstan*: 'to excell in standing still', an ordeal in which the participants had to stand motionless, with their arms stretched sideways.

7   Presenting a gauntlet was a common ritual to symbolize the acknowledgement of a liege lord.

8–10   *Hachense* and *Wachense*: perhaps Hoekens and Waekens, two small *terp* villages in the district of Westergo, of which Franeker was the 'capital' (Noomen 2001).

12   *lethegis landis*: the genitive depends on *fule* 'much' (§183.1).

13   *sawen Seland*: see note on Text XV, line 40

14   *Deldamanes*: the recension in J adds the gloss: *id est Kaldadel*, later a street situated in Franeker. Franeker for a long time was the Frankish king's property and was (for that reason?) also the place where the counts of Holland spoke justice during their active control of Frisia west of the Lauwers.

19–20   *Thit sind tha twa ferst … mei habba:* this episode in the narrative gives an explanation for the two lawful occasions for postponing a legal court session and for the three legal impediments for not appearing at court.

22–26   When put before the choice of being decapitated, serfdom or being pushed out onto sea in a rudderless boat, the 'advocates' take the third option, in effect an ordeal.

27   *fan Widekines slachte*: 'of Widukind's stock'. Widukind was the leader of the great combined Saxo-Frisian rising against Charlemagne just before 800, cf. Meijering (1970).

28–29   See John 20: 26.

34   *ture*: 'turf; sod'. The word shows regular loss of *v* after *l* or *r* (§78.2v). Springs seem to have played a role of some importance in pre-Christian Frisia, cf. Kaufmann (1908). In any case, it seems very appropriate to have the mysterious helmsman expounding the principles of law, the *fons iuris*, near a spring.

35   *Axenhove*: dative of *Axenhof* 'court of axes'. Unidentified. Axes do not seem to figure in any special symbolic or ritual way in medieval Frisia; *Eswei*: Unidentified. The name has tentatively been explained as 'road of the gods', i.e., **ēsaweg*. One of the Germanic words for 'god' was **ans-*. In Frisian, as in English, the vowel first underwent rounding before nasal: **ons*, then lost the nasal before voiceless fricative with compensatory lengthening: **ōs-* (§§28, 30). This element is preserved in some early personal names, such as *ōsgēr*, literally 'divine spear'. As the word underwent *i*-mutation (§45) in NOM/ACC.PL, the outcome is *ēs-*, and as such is recorded in Old English *ēsa* GEN.PL 'of the gods'. If this explanation of *Eswei* is correct, we would here have a reference to pre-Christian religion, but surely people will no longer have been aware of this when the legend was finally written down.

39   *threttene asegan*: 'thirteen asegas'. It is clear why there should be an odd number of judges, as this number would never result in a draw when opinions differed.

XVIII. A Wedding Speech

Three wedding speeches, apparently written down for (private) pastoral purposes, constitute an unexpected, new genre of texts within the corpus of medieval Frisian literature. The scribe and author of one of them, though not the one printed here, identifies himself in the manuscript as 'Bernhardus Rordahusim'. Roordahuizen (ModWFris *Reduzum*) is a small village just south of Leeuwarden in West Frisia. From there, Bernhard wandered off into the wide world. In all probability, he was associated with the Devotio Moderna, a monastic reform movement: at least the monastery in Hildesheim, Germany, where he copied most of his manuscript around 1450, had strong links with this religious reform movement. His having been abroad for so long had an effect on Bernhard's Frisian which is riddled with Middle Dutch/Low German forms. Apart from these three speeches, the texts in the manuscript are either in Middle Dutch, Middle Low German or Latin. Clearly, for Bernhard Frisian had become a language appropriate for a family gathering, but certainly no longer for learning.

The speech given here was designed to be read, or rather performed, by two speakers. The first of these is the groom's marriage broker, the *mekere*, who had discussed the details of the wedding contract with the bride's parents (or relatives). The second speaker is a representative of the bride's relatives. As for the contents of the speech, it is an intriguing mixture of the serious and the jocular, something which still characterizes many wedding speeches today. Note how both speakers cast their arguments in a quasi-scholastic format. Moreover, parts of the text can be read as poetry, and have been printed here accordingly. Even the very beginning of the speech is adorned with a clear rhythm so that, all in all, this text is a real gem. The wedding speeches, which were discovered in Basel (Switzerland) just after World War II, have been edited thus far only according to strictly diplomatic principles (Buma 1957). Some recent studies dealing with the contents, sources, and language, respectively, are van Gelderen and Orbán (1990), Bremmer (1997), Blom (2007) and Langbroek (2007).

The text below is the first critical edition of Speech I. Apart from the improvement of a few obvious scribal errors, the text follows that of the manuscript in order to give a clear insight into the scribe's usage of Frisian, which is mixed with many Middle Low German forms, always indicated as such in the glossary. Some characteristically late OWFris spelling features are: double vowels or post-vocalic ⟨e⟩ to indicate vowel length; voiceless initial fricatives are frequently written as if voiced: *zoe, vrouwe*; initial *v* often appears as ⟨w⟩: *woergaderet*, and conversely, *w* as ⟨v⟩, *ville vy*. Further late features include final devoicing: *tiit, moet*; voiced *th* appears as *d* (passim), voiceless *th* appears as *t*: *tyennya*. OFris *iā* often appears as *iē* ⟨ye⟩: *tyennya* 'serve', *byere* 'beer', but also as *iā* ⟨ya⟩: *byar*. The cluster [sk] is written ⟨sch⟩. See also §§208–11.

[Speaker A] 'Een lutiik by mankes moede, ende bid v dat hy holden hleeste! Soe sprec ik

gherne al dat beste, als van da heiliga aefte daer my thiink dat hiir vorhanden is. God iuwe

dat hiit sillich ende wruchtik moete wessa ende in Diin name begonnen moete wiirda. Dat

darney moete folgya een goet myddel, ende voertmeer een goet eende, zoe hoep ik dat

5 hiit syllich zee.

Vm dat eerwirdicheyt des heyligha aeftes, soe sprek ik aldus als God selue heeft gesproghen in da heyligha ewangelio: 'Soe in wat stede twe woergaderet werden in Myne name, daer bin Ik dy tredda'. Want aldaervm zoe spreck ik, hwerzoe een man ende wiif mit Gode ende ney der ewa thogader komet ende da heyligha boede der ewa halden sint, daer

10   is dye benedide God fan hemelrik ende siin godlike nede ende gracie twyska hoer beyden. Ende dattet waer is, dat is vns in openbarlike ghewiist als in trem puntten.

Alleraerst, dat dye benedide God fan hemelrike dissen orde, dat is dit aefte, zelue heft gheseet ende maket ende anders ghemen. Gheen appostelen neer ewangelisten neer confessoren neer marteren neer een fan da heylighum dan God fan hemelrike zeluen.

15   Aldaervm zoe is disse orde, dat is dat aefte, gheheten een heylich afte.

Lettera tiid, zoe is dat aefte heylich ende dit is thyo saath. Hwant God van hemelrike hat dat aefte ghescapen in da alderheylichsta loghe dat wp ertrike is, dat was in da heylighe paradyse, doe Hy Adam ende Ewe schop ende hoer beyde bad dat hya rochtelike ende redelik daerin solde libba.

20   Tredda punt, zoe is dat aefte oec gheheylighet darwm, hwant God van hemelrike dat aefte ghescoep ende maket in dae alderheylichsta tiid, dat was eer ma a wralde zunde mochte dwan.

Aldarvm zoe mach ik weel spreka dat dit aefte gheheylighet is, als ik gemmen nv weel ghesecht heb. Ende alle daghene daer in da heyligha aefte ruchtelike libbent sint, dat hya

25   bet ende volkomelike Goede tyennya moghen, zoe ghiis in enich ordo ghenet, als ghy nv weel ghehoert hebbet.

Dyt ville vy nv laten stan
ende vollet nv tho kerle faen,
als hoe dat nv is een goet man N.,

30   ende wil dat heyligha aefte begaen,
als dyo jowe byet
ende dat Heylighe Scrift seyt,
ende oec als een heyligha aefte thobehoert.

Ende oeck zoe bytanket hy N., dat hy sin bode eerst wtzantte, dat hyo tha boeden weel

35   ontfengk, ende scengk horen byar ende wr byar ende myt mennichfalde tu dude weel bewyset heeft.

Ende als hy heer byhyagende was tho ener aefter vrouwe,
dat hyo hem ontheet hara trouwa.
Aldaervm wil hy geern dwaan allerlyawst

40   dat hoere erua synt allermaest.

Nv bygheret hy des, dat ma da vrouwe da breyd leta foer hem gaen uelkomen, ende dat ma

zee hem wp jowe

in Godes wald ende in siin wald.

God jowe datze wirda sillich ende ald.

45   God van hemelrike, dy jowe horen oeck dat zelue

dat hya goede kiinden moete tyan,

daer sye ende hoer wrinden thoe thanck

ende thoe thyenste moghe stan,

ende die goede verck alzo halda,

50   dat wy alle Goedes boede forfolla.

Aldaeraefter soe bid ik fol gherne

dat ma hem sonde werne.

Dat ma hem laeste alzoden goet,

als hem myt da N. vnheten wart.

55   Aldus zoe moghen wy vinna siin moet.

God help ons wt aller noet.

Hiirwp zoe beieriet wy dan dat'ter wpstande een goet man, daer ws jowe een goet antwert alhiirfan. God jowe hyaren ende hws allen luck ende willa. Amen.'

[Speaker B] 'By dees schenza moede! Hy habbet wal spritzen fan da heyligh aefte, dat hit
60   heylich ende sillich is. Ick spreck dy staet daer joncfroulikheyt hy arst heylighat heeft, hwant hy bern wolde werda van ener maghet.

Lettera tiit, zoe sprek ik van de staet der wyduan, hwant God benediit wolde wirda fan Anna, daer wydua was. Wm diis willa, zoe is die joncfrouwelike staet Goede byhagheliker dan dy staet des aeftes: 'wnde virginitas opus dictum, etc.' Hwant dyo edelheyt daer vrouvena
65   is openbere in achte puncten.

In die arste punt: want dyo vrouwe is makat fanda ribbe des mannes, ende dye man is ghemaket fanda slike.

Lettera tiit is maket dyo vrouwe in da paradyse, ende dye man buta paradyse.

Tredda tiit, dat God nam dyo manlika natura fan ener vrouwe ende naet fan da mannen.
70   Fyarda tiit, dat neen frouwa consent dede tho Goedes dade ner Pylatus vrouwe, mar konninghen ende foersten.

Fiifta tiid stond dyo starckheyt Goedes by ener vrouwa in *passio Christi* tho de mannen fleeghen.

Sexta tiit, dat God arst openberet is ener vrouwa als sinte Maria Magdalena.

75   Sauenda tiit, hwant een pur vrouwa woerd is buppa da koer ther engelen, ende neen pur man.

Achtenda punt, dat dyo vrouwe hegelkere gret is fan een enghel.

Wm des villa sint da vrouwen aller eera werd, dar ma van hyaren spreka ende zidza mey.'

[Speaker A] 'Meer solde hy mit al dulker tale wntvynna onze vrouwen, dat vare een
80   groet pand! Meer gaet sitta ende drinket ende makyet v blide, want wy wille v een richt andweert gheuen. Ick sprecka in dat aerste dat God van hemelrike alle erga saka wandelghe in dat beste.

Al daerney,

zoe betankya wy da heren abuta

85   ende da vrouwen abynne,

kocken ende schenzen,

dat hya ws edelike hebbet ontfenzen

ende aengenzen

myt dam allermaest,

90   daer hws was allerlyafst.

Ende heed wy aet misdeen, dat volde wy gherne lete betterie als ma sanlaza zaken schildich is tho betterian.

Als der screuen staet fan dat 'disse liafheyt geet buppa alle lyafheyt, der ma spreka mey ende vertellen', wm des willa zoe is hyo likat da golde. Want dat golde gaet bouen allen
95   metael ende copper.

Hiirbuppa, soe staet'ter ghescreuen dat dye menscha schel wrya fader ende moder, suster ende broder, ende alle hyare vrinden. Wm dis villa, zoe bidda wy da frouwen dat hya rede da vrouve da breyd. Als hy sin swird tye, dat hyo mit daem rede zee. Woermeer, zoe biddet wy dat ma hws myt nene byere swynze ende myt brande oeck naet neyzyete. Ende
100   ellic man neem siin eyghen stock, ende daermeed "goed nacht!" Amen.'

Textual notes: 4 hoep MS hoeft; 9 boede der ewa MS boede en*de* des ewa; 20 ghehey-lighet MS gheheylich; 32 seyt MS syet; 35 ontfengk MS ontfegk; 39 geern MS green; 60 hy arst MS arst; 74 openberet is MS openberet; 77 achtenda MS acktenda.

Explanatory notes:

1 *bid v*: the pronoun for 'I' is not expressed; *hy* for *y* 'you' with unhistoric *h*, so too in lines 59, 79; *hws* for *ws* 'us' in lines 50, 90, 99.

3 *in Diin name*: note the change in person; *diin* is either a mistake for *siin*, or, more likely, an instruction for the priest to lift his face towards heaven.

7–8 *Soe in wat stede* … : Matthew 18: 20.

44 *God jowe datze*: 'May God grant that they [i.e., bride and groom]…'.

45 *God van hemelrike, dy* …: 'the God of heaven, He …'. Note the use of the recapitulating relative (§201).

47 *daer sye ende hoer wrinden*: 'who [i.e., the children]' is subject, *sye … wrinden* indirect object in this clause.

60 *Ick spreck dy staet* … : 'I say that the state …'. On the deletion of the conjunction *thet*, see §202.

63 Anna was the old widow who blessed the child Jesus when he was taken to the Temple to be circumcised, see Luke 2: 36–38. In medieval tradition, St Anna was taken as Jesus's (maternal) grandmother.

64 *Wnde virginitas opus dictum, etc.* …: source untraced.

98 *sin swird*: the sword was a symbol of the husband's authority; cf. the following provision concerning an adulterous wife, found in the *West Frisian Sendriocht* (Buma/Ebel 1977: IX.50): *soe aegh di foermond dine ker hor hise fille, so hise haudie mitta swird deerse onder ghing dase dat aefte bighing, so hise to him nimme* 'then the guardian (i.e., husband) has the choice whether he will flog her or decapitate her with the sword under which she passed when she entered into wedlock or whether he will take her back'. Undoubtedly, some wedding guests will have taken the remark as an innuendo.

XIX. The Palm Knight

Among the medieval literary genres, saints' lives no doubt ranked high. It is all the more surprising that no specimen of this genre in Old Frisian has survived. Very close to it comes this episode, taken from *Gesta Fresonum,* an ingeniously construed history of the Frisians, which despite its Latin title is a translation from the Latin *Historia Frisiae*, a fourteenth-century composition. Its popularity also appears from a Middle Dutch prose version, *Gesta Frisionum* and even a Middle Dutch verse translation, *Die olde Freesche Cronike.*

The narrative represents a curious instance of the medieval custom of identifying God's way with the Israelites with a nation's own history. The author of the *Historia* even rearranged the order of events in the history of the Frisians so as to achieve a closer correspondence to the Old Testament narrative, a clear indication of his well-defined ideological intentions with this account.

Also in the episode given below, dealing with one of the many Crusades in which the Frisians participated, the author has not shunned to bend the 'facts' his way. The protagonist,

Poptatus, is said to be a Frisian, whereas the historical palm knight has been identified with a certain Hendricus from Bonn, in Germany (Poortinga 1965). Yet, the Frisian version must have been early since it is also recounted in Emo's thirteenth-century *Bloemhof Chronicle* (Jansen and Janse 1991). The text has been preserved in Codex Aysma, and its language is illustrative of Old West Frisian at the close of the medieval period.

In addition to the numerous instances of Middle Dutch orthography (e.g., ⟨gh⟩, ⟨y⟩, ⟨sch⟩ for [sk]), indication of vowel length by another vowel ⟨ae⟩, ⟨oe⟩, ⟨ee⟩, etc.) and loan forms (e.g., *ghe-*), we also see such internal Frisian developments as *ē* > *īe* [iːə], (e.g., *dien* 'done', *dier* 'there', *wier* 'were').

In eener tyt dae geschiede't, dat een fan dae Friesena steden, gheheten Vlemsborch, fan dae Sarracenen, dat is fan dae heydena, bileyd wart, als dat dae Fresen, dier dier in wiren, dat moed bisweeck. Ende hya nomen fan dae heyden een tyd des fredes ende wolden fan dae crystenhed gaen. Onder dae frede foergaederden dae Fresen .ijC. man ende taghen
5   iens dae heydana om dae sted te onthalden. Disse twa hondert habba alla dae heydana wriaghet fan der sted ende sloghen wal .xxx. tusent daed. Dae heydenen heerden een grymmelick luwd fan wepena folck in der lucht, hwant Sinte Mauricius hulp dae Fresen thoe stride. Aldus worden hya fan disse lude foerfeerd ende sint flechtich wirden wt dae stride. O, hoe graet wonder hat God by ws Fresen dien, dat twa hondert scholden .CM.
10 folkis foeriaya!

In der Fresena heer was een wrste, dier hieten was Poptatus; disse was een ald man ende thoemael godfruchtich ende was barren fan Wirtem. Disse Poptatus riep mit luder stemme, dae hya ghinghen in dae stryd: 'O, myn liauwe broren, alle ws hoep ende traest wolla wy sette aen Goede. Ende stridet Godes stryd mit froliched ende bescermet wse land! Wynna
15 wy't iefta verlese wy't iefte wirda wy foerslayn, altida foercrya wy bata ende wynningha, hwant dat ewighe lyand wert ws sonder twiuel iouwen'. Dae hy dit spretzen hied, dae ward die hymel opdien. Ende Sinte Mauricius mit enen graet scaer ridderen ghinghe in dae lucht foer dae Friesen heer ende habbet al dae heydana wriaghet.

Als dit strid wonnen was ende dyo steed ontset was, dae ontwepende hem dy erbera
20 man Poptatus ende scholde wt een cald born drynthia by enen berch. Doe ward hy schetten fan eenen heyden, dier leyd foerholen oen den bergh. Aldus is hy storuen in God almachtich ende is een merter Godis wirden, hwant hy om den kersten lauwa stritte. Hwant op syn gref vaxet een toemael schien palme, dier een teyken was der verwinninghe. Fan disse palmebaem worden dae Vlixbonenses, dat is dat steedfolck, hemmen seer foerwonderende;
25 dat was hemmen een teyken der grater frede ende resten, hwant eerdertyt worden dae Vlixbonenses ofte oenfochten, bileyd ende byney hara steed alheel foerdoeren ende

foerbarnd, maer dierney hieden hya langhe tyd ewighe resten ende ferd, dat hya Goede

mochte tyaenie. Als dit dy biscop van der sted sach, dat disse begroune man soe fula teykenen

dede – hwant folla dades folkes ward'er op syn gref gheleyd ende hya worden weer toe

30   liwe, dae cranken worden sond – disse biscop hild'en foer een heilich mertir Godes ende dat

hy wirdich wier toe canonisieren, ende hy foercrigh'et fan den pauis, dat me'n canonisiren

scholden. Meer aerst schold men syn gref opgrouwa ende onderfinde wier des bames wirtle

wire. Aldus werd'er dien. Men fant dat dy palmbaem waxen was wyt syn herte, dat sonder

twifel een foerwinninghe ende sterckheit des lauwes biteykent, dier hy in syn herte heed,

35   als hy ghinghe toe stride. Dissen heilighen man Poptatus habbe ya eret ende firet als een

oer martir Godis. Disse palm fierden hya fara in hyara heer in een teyken der foerwinninghe;

ende graten lauwa hieden hya in den palmbaem, als dae kynderen fan Israhel hieden in

Moyses rode, ende hilden'se toemael eerwirdich. Aldus wart dy palma graet era dien.

Explanatory notes:

1   *een fan dae Friesena steden*: i.e., one of the towns by which the Frisians made a name
for themselves during the Crusades. *Vlemsborch*: a vernacular adaptation (by approximation) of Latin *Ulixbona*, i.e., Lisbon. In medieval script, the letters ⟨u⟩ and ⟨v⟩ could each be
used to indicate both the vowel and the consonant. Elsewhere in the text, the inhabitants
of Lisbon are called *Vlixbonenses*. Apparently, the translator did not know what to do with
this word and left it untranslated; *Sarracenen*, i.e., Muslims, Mohammedans. Hence, they are
called 'heathens'.

7   *Sinte Mauricius*: Saint Maurice, leader of the Thebain Legion, was reputedly martyred
c.450. He was especially venerated as a military saint. From the twelfth century onwards, the
Holy Roman Emperors were annointed at the altar of St Maurice in St Peter's, Rome. He was
also known in the later Middle Ages as the 'Duke of the Moors' (i.e., Saracens).

11   *Poptatus*: a latinized form of Frisian *Popta*.

13   *Wirtem*: there are three places with this name: in Frisia west of the Lauwers, in the
Ommelanden, and in Frisia east of the Ems.

17   *Sinte Mauricius … ghinghe … and habbet*: note the switch from singular to plural subject.

22   *stritte*: on the weak past tense, see §155.6.

24   *worden … foerwonderende*: on this construction, see §193.

25   *een teyken der grater frede ende resten*: the gender of *frede* is masculine, but seems here
to be feminine on account of *resten*.

29   *folla dades folkes*: on this genitival construction, see §181R.1.

XX. Hideous Crimes, Cruel Measures

Whereas in the earlier laws all crimes could be redeemed by compensations, gradually corporal punishments were introduced, also under the influence of Roman law. The first two regulations are illustrative, at least from a modern point of view, of the highly detailed and ritualized way in which offenders of such diverse crimes as bestiality and violent robbery were (threatened to be) executed. The third penalty gives a fitting foretaste for those who deviate from the orthodox faith. In D, a selection of capital punishments is offered, while the last measure, E, shows that there was no mercy for stray geese.

Passage A is taken from the *West Lauwers Synodal Law* and B from a set of miscellaneous decrees, both from J, a manuscript copied around 1530, partly at least from a now lost manuscript from 1464 (§14). Its language, therefore, is a hybrid of older and younger forms of Old West Frisian. Passage C is found in *Jurisprudentia Frisica* (§13.21, Codex Roorda), dating from around 1500, written in one hand. Passage D is from the Fivelgo manuscript, while passage E is from the *Snitser Recesboeken* (§13.25).

A.   *Fan wildinghum dera schettena*

Hweersoe en man Godes ewa ende Godes riocht ende Octavianus riocht ende Moyses ewa britzen haet ende al der wralde, dat hi scetten wildath haet, soe aegh him di riochter tre kerren ti delane, als hi en etmel al omme liuwet haet mit twam heldem spanned, ende hi

5   dis alles biechte wert: dat hi dyn kerre habbe, her hi zijn machta weer zijn lyf ofsnide ende sine sonda bettrie, soe dat ma anne kulc dele, deer alle dat quick in moege ende dat ma him al benida brenge, iefta dyn tredda kerre, dat ma alle dat heer gaedrie of dera schettena sterten ende meckie deerof en beynd ende bynde'ne deermey ende berne'ne.

B.   *Hat ma dwaen schil, als ma dae lioede hiare gued mey wyeld benima wil.*

10   Dit is riocht: Hweerso en scip steet ende deer goede lioede binna sint, deer hiara lijf mit riochta thinghum nerra wellath, ieftha en fiuldfarende man, ief hi sine hewa op sine bec bonden haet, ief di man, deer binna zijn huus sit – ief se disse trine mit riochte thinghum binerra wolleth ende deer onriochta liode kommeth, deer himmen hiara hewa binymeth, soe is dat riocht, dat ma hit keda schel mit clockaclinne ende mit wepena rofte, deermey

15   allermaest, deer me't allerwydest mei keda mei. Is hi ald, is hi jong, deer da kedene heerth, is hi torstich, is hi hongerich, is him hete, is him kalde, soe ne ach deer nen man soe lange toe bidiane, dat hi zijn weed bewandelia moeghe. Mer hia schelleth dae Goedis fianda fulghia. Soe agh ma him oen ti faene, deer ma him alleraerst bifaert. Is hi an howe, is hi an huse, is hi an tzercka, is hi op dae altaere, is hi op dae funte, zoe aegh ma him of ti nimane

20   and fyf deda ti dwane, fijf thing: sine tweer eermen [ende] sine tweer tiaechschuncken oen twa te stetene mit ene ielrena stipa ief stile. Soe aegh ma him wtor dike toe ferane ende

deer en baem toe ferene, en tial toe brengane, deer eer oen wayne ne kome, him deer op ti

settane, [ende] hi zijn eynde deerop ti nymane. Him aegh nen wynd ti biwaiane, nen man

ti bisiane, nen dau ti bidauwene, nen senne ti beschinene, mer datt'er alle lioed oen merke,

25 dat ma eergha deda wrmide.

    C. *Dit is riucht.*

Hwaso myt towerie, myt foergiffnisse, myt bothem, myt wytgien ende myt onlawa omgeet –

disse vorscrioune lywd, deer enich fan disse secken dwaed, schel ma altomael op een

roester barna.

30 D. Thene morder regbrek'ma.

Thene rawir vnthaudat ma.

Thene kattere barn'ma jefta siuth'ma, *id est eum qui peccat contra naturam.*

Thene witherstridega and thene hera sunder erum vrsanc'ma.

Fad is bi there ferra hond.

35 E. Het is wr dae tzercka kondiget ende vorbaden dat nemmen nen ghees moet halda

dan elk op syn ayna lande. Ende hwae syn ghees naet hofftiget ende in oer liodena land

byginssen off byfonden wirde, ien moegma daed smyte sonder breeck.

Explanatory notes:

1 *wildinghum* and *wildath* (3): on the stem vowel, see §208.4.

2–3 The four kinds of law enumerated here are: natural law, canon law, Roman law, and
Mosaic (= Old Testament) law, respectively. On having sex with animals, cf. Exodus 22: 19,
Leviticus 18: 23, 20: 15–16.

3 *tre* 'three': notice that in this sixteenth-century manuscript the scribe used initial *t* where
older manuscripts have *th* (so too: *tredda* 8, *trine* 16, *torstich* 20, *tiaech-* 26, *tial* 28). Apparently, the original voiceless fricative had become a stop by this time. Notwithstanding the
fact that the scribe wrote three times *thing-* (14, 16, 25), he will have pronounced these
words as *ting-*.

8 *beynd*: on the vowel, see §208.6.

10–12 Skippers, pedlars and, apparently, farmers and craftsmen respresent the working
part of society.

11 *fiuldfarende*: a south-western form, see §211.

16 *is him hete, is him kalde*: on this impersonal construction, see §203.

21 *wtor dike*: i.e., outside the bounds of ordered society, in no man's land; *tial*: one of the
reflexes of **hwiāl*, see Århammar (1969).

23–24   The wind, the dew and the sun are stock elements of the traditional 'eternity formula' which often concludes an agreement in medieval Frisian charters (Vries 1984). An agreement will last 'as long as the sun shines, the wind blows, etc.' The idea here is that the punishment will grant no such eternity for the convicted thief.

27–29   The Latin glosses which follow this stipulation in *Jurisprudentiae Frisicae* refer to various places in the *Codex iuris civilis*.

30–34   This curious list, found in a long section with miscellaneous legal regulations, has an encyclopaedic ring to it. It seems as if the scribe wrote down the various kinds of capital punishment he knew. The Cathars (like other groups with deviant ideas) were often accused of sodomy. Curiously, hanging, the most popular way of execution in Frisia, is lacking. Striking off the right hand of counterfeiters, however, is regularly encountered, see e.g., Text VIII.20–24.

32   *id est eum qui peccat contra naturam* 'that is he who sins against nature'.

35   Each Sunday before the service, all kind of important information relevant for the community was announced from the pulpit.

36   *Ende hwae syn ghees … byfonden wirde*: a construction in which the subject 'who' is silently switched after *ende* (42) to 'whose geese'; *hofftiget*: from stem *heft-* [< WGmc **haft-*], with south-western *e* > *o* (§211) and additional *-ig-* infix (§164).

Glossary

It should be noted that this glossary occasionally contains normalized forms which do not always occur in the actual manuscripts.

Unless otherwise mentioned, mood is indicative. A verb followed by a Roman numeral (indicating class) is strong, and weak if followed by an Arabic numeral. A form followed by ∞ indicates that it is not Frisian, but either Middle Dutch or Middle Low German. The cognates and etymologies added are intended to help recognition, particularly for those who have already acquired some knowledge of Old English.

The following abbreviations have been used:

ACC	accusative	MDu	Middle Dutch
ADJ	adjective	ML	Medieval Latin
ADV	adverb	MLG	Middle Low German
ANOM	anomalous		
ART	article	N	neuter
AUX	auxiliary	NOM	nominative
		NUM	numeral
COMP	comparative		
CONJ	conjunction	OBL	oblique case
		ODu	Old Dutch
DAT	dative	OE	Old English
DEF	definite	OF	Old French
DEM	demonstrative	OHG	Old High German
Du	Dutch	OIce	Old Icelandic
		OS	Old Saxon
E	English		
ENCL	enclitic	PL	plural
		PP	past participle
F	feminine	PRES	present
		PREP	preposition
G	German	PRET	preterite
GEN	genitive	PRON	pronoun
Goth	Gothic	PTC	participle
Gr	Greek		
		REFL	reflexive
INDEF	indefinite	REL	relative
INS	instrumental		
IMP	imperative	SG	singular
IMPERS.VB	impersonal verb	SB	substantive (noun)
INF	infinitive	SUBJ	subjunctive
INFL	inflected	SUPERL	superlative
INTERJ	interjection		
		VB	verb
L	Latin	VL	Vulgar Latin
M	masculine		

A

a *prep.* + *dat./acc.* in, into; on, onto; at; to (cf. an,
  on) [OE an, on]

ā *interj.* oh!, ah!

abba *m.* abbot [< L < Gr abba < Aramean 'father']

abbet *m.* abbot; *abbete* DAT.SG [< L abbāt-em]

abinna *adv.* inside [OE on-binnan]

abūta *adv.* outside [OE ābūtan]

āch → **āga**

achta *num.* eight [OE eahta]

achtēne *num.* eighteen

achtenda, -unda *num.* eighth

aen *see* on, an

āft(e) *adj.* legal, legitimate, legally valid; *ēftes*
  GEN.SG.N; *āfte* DAT.SG.M; *āftne, ōftne*
  ACC.SG.M (~ *stōl* 'matrimonial position');
  aefter DAT.SG.F; *āfte* ACC.PL [OHG ē-haft]

āfte *n.* matrimony (sacrament); marriage; *aeftes*
  GEN.SG; *āfta, aefte* DAT.SG [from prec.]

āga *pret.pres.* to owe; have to, must (+ INFL.INF);
  hāch, āch, a(e)gh 3SG.PRES; *āch* PL.PRES;
  āge, āg(h)en, hāgon PL.PRES (forms with
  h- typical for R) [OE āgan]

āge[1] *n.* eye; *āgenum, āgnem* DAT.PL; *āgene*
  ACC.PL [OE ēaġe]

āge[2] → **āga**

aider, ei- *pron.* either; both [OE æghwæðer]

āin → **ēin**

ac *conj.* but [OE ac]

āc *conj./adv.* also; nevertheless [OE ēac]

al *adv.* entirely, thoroughly

al(le), ol- *pron./adj.* all; each; entire; *alles*
  GEN.SG.N; *alne* ACC.SG.M; *alle, olle*
  NOM/ACC.SG; *alra, alre, aller(a), alle(re)*
  GEN.PL; *alle* NOM/ACC.PL; *alla, alle* DAT.PL
  [OE eall]

āland *n.* island; coastal land

ald *adj.* old [OE eald]

alderlāsa *m.* orphan [alder 'parent' + lās 'without']

alder(- → **aller(-**

aldēr(- → **althēr(-**

aldulk → **althulk**

aldus → **althus**

alēna, -ll- *adj.* alone [OE eall āna]

algadur, allegather *adv.* completely; together
  [OE eallgædor]

alhēl *adv.* completely

alhīr *adv.* here; for this reason

alhīrfan *adv.* of this, about this

alla = alle + a (PREP)

alle *adv.* universally, commonly

allēn *adv.* equally

allerēk *pron.* each; *allerēkum* DAT.SG [cf. *ēk*]

allerērst, -ārst, -aerst *adv.* first of all

allerhāgest, alrahāgist *adj.superl.* highest of all,
  most important

allerhārist *adj.superl.* most honourable of all,
  most important [OE hār 'grey']

allerhēlichst *adj.superl.* holiest; *alderheylichsta*
  DAT.SG.M

allerliāfst *adj.superl.* dearest, most favourite

allerliāfst *adv.superl.* most of all, by preference;
  allerlyāwst

allerlīk *pron.* each; *allerlīkum* DAT.SG

allermāst *adj.superl./adv.* most important(ly);
  best of all

allerwīdest, -y- *adv.* most widely

allis *adv.* entirely, completely

almachtich → **ellemechtich**

alomme *adv.* completely (cf. **umbe**)

ālong *adj.* eternal, everlasting

alrahāgist allerhāg-

als → **as**

alsā, olsā *adv./conj.* thus, so; like, just as; when;
  alsā thet all that; *alsa ... thet* so ... that;
  alsa ...
  sa such ... as; so/as ... as [OE eall swā]

alsādēn *adj.* such; *alsādēna* DAT.PL [< dēn PP
  of dwā]

alsādēn(e), -zō-∞ *adv.* in such a way; ~ ... sā
  such ... as, those ... which; such

alsā're = alsā + er

alsek *adj.* such [< al-sel(i)k; cf. OE swelċ]

alsemin *adv.* completely

alsō∞ *adv.* so; *alsō ... sō∞* as ... as; so ... if
  (cf. **alsā**)

altāre, -ae- *m./n.* altar [< L altāre]

althēr *adv./rel.* where; wherever; whenever

althērefter *adv.* thereafter; furthermore;
  aldaeraefter

althērnēi *adv.* thereafter

althērum(be), -dār-∞ *adv.* therefore

althulk, -d- *adj.* such; *aldulker* DAT.SG.F [OE
  þulic]

althus, -d- *adv.* thus, in this way [OE þus]

altīda *adv.* always

altōmāl∞ *adv.* completely, altogether; *altomael*

alvene, -w- *num.* eleven [OE endleofan]

an *prep.* + *dat./acc.* in(to); (up)on, on(to); through, by means of; resulting in; at; ~ *kap* for sale [OE on] (cf. **on**)

ān *num./pron.* one; a(n); *ānne* ACC.SG.M (cf. **ēn**) [OE ān]

an(n)a *prep.* + *dat/acc.* in; into; on (cf. **a, on**) [OHG an-an]

and, ande, end(e) *conj.* and; as; if [OE and]

anda¹ = an + thā

anda² = and + a (PREP)

and(a)³, end *prep.* + *dat./acc.* in, on; with respect to (cf. **anna**) [Goth and]

andere = an + there

anders∞, ondris∞ *adv.* otherwise, beside

andlofta *num.* eleventh

andwerd *n.* answer; *andweert* ACC.SG [OE andwyrde]

anfara *adv.* to the front

angān *VII* to entertain, treat; *aengenzen* PP

angel *m.* angel; *anglar* NOM.PL; *anglon* DAT.PL (cf. **engel**) [< L angelus]

angne → ānich

ānich *pron./adj.* any; *angne* ACC.SG.M (cf. **ēnich**)

anna → ana

antes = and + thes

anti = and + thī

apostel *m.* apostle; *apostela, appostelen* NOM.PL [< L apostolus]

ār(i)st, aerst *num.superl./adv.* first; *ārista* DAT.SG; *ārsta* DAT.PL (cf. **ēr(o)st**)

as, als *conj./adv.* as, like; if, provided that; namely, to wit; when; ~ *dat* when; ~ *hoe dat* because (cf. **alsā**)

āsega *m.* legal official, 'lawspeaker' [OS ēo-sago]

āsta *n.* east [OE ēast]

āster *adv.* eastwards [OIce austr]

āt, -ae- *pron.* anything, ought [OE āwiht]

aubēre *adj.* manifest [OE ǣbǣre]

auth → āwia

āwia *2* to show; *auth* 3SG.PRES [OE ēawian]

axe *f.* axe; *axe* DAT.SG [OE æcs]

axle *f.* shoulder; *axla* DAT.SG [OE eaxl]

B

balde *adv.* immediately [OE bealde]

bām, -ae- *m.* tree; *bames* GEN.SG; *bām* ACC.SG; *bāmar* NOM.PL [OE bēam]

band → binda

band're = band er

ban(n) *m.* fine; order, command, injunction; *bannum, -im* DAT.PL (see also **bon(n)**) [OHG bann]

bank *f.* bench [OE benċ]

barna → berna²

barren → bera

bāsfeng *m.* lascivious, indecent grasping [OHG bōsi; OE feng]

bata *m.* profit [OIce báti]

be- see also **bi-**

bebād → bibiāda

bed *n.* bed; *bedde* DAT.SG [OE bedd]

bedda *m.* bed companion, husband [OE ġebedda]

bedinge *f.* prayer [bidda]

befara *VI* to detect, catch (red-handed) [OE faran]

befiuchta, bi- *III* to wound (by fighting); *befuchten* PP

befrēgia *2* to inquire; *befrēgad* PP [OS frāgon]

begān *anom.vb.* to enter; to catch, detect; *byginssen* PP [OE gān]

begr(i)ouwa *VI* to bury; *begroune* PP/ADJ [OE grafan]

begrēta *1* to challenge, summon; *begret* PP [OE grētan]

begrīpa *I* to detect, catch (red-handed) [OE -grīpan]

begunna, bi- *III* to begin; *bigunde* 3SG.PRET; *bigunden* PL.PRET; *begonnen* PP [OE ġinnan]

beieria *2* + *gen.* to desire, wish; *bygheret∞* 3SG.PRES; *beieriet* PL.PRES [OS gēron]

beijlum → bēl

bek, -c *n.* back [OE bæc]

bēl *m./f.* boil; *beijlum* DAT.PL [OE bȳl]

bem → wesa

bēn *n.* bone; *bēnena* GEN.PL [OE bān]

bend, -ey- *m.* bond, fetter; *beynd* ACC.SG [OE bend]

benedīa *1* to bless; *benediit* PP [< L benedīcere]

benedīd *adj./pp.* blessed; *benedīde* NOM.SG.M [from PREC]

bēnete *n.* bones, skeleton [MLG bēnte]

bēnetaburch *f.* body (as protection for the foetus)

benima *IV* to deprive; *binymeth* PL.PRES

benitha, -d- *prep.* + *dat.* underneath [OE bineoðan]

benithim, -da *adv.* below, beneath

bennon → **bonna**

bera *IV* to bear, carry; *(e)bern, barren* PP born [OE beran]

berch *m.* mountain; *berge* DAT.SG; *bergh* DAT/ ACC.SG; *berga* NOM.PL; *bergon* DAT.PL [OE beorg]

berd *f.* foetus; *berde* DAT.SG [OE ġebyrd]

berdwendene *f.* harm to a foetus

bere *f.* (hand-)barrow; *bera* DAT.SG [OE bearwe]

berēda *VII* to demonstrate, prove; *berēt* 3SG.PRES

berenda *1* to destroy; *berant* 3SG.PRES [OE rendan]

bereskintse, -ze *adj.* bare-legged [OE bær; scanca]

berjelda *m.* legal subject; *berieldan* ACC.PL

bern *n.* child; *mith -e* (DAT.SG) pregnant [OE bearn]

berna[1] *adj./pp.* born one (cf. **bera**)

berna[2]**, -a-** *III/1* to burn; *barn'* 3SG.PRES.SUBJ; *bernande* PRES.PTC/DAT.SG; *bernt/barnt* 3SG. PRES; *berne* 3SG.PRES.SUBJ [OE bærnan]

bernde → **berthene**

berne'ne = berne + hine

berthene *f.* burden; *bernde* ACC.SG [OE byrðen]

beskerma *1* to protect; *beskermet* IMP.PL [cf. OHG skirm]

beskīna *I* to shine upon; *beschīnane* INFL.INF [OE scīnan]

beslūta *II* to comprise; lock up; *bislūt* 3SG.PRES; *beslūtath* PL.PRES; *beslāt* 3SG.PRET

besma *m.* besom, rod [OE besma]

best → **gōd**

bet → **wel(l)**

bēta *1* to compensate, pay for an offence; *bētane* INFL.INF; *bēte* 3SG.PRES.SUBJ [OE bētan]

betein → **betiā**

betēna *1* to block (with osiery); *betēnt* 3SG.PRES [cf. *tēn; OE tān 'twig']

bet(t)(e)ria *2* to improve, recompense; *bettrie* 3SG.PRES.SUBJ; *betriane, betterian* INFL.INF [OE beterian]

beth, *n.* bath; *bethe* DAT.SG [OE bæþ]

bethankia *2* to thank; *bytanket* 3SG.PRES; *betankya* PL.PRES [OE þanċian]

bēthe, -eid- *adj./conj./pron.* both; *bēthe ... and* both ... and; *beyde* DAT.PL; *beyden* ACC.PL [OS bēð]

betiā *II* to cover; *betein* PP

betimbria *2* to block (with pile-work); *betimbrath* 3SG.PRES [OE timbrian]

better → **gōd**

bevia *2* to tremble, shake; *beuath* 3SG.PRES [OE bifian]

bewand(e)lia *2* to change [OS wandlon]

bewīsa *1* to prove; *bewyset* PP [OE wīsan]

beyde → **bēthe**

bi- see also **be-**

bī, bij, by *prep. + dat.* according to; by; on pain of; with; near; through; at the rate of [OE bī]

biāda *II* (+ *dat.*) to give, present, offer; order, command; *biād* 1SG.PRES; *biūt, byet* 3SG.PRES; *bād* 3SG.PRET; *bedon* PL.PRET [OE bēodan]

biār *n.* beer; *byēre* DAT.SG [OE bēor]

bibiāda *II* to order; *be-, bibād* 3SG.PRET [OE bēodan]

bidauwa *1* to cover with dew, bedew; *bidauwene* INFL.INF [cf. OE dēaw]

bidda *V* (+ *gen.*) to ask, pray; *bid(de)* 1SG.PRES; *bidda, biddet* PL.PRES; *bidde* 3SG.PRES.SUBJ; *bed* 3SG.PRET; *bēden* PL.PRET [OE biddan]

bīdia *2* to wait, linger; *bīdiane* INFL.INF [OE (and)bidian]

biechte → **bi(j)echte**

bi-era *1* to till, plough; *bi-ere* 3SG.PRES.SUBJ [OE erian]

bifā *VII* to envelop, cover; embrace; *bifangen* PP [OE fōn]

bifara[1] *adv./prep. + dat.* before

bifara[2] *VI* to find, run into, catch; *bifaert* 3SG.PRES

bifela *IV* to recommend; turn over, delegate; *bi-, befel* 3SG.PRET [OE felhan]

bifella *1* to dismiss [OE fellan]

bifinda *III* to find, come upon; *byfonden* PP

bifiuchta *III* to fight, take by fighting; assault; *bifiuchtane* INFL.INF; *bifochten* PL.PRET [OE feohtan]

bigrīpa *I* to contain, include; *bigripen* PP [OE grīpan]

bihagelīk *adj.* pleasing; COMP *byhagheliker* [cf. OE hagian]

bihalda, -e *VII* to safe, keep; retain; withhold; *bihald, behalde* 2SG.PRES.SUBJ [OE healdan]

bihalva, -wa *prep. + dat.* without; apart from

bihrōpa *VII* to raise alarm; *bihrōpe* 3SG.PRES. SUBJ

bijagia *2* to woo, court; *byhyagende* PRES.PTC [OHG jagōn]

bi(j)echte *adj.* manifest, public; ~ *wertha* (+ *gen.*) to confess [OHG bijiht]

bikenna *1* (+ *gen.*) to acknowledge; *bikenne* 1SG.PRES

bikera *1* to convert [OE ċieran]

bicringa *III* to obtain, win; *bicrongen* PL.PRET [OE cringan]

bilethia *2* to form; *bilethad* PP [OHG bilidōn]

bilidza *1* to besiege; *bileyd* PP

bilīva, -w- *I* to remain; stay; *bilēf* 3SG.PRET [OE bilīfan]

binda, -y- *III* to bind; *bynde* 3SG.PRES.SUBJ; *bindande* INFL.INF; *band* 3SG.PRET; *bundin* PL.PRET; *bonden* PP [OE bindan]

binēi *adv. byney* almost

binera¹ *1* to hinder, bother; *binere* 3SG.PRES. SUBJ [OE nierwan]

biner(r)a² *1* to feed oneself, make a living with [OE nerian]

binētha *1* to venture, risk; *binētthen* PL.PRET [OE nēðan]

biniāta *II* + *gen.* to avail oneself of, utilize; *bineten* PP [OE nēotan]

binima, be-, bij- *IV* to deprive, take away from; *benymeth* 3PL.PRES; *bijnom* 3SG.PRET [OE niman]

binna *prep.* + *dat.* within, inside [OE binnan]

biplega *V* to recommend to one's care; *biplach* 3SG.PRET [OE plegan]

biracht → **birētsa**

birāvia, -w- *2* (+ *gen.*) to rob; to deprive of; *birāvath* 3SG.PRES; *birāwade, birāvade* 3SG. PRET; *berāwed, birāvad, birāwd* PP [OE rēafian]

birēda *1* to prepare; prove, confirm; *birēt* 3SG.PRES; *birāt* PP [cf. OE ġerǣde]

birētsa *1* to issue; agree (upon) *biracht* PP [OE rǣċan]

biseka *1* to deny; *biseke* 3SG.PRES.SUBJ; [OE sacan]

bisetta *1* to occupy; *bisette* 3SG.PRET [OE settan]

bisiā *V* to see, behold; *bisīane* INFL.INF [OE sēon]

bisitta *V* to possess; have at one's disposal; *bisittane* INFL.INF; *biseten* PP [OE sittan]

bisionga *III* to read or celebrate mass; *bisonge* 3SG.PRET.SUBJ [OE singan]

biskera *IV* to mow, cut; *bischere* 3SG.PRES.SUBJ [OE scieran]

biscop *m.* bishop; *biscopar* NOM.PL [< L episcopus]

biskrīva *I* to write down; *biskrēf* 3SG.PRET [OE scrīfan]

bislā(n) *VI* to mount; decide; *bislāne* INFL.INF [OE slēan]

bislūta *II* to close, shut

bispreka *V* + *dat.* to utter; swear; *bispreke* 2SG.PRES.SUBJ [OE sprecan]

bistān *VI* to attack, set upon

biswīka *I* to succumb; give way; *bisweeck* 3SG.PRET [OE swīcan]

bitēknia *II* to signify; *biteykent* 3SG.PRES [OE tācnian]

bitella *1* to calculate (a compensation) [OE tellan]

bitetza *1* to take possession of; *biteszie* 3SG. PRES.SUBJ [G zücken]

biteykent → **bitēknia**

bitigia *2* (+ *gen.*) to accuse; *bitig(i)ath, bitig(h) eth* 3SG.PRES [cf. OE an-tiġe]

bitiūna *1* to encroach, infringe upon (somebody's rights); *bitiūne* 3SG.PRES.SUBJ [OE tīenan]

biūt → **biāda**

biwāia *VII* to blow upon; *biwāiane* INFL.INF [OHG wā(h)en]

biwēna *1* (*impers.vb.* + *gen.obj.*) to expect; *biwēne* 3SG.PRES.SUBJ [OE wēnan]

biweria *2* to confirm [OE bewarian]

blāt *adj.* poor [OE blēat]

blāta *m.* poor man; landless man

blēʼrʼem = blē (→ **bliā**) + er + him

bliā *VII* to blow; *blē* 3SG.PRET [OE blāwan]

blīka *I* to be visible; *blīke* 3SG.PRES.SUBJ [OE blīcan]

blīthe, -d- *adj.* glad, happy [OE blīðe]

blōd *n.* blood [OE blōd]

blōdelsa *m.* bloody wound

blōdich *adj.* bloody; *blōdiga* DAT.SG.M/N; ACC.SG.F [OE blōd]

blōdrennand *adj./pres.ptc.* bleeding

blōdrene *m.* bleeding, haemorrhage [OE ryne]

bobbaburch *f.* infant's protection, i.e womb, uterus

bod *n.* commandment, precept; order; *bode* DAT.SG; *boede* ACC.PL [OE bod]

boda *m.* messenger; *bode* DAT.SG; *boede* NOM/ ACC.PL; *boeden* ACC.PL [OE boda]

bodelhūs *n.* brothel [< OF bordel]

bod(i)skip *n.* message [OE bodscipe < OS]

bōc, -k *f./n.* book; *bōc* ACC.PL; *bōkem, bōkon* DAT.PL [OE bōc]

boldbreng *m.* dowry, trousseau; *~brenge* DAT.SG [< *bōdel* 'chattles']

bon *m./n.* ban, order; proclamation, summons; *bonne* DAT.SG [OE ġebann, N.]

bon *m.* legal official

bonna *VII* to proclaim, summon, ban; *bonne* 1SG.PRES; *bennon* PL.PRET; *bonnena* PP/DAT.SG.M/N [OE bannan]

bonnere *m.* magistrate's official, messenger

born → **burna**

bōte *f.* compensation; fine; remedy, cure *bōthem* DAT.PL [OE bōt]

bova, -e, boven∞ *prep.* + *dat.* above [OE bufan]

brand, -o- *m.* fire-brand; *brande* DAT.SG [OE brand]

brēd *adj.* broad; *breida* ACC.SG.N [OE brād]

breeck → **breke**

brēf *m./n.* charter; writ; *brēve* DAT.SG; *brēf* ACC.PL; *brēwm* DAT.PL [< L breve]

breid- see also **brēd**, *adj*

breid *f.* bride; *breyd* ACC.SG [OE brȳd]

breida *III* to draw; *breit* 3SG.PRES; *brudena* PP/DAT.SG.N [OE breġdan]

breinsechte *f.* brain disease; *~sechtum* DAT.PL [OE bræġn; cf. OS suht]

breka *V* to break; trespass; break into; *brecht* 3SG.PRES; *brekath* PL.PRES; *breke* 3SG.PRES. SUBJ; *breken* PRET.PL.SUBJ; *brek'i* = *breke i*; *brekande* INFL.INF; *britzen* PP [OE brecan]

breke *m.* fine, 'breach'; *breeck* [OE bryċe]

brenga, -i-, -a-, brenz(i)a, *1* to bring; *brenge, brange* 3SG.PRES.SUBJ; *brengane* INFL.INF; *brocht(e)* 3SG.PRET; *brocht* PP [OE bringan]

brēve → **brēf**

brēwm → **brēf**

briāst *f.* breast; *briāste* DAT.SG; *briāstem* DAT.PL [OE brēost]

britzen → **breka**

brochte → **brenga**

brond → **brand**

brondrād *adj.* fiery red (cf. **brand**)

brōther, -d- *m.* brother; *brōren* NOM.PL [OE brōðor]

brudena → **breida**

brūca *II* + *gen.* to enjoy; use; *brūc* 2SG.PRES. SUBJ [OE brūcan]

būc *m.* belly, stomach [OE būc]

būclamethe *f.* abdominal paralysis

buppa *prep.* + *dat./acc.* above; over

burch, -(i)g *f.* fortification; city, town; *burga* ACC.PL [OE burg]

burna, born *m.* spring; well [OE burna]

burna *III/1* to burn; *burnth* 3SG.PRES; *burnath* PL.PRES (cf. **berna**)

būta *adv./prep.* + *dat.* outside; from the outside; apart from [OE būtan]

būta *conj.* except, but

byfonden → **bifinda**

bygheret∞ → **bijeria**

byginssen → **begān**

byhyagende → **bijagia**

bynde'ne = **binde** + **hine**

C see K

D

d- see also **th-**

dā → **thī**

dād¹, -th, daed *adj.* dead; *dādes* GEN.SG.N; *dāthon* DAT.PL [OE dēad]

dād² see also **dāth**

dād(d)ēl *n.* manslaughter, murder; wergeld; *dādēle* DAT.SG [< dāthdēl; cf. OE dēaðġedāl]

dan → **than²**

dār- see also **thēr-**

dār∞ *rel.part.* who, that (cf. **thēr**)

dat → **thet** CONJ; → **thī**

dāth¹ see also **dād**

dāth², -d *m.* death; homicide; *dāda, -e* DAT.SG [OE dēað]

datter = DAT + **thēr**

dāw, -au *m./n.* dew; *dāwe* DAT.SG [OE dēaw]

dede(n) → **dwā(n)**

dēd(e) *f.* deed; action; wound, injury; *dēde* DAT.SG; *dēda* ACC.PL [OE dǣd]

deer(-) → **thēr**

dees → **thī**

dega → **dei**

dege → **duga**

dei, dī *m.* day; *deis, dīs* GEN.SG; *dī* DAT.SG; *dega* NOM.ACC.PL [OE dæġ]

decma *m.* tithes [< L decimus]

del *n.* valley, dale; *tō dele* (ADV) down [OE dæl]

dēl *m.* part; share; *tō dēle wertha* to become property of [OE dǣl]

dēla *1* to decide, pronounce judgment or verdict; *dēlane* INFL.INF; *dēled, dēlet* PP [OE dælan]

dele see also **del(v)a**

dēn → **dwā**

del(v)a *III* to delve, dig; *dele* 3SG.PRES.SUBJ [OE delfan]

dēpa *1* to baptize; *dēpe* 3SG.PRES.SUBJ [OE dīepan]

dēpere *m.* Baptist (St John)

dēpinge *f.* baptism

dernfiā *n.* concealment of moveable property; *~fiās* GEN.SG

dernsōne *f.* secret or extra-legal expiation [OE dierne; OHG suone]

dī → **dei**

dier(- → **ther; thēr(-**

dīk *m.* dike; *dīke* DAT.SG; *dīkan* ACC.PL [OE dīċ]

dīkstathul *m.* base, foundation of dike [OE staðol]

diōre *adj.* 'dear', excellent [OE dēore]

diōvel *m.* Devil; *diōwele* DAT.SG [< L diabolus]

dīst(h)ik *adv.* daily; only in: *(to) allera ~* [< ?]

doe → **thō**

dōk *m.* cloth; blindfold; *dōc* ACC.SG [OHG tuoh]

dolch *n.* wound; *dolge* DAT.SG [OE dolg]

dole *?* pride?; *mit ~* [?]

dom *m.* dam, embankment; *domman* ACC.PL [ON dammr]

dōm *m.* judgement; *dōme* DAT.SG; *dōmen* ACC.PL; *dōmum* DAT.PL [OE dōm]

dōmesdei, -dī *m.* Doomsday [OE dōmesdæġ]

drega, -a- *VI* to carry; wear; *dreghe* 2SG.PRES.SUBJ; *drōgin* PL.PRET [OE dragan]

dreppel *m.* threshold; *dreppele* DAT.SG

drinka *III* to drink; *drinket* IMP.PL [OE drincan]

drynthia *1* to drink [OE drenċan]

drīva see also **ofdrīva**

Drochten *m.* Lord; *Drochtenes* GEN.SG; *Drochtene* DAT.SG [OE dryhten]

drynthia → **drinka**

dūde → **thiōde**

duga *pret.pres.* to avail, be profitable; *dege* PL.PRES.SUBJ [OE dugan]

dum *adj.* foolish; *dumme* NOM.PL [OE dumb]

dure *f.* door; *dura* ACC.SG; *durum, durun* DAT.PL [OE duru]

dwā(n), duā(n), -ae- *anom.vb.* to do; *dēth* 3SG.PRES; *dwaed* PL.PRES; *dwē* 3SG.PRES.SUBJ; *dwāne* INFL.INF; *dede* 3SG.PRET; *deden* PL.PRET; *consent ~ to give permission to*; *(e)dēn, gedēn, dien, (ge)dān∞* PP [OE dōn]

dy(n), dyo → **thī**

E

For -ee- see -ē-

ebba *m.* ebb-tide [OE ebba]

ebiāda *II* to order; *ebād* 3SG.PRET [OE ġebēodan]

ēddre *f.* vein, blood-vessel; *ēddra* NOM.PL; *ēdderum* DAT.PL [OE ǣddre]

edel(l)īke → **ethellīke**

een → **ēn**

eflīve *adj.* dead [MHG abe-lībe]

efta *prep. + dat.* behind [OE æftan]

efter *adv.* afterwards [OE æfter]

efter *prep. + gen./dat./ins.* after; throughout; *efterthiu* after that

efterkumand *adj./m.* descendant, PL. posterity

ēftes → **āft(e)**

eg *f.* edge, sword; *egge* DAT.SG [OE ecg]

egadurad → **gaderia**

eider → **aider**

e-ifnad → **ivenia**

eigen∞ *adj.* own [cf. **ēin**]

ēin, āin *adj.* own; unfree; *eines* GEN.SG.M; *ayna* DAT.SG.N; *eina* ACC.PL.F [OE ǣgen, āgen]

ēk, (h)ēc *pron./adj.* each; *allera monna ~* each, everybody [OE ǣlċ]

elāsta *1* to carry out, perform; *elāste* 3SG.PRES.SUBJ [OE ġelǣstan]

eles *adv.* otherwise [OE elles]

elle *adv.* entirely

el(l)emachtiande *adj.* almighty

ellemachtich, al-∞ *adj.* almighty [OE ælmihtig]

ellic, elk *pron.* each, every (cf. **ēk**)

emmer *adv.* ever [OS eomēr]

emmermēr∞, ~mār *adv.* for evermore

en *prep. + dat.* on, at (cf. **an**)

ēn, een *num./indef.art.* one; a(n); *ēn* NOM.SG.M/N; *ēna, ēne* DAT.SG.M; *e(e)nen* DAT/ACC.SG.M; *ēn* NOM.SG.F; *ēner(e), -ir* DAT.SG.F; *ēne* ACC.SG.F; *ēnes* GEN.SG.N; *een* ACC.SG.N (cf. **ān**)

end(e)∞ *conj.* and (cf. **and(e)**)

end (PREP) → **anda²**, **anda³**

ende, ee-, ey- *m.* ending, conclusion; death; *anda ~ lidza* to be dying [OE ende]

enēdgad → **nēdigia**

ēng ➤ ēnich

engel *m.* angel; *enghelen* GEN.PL (cf. **angel**)

ēnich, ēng *adj.* any; *ēniga, -e* DAT.SG [OE ǣniġ]

enōch *adj.* + *gen.* enough [OE ġenōg]

entā = en + thā

enze *f.* ounce; unit of money; *enza* NOM.PL; *enzena* GEN.PL; *enzum* DAT.PL [< L uncia 1/12 pound; cf. OE ynċe]

-er(e) *encl.pron.* he

ēr[1], ee- *prep.* + *dat./adv./conj.* earlier; before; previously [OE ǣr]

ēr[2], ēre, -a *f.* honour; *era* ACC.SG; *eera* GEN.PL; *ērim, -um* DAT.PL [OE ār]

ērber *adj.* honourable; *ērbera* NOM.SG.M

erch *adj.* bad, evil; *ergon* DAT.PL; *erga, eergha* ACC.PL [OE earg]

ērdertīd *adv.* *eerdertyt* previously

ērest, -(o)st *adv./num.* first (cf. **ārst**) [OE ǣrost]

ergon ➤ erch

ēria *2* to honour; *ērie* 3SG.PRES.SUBJ; *ēret* PP [OE ārian]

erisen ➤ rīsa

erm[1] *adj.* poor; wretched; *erma* ACC.S.F [OE earm]

erm[2], ee- *m.* arm; *eermen* ACC.PL [OE earm]

erthe *f.* earth [OE eorðe] (cf. **irth-**)

erthesk *adj.* earthly, mortal; *ertheskera* GEN.PL

erthrīke *n.* earth; *ert(h)rīke* DAT.SG

erve, -w- *m.* heir, child, descendant; *erva, erwa* NOM.PL [OE ierfa]

erve *n.* land, (inherited) property [OE ierfe]

ērwerdich, -wir- *adj.* honourable, venerable

ērwerdichhēd *f.* respectability, honour(ability); *eerwirdicheyt* ACC.SG

eskepin ➤ skeppa

escriuin, eskrivin ➤ skrīva

espen *adj.* aspen [OE æspen]

et, it *prep.* + *dat.* in; at; from; out of [OE æt]

etein ➤ tiā

ēth *m.* oath; *ēth* ACC.SG; *ēthe* DAT.SG; *ēthon, -um* DAT.PL [OE āþ]

ethel *adj.* noble [OE æðele]

ethelhēd, -d- *f.* excellence

etheling *m.* freeman, 'nobleman'; *ethelinga* NOM.PL [OE æðeling]

ethellīke *adv.* nobly

etkēr *m.* spear [< etgēr, cf. OE ætgār]

etmēl(de) *n.* period of 12 or 24 hours; *etmēl* ACC.SG; *etmēldum* DAT.PL [OE edmæl]

etta = et + thā

evangelista, ew- *m.* Gospel writer, evangelist; *ewangelista, -en* NOM.PL [< L evangelista]

evangelium *n.* Gospel; *ewangelio* DAT.SG [< L evangelium]

evel, -w- *n.* evil; disease; *ewele* DAT.SG [OE yfel]

evele, -w- *adv.* evilly, wrongfully

evenhāch *adj.* equally high [OE hēah]

evennacht *f.* (vernal) equinox (21 March) [OE efnniht]

ēwa, jōwe *f.* law; common use, custom; *ēwa* DAT.SG, ACC.SG [OE ǣ(w)]

ewart, ewert ➤ werda

ewele ➤ evele

ēwelīka, -v-, -e, hēwelīke *adv.* eternally

ēwich *adj.* eternal; *ēwighe* NOM.SG.N; *ēwga* DAT.SG [cf. OE ǣwignes]

ewrocht ➤ werka

F

fād *m.* counterfeiting coins of less than official value; counterfeit coin [< *faihōd]

fader ➤ feder

fadera *m.* godparent, esp. godfather; *fadera* NOM.PL; *faderum* DAT.PL [OE ġefædera]

falla *VII* to fall; concern, regard, pertain to; amount to; declare unfounded, reject; *fallanda* PRES.PTC; *falt* 3SG.PRES; *fallath, -eth* PL.PRES; *falle* 3SG.PRES.SUBJ; *fōlen* PL.PRET [OE feallan]

falsk, falesc *adj./sb.n.?* false; falsehood; counterfeit money; *falska, falsk(e), falleske* DAT.SG [< L falsus]

fan ➤ fon

fā(n), -ae-, fōn *VII* to catch, seize; *tho (= tō) kerle ~* to bring the man forward; *fēth* 3SG.PRES; *faene* INFL.INF; *fēng* 3SG.PRET [OE fōn]

fand ➤ finda

fana, -o- *m.* banner, standard [OE fana]

fanare, -o- *m.* standard bearer

fara[1] *prep.* + *dat./acc.* before (cf. **fori**) [OE fore]; *adv.* in front; *an ~* in front

fara[2] *VI* to go, proceed; *farande* INFL.INF; *fer(e)th, far(e)th* 3SG.PRES; *fōr* 3SG.PRET; *fōrin* PL.PRET [OE faran]

farend *m.* ulcerous disease; *farendum* DAT.SG [< fara[2]]

farra ➤ fīr

fatia *2* to seize, get hold of; *fatada* PP/ACC.SG.N [OE fatian] feder, -a- *m.* father [OE fæder]

federerve *f.* paternal inheritance, patrimony; ~erwe DAT.SG

feitha ➤ fēth(e)

fel *n.* skin; *felle* DAT.SG [OE fell]

feld *m.* field; *felda* DAT.SG [OE feld]

fele *adv.* very (see also **fule**) [OE fela]

fēle *f.* touch [*fōli]

fella *1* to pay for; *fellane* INFL.INF [OE fiellan]

fenne *f.* meadow; *fennon* DAT.PL [*fanja]

fēra *1* to carry; lead; *fērane, -ene* INFL.INF; *fērth* 3SG.PRES; *fierden* PL.PRET [OE fēran]

ferd ➤ frethe

fere *f.* profit [OE fyre]

ferech *m./n.* life [OE feorh]

ferest *num./adv.* first [OE fyrest]

ferra, -e ➤ fīr *adj*

ferst *n.* period, interval; delay; *ferstis* GEN.SG [OE fierst]

fest *adj.* firm [OE fæst]

feste *adv.* firmly [OE fæste]

festia *2* to fast; *festade* 3SG.PRET [OE fæst(i)an]

festnia *2* to fasten; *ifestnad* PP [OE fæstnian]

fēth ➤ fā(n)

fēth(e) *f.* feud; *feitha* ACC.PL [OE fæhðu]

fethem *m.* fathom (= six feet, 1.8 m.); *fethma* GEN.PL [OE fæðm]

fiā *n.* moveable property; money; *fiā* DAT.SG [OE feoh]

fiā-ēth *m.* 'property oath'; ~ēthe DAT.SG

fiāl *n.* wheel [OE hwēol] (cf. **thiāl**)

fiand *m.* enemy; *fianda* ACC.PL [OE fēond]

fiarda *num.* fourth [OE feorda]

fiardahalf *num.* 3½

fiardandēl *m./n.* quarter, ¼

fierden ➤ fēra

fīf, -ij-, -y- *num.* five [OE fif]

fīfta, -e *num.* fifth [OE fifta]

fīftahalf *num.* 4½

fīftīnda *num.* fifteenth

fīftīne, -tēne *num.* fifteen

fil(i) *m./n.* grass-land; *fili* ACC.SG [OE fileðe]

finda *III* to find; *fand, -t* 3SG.PRET; *funden* PL.PRET [OE findan]

fiower ➤ fiuwer

fīr *adj.* far; COMP *ferra, -e, farra* right, 'dexter' [OE feorr]

fīr *adv.* far; *(al)sa fīr … sa* in as far as, in so much as

firia *2* to celebrate; *firet* PP [< L fēria]

firne *f.* crime; tresspass; *firna* ACC.PL [OE firen]

fisk *m.* fish; *fiskar* NOM.PL [OE fisc]

fiuchta, -g- *III* to fight; *fiuchtath* PL.PRES; *fugtin* PL.PRET; *fuchten* PP [OE feohtan]

fiuldfarende *adj./pres.ptc.* travelling through the fields; ~ *man* hawker, pedlar

fiūr *n.* fire; *fiūre* DAT.SG [OE fȳr]

fiuwer, -io- *num.* four [OE feower]

fiuwerti(c)h *num.* forty; *fiowertega* DAT.PL

fiuwertīnda *num.* fourteenth

flāsk *n.* flesh; *flāske* DAT.SG [OE flǣsc]

flāt ➤ fliāta

flechtich *adj.* flying; ~ *wesa* to be in flight, on the run [cf. OE flyht]

fliā *II* to fly; to perish; *fliānde* PRES.PTC [OE flēon]

fliāga *II* to flee; *flēgin, fleeghen* PL.PRET [OE flēogan]

fliāta *II* to flow; *flāt* 3SG.PRET [OE flēotan]

flōd *m.* flood-tide [OE flōd]

foer(- ➤ for(-

fōgia *2* to add; *fōgade* 3SG.PRET [OS fōgian]

folgere *m.* assessor; oathhelper, cojuror; *folgerum* DAT.PL

folg(h)erne∞ *adv.* right willingly

fol(g)ia, fulghia *2 + dat.* to follow; *fol(g)iath* PL.PRES; *folgiath* IMP.PL; *folgade* 3SG.PRET [OE folgian]

folk, -ck *n.* people; army; *folkes, -is* GEN.SG; *folke, folck* DAT.SG; *folk* ACC.PL [OE folc]

folkomelīke, v- *adv.* perfectly, completely

folla ➤ fule

fon, fan∞, v-∞ *prep. + dat.* of; by; out of; from; because of; concerning; on behalf of [OS fan]

fōn ➤ fān

font ➤ funt

for- see also ur-

for, -oe- *prep. + dat.* for; before [OE for]

forbarna *1* to burn down; *foerbarnd* PP

fordera ➤ forth

forder(v)a *III* to destroy; *foerdoeren* PP [OE deorfan]

fore ➤ fori

foremund ➤ formund

forespreka *m.* advocate; spokesman; *foresprekan* ACC.PL

forfērd *adj./pp. foerfeerd* afraid [OE fǣran]

forfolla *1* to fulfill; *forfolla* PL.PRES.SUBJ

forgaderia *2* to get together; *foergaederden* PL.PRES; *woergaderet* PP

forgān *VII* to fare with; *forgēn* PP

forgifnisse∞ *f.* poison

forhanden *adv.* at hand, present

forhela *VI* to hide; *foerhoelen* PP [OE helan]

fori, -e *prep.* + *acc.* for (cf. **fara**[1])

foribrenga, -a- *III* testify; *foribrangath* 3SG.PRES

forifongere *m.* substitute, bailsman; *forifongera* ACC.PL

fōr'im = *fōr* + *him*

forjagia, -jaīa *2* to chase away, put to flight [OHG jagōn]

forke *f.* pitchfork; *forka, forke* DAT.SG [< L furca]

forkrīgia, -krīa *2* to obtain; *foercrighet* 3SG.PRES; *foercrya* PL.PRES [MHG kriegen]

forma *num./adj.* first; *forme* NOM.SG.N [OE forma]

formītha *I* to avoid [OE mīðan]

formund *m.* guardian; spouse, husband; *foremunda* DAT.SG [OE mund]

forskriven *pp./adj.* afore-written, afore-mentioned. *vorscrioune*

forslān *VI* to defeat, beat; *foerslayn* PP

forsmāia *2* to despise, reject; *forsmāge* 3SG.PRES. SUBJ [OHG smāhen]

fornima *IV* to learn; *fornōm* 3SG.PRET; *fornāmin* PL.PRET

forsta *m.* prince; *foersten* NOM.PL [cf. OE fyr(e)st]

forstān *VI* to understand

fortella *1* to tell; INF *vertellen*∞ [OE tellan]

forth *adv.* forth; forwards; furthermore; thereupon, later on; henceforth; *alsā ~ deis sā* immediately on the day when; COMP *forthera, -d-* further [OE forð]

fort(h)mēr *adv.* furthermore; *voer(t)meer, woer-*

forthrēd *m.* store, supplies; *~rēde* NOM.PL [OE rǣd]

forthskeft *n.* eternal life; *~skefte* DAT.SG [OE forðgesceaft]

forwinninge, ver- *f.* victory

forwund(e)ria *2* to marvel; *foerwonderende* PRES.PTC.PL

fōr ➔ **fara**

fōt *f.* foot; *fōta* GEN.PL [OE fōt]

foune *f.* girl, virgin; *founa* ACC.SG [OE fæmne]

framede *adj./m.* stranger [OE fremde]

frāna *m.* 'frana', legal official ['(representative) of the lord', cf. OE frēan, GEN.SG]

frēgia *2* (+ *gen.*) to ask; *frēgie* 3SG.PRES.SUBJ [OS frāgon]

frei ➔ **frī**

frethe, -o, -d-, ferd *m.* peace, protection; fine for breach of peace; *fredes* GEN.SG; *frede* DAT.SG; *fretha* ACC.PL [OE freoðu]

fretma *m.* bone-rot; *fretma* DAT.SG [cf. OE fretan]

frī, frei *adj.* free (not under feudal obligation) [OE frēo]

frīlīk *adj.* free; *frīlīke* DAT.SG.N [OE frēolīċ]

frīlīke *adv.* freely

friōnd ➔ **friūnd**

Frīsa ➔ **Frēsa**

frīstōl *m.* right to have tribunals ('free chair') [OE stōl]

friūdelf *m.* lover; husband; abductor [cf. OHG friudil 'lover' + OFris liāf]

friūnd *m.* friend; PL kinsmen, relatives; *wrinden*∞ NOM.PL; *friōnda* GEN.PL [OE frēond]

frō∞ *adj.* happy [OHG frō]

frōlikhēd∞ *f.* happiness

frōwe, -a, -ou- *f.* lady; wife; *vrouwe* DAT.SG; *frōwe* ACC.SG; *frouwa* NOM.PL; *vrouwena* GEN.PL [OHG frouwa]

fruchtich *adj.* fertile, fruitful; *wruchtik* [< L fruct-]

fuchten ➔ **fiuchta**

ful *adj.* full; *fulla* DAT.SG.N [OE full]

fule, -a, folla *adj.* + *gen.* much; many

ful(e) *adv.* much; very (see also **fele**)

fulghia ➔ **fol(g)ia**

fulkuma *IV* to be born alive

fulwunia *2* to persist; *fulwunige* 3SG.PRES.SUBJ [OE wunian]

funden't = funden + hit

funt, -o- *n.* baptismal font; *funte* DAT.SG [< L font-em]

further *adv.*COMP furthermore, in addition (cf. **forth**)

fyf ➔ **fīf**

fyr ➔ **fīr**

G

gā *m.* district; *gā* ACC.SG [Goth gawi, G Gau]

ga(e)d(e)ria *2* to gather; *gaedrie* 3SG.PRES.SUBJ; *egadurad* PP [OE gadrian]

gaderlēda *1* to bring together; *gaderlet* 3SG.PRES [OE lǣdan]

game *f.* favour, pleasure; *gama* ACC.SG [OE gamen]

gān, -ae- *anom.vb.* to go; *geet* 3SG.PRES; *gaet* IMP.PL; *ghinghe* 3SG.PRET; *ghinghen* PL.PRET [OE gān] (cf. **(g)unga**)

gāstelīk *adj.* spiritual; canonical; *gāstelīka* DAT.SG [OE gāstlič]

gē *interj.* yes [OE ġē]

gedēn → **dwā(n)**

gehoert∞ → **hēra²**

gelden *adj.* golden, of gold; *geldene* ACC.SG.M [OE gylden]

gemen∞ *pron.* no one

gemmen → **jemma**

gēn∞ *pron.* nobody; *gheen ... neer* neither ... nor

genēta∞ *II + gen.* to enjoy; *ghenēt* PL.PRES [OE ġenēotan]

gēngen, genth → **gunga**

genima *IV* to take; *genōmin* PRET.PL

genz(i)e *adj.* current [< gunga]

gerdel *m.* girdle; *ger(d)le* DAT.SG [OE gyrdel]

gerne∞ *adv.* gladly; eagerly (cf. **ierne**)

gers *n.* grass, herb; turf, sod; *gerse* DAT.SG; *to gerse* 'for cutting sod(s)'; *gerso* NOM.PL [OE gærs]

gēs *f.pl.* geese; *ghees* [OE gēs]

gesiā(n) *V* to see; *gesēgin* PRET.PL

geskeppa *V* to create, ordain; *ghescoep* 3SG.PRET (*ghe-∞*) [scieppan]

geskīa∞ *1* to happen; *geschiede* 3SG.PRET [OHG giskehan]

geven∞ → **ieva**

gewinna *III* to accept; gain; *gewinne* PL.PRES.SUBJ [OE ġewinnan]

gh- → **g-**

gheheylighet → **hēligia**

ghesecht → **sedza**

ghiis = gī + es

gī∞, gy∞ *pron.* you (PL) (cf. **ī**)

gled *adj.* slippery; *glede* DAT.SG [OE glæd]

God *m.* God; *Godes, -is, -oe-* GEN.SG; *Gode, -i, -oe-* DAT.SG [OE God]

godeskniucht *m.* servant of God, priest, monk

godishūs *n.* church; *~hūses* GEN.SG; *~hūse* DAT.SG; *~hūsum* DAT.PL

godismon *m.* cleric, clergyman; *godismonnum* DAT.PL

gōd¹, -oe- *adj.* good; *alsā ~ sā* as much as; *goet* NOM.SG.M; *gōda* DAT.SG; *gōdne, gōd* ACC.SG.M; *goede* NOM.PL; *gōdera* GEN.PL; *bet(t)era* COMP.ACC.SG.N; *best* SUPERL; *besta* ACC.PL [OE gōd]

gōd², -ue- *n.* property; *gōdes, -is* GEN.SG; *gōde* DAT.SG; *gōd, gued* ACC.SG [OE gōd]

gōdelīk, -ilīk *adv.* goodly [OE gōdlīče]

gōdeweb *n.* gold brocade [OE webb]

godfruchtich *adj.* God-fearing [OE fyrht]

godlīk *adj.* divine; *godlīke* NOM.SG.F

goet → **gōd¹**

gold, -t *n.* gold; *golde* DAT.SG [OE gold]

golde → **ielda**

golden *adj.* of gold (cf. **gelden**)

grācie *f.* grace [< L gratia]

grāt, -ae- *adj.* great, big, large; *graet* NOM.SG.N; *grāta, graet* DAT.SG.M/N; *grāten(e)* ACC.SG.M; *grāter* DAT.SG.F [OE grēat]

gref *m.* grave; *grewe* DAT.SG [OE græf]

grēne *adj.* green; *grēnes* GEN.SG.M [OE grēne]

grēta¹ *1* to greet; accuse; *grēt* PP [OE grētan]

grēta² *1* to enlarge; *grēt* PP [< grāt]

grētene *f.* accusation, charge [< grēta¹]

grēva, -w- *m.* count [OHG grāvo]

grim *adj.* fierce; *grimma* ACC.PL [OE grimm]

grimlīk *adj.* fierce; *grymmelick* ACC.SG.N

grimlīke *adv.* fiercely

grundiet *n.* pool behind a dike caused by dike-burst; *~iete* ACC.PL [OE grund; ġeat]

gundtma = gund (→ **(be-)jenna**) + mā

gued → **gōd²**

gunga, unga *VII* to go; *genth, gunth* 3SG.PRES; *geng, gunge* 3SG.PRES.SUBJ; *gēngen, gengin* PL.PRET [OE gangan]; cf. **gān**

gunth → **gunga**

H

hā *interj.* ha!

habba → **hebba**

hāch¹, hāgon → **āga**, *vb.*

hāch² *adj.* high; *hāga* ACC.SG.M; *hācha* NOM.PL; *hār* COMP; *hāgist, -est* SUPERL [OE hēah]

hade → **hebba**

haet → **hebba**

hāge *adv.* highly; solemnly

hāgere = hāch² + er

halda *VII* to hold; keep, maintain; retain; *hal(d)st* 2SG.PRES; *hald* 2SG.PRES.SUBJ; *halde,*

holden∞ PL.PRES.SUBJ; *haldane* INFL.INF;
hīldon, -en PL.PRET; *hīlde, hēlde*
PL.PRET.SUBJ; *halden* PP [OE healdan]

hāle *adv.* much, far ('whole') [cf. OE hāl]

half *adj.* half [OE healf]

hālīk *adj.* high; *hālīka* DAT.SG; *hālīke* ACC.PL
[OE hēah-]

hals *m.* neck; body; life; *halse* DAT.SG [OE heals]

halst → **halda**

halve *f.* side; *halvem* DAT.PL in: *fon Godes* ~ on
God's behalf [OE healf]

hand *f.* hand; kind; *handa* GEN.PL; *aller* ~
all kind of; *handum* DAT.PL [OE hand]
(cf. **hond**)

handskōch *m.* glove [OE scōh]

hār → **hāch²**

har(a) *pron.* her; their; theirs (cf. **hira, hire**)

harkia *2* to listen, hark [cf. OE heorcnian]

hāstelīke *adv.* vehemently, violently [OE
hǣstelīċe]

hat → **hwet**

hat → **hebba**

hāt → **hēta**

haud → **hāved**

haudia *2* to behead, decapitate; *haudie*
3SG.PRES.SUBJ

haudlēs(e)ne *f.* head ransom, money paid to
avert capital punishment [OIce höfuð-
lausn]

haudstō *f.* cathedral, see [OE stōw]

hāved, -th, haud, hāwid *n.* head; *hāveth* ACC.SG
[OE hēafod]

hāveddēd *f.* capital crime; *~dēda* ACC.PL

hāvedlās *adj.* 'headless', without a leader;
hauedlāsa DAT.SG.M

hāvednēd *f.* case of emergency; *-nēda* ACC.PL

hava, hawa → **heve**

hāveth → **hāved**

hāwid → **hāved**

hē → **hī**

hebba, habba *1* to have; *habbe, heb(be)* 1SG.
PRES; *he(e)ft*∞*, hewet*∞*, het(h), hat, haet*
3SG.PRES; *hebbat(h), -et, habbet, habba, -e,
hebb'* (= *hebbe*) PL.PRES; *hebbe, habbe* 3SG.
PRES.SUBJ; *hebben* PL.PRES.SUBJ; *hebbane*
INFL.INF; *hede, hade, heed, hied* 3SG.PRET.
IND/SUBJ; *hieden, heed* PL.PRET.IND/SUBJ
[OE habban]

hēc → **ēk**

hēd *f.* skin [OE hȳd]

hede → **hebba**

heed → **hebba**

heer → **here**

heer → **hēr**

hef *n.* sea [OE hæf]

hēgelīke *adv.* solemnly, reverendly; COMP
hēgelkere

hei *m.* thought, mind, heart [OE hyge]

hēia *1* to open a court session with all the
necessary rites and prescriptions; *hēida*
PP/DAT.SG [OE hieġan]

heila → **hēla**

heilig → **hēlich**

hēc → **ēk**

hēl *adj.* whole; firm; dry; *hēles* GEN.SG.N
(cf. **hāle**)

hēla, heila *m.* heel [OE hēla]

helde¹ *f.* grace, divine clemency; favour, loyalty
[OE hyldo]

helde² *f.* 1. hiding-place; trunk, chest; 2. fetter;
heldem DAT.PL [OHG halti]

helde³ → **halda**

hēlich, -ech, hilg-, -ei- *adj.* 1. holy; *hēl(e)ga,
heiliga, heilighen, hēlege, heyligha* OBL;
hēliga, hilgha M.PL saints; *hēligon, hēlgum,
heylighum* DAT.PL; 2. PL *thā -a* the church;
the host, Eucharist [OE hāliġ]

hēligia *2* to sanctify; *gheheylighet*∞*, heyligat*
PP [OE hālgian]

helm *m.* helmet [OE helm]

helpa *III + dat.* to help; *helpande* PRES.PTC;
help(e) 3SG.PRES.SUBJ [OE helpan]

hemethe *f.* undershirt, undergarment [OE
hemeðe]

hemliācht *adj.* clear; *hemliāchtes* GEN.SG.M
[hem 'village']

hemel- → **himil-**

hēmeswei *m.* village road, local road; *~wegan*
ACC.PL

hēr¹, -ee- *n.* hair [OE hær]

hēr² → **hwether**

hēr(a)¹ *m.* lord; Lord; landlord; *hēra(n)* NOM/
ACC.PL; *hērum, hērim* DAT.PL [OE hēarra
< OS hērro]

hēra², -ee- *1* to hear; belong to; *heerth* 3SG.PRES;
hērden, heerden PL.PRET; *hērd, ghehoert*∞
PP [OE hēran]

hēre *f.* hearing

here, hiri, heer *m.* army, armed band; *hiri, heer* DAT.SG [OE here]

herefona *m.* army banner; *hirifona* ACC.SG; *~fonan* ACC.PL [OE fana]

hereferd *m.* military expedition, campaign; *~ferd* DAT.SG [OE fyrd]

herenāt *m.* comrade in arms; *~nātan* NOM.PL [OE ġenēat]

hereskild *m.* band of soldiers; *~skilde* DAT.SG

heretēken *n.* banner, standard [OE tācn]

herewei *m.* highroad, military road

hēre *f.* rent [OE hȳr]

hērewere *f.* leased property; *hērwerum* DAT.PL

hērich *adj.* + *dat.* obedient [cf. OE hīeran]

herne *f.* corner; *herna* ACC.PL [OE hyrne]

herte *f.* heart; *herta, -e* DAT/ACC.SG [OE heorte]

hertoga *m.* duke; *hertigan* ACC.PL [OE heretoga]

hērskipi *n.* dominion, rule (cf. hēr[a])

het → hit

hēt *adj.* hot; *hēta* ACC.PL [OE hāt]

hēta *VII* to call, be called; order; *hāt, hēt* 3SG.PRES; *hēte* 3SG.PRES.SUBJ; *hīton* PL.PRET; *ehētin, hieten, ghehēten*∞ PP [OE hātan]

hēte *f.* heat [OE hǣtu]

het(h) → hebba

hēthen, heyden *adj.* heathen, pagan (not Christian); PL *heydana, -ena, -enen* heathens [OE hǣðen]

heth'ere = heth (→ hebba) + -er

heve, ha-, -w- *f.* possessions, property, goods, stock; *hava* DAT.SG; *hewa* NOM/ACC.PL; *hewena* GEN.PL; *hevum* DAT.PL; *hava* ACC.PL [OHG haba]

hēwelīke → ēwelīke

hī → see also ī

hī, hy *pron.* he; *him, hem* DAT.SG; *hini, hine, -ne* (ENCL), *hem* ACC.SG; REFL himself [OE hē]

hia, hya, iha, ia, ya *pron.* they; *se, sye*∞ NOM/ACC (ENCL; unstressed); *him, himmen, hemmen, hyaren, hoer*∞, *hōren*∞ DAT; *har* DAT/ACC; *hia* ACC; REFL themselves [OE hīe]

hia's = hia + se

hia't = hia + hit

hiit → hit

hied → hebba

hild → helde[1]

hilde, hildon → halda

hilg- → hēlich

hille *f.* hell [OE hell]

hilleporte *f.* gate of hell; *~porta* DAT.SG [< L porta]

him → hī, hia

himmen → hia

himel, -ul, -y- *m.* heaven; sky; *himule* DAT.SG [OS himil]

himelscilde *f.* church tax; *~scilda* ACC.SG [OE scyld]

himelrīke *n.* heaven, heavenly kingdom; *himulrīkes* GEN.SG; *himelrīke, hemelrīk(e)* DAT.SG [OE rīċe]

hī'ne = hī + hine

hini → hī

hio[1] = io → iuwe

hio[2] → hiu

hīr, -ii- *adv.* here [OE hēr]

hira, ihera, hyara, -e *pron.* their [OE hiera]

hīrbuppa, *adv.* above, supra

hire *pron.* her; *hires* GEN.SG.M; *hara* ACC.SG (cf. hiu)

hiri(-) → here(-)

hirte *f.* heart [OE heorte]

hīrtō *adv.* to this

hīrumbe *adv.* about this, because of this

hīrup *adv.* hereupon, after this; *hiirwp* [OE upp]

his → wesa

hī't = hī + hit

hit, -ii-, het ∞ *pron.* it [OE hit]

hit ne sē *conj.* unless

hiu *pron.* she; *se, zee* NOM/ACC (ENCL); *hire, heer* ACC [OE hēo]

hiūde *adv.* today; *~ te dei* today, this very day [OHG hiuta]

hiūdega *adv.* today

hlakkia *2* to laugh; *hlakkade* 3SG.PRET [OIce hlakka]

hlāpa *VII* to leap, jump; attack; *hlāpth, hlēpth* 3SG.PRES [OE hlēapan]

hleste *f.* attention, silence; *hleeste* ACC.SG [OE hlyst]

hlidia *2* to provide with a flap-valve or clack (see explanary note); *hlidiane* INFL.INF [OE ġehlidian]

(h)lūd *adj.* loud, noisy; *lūder* DAT.SG.F [OE hlūde]

(h)lūd, -uw- *n.* noise, sound; *lūde* DAT.SG [OE hlūd]

hnekka *m.* neck [OE hnecca]

hō, hoe → hū

hocca, -ck- *m.* headgear, coif [< OF huque?]

hōd *m.* hat [OE hōd]

hoder → hwether

hoep → hope, hopia

hoer(e)∞ *pron.* their (cf. hia)

hof *n.* court; courtyard; *hove, howe* DAT.SG [OE hof]

hoftigia *2* to pen up, confine; *hofftiget* 3SG.PRES [OE hæftan]

hōf up → upheffa

hol *n.* hole, gap; *hole* ACC.PL [OE hol]

hold *adj.* loyal, faithful, dutiful [OE hold]

holda *m.* kinsman, relative [from prec.]

holt *n.* wood; *holte* DAT.SG [OE holt]

holten *adj.* wooden; *holtena* ACC.SG.F

hond *f.* hand; *hond* DAT.SG; *honda* ACC.PL; *hondum, -on* DAT.PL (cf. hand)

hongia *2* to hang; *hongath* 3SG.PRES [OE hangian]

hōp *m.* ring, 'hoop' [OE hōp]

hope, hoep *f.* hope [OE hope]

hopia *2* to hope; *hoep* 1SG.PRES [OE hopian]

hōr *n.* fornication [OE hōr]

horen → hia

hot → hwet

hove → hof

howe → hof

(h)regbreka *V* to break someone's back on the wheel; *regbrek'* 3SG.PRES.SUBJ [OE hrycg]

(h)reil *m.* cloth (cf. note to *Statutes of Magnus*) [OE hrægl]

(h)reilmerk *f.* 'cloth-mark', certain currency; *reilmerk* ACC.PL

hrene *m.* smell [cf. OE hrenian]

hrīf *m./n.* rake; *rhīve* DAT.SG [OIce hrífa]

(h)rīvia *2* to rake, level by raking; *rīwat* PP

(h)rōft *f.* cry, shout; *wēpena rōfte* DAT.SG call to arms, alarm [from foll.]

(h)rōpa *VII* to call; *hrōpath* PL.PRES; *rōpande* PRES.PTC; *hrīep* 3SG.PRET [OE hrōpan]

hū, hō, hoe *pron./conj.* how; why; so that [OE hū]

hulp∞ *f.* help

hunderd, hondert *num.* hundred [OE hundred]

hungerich, hon- *adj.* hungry [OE hungry]

hunich *m.* honey; *hunige* DAT.SG [OE hunig]

hūs, -uu- *n.* house; *hūse* DAT.SG [OE hūs]

hūsing *m.* freeholder; freeholding peasant; *hūsingar* ACC.PL

hūslāda m. tax on houses [mix of ~*lōtha* and ~*laga*?]

hūsliūde *m.pl.* landowning freemen, 'householders'; ~*liūdum* DAT.PL

hūsmon *m.* free peasant, owner of farmstead

hūtā = hū + hit + thā

hvanne → hwand(e)

hwǎ *pron.* who; whoever; anyone, *hwae* [OE hwā]

hwā(n) *VII* to hang; *hwānde* INFL.INF [OE hōn]

hwand(e), (h)want(e), hvanne *conj.* for, because [OS hwande]

hwarl *m.* turn(ing), rotation; *hwarlar* NOM.PL [OHG hwirvil]

hwāsā *pron.* whoever (often preceded by sā)

hwēlik, -c *pron.* whoever, whichever; + GEN.PL: each, every; *hwēlikera* GEN.SG.F; *hwēlikum* DAT.SG [OE hwælċ]

hwēr, -ee-, wier *adv./pron.* where [OE hwær]

hwērsā *adv.* when(ever); *hwērzoe∞, hweersoe*

hwērsā'r = hwērsā + thēr

hwērum(be) *pron.* why

hwet, hot(sō), hat *pron.* what; whatever; ~ *wi Frīsa* all we Frisians; *wat∞* [OE hwæt]

hwether, -d(d)-, hēr, hoder, -ir, hōr *conj.* whether; which of two; *(sa)* ~ *sa ... sa, soe* whether ... or; *hēr ... soe ... iefta* whether ... or ... or; *hoder ... than* whether ... or [OE hwæðer]

hwīla *1* to remain, stay; *hwīle* 3SG.PRES.SUBJ [cf. OE hwīl]

hwīt *adj.* white; *witta∞* DAT.SG [OE hwīt]

hws → wī

hya → hia

I and J

ī, hī, hy, J *pron.* 1. you (PL); 2. you (SG polite); *iū, jō, ū∞* DAT/ACC [OE ġē]

ia → hia

iā(n) *V* (+ gen./acc.) to admit, plead guilty; *an ... iēth* 3SG.PRES agrees with; *iē* 3SG.PRES.SUBJ; *jēn* PL.PRET [OHG jehan]

iāhwēlik *pron./adj.* each [OE ǽghwælċ]

īdle *adv.* vainly [OE īdel]

iē → iā(n)

iecht *pp./adj.* proven; *jechta* NOM.SG.N

iechta *m.* confession; *a iechta* undeniably [cf. OHG bī-jiht]

iechta *1* to prove, demonstrate (in court)

iechtech *adj.* proven, manifest

ief see also ieva

ief *conj.* 1. if, in case; 2. or (see ieftha) [OE ġif]

ieft(h)a, -e *conj.* or [OS eftha, -o]

iefte *f.* gift; privilege; *jefte* DAT.SG; *iefta, jefta*
    ACC.PL; *ieftum* DAT.PL [OE ġift]

ield *n.* money; wergeld; *ieldes*; GEN.SG; *ielde*
    DAT.SG; *ieldem* DAT.PL [OE ġield]

ielda *III* to pay; *ieldane* INFL.INF; *ield, ielt*
    3SG.PRES; *golde* PL.PRET.SUBJ [OE ġieldan]

ieldebrōther *m.* guild-brother; ~*brōtheron*
    DAT.PL [OE ġild-]

ieldeswester *f.* guild-sister; ~*swesteron* DAT.PL

ielren *adj.* (of) alder wood; *ielrena* DAT.SG.M
    [OE ælren]

ielťer = ielt (→ ielda) + er

iemma *pron.* you (PL); *gemmen* DAT [< ī + man]

iena *pron.* that, those; *ien* PL [OHG jenēr]

jēn → iā(n)

iens *prep.* + *acc.* against [cf. OE (on-)ġeġn]

iēr *n.* year, *iēre* DAT.SG; *iēra* ACC.PL; *iēra* GEN.PL
    (*iēra hēc* each year) [OE ġēar]

iērich *adj.* adult, of years

ierde *f.* rod; yard; *allera ierdik* [< *ierda* GEN.PL
    + *ek*] each yard [OE ġierd]

ierdik → ierde

ieria *2* (+ *gen.*) to covet; ~ *ova* to yearn
    for, hanker after; *ieraden* PL.PRET
    [OHG gerōn]

ierne *adv.* eagerly [OE ġeorne]

iēth → iā(n)

ieva, jowa *V* to give; *gheven∞* INF; *ievene*
    INFL.INF; *iefth* 3SG.PRES; *ieve, iuwe, jowe*
    3SG.PRES.SUBJ; *ief, jef, iof, gaf∞* 3SG.PRET;
    iouwen, geven∞ PP [OE ġiefan]

ieve¹ *f.* gift; *ievem* DAT.PL [OE ġiefu]

iēve² *adj.* acceptable, good [MHG gæbe]

ic, i(c)k *pron.* I; *mī, my* DAT.SG [OE iċ]

il *m.* footsole [OE ile]

in *prep.* + *dat./acc.* in, into [OE in]

ina → in(n)a

inda = in + thā

infiuchta *III* to fight oneself into; *infiuchte*
    3SG.PRES.SUBJ

ingunga *VII* to (re-)enter; *ingenth* 3SG.PRES

inhalia *2* to overrule; *in ... haliane* INFL.INF
    [OS halon]

inledza *1* to deposit

inlēge *f.* deposit; *inlēgum* DAT.PL [OHG lāge]

inlīke *adv.* intensely; piously

in(n)a *prep.* + *dat./acc.* in; into [OE innan]

inōr, -ūr *prep.* + *acc.* to; across [< in + over]

inra *adj.*COMP interior

inrost *adj.superl.* he who lives most land
    inwards; *inrosta* DAT.SG; *inreste*
    ACC.SG. innermost

insigel *n.* seal [< L insigillum]

inūr → inōr

inweter *m.* inland waterway; *inwetir* ACC.PL

inwrētse *adj.* piercing, penetrating [cf. wreka *V*]

ioldfretho *m.* fine for breach of the peace of the
    guild; ~*fretho* ACC.SG (cf. ielde-)

ioldskipi *n.* guild, brotherhood; ~*skipi* ACC.SG

iōn *prep.* + *acc.* against [OE ġeġn, ġēn]

jonkfroulikheit *f.* virginity; *jonckfroulikheyt*
    DAT.SG [< MHG junkfroue]

jonkfrowelīk *adj.* virgin, virginal

iowa → ieva

jōwe → ēwa

irthbivinge *f.* earthquake [cf. OE bifian]

irthkining *m.* earthly king

irthrīke *n.* earthly kingdom, earth; -*rīkes* GEN.SG

is → wesa

īs *n.* ice; *īse* DAT.SG [OE īs]

is't = is + hit

it(t)a = it (→ et) + thā

iung, -o- *adj.* young [OE ġeong, ġung]

iungera *adj./*COMP disciple; *jungeran* ACC.PL

iūwe, iū *pron.* your (PL)

ivenes *adv.* equally (cf. even-)

ivinhār *adj.* + *dat.* equally high

ivenia *2* to level, make even; *e-ifnad, e-ivenad*
    PP [OE efnian]

ivenkerstena *m.* fellow Christian

C and K

kairscip → keiser-

cald *adj.* cold [OE ċeald]

kalde *f.* cold [OHG kaltī]

kampa → kempa²

canonisi(e)ren∞ *1* to canonize [< L canonisēre]

cāp, k- *m.* purchase, buying; *cāp(e)* DAT.SG [OE
    ċēap]

cāpia, k- *2* to buy; buy off; *cāpeden* PL.PRET [OE
    ċīepan]

karan → kere

cās → kiāsa

kāse *f.* quarrel, dispute; *cāse* DAT.SG [< L causa]

kāte *f.* knuckle-bone; PL bones; *kāta* NOM.PL
    [MDu kôte]

kattere *m.* sodomite, homosexual [L catharus]

kēda → kētha

kedde *m.* group; faction, party [OHG kutti, Du kudde]

kēi *m.* key; *kēia* GEN.PL; *kēiem* DAT.PL [OE cǣġ]

keisere *m.* emperor; *keyseres* GEN.SG [< G < L caesar]

keiserlīk, kairs- *adj.* imperial; *kairslīka* DAT/ACC.SG; *kairslīke* ACC.SG.N

keiserlīke, kairs- *adv.* imperially

keiserscip, kairs- *m.* empire, imperial power

kēla *1* to compensate, 'cool' [cf. OE cōl]

kēma *1* to charge, complain, claim; *kēmth* 3SG.PRES [OS cūmian]

kempa¹ *m.* champion, duelist [OE cempa]

kempa², -a- *1* to fight a duel

kemth → kēma

kempth → kuma

ken *n.* kindred; *kenne* DAT.SG [OE cynn]

kening, -eng, kin- *m.* king; *kin-, keninges, -enges* GEN.SG; *kening(g)e* DAT.SG; *keningan* ACC.PL [OE cyning]

keninglīk *adj.* royal

keninglīke *adv.* royally

keningrīke *n.* kingdom; *keningrīke* DAT.SG [OE cyneríċe]

kere, -a-, -rr- *m./f.* choice; statute; legal decree; *mith* ~ of one's own free will; *karan* NOM.PL; *kerren* ACC.PL [OE cyre]

kere → kerf

kere(n) → kiāsa

kerf *f.* cut, gash; *kere* ACC.SG [OE cyrf]

kerl *m.* man; *kerle* DAT.SG [OE ċeorl]

kerrin → kiāsa

kersten *adj.* Christian [cf. **Cristen**]

kerva *III* to cut; *kerft* 3SG.PRES [OE ċierfan]

kest *f.* statute; legal decree; *kest* DAT.SG; *kesta* NOM/ACC.PL [OE cyst]

kētha, -d- *1* to announce, proclaim, make known; *keth* PP [OE cȳðan]

kēdene *f.* announcement, alarm

kiāsa, sz-, ts- *II* to choose, decide (by common consent); *kiāse* PL.PRES.SUBJ; *cās, kās* 3SG.PRET; *keren, kerrin* PRET.PL; *kere* PRET.SUBJ.PL [OE ċēosan]

kind *m./n.* child; *kindar, kiinden, kynderen∞* ACC.PL [< OS kind]

kining → kening

clage *f.* complaint; *clagi* DAT.SG [OHG klaga]

clagere *m.* plaintiff

clagia *2* to raise a complaint because of; *clagath* 3SG.PRES [OHG klagōn]

clāster *m.* monastery [< L claustrum]

clāth *n.* cloth; PL clothes; *clāthar* NOM.PL; *clāthum* DAT.PL [OE clāð]

clockaclin *m.* chiming, bell-ringing [OIrish *clocc* + OHG klingan]

knē *n.* knee; *knē* ACC.PL [OE cnēow]

koer → kōr

kok *m.* cook; *kocken* DAT.PL [< VL cocus]

cōm, koma → kuma

comp *n.* duel, single combat; *compe* DAT.SG [< L campus]

kondigia∞ → kundigia

confessor *m.* confessor, Church Father; *confessoren* NOM.PL [< L confessor]

koning∞ *m.* king; *koninges* GEN.SG; *koninge* DAT.SG; *konnighen* NOM.PL; *koningen* DAT.PL (cf. kining, -e-)

koningscilde *f.* tax paid to the king; *~scilda* ACC.SG [OE scyld]

consent *m.* consent, permission; *consent* ACC.SG [< L consentus]

copper *n.* brass, copper [< L cuprum]

kōr *n.* choir; *koer* DAT.SG [< L chorus]

corn *n.* grain [OE corn]

crank *adj.* ill, diseased; *cranken* PL [OHG kranc]

kreftlik *adj.* violent [OE cræft]

kreftlike *adv.* violently, forcefully

kriāpa *II* to creep, crawl [OE crēopan]

criōse, *n.* cross [L crūcem]

crisma *m.* consecrated oil, (sacrament of) chrism [< L c(h)rīsma]

Cristen *adj.* Christian; *cristena* ACC.SG.M [L chrīstiānus]

cristenēde, crystenhēd *f.* 1. christening, (sacrament of) baptism 2. Christian faith [-ēde < -hēde]

cristnia *2* to baptize, christen; *cristnede* 3SG.PRET

crōna, -e *f.* crown [< L corōna]

cū *f.* cow [OE cū]

kūden → kunna

kulc, -o- *m.* pit, hole [MLG kolk]

kuma, koma *IV* to come; amount; *cumest* 2SG.PRES; *kempth, cumth* 3SG.PRES; *komet, kommeth* PL.PRES; *kome, kume* 2,3SG.PRES. SUBJ; *cōm, kōm* 3SG.PRET; *kōmon, kōmen,*

-in PL.PRET; *kōme* 3SG.PRET.SUBJ; *kōmen*
PL.PRET.SUBJ; *ekimin, komen* PP [OE
cuman]

kundig∞ *adj.* public, known [< MLG]

kundegia∞, kon-∞ *2* to announce, make
known, *kondiget* PP [< PREC]

kunna *pret.pres.* can, to be able; *kūden* PL.PRET
[OE cann, cunnon]

kyrioleys 'Lord have mercy' [< L < Gk
Kyrie eleison]

L

lāf *n.* leaf [OE lēaf]

lamethe *f.* paralysis, crippling; any serious
wound; *lametha* ACC.PL [cf. OE lama]

land(- → lond(-

lang(- → long(-

lānia *2* to reward [OE lēanian]

lāsta, -ae- *1* to perform, carry out; give, pay;
laeste 3SG.PRES.SUBJ; *lāstane, lāstene*
INFL.INF [OE lǣstan]

lāten → lēta

lathia *2* to invite; summon, cite; *lathath* 3SG.
PRES; *lathade* 3SG.PRET [OE laðian]

lat, latte(n) → lēda

latt'ene = lat (→ lēda) + hine

lauwe *f.* lioness; *lauwa* GEN.SG [< L leoa]

lāva¹, lauwa *m.* belief, faith; *lauwes* GEN.SG [OE
ġelēafa]

lāva², -w- *f.pl.* inheritance; *lāwem* DAT.PL
[cf. OE lāf]

lēda *1* to lead; bring to court; *lat* 3SG.PRES;
lēde 3SG.PRES.SUBJ; *latte* 3SG.PRET; *latten*
PL.PRET [OE lǣdan]

ledza, -i- *1* to lay; *bon* ~ to order or prohibit
sth. under threat of punishment; *frethe* ~
to place under legal protection; *ledzane*
INFL.INF; *lidze* 1SG.PRES; *gheleyd∞* PP [OE
lecgan]

leid *pp./adj.* imposed, proclaimed; *leida*
DAT.SG.F [from prec.]

leith → lēth; lidza

lēka *m.* layman; *lēcan* NOM.PL [< L lāicus]

lēra *1* + *dat.* to teach; *lēre* 3SG.PRES.SUBJ; *lērde*
3SG.PRET [OE lǣran]

lērest *adj.superl.* smallest

lernia *2* to learn; *gelernad* PP [OE leornian]

lesa *V* to read; *lest* 3SG.PRES; *les(e)*
3SG.PRES.SUBJ; *gelesen* PP [OE lesan]

lēsa *1* to ransom; *lēsane* INFL.INF [OE līesan]

lesma = lese + ma

lessera *adj.*COMP smaller

lēst *m.* track, footstep; *lēstum* DAT.PL; *lēsta*
ACC.PL; *an, thruch thiāves* ~ thievishly
[OE lāst]

lest *adj.superl.* latest; last; *tō thā lesta* at last;
uppa thet leste at last [cf. let]

let *adj.* late; COMP *let(t)era* next, second; SUPERL
lest(a) [OE lǣt]

lēta *VII/1* to let, have; *lāta∞* 3SG.PRES.SUBJ;
lēta IMP.PL; *lēt* 3SG.PRET; *lette* 3SG.PRET;
lāten∞ PP [OE lǣtan]

lēth(e), -ei- *adj.* loathsome, unpleasant; *lētha*
DAT.SG [OE lāð]

lethich *adj.* empty; unoccupied, free; without
a lord; *letheges* GEN.SG [ON liðugr]

lethogia *2* to redeem, deliver; *lethogade*
3SG.PRET [from prec.]

lētsa *m.* doctor, physician [OE lǣċe]

leyd → lidz(i)a

liāchtere *m.* candle; *liāchtera* DAT.SG [G Leuchter]

liāf *adj.* dear, beloved; *liauwe* NOM.PL; COMP
liāvera [OE lēof]

liāfhēd *f.* charm, grace

līand, -y- *n.* life [< MLG levent]

liāt *adj.* lying [Goth liuts, OIce ljótr]

liāva *f.* 'beloved', wife

libba *1* to live; *liuwet* 3SG.PRES; *libbe*
SG/PL.PRES.SUBJ; *libbent* PRES.PTC;
lifde PL.PRET.SUBJ; *liuwet* PP [OE libban]

licht *adj.* light (in weight); COMP *lichtera*
[OE leoht]

lidz(i)a *V* to lie; *līth, leith* 3SG.PRES; *leyd*
3SG.PRET [OE licgan]

līf, -ij-, -y- *n.* body; life; wergeld; *līwes, -is*
GEN.SG; *līve, līwe* DAT.SG [OE līf]

lifde → libba

līfheftich *adj.* alive

līk *adj.* (+ *dat.*) same; equal to, like; *līkere*
DAT.SG.F; *te līke* equally [OE ġelīċ]

līke *conj.* like

līkia *2* to compare; *līkat* PP

līk(h)oma, -kk- *m.* body; *līckoma* DAT.SG,
līcoma ACC.SG [OE līchoma]

liōd- → liūd-

liūde, -iō-, -a, lioed *n.pl.* people; *liōda, liūda,
liōdena* GEN.PL; *liōdon, -em* DAT.PL [OE
lēode]

liŏdfretho, -e *m.* (fine for breach of) the people's peace; *~fretho* ACC.SG

liŏdkest *f.* people's statute

liŭdmerk *f.* kind of money, coin ('people's mark')

liŏdthing *n.* people's convention; *~thinge* DAT.SG

liŭdwurpen *pp./adj.* convened by the people

lith *n.* part (of body); *lithona, -ena* GEN.PL; *lithum* DAT.PL [OE lið]

lithalēt *n.* joint; *~lētum* DAT.PL OHG lidagilāz]

lithmata *m.* member (of body); *~mata* NOM.PL [MHG (ge)lidemæze]

lītsa *1* to level; *lītsed* PP (see note) [< *līk,* ADJ]

littec *adj.* small; *litteca* DAT.SG (cf. **lutik**)

liŭd ‑► **liŏd**

liuwet ‑► **libba**

livere *f.* liver; *liwera* DAT.SG [OE lifere]

lof *m.* praise, glory; *love, lowe* DAT.SG [OE lof]

lofleisasang *m.* song of praise (cf. **kyrio-leys**)

lōg *n.* place; *lōghe* DAT.SG [OE lōg]

lok *m.* lock (of hair); *lokkar* ACC.PL [OE locc]

lond, -a- *n.* land; *landis, londes* GEN.SG; *lande, londe* DAT.SG; *londa* GEN.PL [OE land]

londriucht, land- *n.* customary law, land-law (i.e., law pertaining to a particular land or district); *~riuchta* ACC.PL

long, -a- *adj.* long; *langhe* ACC.SG.F [OE long]

long(e), -a- *adv.* long; *langor* COMP [OE longe]

lovia *2* to promise, pledge; decide, establish; *loviane* INFL.INF; *loviath* PL.PRES; *lovade* PL.PRET.SUBJ; *lovad* PP [OE lofian]

lowe ‑► **lof**

lucht∞ *f.* air, sky

lūd ‑► **(h)lūd**

luk *n.* good luck, happiness; *luck* [MLG gelucke]

lungi(r)nsiāma *m.* discharge of pus from lungs [cf. OE sēon 'to drip']

lutik∞ *adj./n.* (a) little; *lutiik* ACC.SG [cf. OE luttuc]

M

ma *pron.* one; men, people, they [OE man]

macht *f.* power; PL genitals; *macht* ACC.SG; *machtem* DAT.PL; *machta* ACC.PL [OE meaht]

machte ‑► **muga**

maga *m.* 'maw', stomach [OE maga]

mageth ‑► **megeth**

magte ‑► **muga**

makia, -e- *2* to make; establish, demonstrate; declare; *meckie* 3SG.PRES.SUBJ; *makyet* IMP.PL; *makad, maket, ghemaket∞* PP [OE macian]

māl, -ae-∞ *n.* time, period; *t(h)oe ~* especially, particularly

maledīa *1/2* to condemn; *maledīad* PP [< L maledīcere]

man ‑► **mon**

manich ‑► **monich**

manichfald, mennich- *adj.* various; *myt mennichfalde* with all kinds of everything [OE manigfeald]

mankes ‑► **mannik**

manlīk *adj.* male

manlīke *adv.* manly, valiantly

mannesklīk *adj.* human

mannik *pron.* everyone, each; *mankes* GEN.SG [< *manna* + e(l)k]

manniska *m.* man, human being [OHG men(n)isco]

mar *m.* horse [OE mearh]

mā(r) *adv.*COMP more, greater

mār(r)a *adj.*COMP more [OE māra, mæra]

marter, mert-, -ir *m.* martyr; *marter, merter, -ir* OBL.SG; *martilar, marteren* NOM.PL [< L martyr]

māst(a) *adj.*superl. most; greatest, most important [OE mæst]

māstere *m.* master; leader, commissioner [< L magister]

ma't = *ma* + *hit*

meckie ‑► **makia**

mede *m./n.* mead [OE medu]

mēde, -ei- *f.* present, bribe; *meidem* DAT.PL [OE mēd]

megeth, ma- *f.* virgin; *maghet* DAT.SG; *megetha* NOM.PL [OE mæġeð]

mei, mey ‑► **muga**

mei, mey ‑► **mith**

mei- see also **mē-**

meiden *n.* girl, virgin [OE mæġden]

mek *n.* marriage; *meke* DAT.SG [< makia, cf. OE mæcca]

mekere *m.* marriage broker [from prec.]

mēlia *2* to paint [OS mālon]

melok *f.* milk; *melokon* DAT.PL [OE meoloc]

men∞ *pron.* one, they

mēn, meyn *adj.* common; 'mean' [OE ġemæne]

mene *f.* intention [OE myne]

menete *f.* mint; coin, currency; *meneta* DAT.SG [< L monēta]

menetere *m.* mintmaster, moneyer; *menetare* DAT.SG

mēnēth *m.* perjury; *mēnēth* ACC.SG

mēnis *adv.* falsly [< mēn]

mēnlīke *adv.* together

mennich- → manich-

men(e)ska *m.* man, human being (cf. **manniska**)

mēnwīf *n.* whore

mer, meer, maer∞ *conj./adv.* but [< ne wēre]

mēre *m./n.* rope; *mēre* DAT.SG [cf. OE mǣrels]

mēre *f.* message; news; rumour [OHG māri]

merch *n.* marrow [OE mearg]

merik → merke

merk *f.* mark, certain currency; *merka* ACC.PL; *merkum* DAT.PL [OE mearc]

merka *1* to observe; *merke* PL.PRES.SUBJ [OHG merken]

merke *f.* border; *merik* DAT.SG; also PL district, land; *merka* ACC.PL; *merkon* DAT.PL [OE mearc]

merter → marter

mēse *f.* urine [OE mēsa PL 'dung']

mēster *m.* master (cf. **māstere**)

mēsterskip *m.* authority; *~skipe* ACC.PL

me't = ma + hit

mēta¹ *1* to meet; pass by [OE mētan]

mēta² → mēte

metāl *n.* metal; *metael* DAT.SG [< L metallum]

mēte *f.* measure, quality; *mēta* GEN.SG [< meta V to measure]

mey → mit(h)

meyn → mēn

mī → muga

middel *n.* middle, middle part [OE middel]

middesumer *m.* midsummer (24 June) [OE midde-]

mīn, -y- *pron.* my, mine; *mīnem, myne* DAT.SG [OE mīn]

minnera *adv.* COMP lesser

minnia *2* to love; *minnie* 3SG.PRES.SUBJ [OS minnian]

mīre = mī + er

misdītsa *1* to build or repair a dike poorly; *misdītsed* PP (cf. **dīk**)

misdommia *2* to dig a ditch poorly; *misdommad* PP [E dam < MDu]

misdwā(n) *anom.vb.* to do wrong; *misdeen* PP

misera *1* to plough poorly; *misered* PP [OE erian]

misielda *III* to pay poorly; *misgulden* PP [OE ġieldan]

misskera *IV* to mow poorly; *misskerid* PP [OE scieran]

mit(h), mei, mey *prep.* + *dat.* with, through, by means of; *~ daem* with it [OE mið]

mitha = mith + thā

mithe, -i *adv.* with; *ther ... mithe* with which

mōd, -oe- *n.* heart, mind; courage; approval; *mōde, moede* DAT.SG; *moet* ACC.SG [OE mōd]

mōder, -ir *f.* mother; *mōdere* DAT.SG [OE mōdor]

mōdwilla *m.* willfulness; *mōdwilla* ACC.SG [OHG muotwillo]

moeg, -e → muga

moet(-) → mōd, mōta

mon, -a- *m.* man; vassal; *monnes, mannes* GEN. SG; *monne* DAT.SG; *man* NOM/ACC.PL; *monna* GEN.PL; *monnum, -em, -on, mannon, -en* DAT.PL; *to mannon branga* to give birth to [OE mann]

mōnath *m.* month; *mōnathe* DAT.SG; *mōnath* ACC.PL [OE mōnað]

monich, -a-, -g *adj.* many; *monigere* DAT.SG.F; *monege* ACC.PL [OE maniġ]

monslaga *m.* manslaughter

morth *m.* murder; abortion, stillborn child; *morthe* DAT.SG [OE morð]

morthdēd *f.* hidden crime; *~dēda* ACC.PL

morther(e) *m.* murderer, miscreant; *morder* ACC.SG

morthia *2* to kill; *morthat(h)* 3SG.PRES

morthkāse *f.* fight resulting in manslaughter

mōs *n.* meal [OE mōs]

mōste → mōta

mōstere = mōste + -er(e)

mōta *pret.pres.* to be allowed to; may; must; *moet* 3SG.PRES; *mōte, moete* 3SG.PRES. SUBJ; *moete* PL.PRES.SUBJ; *mōste* 3SG.PRET; *mōstin* PL.PRET; *mōste* PL.PRET SUBJ [OE mōtan]

muga, -o-, -oe- *pret.pres.* can, to be able; be allowed; *mei, mey, mī, mach∞* 1,3SG.PRES; *mugun, -en, -in* PL.PRES; *mugi, moeg(h)e, moeg* 3SG.PRES.SUBJ; *moghe(n)* PL.PRES.

SUBJ; *machte, magte, mochte* 3SG.PRET;
muchten PL.PRET; *mochte* PL.PRET.SUBJ [OE
mugan]

mund∞ *m.* mouth; *munde* DAT.SG [< MLG
mund]

mundlās *adj.* without a guardian; unmarried

mūre *f.* wall [< L mūrus]

my → **ic**

N

nā *adv.* never [OE nā]

nā∞ *prep.* + *dat.* after, according to (cf. **nēi**)

nacht *f.* night; *nachtes, nachtis* GEN.SG; *nachte*
DAT.SG [OE neaht]

nachtbrond *m.* nightly arson

nāhwedder, nauder *conj.* neither; *nauder ...
thēr* neither ... nor [OE nāhweðer]

naked *adj.* naked; *nakeda* ACC.PL [OE nacod]

nama → **noma**

nammermār *adv.* nevermore

nān → **nēn**

nas (< ne was) → **wesa**

nānēn *adj.pron.* no; *nānēne* DAT.SG.N; *mith
nānēne thinge* on no condition

nāt¹ *adv.* → **nāwet**

nāt² *m.* companion; relative; *nāta* GEN.PL [OE
ġenēat]

nāthe∞ *f.* mercy; grace, favour; *nātha* NOM.PL;
to nāthon DAT.PL 'as a benefit' (cf. **nēthe**)

natūra *f.* nature, quality; *natūra* ACC.SG [< L
natūra]

nauder → **nāhwedder**

naut → **nāwet**

nāwet, naut, nauwet, -it, nout, nowet, nāt *adv.*
not [OE nāwiht]

ne, ni *adv./conj.* not, no (usually with double
negation); nor; *ne ... nāwet* not (at all)
[OE ne]

nebba *1* to have not; *nebbe, -a* 1SG.PRES;
neth 3SG.PRES; *nebbe* 3SG.PRES.SUBJ [<
ne hebba]

nēd *f.* fear, danger; hardship, force; *nēde* ACC.SG;
nēde DAT.SG; *nēde nima* to take by force,
rape [OE nīed]

nēdgia *2* to rape; *enēdgad* PP

nēdkest *f.* rape; *~kestum* DAT.PL; *~kesta*
ACC.PL

nēdmonda *m.* rape; *~monda* DAT.SG [mund
'guardianship, marriage']

nēdskīn *n.* (proof of) force majeur, legal
impediment

neem → **nima**

nēi¹ *adj.* near, nigh; COMP *niār* + *dat.* more
entitled to; SUPERL *nēsta, -e* ACC.PL next
[OE nēah]

nēi², nēy *prep.* + *dat.* in accordance with,
according to; after [OE nēah]

neil, nīl *m.* nail; *neilar, -an* NOM/ACC.PL; *neylon*
DAT.PL; *nīla* ACC.PL [OE næġl]

nēiskiāta *II* to shoot after, in pursuit; *neyzyete*
3SG.PRES.SUBJ [OE scēotan]

nella *anom.vb.* to be unwilling, not want; *neli,
nel* 3SG.PRES [OE nyllan]

nemma, nemmen *pron.* no one [OHG nioman]

nemmer *adv.* never [OHG niomēr]

nēn, nān *pron./adj.* no; *nēne* DAT.SG.M/N; *nānne,
nēn(n)e* ACC.SG.M; *neen* NOM.SG.F; *nēne* ACC.
SG.F; *nēna* ACC.PL; *nēne* DAT.PL, ACC.PL [OE
nān]

nēn *conj.* neither, nor; *nēn ... thā nēn* neither
... nor

nēr *adv./conj.* neither, not even; not, nor; *neer*
[OE nēar]

nera, -rr- *1* to feed, sustain [OE nerian]

nēren → **wesa**

nerthe = ne + werthe

nēst → **nēi¹**

nēt (< ne + wēt) → **wita**

nēthe *f.* grace, favour; profit; *nēthum* DAT.PL
[OS nāða]

nēthelīk *adj.* fitting, reasonable

neth'ere = neth (→ **nebba**) + -er(e)

nette *adj.* useful [OE nytt]

nēy → **nēi²**

nī *adj.* new; *nīe* DAT.SG; *nīa* ACC.SG.M; *nīge*
ACC.PL [OE nīwe]

ni → **ne**

niār → **nēi**

nīge → **nī**

nīl → **neil**

nima *IV* to take; *nimpth* 3SG.PRES; *nime, neem*
3SG.PRES.SUBJ; *nim-, nymane* INFL.INF;
nam, nōm 3SG.PRET; *nōmen, -in* PL.PRET;
nimen PP [OE niman]

nis = ne + is

nither *adv.* down [OE niðer]

niugenspatze *adj.* with nine spokes [cf.
OE spǣc]

niugun, -en *num.* nine [OE nigon]

niugenda, -e, *num.* ninth

nōd∞ *f.* need, distress; *noet* DAT.SG (cf. nēd)

nōgia *2* to please (impers.vb.); *nōgade* 3SG.PRET [cf. OE ġenōg]

noma, -a- *m.* name; *name* DAT.SG; *noma* ACC.SG [OE nama]

nōm(en) → nima

nomia *2* to name; mention, enumerate; *nomad* PP [OS namon]

nordkoning∞ *m.* northern king

nordkoningrīke∞ *n.* northern kingdom

north *adv.* north [OE norð]

northhald *adj.* northward, directed to the north; *northalda* ACC.SG.M

nout, nowet → nāwet

nū *adv.* now; CONJ *nū thēr* because, since [OE nū]

o

o- see also u-

oen → on

oer → ōther

of *adv.* off

of *prep.* + *dat.* out of; from [OE of]

ofdrīva *I* to drive away, dislodge, expel; *ofdrīvane* INFL.INF [OE drīfan]

oferawad → ofrāvia

ofkerva *III* to cut off, draw off; *ofkerft* 3SG.PRES [OE ċierfan]

oflēdene *f.* raid; liability for damage done during raid; *oflēdene* ACC.SG [cf. lēda]

ofslā(n) *VI* to kill; *ofslōg* 3SG.PRET

ofsnīda *I* to cut off; *ofsnīde* 3SG.PRES.SUBJ [OE snīðan]

ofrāvia *2* to rob away; *oferāwad* PP [OE rēafian]

ofstonda *VI* + *dat.* to forsake

ofte *adv.* often [OE oft]

ōftne → āft(e)

ōk∞, -oe- *conj.* also, too (cf. āc)

ol- → al-

oliene *f.* (sacrament of) extreme unction [olie- < L oleum + -ne]

olcnum → wolken

olsā → alsā

ologia *2* to administer the extreme unction; *ologad* PP

om¹ *m.* breath; *om(me)* ACC.SG [< *omma < *on-ma; cf. Goth uz-anan]

om² → umbe

ombecht *n.* sacrament (here: of last rites) [OE ambyht]

omme¹ → om¹

omme² → umbe

on- → un-

on, oen *prep.* + *dat./acc.* in; to; on; against; at, during; *thēr ... on* on which [OE on] (cf. an)

onbi-ien *m.* beginning

onderd *n.* answer; *onderdes* GEN.SG [OE andwyrde]

ondlete *n.* face, countenance; *ondleta* DAT.SG [OE andwlite]

ondris → anders

ondwardia *2* to answer [OE andweardian]

onfā(n) *VII* to seize; *oen ti fāne* INFL.INF

onfiuchta *III* to attack; *onefuchten, oenfochten* PP

ongost *m.* fear, 'Angst' [cf. OE angian]

onkuma *IV* to come by, obtain, acquire; *onkemen* PP

onlāwa *m.* unbelief [OE ungelēafa]

onlēda *1* to prove by oath, confirm; *onlet* 3SG.PRES

onledza *1* to lay on; administer; *onleijde* 3SG.PRET

ons → wī

onspreka *V* to accuse

onspreke *f.* complaint; accusation

ont- see also un(t)-

ontiā *II* to put on; *ontāch* 3SG.PRET

onze → ūse

op, op(p)a → uppa

openbārlīk∞ *adj.* clear, public, manifest; *in -e* manifestly

openbēr∞ *adj.* clear, obvious, manifest

opinbēre *adv.* publicly

openbēria∞ *2* + *dat.* to reveal, make known; *openberet* PP

oppermon *m.* verger, saxton

ōr → ōther

ord *n.* point, spear; *orda* DAT.SG [OE ord]

orde *m.* state, condition [< F < L ordo]

ordēl, -dil *n.* judgement, verdict; ordeal; *ordēla* GEN.PL; *ordēlim* DAT.PL [OE ordāl, -dēl]

ordo *m.* monastic order; *ordo* DAT.SG [< L ordo]

orlef, -lof *n.* consent, permission; *orleve, orlovi* DAT.SG [OE -lof]

ōrne → ōther

ōther, ōr, oer *adj./num.* other; second; another,
  someone else; *ōtheres* GEN.SG.M; *ōra* GEN.
  SG.M (weak); *ōtheron, ōron* DAT.SG.M (strong);
  ōtherne, ōrne ACC.SG.M; *ōthere* DAT.SG.F; *ōr*
  ACC.SG.N; *ōthera* DAT/ACC.PL [OE ōðer]
ova *adv.* land inwards [OE ufan(e)]
ova *prep.* + *dat.* on, concerning (see also *ieria*)
ōver, -w- *m.* shore, coast, border [OE ōfer]
over, -w- *prep.* + *dat.* over [OE ofer]
overhōr *n.* adultery
ovirbulgen *pp./adj.* very angered
ovirfiuchta *III* to waste by fighting

P

palas *n.* palace [< L palātium]
palma, -e *m.* palm [< L palma]
palm(e)bām *m.* palm-tree
pand *n.* inconvenience, discomfort [OHG pfant]
pāpa *m.* priest; clergyman, cleric; *pāpena*
  GEN.PL [< L pāpa]
patriarcha *m.* patriarch; *patriarcha* NOM.PL
  [< L patriarcha]
pāwis *m.* Pope; *pāwis* GEN.SG; *pāwis, pāuis*
  DAT.SG [< L pāpa]
paradīs *n.* paradise; *paradyse* DAT.SG [< L
  paradīsus]
penda *1* to secure with a pledge; *pend* PP [< pand]
penning, -eng *m.* penny; part; *pennengar* NOM.PL;
  pennegum DAT.PL [OE penning]
pennigia *2* to pay out; *pennegad* PP
pīne *f.* corporal punishment [< VL pēna, L pœna]
plichtich *adj.* + *gen.* responsible for, under
  obligation (to maintain) [cf. OE pliht]
porte *f.* gate [< L porta]
pote *f.* skull ('pot'); *pota* DAT.SG [OE pott]
pralling *m.* testicle [< ?]
prēster(e) *m.* priest; *prēstere* DAT.SG [< L presbyter]
progost *m.* provost, dean; *progostes* GEN.SG
  [< ML propositus]
propheta *m.* prophet; *propheta* NOM.PL
  [< L propheta]
pund *n.* pound, monetary unit [< L pondo]
punt *m.* point; *puntten* DAT.PL [< L punctus]
pūr *adj.* pure, immaculate [L pūrus]

Q

quetha *V* to say; *queth* 3SG.PRES; *quath*
  3SG.PRET [OE cweðan]
qui(c)k *n.* cattle [cf. OE cwicfeoh]

R

r- see also hr-
racht'ene = rachte (→ rētsa) + hine
rād *adj.* red; *rāda* ACC.SG.M [OE rēad]
rāf *n.* robbery; *rāve* DAT.SG [OE rēaf]
ramia *2* to build, construct; *ramed* PP [OHG
  ram(a) 'supporting beam']
rathia *2* to tell [OS reðion]
rāvia *2* to rob, plunder; *rāwath* 3SG.PRES [OE
  rēafian]
rāver(e, -w- *m.* robber, plunderer; *rāwir* ACC.SG
  [OE rēafere]
rēd *m.* counsel, advice; agreement, consent;
  rēde DAT.SG [OE rǣd]
rēda¹ *1* to speak [OE rǣdan]
rēda² *1* to prepare, make ready; *rēde* PL.PRES.
  SUBJ [OE rǣdan]
rēde *adj.* ready, prepared [OE ġerǣde]
rēdelīk(e) *adv.* sincerely, righteously
rēdieva, -w-, rēdia *m.* 'counsel giver', judge;
  rēdiem DAT.PL; *rēdian* ACC.PL
reg- → (h)reg-
reil(-) → (h)reil(-)
rēma¹ *m.* oar [< L rēmus]
rēma² *1* to vacate, clear, leave; (of ditches) to
  deepen; *rēmane* INFL.INF; *rēmden* PL.PRET
  [OE rǣman]
rēne *adj.* pure, clean; *rēnere* DAT.SG.F
  [G rein]
renna *III* to run; *rent* 3SG.PRES [OE iernan]
resta *1* (*refl.*) to rest; *reste* 3SG.PRET [OE restan]
resten(e) *f.* rest [cf. OE reste(n-)]
rēsze → rētsa
reth *n.* wheel [< OS rað]
rētsa, -sz- *1* to reach; place; hand; *rētse, rēsze*
  3SG.PRES.SUBJ; *rachte* 3SG.PRET [OE
  rǣċan]
rētse't = rētse + hit
rhīve → hrīf
rī *adj.* perishable [?cf. Goth riurs]
riāka *1* to smoke; *riākande* PRES.PTC/DAT.SG.N
  [OE rēocan]
rib *m.* rib; *ribbe* DAT.SG [OE ribb]
richt → riucht
ridder(e) *m.* knight; *ridderen* GEN.PL; *ridderan*
  ACC.PL [OE rīdere]
rīep → (h)rōpa
rīke *adj.* powerful, influential; rich; *rīka* ACC.
  SG.M; *rīkera* GEN.PL [OE rīċe]

rīke *n.* kingdom; realm, empire; *rīke* DAT.SG; *rīza* NOM.PL riches [OE rīċe]

rīkedōm *m.* riches, wealth; *~dōmar* ACC.PL

riocht → riucht

rīsa *I* to rise, originate [OE rīsan]

riu(c)ht¹, -io- *adj.* just, right, rightful; lawful; legal; *riuchtne* ACC.SG.M; *riuchta* NOM.SG.F; *riuchtere* DAT.SG.F; *richt∞* ACC.SG.N; *riochta, -e* DAT.PL [OE reoht, riht]

riucht², -io- *n.* law, right, justice; oath of exoneration; *riuchte* DAT.SG, ACC.PL; *riuchtum* DAT.PL; *riuchta* ACC.PL; *bī ~* according to law; *fon ~* of right, legally; *tō ~* as law [OE riht]

riuchta *1* to administer justice; swear an oath of exoneration

riuchte *adv.* justly, according to law

riuchter(e), -io- *m.* judge

riuchtlīk *adj.* legal

riuchtlīke *adv.* rightly, according to right; *rochtelīke, ruchtelīke*

rīwat → hrīvia

rīza → rīke

rocht- → riucht-

rōd(e) *f.* rod; *rōde* DAT.SG [OE rōd]

rōft → (h)rōft

rōster *n.* gridiron [OHG rost]

rōther *m.* rudder; *rōther* DAT.SG [OE rōðor]

ruald → wrald

rucht- → riucht-

S

sā *adv./conj.* then; so, in that case; as; if (introduces main clause after subclauses or adjuncts of time, condition, etc; often redundant in ModE) [OE swā]

saath → sate

sach → siā(n)

sādēn *adj.* such ('so done')

sake *f.* sake, thing; *secken* DAT.PL; *saka, zaken* ACC.PL [OE sacu]

salt *adj.* salty [OE sealt]

sanlās *adj.* uncontested; unimportant, insignificant; *sanlāza* ACC.PL [OIce senna]

sansane → sentsa

santen → senda

sant'ere = sant(e) (→ **senda**) + -er

sara → sera

sā'r(e) = sā + er

sareda → sera

sā'r'et = sā + er + hit

sā't = sā + hit

sate *f.* place; *saath*

sawen, -in *num.* seven [OE seofon]

sawenda *num.* seventh

sax *n.* knife, short sword; *saxe* DAT.SG [OE seax]

sch- → sk-

schien → skēne

se → hia, hiu

sē → wesa

sē *m./f.* sea; *sēs* GEN.SG [OE sǣ]

sēburch *f.* sea-fortress: dike; *~burch* ACC.SG

secken → sake

sēd(e) *f.* meal ('satiation'); *sēde* DAT.SG [cf. OE sǣd]

sedza, sidza, z- *1* to say; *seith, seyt* 3SG.PRES; *ghesecht∞* PP [OE secgan]

seith → sedza

sēle *f.* soul; *sēle* ACC.SG [OE sāwol]

self *adj./pron.* self, same; *selwis* GEN.SG.M; *selva* OBL (weak); *selve, zelve* (in postposition) used to re-inforce DEM.PRON [OE self]

sēlich *adj.* pious, righteous; *sillich* happy, blessed [OE sǣliġ]

sella *1* to sell, dispose of, part with, hand over [OE syllan]

selver, -w- *n.* silver [OE seolfer]

sēna *1* to reconcile, compromise; *sende* PP/ADJ (F.PL) [OS sōnian]

send → wesa

send'ti = send (→ **wesa**) + thī

senda *1* to send; *sende* 3SG.PRES.SUBJ; *sant* 3SG.PRET; *santen* PL.PRET [OE sendan]

senne → sunne

sente *adj.* saint [< L sanct-us, -a]

sentsa, sansa *1* to (make) sink; be drowned; *sansane* INFL.INF [OE senċan]

sent(t)i = send(e) + thī

sera, -a- *1* to equip; *sareda* PP/ACC.SG.M [OE sierwan]

sēre, seer *adv.* painfully; firmly; very [OE sāre]

sērlīke *adv.* carefully; expressly

sē't = sē + hit

set → sitta

setta, -e *1* to set, establish; place; *sette* 3SG.PRET; *settane* INFL.INF; *gheseet∞* PP [OE settan]

sex *num.* six [OE seox]

sexta, -e *num.* sixth

sextinde *num.* sixteenth

sextendesta *num.* sixteenth

sī → **wesa**

siā(n) *V* to see; *siāth* PL.PRES; *sach∞* 3SG.PRET; *sēgen, -in* PL.PRET [OE sēon]

siātha *II* to boil, 'seethe'; *siāthane* INFL.INF [OE sēoðan]

sibbe *adj./sb.* related, akin; kinsman, kinswoman [OE sibb]

sīde *adv.* low, deep [OE sīde]

sīde *f.* side [OE sīde]

sidza → **sedza**

sigun → **siugun**

siker *adj.* unchallenged, undisputed [< L *sēcūrus*]

sik(e)ria *2* to redeem; *sikerie* 3SG.PRES.SUBJ

sīl *m.* drain, water outlet; *sīlan* ACC.PL [cf. OE sēon 'drip']

sillich → **sēlich**

sin *m.* sense; determination; *sinne* DAT.SG; *sinna* GEN.PL [OHG sin]

sīn, -ij-, -y-, z- *pron.* his; *sīn(n)e* ACC.SG.M; *sīnes* GEN.SG.M; *sīne* DAT.SG.M./N; *sijn* NOM.SG.F; *sīne* ACC.SG.F; *sīner, sīn(e)re* DAT.SG.F; *sīn* NOM.SG.N; *syn* OBL.SG; *sīne, -a* NOM/ACC.PL; *sīnera* GEN.PL; *sīna* DAT.PL [OE sīn]

sine *f.* sinew; *sina* NOM.PL; *sinum* DAT.PL [OE sinu]

sineth *m./n.* synodical, ecclesiastical court; *sinethe* DAT.SG [cf. OE sinoð; < L synodus]

sinithriucht *n.* synodical, ecclesiastical law; *~riuchta* ACC.PL

sin *m.* senses, wits; *sinnes* GEN.SG [OHG sin]

sint(e) *m.* saint [< OF seint]

sinte, -ii- *f.* female saint [< OF seinte]

sitta *V* to sit; *sit* 3SG.PRES; *set* 3SG.PRET; *sēten* PL.PRET [OE sittan]

si(u)gun *num.* seven (cf. **sawen**)

siugentēn, so- *num.* seventeen

siugunda, -e, sog- *num.* seventh (cf. **sawenda**)

siūne *f.* sight; *siūne* GEN.SG [Goth siuns]

scalk *m.* servant [OE scealc]

scancťim = scancte (→ **skenka**) + him

skār, -ae-∞ *m.* multitude, throng; *scaer* DAT.SG [MDu schār]

skatha *m.* injury, damage; *skatha* DAT.SG [OE sceaðu]

skathia *2 + dat.* to harm, injure [OE sceaðian]

skeft *m.* shaft (of spear) [OE sceaft]

skeka *VI* to elope, allow to be abducted; *skecht* 3SG.PRES [OE scacan]

skekmek *n.* marriage after abduction or elopement; *~meke* DAT.SG [cf. mek]

skela *pret.pres.* will, shall; have to, must; *scalt, skalt, skaltū* 2SG.PRES (+ *thū*); *scel, skel, skil(e), schil* 3SG.PRES; *scele, skelen, skilun* PL.PRES; *scel'i* = scele i; *scele* 3SG.PRES.SUBJ; *skelen* PL.PRES.SUBJ; *sc(h)old(e)* 3SG.PRET. IND/SUBJ; *scholden, solde* SG/PL.PRET.IND/SUBJ; *sculde* 3SG.PRET.SUBJ [OE sculan]

sceld, -i- *m./n.* shield; *scelde, scilde* DAT.SG; *skeld* ACC.SG [OE scield]

scel't = skel + hit

skelta(ta) *m.* legal magistrate, sherrif, bailiff [OE scyldhāta)

skēne, -ie- *adj.* beautiful; *schien* NOM.SG.F; *skēna* DAT.SG.F, ACC.PL [OS skōni]

skenka *VII/1* to pour, serve drinks; *skēngk* 3SG.PRET; *scancte* 3SG.PRET [OE scenċan]

skentsa, -z- *m.* butler; host, master of ceremonies; *schenza* GEN.SG; *schenzen* DAT.PL

skeppa *VI* to create; fix, appoint; *skeppe* 3SG. PRES.SUBJ; *sc(h)ōp* 3SG.PRET; *eskipin, eskepin, ghescapen∞* PP [OE scieppan]

scera *IV* to cut [OE scieran]

skēre *f.* ploughshare; ordeal with hot ploughshares; *skēra* ACC.SG/ACC.PL; *skērem, -on* DAT.PL [OE scear]

scerp *adj.* sharp; *scerpa* ACC.PL [OE scearp]

sket *m.* treasure; cattle; *skettis* GEN.SG; *skette* DAT.SG; *schettena* GEN.PL; *scetten* ACC.PL [OE sceatt]

sketfiā *n.* cattle

skētha *1* to separate; *sketh* PP [Goth skaidan]

skethelīc *adj.* harmful

skiā *V* to happen; *scē* 3SG.PRET [OE scēon]

skiāta *II* to shoot; contribute, procure, pay; *schetten* PP [OE scēotan]

skila → **skela**

scild → **sceld**

skildich *adj.* due, indebted; *~ wesa* to owe [OE scyld]

skilling *m.* shilling; *skillinge* DAT.SG; *skillingar* NOM/ACC.PL; *skillinga* GEN.PL [OE scilling]

skīna *I* to shine; *scīnandere* PRES.PTC/DAT.SG.F [OE scīnan]

skip, sc- *n.* ship [OE scip]

skippere *m.* creator [cf. **skeppa**]

skipnese *f.* shape, form

skolde → **skela**

scondlīk *adj.* shameful [OE sceand]

scōne∞ *adj.* beautiful, bright [cf. **skēne**]

sc(h)ōp → **skeppa**

scrēf → **skrīva**

scrift *n.* book, writ; (Holy) Scripture, Bible;
    scrifta ACC.PL; *scriftem* DAT.PL
    [< L scriptum]

skrīva *I* to write; prescribe penance (in
    confession); *scrēf, skrēf* 3SG.PRET; *eskrivin,
    escriuin, (ghe)screven*∞ PP [< L scribere]

skrīvere *m.* clerk (of the court); *scrīveres*
    GEN.SG; *scrīvere* DAT.SG

sculde → **skella**

slā(n) *VI* to strike; kill; fill up with sand, stop
    up; *slān(d)e* INFL.INF; *sleith* 3SG.PRES;
    sloghen PL.PRET; *geslagin*∞ PP [OE slēan]

slacht(e) *n.* race; generation; stock [OHG
    gislahti]

slēpa *VII* to sleep; *slēpandera* PRES.PTC/DAT.
    SG.F; *slēpande* PRES.PTC/DAT.PL [OE slpan]

sletel *m.* key; *sletela* NOM.PL; *sletelon* DAT.PL
    [< OS slutil]

slīk *n.* mud; *slīke* DAT.SG [cf. OE slic]

slūta *II* to lock; *sleten* PP [OS slūtan]

smek *m.* taste; *smekkes* GEN.SG [OE smæc]

smere *n.* pus [OE smeoru]

smīta *I* to kill, smite [OE smītan]

snabba *m.* mouth [cf. OE nebb]

sō∞, -oe, z- *conj./adv.* as; so (cf. **sā**)

sogen(- → **sawen**(-, **siugen**

somnia *2 (refl.)* to gather, assemble; *somnath*
    3SG.PRES (not refl.); *somniath* PL.PRES;
    somnie 3SG.PRES.SUBJ; *somnad* [OE
    samnian]

sond *adj.* healthy, sound [OE sund]

sonde[1] *f.* well-being, prosperity [from prec.]

sonde[2]∞, **zunde** *f.* sin; *sonda* ACC.PL [< MDu/
    MLG]

sonder → **sunder**

sōne *f.* reconciliation, compromise; *sōne* ACC.
    SG; *sōna* GEN.PL [OHG suona]

soth *n.* porridge; *sothe* DAT.SG [< siātha; cf. OE
    ġesod]

spada *m.* spade [OE spada]

spanna *1* to fasten, attach; *spande* 3SG.PRET.
    SUBJ; *spanned* PP [OE spannan]

spiri *n.* spear [OE spere]

spona *VI* to lure away; *spont* 3SG.PRES [OE spanan]

sprack → **spreka**

spreka *IV/V* to speak; *sprekth* 3SG.PRES;
    sprekath PL.PRES; *sprec(k)* 1SG.PRET;
    sprec, sprack∞ 3SG.PRET; *sprēkin* PL.PRET;
    spritzen, ghesproghen∞ PP [OE sprecan]

spreke *f.* accusation, charge

sprūta *II* to come forth; generate; *sprūte* 3SG.
    PRES.SUBJ [OE sprūtan]

stal *m.* 1. (the act of) standing; 2. stall, stable
    [OE steall]

stān *anom.vb.* to stand; *staet, steet* 3SG.PRES
    (cf. **stonda**)

stark → **sterk**

stāt *m.* state, condition [< L stātus]

sted(e), -i-, -ee- *f.* place, spot; town *stidi* [OE stede]

ste(e)dfolk *n.* citizens, townspeople

steet → **stān**

stefne, -i-, **stemme** *f.* voice; *stemme* DAT.SG;
    stifne ACC.SG [OE stefn]

steka *IV/V* to raise, put on (a hat) [OE stecan]

stela *IV/V* to steal; *stēlth* 3SG.PRES; *stelin* PP [OE
    stelan]

stemme → **stefne**

stēn *m.* stone; *stēne* DAT.SG [OE stān]

stēnen *adj.* stone; *stenena* ACC.PL [OE stnen]

stera *m.* star [OE steorra]

stēra *1* to fortify; *stērande* INFL.INF [< stōr 'big']

sterk, -a-, **steric** *adj.* strong [OE steorc]

sterkhēd, -heyd *f.* strength

stert *m.* tail; *sterten* DAT/ACC.PL [OE steort]

sterva *III* to die; *steruath* PL.PRES; *storuen* PP
    [OE steorfan]

stēta *1* to thrust, pierce; *stētene* INFL.INF; *stet* PP
    [OS stōtan]

stherkhof *n.* churchyard; ~*hovi* DAT.SG (cf. **tsiurce**)

sti- see also **ste-**

stifta *1* to maintain; found; make, build;
    stiftan(d)e
    INFL.INF; *stifton* PL.PRET [OHG stiftan]

stīga *I* to rise; *stīgath* PL.PRES [OE stīgan]

stīl *m.* (door)post, beam; *stile* DAT.SG [< L stilus]

stil *adj.* quiet, still; *stille* DAT.SG.M [OE still]

stilnes *f.* (period of) menstruation; *stilnese* DAT.SG

stiōra, -iū- *1* to steer; *stiōre* 3SG.PRES.SUBJ;
    stiūrde 3SG.PRET [OE stīeran]

stiōrne *f.* stern, rudder [OIce stiórn]

stīpa *m.* pole, beam [< L stipes]

stīth *adj.* stern, severe [OE stīð]

stō *f.* place [OE stōw]

stōde → **stonda**

stok *m.* stick; stocks (instrument of punishment); *stock* ACC.SG [OE stocc]

stōl *m.* chair [OE stōl]

stonda *VI* to stand; *stont* 3SG.PRES; *stondath* PL.PRES; *stond∞* 3SG.PRET; *stōden* PL.PRET; *stōde* 3SG.PRET.SUBJ [OE standan]

stōr *adj.* big, large [OE stōr < OIce]

strām *m.* stream, current [OE strēam]

strēte *f.* (paved) road; *strēte* ACC.SG [< L strāta]

strīd, -y- *n.* battle, fight; duel (as ordeal) *strīde* DAT.SG; *māra ~* judical duel [OS strīd]

strīda *I/1* to fight; *strīdet* IMP.PL; *stritte* 3SG. PRET [OHG strītan, cf. OE strīdan]

strīdēth *m.* oath preceding a duel

stult *adj.* proud; brave; *stultere* DAT.SG.F; *stulta* ACC.PL [MHG stolz]

stultlīke *adv.* proudly

stunde *f.* time; *stunda* ACC.PL [OE stund]

stūpe *f.* pole; flagellation; *stūpa* ACC.SG [cf. OE stūpian]

suerde → **swerd**

sumeresnacht *f.* summer solstice (21 June)

sumur *m.* summer; *sumures* GEN.SG [OE sumor]

sunder, -o- *prep.* + *dat.* without [cf. OE sunder, ADV]

sunderacht *f.* extra-legal consultation [OE eaht]

sundrich *adj.* special, separate, 'sundry'; *sunderge* ACC.SG.F [OE syndriġ]

sunnandī *m.* Sunday [OE sunnandæġ]

sunne, -e- *f.* sun; *sunna* DAT.SG [OE sunne]

sūthern *adj.* southern; *sūthirna* ACC.SG.M [OE sūðerne]

sward(e) *f.* scalp; *sward* ACC.SG [OE sweard]

swart *adj.* black; *swarta* ACC.SG [OE sweart]

swella *III* to swell, increase; *swilth* 3SG.PRES [OE swellan]

swen(d)za, -i- *1* to throw, swing; *swynze* 3SG. PRES.SUBJ [OE swenġan]

swerd *n.* sword; *swerde, suerde* DAT.SG; *suerd* ACC.PL [OE sweord]

swera *IV/V* to swear; *swerane* INFL.INF; *swere* 2,3SG.PRES.SUBJ; *(e)sweren* PP [OE swerian]

swester *f.* sister; *swester* ACC.SG [OE sweostor]

swēt *n.* sweat [OE swāt]

szere- → **tsere-**

szetele → **tsietel**

sziāsa → **kiāza**

szīwe → **tsīva**

T

t- see also **th-**

tāghen → **tiā**

tale → **tele**

tāne *f.* toe; *tāne* DAT.SG [OE tā]

tāwe *f.* instrument, utensil; tackle; *tōwe* DAT.SG; *tauwon* DAT.PL [OE ġetāwe, PL.]

te → **tō**

teddre *adj.* weak, tender; *teddera* GEN.SG [OE tīedre]

tefle *f.* tablet; *teula* DAT.SG; *tefla* ACC.PL [< L tabula]

tegen → **tiā(n)**

tegetha *m.* tithes; *tegethan* ACC.PL [OE teogoða]

tēken, -ey- *n.* sign; *tēkna, teykenen* PL [OE tācen]

tele, -a- *f.* talk, words; accusation; *tale, tele* DAT. SG; *bi twīra ~* by accusation and defence [OE talu]

teula → **tefle**

th- see also **t-** and **d-**

thā → **thī**

thā¹ *adv.* then [OE þā]

thā² *conj.* when; than; (n)or; *thā ... jefta* either ... or [OE þā]

thāch, -g *adv.* however, yet, nonetheless [OE þēah]

thāch *conj.* even though

than- → **then-**

than¹ *conj.* than; *hoder ... than* whether ... or [OE þonne]

than² *adv.* except, but (after negation); or; *dan*

thank → **thonk**

thanne → **thenna**

thantse → **thentsa**

that∞ *pron.n.* the, that (cf. **thī**)

thē *rel.particle* who, which, that (< OS ðē)

thene, -a → **thi**

thenna, -e, thanne *adv.* then [OE þonne]

thentsa, -a-, -z- *1* to think; remember; *thantse, thanze* 2SG.PRES.SUBJ; *thenzie* 3SG.PRES. SUBJ; *thogte* 3SG.PRET [OE þenċan]

thēr¹ *rel. particle* who, that, which; *daer∞*

thēr², deer *adv.* there; then [OE þǣr]

thera, -e, ther → **thiu, thī**

thērabūta *adv.* besides, in addition

thērbinna *adv.* inside

thērefter *adv.* after that, thereupon

thērin *adv.* therein, in it; *daerin∞*

therm *m.* bowel, intestines; *thermar* NOM.PL [OE ðearm]

thērmithe, -i *adv.* with it, therewith; CONJ therefore *deermey, daermeed∞*

thērnēi, -nā∞ *adv.* thereafter, after that; *dār∞ney*

thērof, deer- *adv.* from there

thēron *adv.* thereon, on it; in it

thērop *adv.* thereon, on it

thērtō *adv.* in addition

thērum(be) *adv./conj.* for it; therefore, that's why; *dārum∞*

thērunder *adv.* meanwhile

thēruppa *adv.* thereon, on it

thes → thī, thet

thes *adv.* accordingly

thesse → this

theste *adv.* the (+ ADV.COMP) [thes GEN.SG + *the < *thī; OE þȳ]

thet[1] *conj.* that, so that; *dat∞* [OE þæt]

thet[2] → thī

thetta = thet + thā

thette = thet + hī

thettet = thet + thet

thet(t)'er, datt'er = thet + thēr, thet + er

thetter'ne = thet + er + hine

thetti = thet + thī

thet'tu = thet + thū

thī, dye, di *pron.m.* that, the; *thes, this, dees, dis* GEN.SG.M/N; *thā(m)* DAT.SG.M/N; *then(e), dyn* ACC.SG.M; *thiu, thyo* NOM.SG.F; *there, ther(a), thirre, der, daer∞* GEN/DAT.SG.F; *thā* ACC.SG.F; *thet, that, dat∞* NOM/ACC. SCR.N; *es* GEN.SG.N (ENCL); *thet … thēr* that … which; *thā, dā, die∞* NOM/ACC.PL; *thera, -e, dera* GEN.PL

t(h)iāchskunk(a) *m.* thigh, upper leg; *tiāch-skuncken* ACC.PL [OE þēohscanca]

thiād *f.* people [OE þēod]

thiāf *m.* thief; *thiāves* GEN.SG [OE þēof]

t(h)iāl *n.* wheel; *tiāl* ACC.SG (OE hwēol) (cf. fiāl)

thiānia *2 + dat.* to serve; obey; *tyennya, tyaenie* INF; *thiānade* 3SG.PRET.SUBJ [cf. OE þēow]

thiānst *m.* service; *tho thyenste stān tā* to be of help to someone [OE þēonest]

thījena, -e *pron.* the one; *dāghene∞* DAT.PL; *thījena … thēr* he who, PL those who [OE ġeon]

thīn *pron.* your, 'thy'; *thīnes, thīnis* GEN.SG; *diin, thīn(n)e, thīna* ACC.SG.M; *thīnere* DAT.SG.F; *thīne* ACC.SG.F; *thīna* DAT.SG.N; *thīna* NOM/ACC.PL; *thīnra* GEN.PL [OE þīn]

thīne → thī

thing *n.* thing; (legal) provision; assembly; court of justice; *thinges* GEN.SG; *thinge* DAT. SG; *thing(h)um* DAT.PL [OE þing]

thingad'ere = thingade + ere

thingia *2* to proceed, sue; administer justice, sit in judgment; *thingie* PL.PRES.SUBJ; *thingade* 3SG.PRET [OE þingian]

thingslītene *f.* disturbance of court session [cf. OE slītan]

thingstapul *m.* scaffold; *~stapule* DAT.SG [OE stapol]

thingtīd *f.* time for holding court

thintsa, -k- *1* to seem (IMPERS.VB + DAT); *thiink* 3SG.PRES.SUBJ [OE þynċan]

thiōde *f.* meaning, explanation; *tō dūde∞, tū dūde∞* in the vernacular [OE þēod]

thirre → thī

this(se), d- *pron.* this; *thisse* DAT.SG.M./N; *dissen* ACC.SG.M; *thius* NOM.SG.F; *thissa* ACC.SG.F; *thit, dit* NOM/ACC.SG.N; *thesse, thisse, disse* NOM/DAT/ACC.PL [OE þis]

thit → this(se)

thiu → thī

thius → this(se)

thiūft(h)e *f.* theft; stolen property; *thiūvethe* ACC.SG; *thiūftem* DAT.PL [OE þiefð]

thiūvethe → thiūft(h)e

thō[1] → tō

thō[2]∞ *adv./conj.* then; when; *doe* (cf. thā)

thochta *m.* thought, mind; memory [OE þoht]

tholia *2* to suffer; *tholade* 3SG.PRET [OE þolian]

thonk *m.* thanks; *te thonke* as satisfaction; *tho ~ stān + ACC* to meet someone's wishes [OE þanc]

thor(f) → thur(v)a

thornen *adj.* thorny; *thornena* DAT.SG.F [cf. OE þyrnen]

thorpemār *m.* village-ditch; *~māran* ACC.PL [OE þorp; ?mǣre]

t(h)orstich *adj.* thursty [OE þurstiġ]

t(h)rē *num.* three; *thrēm, thrīm, thrīum* DAT.M; *thrē* ACC.M; *thriū* ACC.F [OE þrēo]

t(h)redda, -e *num.* third [OE þridda]

threttēne *num.* thirteen

thredtinda *num.* thirteenth

threttundista *num.* thirteenth

thria *adv.* thrice, three times [OE þriwa]

thribēte *adv.* three times (the compensation)

thrimen(e) *adj./num.* one third; ~ *forthera* ½ times as much [OE þrimen]

t(h)rina, -e *num.* three each, three; *trine* [OE þrinen]

thritich *num.* thirty [OE þritiġ]

thriū → **t(h)rē**

thruch *prep. + acc.* through; because of; CONJ *thruch thet,* ~ *that∞* because [OE þurh]

thruchskīnich *adj.* transparent; indecently exposed [cf. OE scīnan]

thruchsnītha *I* to cut through; *thruchsnithin* PP [OE snīðan]

thruchstēta *1* to thrust through, pierce; *thruchstēt* PP

thū *pron.* you, thou; *t(h)ī, dij∞* DAT/ACC [OE þū]

thur(v)a, -o- *pret.pres.* to need; be allowed, may; *thor(f)* 3SG.PRES [OE þurfan]

t(h)ūsend, -t *num.* thousand [OE þūsand]

thuwingga → **thwinga**

th(u)win(g)ga *III* to force

ti → **tō**

-ti = **thī** → **thū**

tiāch → **thiāch**

tiāl → **thiāl**

tiā(n) *II* to pull, draw; bring forth; beget, procreate; march against; appeal to, plead; *tiānde* INFL.INF; *tye* 3SG.PRES.SUBJ; *tēgen, -in, tāghen* PL.PRET; *etein* PP [OE tēon]

tiān *num.* ten [OE tēon]

tiānda, -e *num.* tenth

tichta *m.* accusation; *tichtan* ACC.PL [cf. OE tihte, f.]

tichtega *m.* accusation; *tigtega* ACC.SG

tīd, tiid, tyd, -t *f.* time; hour [OE tīd]

tig- → **tich-**

til *prep. + dat./ins.* to; *til thiu* in order that [OE til]

tilath *f.* labour; yield; *tilathe* DAT.SG [cf. OE tilð]

timber *n.* building; *timber* NOM.PL [OE timber]

tins *m.* tax, tribute [< OS < OHG zins < L cēnsus]

tiūch *n.* witness [OHG giziug]

tō, thō, -oe-, te, ti *prep. + dat./acc.* to; up to; until; towards; at; in; for, as [OE tō]

tōbehōra∞ *1* (*impers.vb. + dat.*) to befit; *thōbehoert∞* 3SG.PRES (cf. **hēra**)

tōbreka *V* to break in pieces, destroy; *tōbrekth* 3SG.PRES; *tōbretzen, -breken* PP

tōbrendza *1* to inflict; *tōbrogte* 3SG.PRET.IND/SUBJ

tōfara¹ *prep. + acc.* before, in front of [OE tōforan]

tōfara² *VI* to go to; *tōfōren* PRET.PL.SUBJ

tōfarastonda *VI* to represent, be substitute

tōgader(e), -th- *adv.* together [OE tōgædre]

tōhlāpa *VII* to walk up to; *tōhlapt* 3SG.PRES [OE hlēapan]

tōiōniskuma *IV + dat.* to meet; *~kōmin* PL.PRET [OE tōġeġn]

tolef → **twelef**

tōmāl∞ *adv.* great; *t(h)oemael*

tor *m.* tower [< L turris]

tōre = **tō** + **there** (→ **thī**)

tōrenda *1* to rend apart, wound badly; *tōrent* PP [OE rendan]

tornig *adj.* angry [cf. OE torn]

tōsamene, -semine *adv.* together [OE samin]

tōsēka *1* to sue for, demand; *tōsocht* PP [OE sēċan]

tōsetta *1* to appoint

tōsocht → **tōsēka**

tōspreka *V* to accuse; *spreke ... to* 1SG.PRES

tōwe → **tāwe**

tōwerīe∞ *f.* sorcery [OE tēafor]

trāst, -ae- *f.* help, support [OIce traust]

trāsta *1* to comfort; encourage; *trāste* 3SG.PRET

trē *n.* tree [OE trēow]

tribēte → **thribēte**

trindumbe *adv.* roundabout [cf. OE trendel]

trine → **thrina**

triūwe, trōwe, -ou- *adj.* reliable, trustworthy [OE trīewe]

trōwe *f.* faithfulness; *trouwa* ACC.SG [OE trēow]

tseremon *m.* (free) man; *szeremonnis* GEN.SG [szere < tserl; cf. OE ċeorl]

tsiāsa → **kiāsa**

tsietel *m.* cauldron; kettle; *tsietele, szetele* DAT.SG [< L catīnum]

tsiurce, tzer(c)ke *f.* church; *tsiurca, tzercka* DAT.SG [< OE ċyriċe]

tsīvia *2* to quarrel; *szīwe* 3SG.PRES.SUBJ [OIce kífa]

tu- see also **tw-**

tuischa → **twiska**

ture → **turve**

tuchtelās *adj.* impotent, infertile [cf. **tiā**]

tunge *f.* tongue; *tunga* DAT.SG [OE tunge]

turf *m.* grassland; *turves* GEN.SG [cf. OE turf]

tur(v)e *f.* turf; sod; grass land; *ture* ACC.SG

twēde *adj./num.* two-thirds [OE twǣde]

twel(e)f, twilif, tu- *num.* twelve [OE tweolf]

twēne, twā *num.* two; *twīra* GEN; *tuām, twām*
  DAT.M; *tuĕn(e), tuĕr, twe(e)r* ACC.M; *tvā*
  F./N; *twē∞; twām* DAT.PL; *an twā spreka* to
  disagree; *oen twā* into two [OE twēġen, twā]

twēra *adv.* truly [< tō + wēr]

twīa *adv.* twice [OE twiwa]

twifald *adj.* double, twofold [OE twifeald]

twīfel, -u- *m.* doubt [OHG zwival]

twilifta *num.* twelfth [OE twelfta]

twintich, -ech *num.* twenty; *twintege* DAT.SG.M;
  twintega DAT.PL [OE twēntiġ]

twintigesta *num.* twentieth

twisk(a), -y- *prep. + acc.* between; *tuischa* [cf.
  OE betwix]

tye → tiā

tyaenie, tyennia → thiānia

tzercka → tsiurce

U

u- see also o-

umbe *adv.* around; *al ~, omme* through

um(be), om *prep. + acc.* around; because of;
  concerning, about [OE umbe]

umbekera *1* to turn around, over [OE ċieran]

un- see also und-, une-, unt-

unbern → un(e)berna

undad → (w)undia

under, on- *prep. + dat.* under; among [OE
  under]

underdēnoch *adj. + dat.* obedient to

underfinda, on- *III* to find out

understonda *VI* to understand; *understōd*
  3SG.PRET

undfā → untfā(n)

undfēngnesse *f.* conception [cf. untfā(n)]

undhwerva *III* to escape, evade; *undhverwe*
  2SG.PRES.SUBJ [OE hweorfan]

un(e)berna *adj./pp.* unborn one [< bera, IV;
  OE beran]

unelathadis *adv.* uninvitedly [cf. OE laðian]

unewaxen *adj./pp.* not fully grown; *unewaxena*
  DAT.PL [< waxa *vb.*]

un(e)wis *adj.* uncertain; *un(e)wissa* DAT.PL [OE
  (ġe)wiss]

unga → gunga

unhēten → un(t)hēta

unhlest *m./f.* noise, unrest; breach of the peace
  [OE hlyst]

uniĕrich *adj.* under age, minor

unriucht, -io- *adj.* unjust, unlawful, false;
  onriochta, -e NOM.PL

uns, vns → wī

untfā(n), und- *VI* to receive; listen to; *undfēth*
  3SG.PRES; *ontfēngk* 3SG.PRET; *ontfenzen* PP

untgunga *VII + gen.* to exonerate oneself

unthalda, ont- *VII* to relieve; *onthalden* INFL.
  INF

unthaudia *1* to decapitate, behead; *vnthaudat*
  3SG.PRES

unthelande *adj./pres.ptc. IV* not concealing,
  public, manifest [cf. OE helan]

un(t)hēta *VII* to promise, pledge; *ontheet*
  3SG.PRET; *unhēten* PP

un(t)ielda *III* to pay (up), recompense; *untgolde* PL.PRET.SUBJ

untsetta, ont- *1* to relieve; *ontset* PP

untslūta *II* to unlock

untspringa *III* to spring up [OE springan]

untswera *IV/V + gen.* to swear innocence

untwēp(e)nia *2* to disarm; *ontwēpende* 3SG.PRET

untwīvelīke *adv.* undoubtedly [cf. OHG zwival]

untwinna *III* to take away from, deprive [OE
  winnan]

unwilla *m.* disapproval [OE unwilla]

unwis → un(e)wis

up *adv.* up, upon; upwards, inland, upcountry
  [OE upp]

up, wp, op *prep. + dat.* upon, on

updwā(n), op- *anom.vb.* to open; *opdien* PP

up(g)ehewen → upheffa

upfā(n) *VII* to raise hands; *fā up* IMP.PL

upgreva, opgrouwa *V* to dig up

upheffa *VI* to raise, begin; *hōf up* 3SG.PRET;
  up(g)ehewen PP [OE hebban]

upiowa *V* to present, hand over; *wpjowe* 3SG.
  PRES.SUBJ [cf. ieva]

uppa[1] *adv.* on top, at the top

uppa[2], op(p)a *prep. + dat./acc.* on; upon; at the
  risk of losing [OE uppan]

upriuchta *1* to raise; erect; *upriucht* 3SG.PRES

upstonda *VII* to rise; stand up; *wpstande* 3SG.
  PRES.SUBJ

uptiā *V* to draw up; *uptīe* 3SG.PRES.SUBJ

ūr *prep. + dat./acc. wr* over; *wr* (ADV) over and
  again (cf. over) [OE ofer]

ūrbec *II* to turn backwards [cf. OE bæc]

urbera *1* (*refl.*) to forfeit; incur a fine by trespassing; *urber(e)de* PL.PRET.SUBJ [OE byrian]

urbiāda *II* to forbid; *urbeden, vorbaden*∞ PP

urbonna *VII* to prohibit; *urbonnane* INFL.INF

urde → wertha

urdēla *1* to sentence (to lose); *urdēl(e)* 3SG.PRES. SUBJ; *urdēld* PP

urevelia *2* to mistreat; *urevelad* PP

urflōka *VII* to curse; *urflōkin* PP [OS flōkan]

urgulden → urielda

urhela *IV* to conceal; *urhelin* PP [OE helan]

ūrhēra *1* to hear fully; *ūrhēred* PP

urjagīa, wr- *2* to drive, chase away; *wrjaghet* PP

ūrjā(n), -y- *V* to give up, leave (cf. **ūrieva**)

ūrield *n.* additional wergeld; *urielde* DAT.SG

urielda *III* to compensate; *urgolden, -gulden* PP

urieta *V* to forget; *urietin* PP [OE forġietan]

ūrieva *V* to give, hand over; *urief* 3SG.PRET (cf. **ūrjā(n)**)

ūrlest *m.* prayer for dying or deceased [< lesa]

urliāsa, ver- *II* to lose; *verlēse* PL.PRES.SUBJ; *urlerin* PP [OE forlēosan]

urmaledīa *1/2* to condemn; *urmaledīad* PP

urmēla *1* to give up, renounce [OE mǣlan]

urmīda *I* to avoid; *wrmīde* 3SG.PRES.SUBJ [OE mīðan]

urnima *IV* to learn (by hearing); *urnomin* PL.PRET

urpena → werpa

urrēda *1* to betray; *urret* 3SG.PRES [OE forrǣdan]

urrēdere *m.* traitor

ursanka *1* to drown; *vrsank'* 3SG.PRES.SUBJ

ūrsiā *V* to see (clearly); *ūrsīe* 3SG.PRES.SUBJ; *ūrsien* PP

urslā(n) *VI* to defeat; *urslain* PP

urstān *VI* to hear, learn; *urstēn* PP

ūrstanda *VI* to surpass, excel; *ūrstōde* 3SG.PRET. SUBJ

ūrste, wr- *adj.superl./sb.m.* leader, officer

urstela *IV* (+ gen.) to steal

urtiā *II* to give up, abandon; *urtiucht* 3SG.PRES; *urtiath* PL.PRES

ūrwald *f.* violence

urweddia *2* to renounce; pawn; mortgage

urwinna *III* to prove guilty; *urwunnen* PP

ūs → wī

ūse, wse *pron.* our; *ūses* GEN.SG; *onze*∞ [OE ūre]

ūt¹ *adj.* finished

ūt² *adv.* outwards, seawards; *wth*

ūt³, vt, wt, wyt *prep.* + *dat.* out; out of, from; *vt'er = ūt + ther(e); ūt'en = ūt + den*∞ (DAT. SG.N) [OE ūt]

ūta¹ *adv.* outwards, towards the sea; from outside [OE ūtan]

ūta² = ūt + thā

ūten = ūt + den

ūtbreka *V* to put out, gouge out; *ūtbrēcon* PRET.PL

ūter¹, wtor *prep.* + *acc.* without; outside [OS ūtar]

ūter² = ūt + ther

ūtes = ūt + thes

ūthalia *2* to fetch, invite; *ūthalath* 3SG.PRES [OS halōn]

ūtieva *V* to mete out, 'give out'

ūtrost *adj.superl./sb.m.* he who lives closest to the sea; *ūtrosta* DAT.SG

ūtsenda *1* to send out, dispatch; *wtzantte* 3SG.PRET

V see also **F** or **W**

vare → wesa

ver- → for-, ur-

Vitesdī *m.* St Vitus's day (15 June)

vlcnum → wolken

volde → willa

vor- → for-

vorbaden → urbiāda

W (see also **F, HW,** and **U**)

wach *interj./adj.* woe [OS wah]

wāch *m.* wall; abdominal wall [OE wāg]

waer → wēr

wakia *2* to be awake; keep watch; *wakandum* PRES.PTC/DAT.PL [OE wacian]

wal → wel(l)

walbera *m.* 'staff-bearer', i.e., pilgrim or beggar [OE wala, -u]

wald¹ *m.* wasteland, moors [OE weald]

wald², -e-, -ye- *f.* power; corporeal faculty; violence; *wyeld* DAT.SG; *wald* ACC.SG; *welde* NOM.PL [cf. OE ġeweald]

walda *VII* + *gen.* to rule [OE wealdan]

wald(e)līk *adj.* powerful, forceful

waldelīka *adv.* powerfully, forcefully

waldewaxe *f.* spine; dorsal muscles; *waldewaxa* DAT.SG [OE wealdweaxe]

*wā(n) *VII* to blow; *woe, wē* 3SG.PRET.SUBJ [OE wāwan]

wandelia *2* to change, turn; *wandelghe* 3sg.
PRES.SUBJ [cf. OE wandlung]

want → hwande

wāra → wēra

ward, -th → wertha

ware → warf

ware(n) → wesa

warf *m.* court, court session; law assembly;
place of execution; *war(v)e* DAT.SG [OE
wearf]

waria *2* to protect; *wariad* PL.PRES
[OE warian]

wart → werda, wertha

warte *f.* 'wart', nipple [OE weart]

warve → warf

wasa → wesa

wāsā → hwāsā

wat → hwet

was'ter = was (→ wesa) + thēr²

wathemhūs *n.* vicarage, parsonage; *-hūse* DAT.SG
[Gmc *weþma- 'gift; dotation'; cf. witma]

waxa, -e- *VII* to grow; *wext, vaxet* 3sg.PRES;
waxen PP [OE weaxan]

wayne → wein

wē → *wā(n)

wed *n.* pledge, promise (with slap of hand);
compensation; ~ *dwā* to give surety;
weddes GEN.SG; *wedde* DAT.SG; *wed*
ACC.PL [OE wedd]

weddia *2* to pledge; *weddath* PL.PRES; *weddaden*
PL.PRET; *weddade* PP/ACC.PL [OE weddian]

wēd(e), -ee- *n.* cloth; dress; means of payment
(worth 12 pence); *wēdis* GEN.SG; *wēda* DAT.
SG; [OE wǣd]

weder∞, -i-, weer¹ *adv.* again (cf. **wither**)

weer² → wither

wegk → widze

wei, wī *m.* road, way; *wīe* DAT.SG [OE weġ]

wein *m.* cart, wain; *weine, wayne* DAT.SG [OE
wæġn]

wel → wel(l)

welde¹ → wald²

welde² → wella

weldich *adj.* powerful, mighty; authorized;
weldega, -iga DAT.SG

welkoma *IV* to (say) welcome; *velkomen∞* INF
[cf. OE wilcuma]

wel(l), -a-, -ee- *adv.* well, rightly; even;
thoroughly; after all; COMP *bet* [OE well]

wella, -i- *anom.vb.* to want to, wish, will; *welt*;
2sg.PRES; *wel, wil* 3sg.PRES; *wellat(h),
ville* PL PRES; *wele, wili* 3sg.PRES.SUBJ;
welle, wolla PL.PRES.SUBJ; *wella, vollet* IMP.
PL; *wolde* 3sg.PRET; *weldon, -in* PL.PRET;
welde(n), wolde(n), volde PL.PRET.IND/SUBJ
[OE willan]

wēna *1* to think [OE wēnan]

wend, *m.* matter, thing; exception; *wendar, -er*
NOM/ACC.PL; *wenda* GEN.PL [OE wend]

wēn'ik = wēne (ē **wēna**) + ik

wēpa *VII* to cry, weep; *wēpande* PRES.PTC [OE
wēpan]

wēpen, -in *n.* weapon; *wēpena* GEN.PL; *wēpnum*
DAT.PL [OE wǣpen]

wēpenia *2* to arm; *wēpena* PP.PL [OE wǣpnian]

wēr *adj.* true; *waer∞* [OE wǣr < OS wār]

wēra, -ā- *conj.* but, except [< ne wēre]

wera *1* to defend [OE werian]

werda, -a- *1* to injure; obstruct; decrease; *ewert,
(e)wart* PP [OE wierdan]

wērde *f.* truth; *werde* DAT.SG [< wēr]

wēre → wesa

were *f.* authority; (authority over) landed
property, estate; *werum, -em* DAT.PL
[OHG giwerī]

were *n.* verification, acknowledgement
[OIce vera]

wergeld *n.* wergild, full compensation [OE
werġield]

werk *n.* work; *werkes* GEN.SG; *wirke* DAT.SG;
verck ACC.PL [OE weorc]

werk(i)a *1/2* to work, labour; *(e)wrocht* PP
(cf. **wir(t)sa**)

werna *1* to warn; take care of; *werne* 3sg.PRES.
SUBJ [OE wearnian]

wēron → wesa

werp *m.* place of execution [OE wyrp]

werpa *III* to throw; summon; *warp* 3sg.PRET;
wurpen PP; *urpena* PP/DAT.SG [OE weorpan]

werth, -d *adj.* + *gen.* worthy of [OE weorð]

wertha, -d-, wirda *III* 1. to become, be (AUX
of passive); *wert(h)* 3sg.PRES; *werthath*
PL.PRES; *werth(e)* 3sg.PRES.SUBJ; *werden,
wir-, wirda* PL.PRES.SUBJ; *warth, ward, wart,
werd∞* 3sg.PRET; *worden* PL.PRET; *wurthe,
urde* 3sg.PRET.SUBJ; *wur-, wor-, wirden* PP
[OE weorðan] 2. + DAT to befall; *nerthe*
3sg.PRES.SUBJ [cf. MDu gewerden]

werther = werth + thēr

werthich, wird- *adj.* worthy

wesa, wasa *V/anom.vb.* to be; *bin, bem* 1SG.
    PRES; *is, his* 3SG.PRES; *send, sint* PL.PRES;
    sē, sī, zee 3SG/PL.PRES.SUBJ; *was* 3SG.PRET;
    wēron, -in, wīren, wāren∞ PL.PRET; neg.
    nēren PL PRET; *wēre, wier, wire* 3SG.PRET.
    SUBJ; *wāre∞, vāre∞, wēre* PL.PRET.SUBJ
    [OE wesan]

wēsklin *n.* orphan; *wēsclinum* DAT.PL [cf.
    OE wāsa]

westa *n.* west [OE westan]

wester *adv.* westwards [cf. OE westerra]

weter → wetir

wether *adv.* again; back [OE wiðer]

wetir, -er *n.* water; water course; *wetere* DAT.
    SG; *wetir* NOM/ACC.PL; *wetiron* DAT.PL [OE
    wæter]

wetma → witma

wexa → waxa

wī[1]**, vy, wy** *pron.* we; *ūser* GEN; *ūs, (h)ws, ons∞,
    uns∞* DAT/ACC [OE wē]

wī[2] **→ wei**

wīa *1* to consecrate; *wīede* PP/DAT.SG.M [cf. OE
    wīh 'idol']

wiāka *II* to escape, evade; *wiākande* PRES.PTC
    [cf. OE wīcan]

wider → weder

widz(i)e, wegk *n.* horse; *widzie, wegke* DAT.SG
    [OE wicg]

wid(w)e *f.* widow; *wyduan* GEN.PL; *widum* DAT.
    PL [OE widwe]

wīe → wei

wier → wesa; hwēr

wīf, -ii- *n.* woman; wife; *wīve, -w-* DAT.SG;
    wīwem DAT.PL [OE wīf]

wīgand m. warrior [OE wīgend]

wīgandlike *adv.* valiantly

wīlās *adj.* unconsecrated; *wīlāse* DAT.SG [cf. OE
    weoh; -lēas]

wild *adj.* wild [OE wild]

wildia *2* to abuse sexually; *wildath* PP [< wald[2]]

wildinge *f.* sexual abuse; *wildinghum* DAT.PL

willa[1] *m.* goodwill, joy; will, wish; *bī ~* with
    consent; *um diis ~* therefore [OE willa]

willa[2] *vb.* **→ wella**

wilmek *n.* voluntary marriage

wīn *m.* wine [< L vīnum]

wind, -y- *m.* wind; *wind(e)* DAT.SG [OE wind]

winna, vynna *III* to win, gain; seize; obtain;
    find; *winnan(d)e, winnende* INFL.INF;
    wynna PL.PRES.SUBJ; *wunnen, wonnen*
    PL.PRET; *wunne* PRET PL.SUBJ; *wonnen* PP
    [OE winnan]

winninge *f.* gain, profit

winster *adj.* left [OE winstre]

winter *m.* winter; *wintres* GEN.SG [OE winter]

wirda → wertha

wirke → werk

wirra *adj.*COMP worse, more evil [cf. OE wiersa]

wirt(e)l(e) *m.* root [cf. OE wyrt]

wir(t)sa, wirza *1* to work [OE wyrčan]

wīs *adj.* wise; *wīse* NOM.PL [OE wīs]

wīs *f.* way, manner; *to likere ~ and* like
    [OE wīs]

wīsa, -ia *1/2* (+ *gen.*) to show; prescribe, decree;
    conduce; *wīsie* 3SG.PRES.SUBJ; *wijse* PL
    PRES.SUBJ; *wīsade* 3SG.PRET; *wīsid, ghe-
    wiist∞* PP [OE wīsian]

wīsdōm *m.* wisdom [OE wīsdōm]

wīshēd *f.* wisdom

wīsie're = wīsie + -re

wiste → wita[2]

wit *n.* sense; *wittes* GEN.SG [OE witt]

wita[1] *1* to acknowledge

wita[2] *pret.pres.* to know; *nēt* 3SG.PRES (< ne +
    wēt) knows not; *wite* 3SG.PRES.SUBJ; *wiste*
    3SG.PRET [OE witan]

wita[3] *m.* witness; *witem* DAT.PL [OE ġewita]

wit(i)gia *2* to predict; *wytgien* INF/SB (the
    act of) predicting [< wit; cf. OIce vittugr
    'skilled in witchcraft']

with *prep.* + *acc.* against; towards [OE wið]

wīthe *f.* anything consecrated; (sacrament
    of) baptism; relics; oath of innocence
    sworn on relics; *wītha* DAT.SG; *wīthe*
    ACC.PL; *wīthon, -em* DAT.PL [OS
    wīhitha]

withedrīva, -w- *I* to force back; *withedrīwe* PL.
    PRES.SUBJ

withecuma *IV* to return, come back

wither, weer *prep.* + *acc.* against; from

witherield *n.* compensation, indemnity

witherstrīdega *m.* rebellious, contumacious
    person

witherweddia *2* to pledge to return

wīthēth *m.* oath (of innocence) sworn on relics;
    -ētha(r) ACC.PL

withspreka *V* to decline, reject; *withsprec* 3SG. PRET

withstān *VI* to withstand

withstonda *VI* to withstand, resist

wit(h)the *f.* collar, *wittha* ACC.SG [OE wiððe]

witma, -e- *m.* dowry; woman's wergeld; wife's legal portion [OE wituma]

wītnia *2* to warn solemnly; *wītnie* 1SG.PRES [OE wītnian]

witscipe *n.* witness [OE witscipe]

witte → hwīt

witzing *m.* pirate; Viking; *witzing* ACC.SG [OE wiċing]

wixel *n.* exchange, interchange; *wix(i)le* DAT.SG [cf. OE wixlan]

woe → wā(n)

wōker *m./n.* usury; *wōkere* DAT.SG [OE wōcor]

wolde → wella

woldsket *n.* 'forest cattle', pigs (cf. **wald, sket**)

wolken *n.* sky; cloud; *wolkem, olcnum, vlcnum* DAT.PL [OE wolcen]

wonder *m.* miracle; *wonder* ACC.SG [OE wundor]

wondria *II* to wander [OE wandrian]

wonnen → winna

word *n.* word; *worde* DAT.SG; *wordem* DAT.PL [OE word]

worde see also **wertha**

wōstene *f.* desert [OE wēsten]

wr(-) → ūr, ur- or for-

wrald *f.* world; *wralde* GEN/DAT.SG; *ruald* ACC. SG; *a ~* in the world, forever [OE weorold]

wrinden → friūnd

wrocht → werkia

wrya → ūrjā(n)

wt(h) → ūt

wt'a = ūt + thā

wtzantte → ūtsenda

wunde *f.* wound; *wndon* DAT.PL [OE wund]

wunder, -o- *n.* miracle [OE wundor]

(w)undia *2* to wound; *undad* PP [OE wundian]

wurthe're = wurthe (→ **wertha**) + -er(e)

wurth *m.* dwelling mound, *terp* [OE wurð]

wyeld → wald²

wyt → ūt

Y

ya → hia

Z

see also **S** and **TS**

zee → hiu or wesa

zunde → sonde²

Glossary of Names

Ādam *m.* Adam

Almēnum *m.* Almenum, district in Westergo, now Harlingen

Anna *f.* St Anna

Augustīnus *m.* St Augustine of Hippo

Axenhof *n.* Axenhof (unidentified place in Westergo), ?'court of axes'; *Axenhove* DAT.SG

Baptista *m.* (St John the) Baptist [< L baptista]

Danemerke *f.pl.* Denmark; *Danemerkum* DAT.PL

Dēldamanes *m.* Deldemanes (perhaps a street in Franeker)

Egypte *m.pl.* Egyptians; *Egypta* GEN.PL [< L Ægyptus]

Êswei *m.* Eswei (unidentified place), ?'road of the gods'; *Êswei* DAT.SG [cf. OE ēsa 'of the gods']

Êva, Êwe *f.* Eve

Flē *f.* the river Flie (Du Vlie)

Frānekere *m.* inhabitant of Franeker (ModWFris Frentsjer); *Frānekra* GEN.PL [< frāna + ekker 'field']

Frēsa, -ī-, -ie- *m.* Frisian; *Frēsan, -en, Friesen* NOM/ACC.PL; *Frēsena,-ie-, Frīsona* GEN.PL; *Frēsum* DAT.PL [OE Frēsa, -ī-]

Frēsland *n.* Frisia, Friesland; *Frēslande* DAT.SG [OE Frēslond]

Gregorius *m.* Gregory the Great (pope 590–606)

Hāchense *m.?* Hoekens (place in Westergo)

Iēronimus *m.* St Jerome

Iohannes *m.* St John

Iotha *m.* Jew; *Iothana* GEN.PL [L Iūdaeus]

Israhel *m.* Israel

Israhelisk *adj.* Israelite

Karle → Kerl

Katherīna *f.* St Catherine

Kerl, Karl(e)∞ *m.* Charles, Charlemagne; *Kerles, -is* GEN.SG; *Kerl(e)* DAT.SG

Crist *m.* Christ [< L Christus]

Leo *m.* Pope Leo III

Liūdingērus *m.* Liudinger, a Saxon rebel

Magnus *m.* Magnus, leader of the Frisians; *Magnus* GEN.SG

Marīe *f.* Mary (Holy Virgin)

Mauricius *m.* St Maurice

Michael *m.* St Michael, archangel; *Michaelis* GEN.SG

Moyses *m.* Moses; *Moyses* GEN.SG; *Moysese, Moysi* DAT.SG

Nīclaus, -ij- *m.* St Nicholas

Octaviānus *m.* Octavian (= Emperor Augustus); *Octaviānus* GEN.SG

Peder, -ir *m.* St Peter [< L Petrus]

Poptatus *m.* Frisian crusader

Pylātus *m.* Pontius Pilate; *Pylātus* GEN.SG

Rēdbād *m.* (King) Redbad

Rōmere *m.* Roman, inhabitant of Rome; *Rōmera, Rūmera* GEN.PL

Rūme *f.* Rome [< L Rōma]

Rūmera → Rōmere

Salomon *m.* King Solomon

Sarracēne *m.* Saracen; *Sarracēnen* PL

Sassisk∞ *adj.* Saxon

Saxa *m.* Saxon; *Saxsona, -enna, -inna* GEN.PL; *Saxum* DAT.PL [OE Seaxe, -an, PL.]

Sēland *n.* coastal district, 'sealand'; *Sēland* ACC. PL; *Sēlandum, -on* DAT.PL

Sinay *f.*(?) Mount Sinai

Stephin *m.* St Stephen, proto-martyr

Vlemsborch *f.* Lisbon

Vlixbonenses *pl.* Lisboans [L]

Wachense *m.*(?) Waekens (place in Westergo)

Widekin *m.* Widukind; *Widekines* GEN.SG [< OS]

Wirtem *m.* Wirdum (place)

Wisere *f.* the river Weser

Bibliography

Ahlsson, Lars-Erik (1960). *Altfriesische Abstraktbildungen*. Uppsala.

—— (1991). 'Untersuchungen zum suffigierten Adjektiv im Altniederdeutschen und Altfriesischen unter Berücksichtigung des Altenglischen', *Niederdeutsches Wort* 31, 77–122.

Alma, Redmer (2000). 'Het Oudfriese Landrecht van het Oldambt', *Us Wurk* 49: 2–45.

—— and Oebele Vries, eds. (1990). '*Summa Agrorum in Slochtra*. Een gedeeltelijke Oudfriese tekst uit de Ommelanden', *Us Wurk* 39, 1–33.

Århammar, Nils R. (1960). 'Zur inselnordfriesischen Wortkunde', *Fryske Stúdzjes oanbean oan Prof. Dr. J.H. Brouwer*, ed. K. Dykstra *et al.* Assen, 279–86.

—— (1969). 'Die friesischen Wörter für "Rad" ("Wheel")', *Kopenhagener germanistische Studien* 1, 35–84.

—— (1977). 'Die *Wurt*-Namen der nordfriesischen Geestinseln und der initiale *w*-Schwund vor *u* im Friesischen', *Onoma* 21, 57–65.

—— (1984). 'Die Lerche (Alauda) im Friesischen … Über Inlautassibilierung, unregelmäßige Lautentwicklung und "Lehnlautungen"', in Århammar *et al.* (1984), 137–52.

—— (1990). 'Friesisch und Sächsisch. Zur Problematik ihrer gegenseitigen Abgrenzung im Früh- und Hochmittelalter', in Bremmer *et al.* (1990), 1–25.

—— (2001a). 'Die Herkunft der Nordfriesen und des Nordfriesischen', in Munske (2001), §50.

—— (2001b). 'Grundzüge nordfriesischer Sprachgeschichte', in Munske (2001), §75.

—— (2004). 'Etymologische und lautgeschichtliche Randbemerkungen zu Band 19 (2003) des "Wurdboek fan de Fryske Taal"', *Us Wurk* 53, 106–43.

—— *et al.*, eds. (1984). *Miscellanea Frisica. A New Collection of Frisian Studies*. Assen.

Blok, P.J. *et al.*, eds. (1896–99). *Oorkondenboek van Groningen en Drente*, 2 vols. Groningen.

Blom, Alderik H. (2007). 'Language Admixture in the Old West Frisian *Basle Wedding Speeches*?', in Bremmer *et al.* (2007), 1–27.

Bor, Arie (1990). 'The Use of the Negative Adverbs *ne* and *nawet* in Old Frisian', in Bremmer *et al.* (1990), 26–41.

Bos-Van der Heide, H.S.E., ed. (1937). *Het Rudolfsboek*. Assen.

Bosworth, Joseph and T. Northcote Toller (1898). *An Anglo-Saxon Dictionary*. Oxford; T.N. Toller, *Supplement*. Oxford, 1920; A. Campbell, *Addenda and Corrigenda*. Oxford, 1972.

Boutkan, Dirk (1996). *A Concise Grammar of the Old Frisian Dialect of the First Riustring Manuscript*. Odense.

—— (1997). 'The Origin of *mon*', *It Beaken* 59, 1–13.

—— and Sjoerd M. Siebinga (2005). *Old Frisian Etymological Dictionary*, Leiden Indo-European Etymological Dictionary Series 1. Leiden and Boston.

Bremmer Jr, Rolf H. (1982). 'Old English – Old Frisian: The Relationship Reviewed', *Philologia Frisica Anno 1981*, 79–88.

—— (1983). 'Old English *feoh and feorh*, Old Norse *fé ok fjǫr*, Ergo: Old Frisian *fiā and ferech* "money and life"', *Us Wurk* 32, 55–62.

—— (1984). '"Substantival Adverbs" and "Prepositionalization" in Old Frisian, Compared with Old English in Particular', *Neuphilologische Mitteilungen* 85, 411–21.

—— (1986). 'The So-called "Impersonal Verb"-Construction in Old Frisian', *NOWELE* 8, 71–95.

—— (1989a). 'Late Medieval and Early Modern Opinions on the Affinity between English and Frisian: The Growth of a Commonplace', *Folia Linguistica Historica* 9, 167–91.

—— (1989b). 'Late Old Frisian *ay* 'yes': An Unnoticed Parallel to Early Modern English *ay(e)* 'yes' (of Obscure Origin)', *NOWELE* 13, 87–105.

—— (1990). 'The Nature of the Evidence for a Frisian Participation in the *Adventus Saxonum*', *Britain 400–600: Language and History*, ed. A. Bammesberger and A. Wollmann. Heidelberg, 353–71.

—— (1992). *A Bibliographical Guide to Old Frisian Studies*. Odense.

—— (1996). 'Old Frisian Dialectology and the Position of the "Ommelanden"', *A Frisian and Germanic Miscellany, Published in Honour of Nils Århammar* (= *NOWELE* 28/29), 1–18.

—— (1997). 'Bad Frisian and Bad Low German: Interference in the Writings of a Medieval West Frisian', *Multilingua* 16, 375–88.

—— (1998). 'Insults Hurt: Verbal Injury in Late Medieval Frisia', in Bremmer *et al.* (1998), 89–112.

—— (2001). 'The Study of Frisian to the End of the 19th Century', in Munske (2001), §1.

——— (2004). *'Hir is eskriven'. Lezen en schrijven in de Friese landen rond 1300*. Hilversum and Leeuwarden.

—— (2005). 'Old Frisian *fule* and *felo* 'much, many': An Ideosyncracy in Germanic and Frisian Perspective', *Papers on Scandinavian and Germanic Language and Culture, Published in Honour of Michael Barnes* (= *NOWELE* 46/47), 31–40.

—— (2007a). 'Language and Content of the Old Frisian Manuscripts from Rüstringen (*c.*1300): A "Veritable *Mixtum Compositum*"', in Bremmer *et al.* (2007), 29–64.

—— (2007b). 'Footprints of Monastic Instruction: A Latin Psalter with Interverbal Old Frisian Glosses', *Signs on the Edge. Space, Text and Margin in Medieval Manuscripts*, ed. S.L. Keefer and R.H. Bremmer Jr. Mediaevalia Groningana N.S. 10. Paris, Louvain and Dudley, MA, 203–34.

—— (2008a). 'Saxon Loans in Rüstring Old Frisian', *Northern Voices: Essays on Old Germanic and Related Topics, Offered to Professor Tette Hofstra*, ed. K. Dekker, A.A. MacDonald and H. Niebaum. Mediaevalia Groningana N.S. 11. Paris, Louvain and Dudley, MA, 191–201.

—— (2008b). 'North-Sea Germanic at the Cross-Roads: The Emergence of Frisian and Hollandish'. *NOWELE* 54–55, 279–308.

——, Geart van der Meer and Oebele Vries, eds. (1990). *Aspects of Old Frisian Philology*. Amsterdamer Beiträge zur älteren Germanistik 31–32/Estrikken 60. Amsterdam, Atlanta, GA and Groningen; repr. 2007.

——, Thomas S.D. Johnston and Oebele Vries, eds. (1998). *Approaches to Old Frisian Philology*. Amsterdamer Beiträge zur älteren Germanistik 49/Estrikken 72. Amsterdam, Atlanta, GA and Groningen.

——, Stephen Laker and Oebele Vries, eds. (2007). *Advances in Old Frisian Philology*. Amsterdamer Beiträge zur älteren Germanistik 64/Estrikken 80. Amsterdam and New York.

Breuker, Philippus H., ed. (1996). *'Landrecht der Vriesne'. Tekstuitgave en commentaar*. Leeuwarden.

Brouwer, Jelle H., ed. (1941). *Thet Autentica Riocht*. Assen.

Buijtenen, Maria P. van (1953). *De grondslag van de Friese vrijheid*. Assen.

Buma, Wybren Jan (1949a). *Die Brokmer Rechtshandschriften*. OTR 5. The Hague.

—— (1949b). *Het godsoordeel in de Oud-Friese literatuur*. Groningen and Batavia.

——— (1950). 'Geestelijke literatuur in Oud-Friesland', *Trijeresom*. Grins [Groningen] and Djakarta, 5–50.

—— (1954). *Het Tweede Rüstringer Handschrift*. OTR 8. The Hague.

—— (1957). *Aldfryske Houlikstapraken*. Assen.

——, ed. (1961). *De Eerste Riustringer Codex*. OTR 11. The Hague.

—— and Wilhelm Ebel. *Altfriesische Rechtsquellen*, Göttingen:

Vol. 1: *Das Rüstringer Recht*. 1963.

Vol. 2: *Das Brokmer Recht*. 1965.

Vol. 3: *Das Emsinger Recht*. 1967.

Vol. 4: *Das Hunsinger Recht*. 1969.

Vol. 5: *Das Fivelgoer Recht*. 1972.

Vol. 6, 1–2: *Jus Municipale Frisionum I–II*. 1977.

——, P. Gerbenzon *et al.*, eds. (1963). *Fryske Stikken út Codex Furmerius, I–II*. Estrikken 33–34. Grins [= Groningen].

——, P. Gerbenzon and M. Tragter-Schubert, eds. (1993). *Codex Aysma*. Leeuwarden and Maastricht.

Caie, Graham D. (1976). *The Judegement Day Theme in Old English Poetry*. Copenhagen.

Campbell, Alistair (1939). 'Some Old Frisian Sound-Changes', *Transactions of the Philological Society* 1939, 78–107.

——, ed. (1952). *Thet Freske Riim. Tractatus Alvini*. The Hague.

—— (1959). *Old English Grammar*. Oxford.

Dekker, Kees (2000). 'Between Rome and Rüstringen: Latin Loan Words in Old Frisian', *Philologia Frisica Anno 1999*, 27–56.

Dyk, Siebren (2007). 'Jorwert Breaking: A Late Old West Frisian Sound Change', in Bremmer *et al.* (2007), 91–128.

Elsakkers, Marianne (2004). '*Her anda neylar*: An Intriguing Criterion for Abortion in Old Frisian Law', *Scientiarum Historica* 30, 107–54.

Ernst, Peter (2005). *Deutsche Sprachgeschichte*. Vienna.

Fairbanks, Sidney, ed. (1939). *The Old West Frisian 'Skeltana Riucht'*. Cambridge, MA.

Faltings, Volkert F. (1987). 'Zum *-el-* Einschub bei der Kompositumsbildung im Nordfriesischen unter besonderer Berücksichtigung der Flurnamen', *Sprachwissenschaft* 12, 381–95.

—— (1996). 'Zur Bildung desubstantivischer Adjektiva mit dem Derivationssuffix *-ed/-et* im Friesischen und in verwandten Sprachen', *Us Wurk* 45, 79–113.

Feitsma, Anthonia (2001). 'Von der Friesischen Philologie zur Frisistik im 20. Jahrhundert', in Munske (2001), §2.

Fell, Christine (1986). 'Old English *wicing*: A Question of Semantics', *Proceedings of the British Academy*, 295–316.

Fokkema, Klaas, ed. (1953). *De Tweede Emsinger Codex*. OTR 7. The Hague.

——, ed. (1959). *De Derde Emsinger Codex*. OTR 10. The Hague.

Fulk, Robert D. (1998). 'The Chronology of Anglo-Frisian Sound Changes', in Bremmer *et al.* (1998), 139–54.

Galama, E.G.A. (1990). 'Altfriesisch *tha heliga* "H.Hostie, das Allerheiligste"', in Bremmer *et al.* 1990, 85–101.

Gelderen, Margreet van, and Árpád P. Orbán (1990). 'Ein lateinisches Ehetrakt und dessen Beziehung zu den drei altfriesischen Traureden in dem Manuskript', in Bremmer *et al.* (1990), 102–24.

Gerbenzon, Pieter, ed. (1954). *Codex Parisiensis*. OTR 9. The Hague.

—— (1956). *Excerpta legum. Onderzoekingen betreffende enkele Friese rechtsboeken uit de vijftiende eeuw*. Groningen and Djakarta.

—— (1958). *Friese rechtstaal en vreemd recht*. Groningen.

—— (1960). 'Oudfries *lest* "lust" en/of Oudfries *lâst, lêst* "voetstap"', *Us Wurk* 9, 76–79.

——, ed. (1961). *Rudolfsboekmateriael*. Estrikken 32. Groningen.

—— (1965). *Kleine Oudfriese kronieken*. Groningen.

—— ed. (1967). *Friese Brieven uit de vijftiende en zestiende eeuw*. Estrikken 42. Grins [Groningen].

—— (1982). 'Oudfriese handschriftfragmenten in de Koninklijke Bibliotheek te 's-Gravenhage', *Tijdschrift voor Rechtsgeschiedenis/Legal History Review* 50, 263–77.

Geuenich, Dieter (1985). 'Soziokulturelle Voraussetzungen, Sprachraum und Diagliederung des Althochdeutschen', *Sprachgeschichte. Ein Handbuch zur Geschichte der deutschen Sprache und ihrer Erforschung*, ed. W. Besch, O. Reichmann and S. Sonдеregger, 2 vols. (Berlin and New York) II, 982–93.

Giliberto, Concetta (2007). 'The Fifteen Signs of Doomsday of the First Riustring Manuscript', in Bremmer *et al.* (2007), 129–52.

Gosses, Godard (1928). *De Friesche Oorkonden uit het Archief van het St Anthony-Gasthuis te Leeuwarden. I. Een bijdrage tot de kennis der historische grammatika van het Westfriesch*. Bolsward.

Haan, Germen de (2001a). 'Recent Trends in Frisian Linguistics', in Munske (2001), §4.

—— (2001b). 'Syntax of Old Frisian', in Munske (2001), §61.

—— (2001c). 'Why Old Frisian Is Really Middle Frisian', *Folia Linguistica Historica* 22, 179–206.

Harbert, Wayne (2007). *The Germanic Languages*. Cambridge.

Helten, Willem L. van (1890). *Altostfriesische Grammatik*. Leeuwarden. [repr. 1970]

—— (1907). *Zur Lexikographie des Altostfriesischen*. Amsterdam. [repr. 1984]

Hettema, Montanus de Haan, ed. (1834–35). *Jurisprudentia Frisica of Friesche Regtkennis. Een handschrift uit de vijftiende eeuw*, 3 vols. Leeuwarden.

Heuser, Wilhelm (1903). *Altfriesisches Lesebuch mit Grammatik und Glossar*. Heidelberg.

Hill, Thomas D. (1998). 'Two Notes on the Old Frisian *Fiā-ēth*', in Bremmer *et al.* (1998), 169–78.

His, Rudolph (1901). *Das Strafrecht der Friesen im Mittelalter*. Leipzig.

Hoekstra, Eric (2001). 'Frisian Relicts in the Dutch Dialects', in Munske (2001), §17.

Hoekstra, Jarich (1993a). '*Ik woe ik ien zoepke hie*: winskjende sinnen sûnder *dat* yn it Midfrysk', *Tydskrift foar Fryske Taalkunde* 8, 34–42.

—— (1993b). '*Ig*-tiidwurden en *g*-tiidwurden', *Us Wurk* 42, 1–68.

—— (1996). 'Transitive Pronouns and Gender Syncretism in Fering-Öömrang (North Frisian)'. *NOWELE* 27, 45–66.

—— (2000). 'Ta Aldfrysk *t(h)riuch* njonken *t(h)ruch* "per"', *Us Wurk* 49, 114–20.

—— (2001). 'Outline History of West Frisian', in Munske (2001), §72.

Hoekstra, Jelle, ed. (1940). *Die gemeinfriesischen Siebzehn Küren*. Assen.

——, ed. (1950). *De eerste en de tweede Hunsinger Codex*. OTR 6. The Hague.

Hofmann, Dietrich (1964/1989). '"Germanisch" *ē*₂ im Friesischen', in *idem, Gesammelte Schriften II*, 165–90.

—— (1969/1989). 'Urgermanisch *wesar* "Frühling"?', in *idem, Gesammelte Schriften II*, 215–27.

—— (1970/1989). 'Die osterlauwerssche Urkundenüberlieferung als Quelle für das Altfriesische', in *idem, Gesammelte Schriften II*, 260–71.

—— (1971/1989). 'Die Sprache der Fivelgoer Handschrift und die Gliederung des Altfriesischen. Zu Bo Sjölins AuSgabe', in *idem, Gesammelte Schriften II*, 284–306.

—— (1972–73/1989). 'Fries. *tiuche*, deutsch *zeche*, griech. *díkē* und Verwandte', in *idem, Gesammelte Schriften II*, 307–32.

—— (1976/1989). '"Thor", "Donnerstag"und "Donner" in Friesland', in *idem, Gesammelte Schriften II*, 366–75.

—— (1982/1989). 'Zur Syntax der Zehnerzahlen mit Substantiv in den altgermanischen Sprachen, insbesondere im Altfriesischen', in *idem, Gesammelte Schriften*, 566–87.

—— (1989). *Gesammelte Schriften. II. Studien zur friesischen und niederdeutschen Philologie*. Hamburg.

—— (1995). 'Zur Monophthongierung von germanisch *ai* und *au* im Altfriesischen und in seinen Nachbarsprachen', *Lingua Theodisca. Beiträge zur Sprach- und Literaturwissenschaft*, ed. J. Cajot, L. Kremer and H. Niebaum. Münster and Hamburg, 23–36.

—— (1998). 'Altriustringisch *fili* "Grasland"', *Us Wurk* 47, 117–28.

Hofmann, Dietrich, and Anne T. Popkema (2008). *Altfriesisches Handwörterbuch*. Heidelberg.

Holthausen, Ferdinand (1925/1984). *Altfriesisches Wörterbuch*, 2nd ed. D. Hofmann. Heidelberg.

—— (1934). *Altenglisches etymologisches Wörterbuch*. Heidelberg.

—— (1936). 'Altfriesische Münzwerte und Bußsätze', *Beiträge zur Geschichte der deutschen Sprache und Literatur* 60, 458–60.

Jansen, H.P.H., and A. Janse, eds. and trans. (1991). *Kroniek van het klooster Bloemhof te Wittewierum*. Hilversum.

Johnston, Thomas S.B. (1993). 'Aldfryske trijeliddige foarmen mei de ôfslutende mulwurden fan *wesa* en *wertha*', *Tydskrift foar Fryske Taalkunde* 8, 52–62.

—— (1994). 'Hoe hat it winliks west? De konstruksje fan de folsleine tiid fan it Aldfryske *wesa* en it Midfryske *wezze*', *Tydskrift foar Fryske Taalkunde*, 9, 1–23.

—— (1995). '*Ene Zie Borch tho Bowenn* … : A New Look at the Pan-Frisian Dike Law in Light of a Low Saxon Ommeland Version', *Us Wurk* 44, 1–37.

—— (1998a). 'Old Frisian Law and the Frisian Freedom Ideology: Text and Manuscript Composition as a Marketing Device', in Bremmer *et al.* (1998), 179–214.

—— (1998b). *Codex Hummercensis. An Old Frisian Manuscript in Low Saxon Guise*. Leeuwarden.

—— (2001a). 'The Old Frisian Law Manuscripts and Law Texts', in Munske (2001), §54.

—— (2001b). 'The Middle Low German Translations of Old Frisian Legal Texts', in Munske (2001), §55.

Kaufmann, Friedrich (1908). 'Altgermanische Religion', *Archiv für Religionswissenschaft* 11, 105–26.

Klaarbergen, Berend W. van, ed. (1947). *Das altwestfriesische jüngere Schulzenrecht*. Drachten.

Krolis-Sytsema, Johanneke C. (1989). '*Quetha, sidza* und *spreka*: ein altfriesisches Wortfeld besprochen', *Frysk & Vrije Universiteit (1949–1989)*, ed. A.M.J. Riemersma *et al.* Amsterdam, 109–23.

Laker, Stephen (2007). 'Palatalization of Velars: A Major Link of Old English and Old Frisian', in Bremmer *et al.* (2007), 165–84.

Langbroek, Erika (1990). '*Condensa atque tenebrosa*. Die altfriesischen Psalmen: Neulesung und Rekonstruktion (UB Groningen Hs 404)', in Bremmer *et al.* (1990), 255–84.

—— (2007). 'Die Sprache von Bernardus Rordahuzim in der niederdeutschen Apokalypse der Baseler Handschrift F.VII.12, folio 211rB217r', in Bremmer *et al.* (2007), 185–212.

Lass, Roger (2000). 'Language Periodization and the Concept of "Middle"', *Placing Middle English in Context*, ed. I. Taavitsainen, T. Nevalainen, P. Pahta and M. Rissanen. Berlin and New York, 7–41.

Löfstedt, Ernst (1928–1931). *Nordfriesische Dialektstudien. Die nordfriesische Mundart des Dorfes Ockholm und der Halligen*, 2 vols. Lund.

—— (1932). 'Zur Lautgeschichte der Mundart von Wangerooge', in *idem, Zwei Beiträge zur friesischen Sprachgeschichte*. Lund, 3–33.

—— (1963–69). 'Beiträge zur nordseegermanischen und nordseegermanisch-nordischen Lexikographie', *Niederdeutsche Mitteilungen* 19–21, 281–345; 22, 39–64; 23, 11–61; 25, 25–39.

Looijenga, Tineke, and Arend Quak, eds. (1996). *Frisian Runes and Neighbouring Traditions*. Amsterdamer Beiträge zur älteren Germanistik 45.

Lühr, Rosemarie (2007). 'Bedingungssätze in altfriesischen Rechtstexten', in Bremmer *et al.* (2007), 213–38.

Luick, Karl (1914–1940). *Historische Grammatik der englischen Sprache. I–II.* Repr. as one volume Oxford, 1964.

Markey, Thomas L. (1981). *Frisian.* Trends in Linguistics. State-of-the-Art Reports 13. The Hague, Paris and New York.

Meer, Geart van der (1990). 'On the Position of the Old Frisian Verbs and Pronouns', in Bremmer *et al.* (1990), 311–35.

Meijering, Henk D. (1970). '*Widekin, thi forma asega*, Flecht op 'e koai. *Stúdzjes oanbean oan Prof. Dr. W.J. Buma ta syn sechstichste jierdei*, ed. T. Hoekema *et al.* Groningen, 53–61.

——, ed. (1974). *De Willekeuren van de Opstalsboom (1323). Een filologisch-historische monografie.* Groningen.

—— (1980). '*d(e)*-Deletion in the Past Tense of the Class II Weak Verbs in Old Frisian', *Linguistic Studies Offered to Berthe Siertsema*, ed. D.J. van Alkemade *et al.* Amsterdam, 277–86.

—— (1986). *Oudfriese kronieken uit het Handschrift Leeuwarden RA Schw. 3992.* Co-Frisica 1A–B. Amsterdam and Kiel.

—— (1989). 'Het Oudfriese *ar*-meervoud. Feiten en interpretaties.' *Amsterdamer Beiträge zur älteren Germanistik* 28, 21–41.

—— (1990). 'Die altfriesischen monosyllabischen Infinitive auf -*n* und die Gliederung des Altfriesischen', in Bremmer *et al.* 1990, 335–48.

Miedema, Hendricus T.J. (1977). 'De breking en zijn uitwerking in Oudfriese namen met *Briocht* (naast *Brecht*).' *Naamkunde* 9, 79–88.

—— (1986). 'Oorkonde, dialekt en kaart. Taljochting by in kaart fan Aldfryske dialektfoarmen út 1402–1544', *Us Wurk* 35, 12–26.

Mitchell, Bruce (1985). *Old English Syntax*, 2 vols. Oxford.

Moulton, William G. (1972). 'The Proto-Germanic Non-syllabics (Consonants)', *Toward a Grammar of Proto-Germanic*, ed. F. van Coetsem and H.L. Kufner. Tübingen, 141–73.

Munske, Horst H. (1973). *Der germanische Rechtswortschatz im Bereich der Missetaten. Philologische und sprachgeographische Untersuchungen. I. Die Terminologie der älteren westgermanischen Rechtsquellen.* Berlin and New York.

——, gen. ed. (2001). *Handbuch des Friesischen/Handbook of Frisian Studies.* Tübingen.

—— (2001a). 'Wortbildung des Altfriesischen', in Munske (2001), §62.

Murdoch, Brian (1994). 'The Old Frisian *Adam octopartitus*', *Amsterdamer Beiträge zur älteren Germanistik* 40, 131–38.

—— (1998). 'Authority and Authenticity: Comments on the Prologues to the Old Frisian Laws', in Bremmer *et al.* (1998), 215–44.

Nauta, K. (1941). *Die altfriesischen allgemeinen Bußtaxen: Texte und Untersuchungen.* Assen.

Nielsen, Hans F. (1985). *Old English and the Continental Germanic Languages*, 2nd ed. Innsbruck.

—— (1994). 'Ante-Old Frisian', *NOWELE* 24, 91–136.

—— (2001). 'Frisian and the Grouping of the Older Germanic Languages', in Munske (2001), §48.

Nijdam, Han (1999). 'The Loss of Old Frisian *h* in Initial Consonant Clusters', *Amsterdamer Beiträge zur älteren Germanistik* 51, 81–104.

Noomen, Paul N. (1989). 'St Magnus van Hollum en Celdui van Esens: Bijdrage tot de chronologie van de Magnustraditie', *De Vrije Fries* 69, 7–32.

—— (2001). '*Hachens* en *Wachens*: Feit en fiksje yn midsieusk Fryslân.' *Speculum Frisicum. Stúdzjes oanbean oan Philippus H. Breuker*, ed. R.H. Bremmer Jr, L.G. Jansma and P. Visser. Leeuwarden and Leiden, 3–22.

Oosterhout, Meinte, ed. (1960–64). (I): *Snitser Recesboeken 1490–1517.* (II): *Nammeregister op de Snitser Recesboeken.* Assen.

—— 'Aldfrysk *a* "ivich, lang, duorjend, fêst" yn gearstallingen.' *Studia Frisica in memoriam Prof. Dr. K. Fokkema 1898–1967 scripta*, ed. H.D. Meijering, H.T.J. Miedema and Y. Poortinga. Groningen, 88–99.

Page, R.I. (2001). 'Frisian Runic Inscriptions', in Munske (2001), §49.

Poortinga, Ype (1965). *De palmridder van Lissabon*. Leeuwarden.

Popkema, Anne T. (2007). 'Die altfriesischen Eidesbezeichnungen', in Bremmer *et al.* (2007), 324–55.

Quak, Arend (1990). 'Runica Frisica', in Bremmer *et al.* (1990), 357–70.

Ramat, Paolo (1976). *Das Friesische. Eine sprachliche und kulturgeschichtliche Einführung.* Innsbruck.

Rauch, Irmengard (2007). 'Gender Semiotics, Anglo-Frisian *wīf*, and Old Frisian Noun Gender', in Bremmer *et al.* (2007), 357–66.

Reinders, H.R. (1988). 'Een dertiende-eeuwse sluis in de Oude Ried bij Buitenpost', *Terpen en wierden in het Fries-Groningse kustgebied*, ed. M. Bierma *et al.* Groningen, 260–69.

Rhee, Florus van der (1974). 'Die starken Verben der IV. und V. Klasse im Altfriesischen', *Us Wurk* 23, 123–27; 24 (1975), 160.

Richthofen, Karl von, ed. (1840a). *Friesische Rechtsquellen*. Göttingen. [repr. Aalen, 1960]

—— (1840b). *Altfriesisches Wörterbuch*. Göttingen. [repr. Aalen, 1961, 1970]

Scheuermann, Ulrich (2001). 'Friesische Relikte im ostfriesischen Niederdeutsch', in Munske (2001), §39.

Schilt, Jelka (1990). 'Zur Verteilung der syntaktischen Fügung *aga te* 'müssen' + Gerundium und ihren semantischen Konkurrenten in einigen altfriesischen Texten', in Bremmer *et al.* (1990), 391–407.

Siebs, Theodor (1901). 'Geschichte der friesischen Sprache', *Grundriss der germanischen Philologie I*, ed. H. Paul, 2nd Edn., Strassburg, 1152–464.

Simonides, Dina, ed. (1938). *Die Hunsingoer Küren vom Jahre 1252 und das Ommelander Landrecht vom Jahre 1448*. Assen.

Sipma, Pieter, ed. (1927, 1933, 1941). *Oudfriesche Oorkonden, I–III*. OTR 1–3. The Hague.

——, ed. (1943). *De eerste Emsinger Codex*. OTR 4. The Hague.

—— (1947). *Fon Alra Fresena Fridome. In ynlieding yn it Aldfrysk*. Snits [Sneek].

Sjölin, Bo (1966). 'Zur Gliederung des Altfriesischen', *Us Wurk* 15, 25–38.

—— (1969). *Einführung in das Friesische*. Stuttgart.

——, ed. (1970–75). *Die 'Fivelgoer' Handschrift, I–II*. OTR 12–13. The Hague.

—— (1984). 'Die Gliederung des Altfriesischen – ein Rückblick', in Åhrhammar *et al.* (1984), 55–66.

Smith, Laura C. (2007). 'Old Frisian Vowel Balance and its Relationship to West Germanic Apocope and Syncope', in Bremmer *et al.* (2007), 379–410.

Smith, Norval, and Klaske van Leyden (2007). 'The Unusual Outcome of a Level-Stress Situation: The Case of Wursten Frisian'. *NOWELE* 52, 31–66.

Spenter, Arne (1968). *Der Vokalismus der akzentuierten Silben in der Schiermonnikooger Mundart. Eine geschichtliche Studie des autochthonen westfriesischen Inseldialekts.* Copenhagen

Stanley, Eric G. (1979). 'Two Old English Phrases Insufficiently Understood for Literary Criticism: *þing gehegan* and *seonoþ gehegan*', *Old English Poetry: Essays on Style*, ed. D.C. Calder. Berkeley, Los Angeles, and London, 67–90.

—— (1984). 'Alliterative Ornament and Alliterative Rhythmical Discourse in Old High German and Old Frisian Compared with Similar Manifestations in Old English', *Beiträge zur Geschichte der deutschen Sprache und Literatur* 106, 184–217.

Steller, Walther, ed. (1926). *Das altwestfriesische Schulzenrecht*. Breslau. [repr. Hildesheim and New York, 1977].

—— (1928). *Abriß der altfriesischen Grammatik*. Halle.

Stiles, Patrick V. (1985–86). 'The Fate of the Numeral "4" in Germanic I–III', *NOWELE* 6, 81–104; 7, 3–21; 8, 3–25.

—— (1995). 'Remarks on the "Anglo-Frisian" Thesis', *Friesische Studien II*, ed. V.F. Faltings, A.G.H. Walker and O. Wilts, 177–220.

Versloot, Arjen (2001a). 'Grundzüge ostfriesischer Sprachgeschichte', in Munske (2001), §73.

—— (2001b). 'Vergleichende Aspekte friesischer Lautgeschichte', in Munske (2001), §76.

—— (2003). 'Fries in Holland in de 17e eeuw', *Taal & Tongval* 55, 1–40.

—— (2004). 'Why Old Frisian is Still Quite Old', *Folia Linguistica Historica* 25, 253–98.

Vries, Oebele, ed. (1977). *Oudfriese Oorkonden IV*. OTR 14. The Hague.

—— (1984). 'De âldfryske ivichheidsformule', in Århammar *et al.* (1984), 89–96.

—— (1993). *'Naar ploeg en koestal vluchtte uw taal'. De verdringing van het Fries als schrijftaal door het Nederlands (tot 1580)*. Leeuwarden.

—— (1998). 'Ist im Altfriesischen die Dualform *wit* belegt?', *Us Wurk* 47, 129–35.

—— (2001a). 'Die Verdrängung des Altfriesischen als Schreibsprache', in Munske (2001), §58.

—— (2001b). 'Die altfriesischen Urkunden', in Munske (2001), §56.

—— (2007). *Asega, is het dingtijd? De hoogtepunten van de Oudfriese tekstoverlevering*. Leeuwarden.

Wollmann, Alfred (1990). 'Zu den frühesten lateinischen Lehnwörtern im Altfriesischen', in Bremmer *et al.* (1990), 506–36.

Index of forms in chapters on grammar

For reasons of relevance (and space), this index of forms is based on Chapters II 'Phonology', III 'Morphology', and V 'Dialectology'. References are to the numbered sections. R = Remark, n = footnote. For reference, also consult the rather detailed table of contents at the beginning of the book. Modern Frisian forms appear on p. 237.

A

ā-, -burch, -lond, -pāl 75
a twēra wegena 125
acht(a) 40, 124
achta hwarve 125
achta(n)tich, achtich ➤ tachtich
aeng ➤ ēnich
āfte 37, ōftne 206.6
āga (tō) 37, 143, hāga 143R.2, 205.8, āch 78.2ch, āchte, ōchte 143R.3
āge 37, 98, 99
āhwedder (āuder) 96
āhwet, āwet 76.4
āider ➤ iāhweder
āin ➤ ēin
āk 37
āka 62, 137
al(l) 40, 96, alra, alder 78.dR, ōlle 206.6
ald 40, 69, 118, 204.a
alder ➤ al(l)
alder 116
aldra ➤ eldra
alsā, ōlsā 206.6
ammon 96
amīe 76.2
ān ➤ ēn
anch ➤ ēnich
andlova, elleva 124
angel 100
ānich, āng 37
anne 37
antwert 208.10
āre 98, 99, 99R.5
arra ➤ erra
arst 37
āsega 99
askia 37

āst 120
aththa 37
āthum 37
āuder ➤ āhwedder
āut, āwet ➤ āhwet
āuwa 76.4

B

baem ➤ bām
*baka, backen, batzen 136.a
bām 37, 75, 100, 204.a, bāmar 204.c, baem 207
bāne 37
batzen ➤ baka
bed 104, bedde 46
bēde 208.9
begunde 133R.2
bēia 76.2
beil 206.2
bēken 103
belga 133
bēn 37, 103, 204a
bera 134.b
berch, berge 78.1g
berdene 66
bereskintse 44R.2
bern 66, bērn 75, bren 66
berna 66
bernde 66
bersta 66, 133.b, 133R.2
(be)skrīa 137c
best 119, 121
bet 121
bet(te)ra 119
beynd 208.6
bi 84R.5
biāda 37, 46, 76.2, 128R, 130, 132, biu(d)th 46.c, 76.2, 132
bidda 135.b

bifara 78.2v
bifela 57, 134.b, 134.bR
bigunna 133R.2
(bi)kringa 133.a
bi-ienna 133R.2
binda 130, 133.a
binetha, binitha 73.e, 205.5
binna 69, 204.a
birch ➤ berch
bisaka/-seka 136.a
biskop 42
bīta 131
biu(d)th ➤ biāda
biūsterlik 76.2
bletsa 44R.2
bliuwa 131
bliā 137.c
blēda 46.b, 75
blīka 131
blōdelsa 66
boda 98, 99, 128R, 204.a
bōdel 66
bōgia 204, 222
bōk 113R.1, boek 207
bold 66
bonna 137.a
borst ➤ burst
bōs 31, 75
bōste 31
bōte 75, 105
brād 37
brast 73
brecht ➤ breka
brēd *adj.* 37, breid 206.2
brēd *sb.* 46.b, 75, 76.2, 206.2
brēda 137.c
brēde *sb.* 107
brēf 75, 103
bregge 106

breid → brēd
breida 133.b
brein 205.6, 222, brīn 205.6
breka 44R.2, 78.1*k*, 135.a, brecht
    78.1*k*, bretsen/britsen 44.1,
    135.a, 204.b
breke, bretse 43.b, 44R.2, 108
bren → bern
brenga, bringa, bren(d)za 78.1*ng*,
    141, brōchte 31, 140
bretse → breke
bretsen/britsen → breka
Briocht 49, 66, 67
briāst 73
brīn → brein
brōchte → brenga
broer → brōther
brōk 113
*brōm 29n
brōr → brōther
brōther 78.2*th*, 110, 208.11, brōr
    208.11, broer 78.2*th*
brouwa 132.a
brūka 75
burna 133.a
burst/borst 66
būta 204.a

D
dād 78.1*d*
dalf → delva
dēd(e) 34, 108
deel → dēl
dei 40, 43, 76.2, 101, dī 75,
    205.6
dēl 108, 125, deel 207
dēla 46.b, 75, 153, 210.6
del(v)a 78.2*v*, 133.b, 133R3
dēma 139.1, dēmande 205.12
dēpa 75
der 78.2*th*
det 208.9
Dichursa 66
Dichusum 66
dī → dei
dīen → dwa(n) 76.2, 149.c
dīk 44R.1
dītsa 43.b
diunk 52
diurra 117
dochter 73, 110
dōm 139.a
dora → dure

draga → drega
drega 40R, 136, draga 136, dre-
    gen/drein 204.b
driāga 132
driuwa → drīva
drīva, driuwa 131
Drochten 73
dū → thū
duga 144
*dura 145
dure 109, dura 73, durun 205.11,
    dora 73, 205.5
dus 78.2*th*
dūst(slēk) 31
dwā(n) 29, 55, 69, 136, 149.c,
    150, 210, dēde 149.c, (e)dēn
    29, 59, 76.2, 136.a, 149.c,
    dīen 76.2

E
ē- 75
ebba 99.1
edēn → dwā(n)
edze 106
efter 84.5
egge 106
ei 76.2
ēin 37, 76.2, āin (ayn) 37, 76.2
einda 208.6
einde → ende
ēinebern 59
ei-lond 76.2
einde → ende
ek, elk, ellic 96, hec 78.2*h*
elde 107
eldest 118
eldra, aldra 118
ele 46.1
elleva → andlova
emma(n), immen 96
ēn, ān 37, 96, 122, 124
ende 76.4, ēnde 75, 76.4,
    einde 76.4
enēdgad 59
ēnes 125
ēnfald, ēnfaldich 125
ēnich (ēng, aeng, anch, ing)
    37, 96
enōch 59
epen 46, 204.b, epern 206.3
ēr 37, 120, 121, ērest, ār(i)st, 37,
    120, 121
-er(e) 91

ēre 37
erm 40, 100
erra, arra 120
ers 40
erthe 75, 99, ērthe 75, irthe 205.3
erva 99
erve 104
esīn → *sīa
escriuen → skrīva
eskepin → skeppa
etgēr 100
ēth 100, ēthon 205.11
ētsen 44R.2
evangelia, ewangelia 78.2*v*
evel 119, wirra/werra 119, wǐrst/
    wěrst 119
ēvend, ioun 76.2
ev-ēst 31
ēwe, iouwe 76.2, 208.3
ēwelīk 208.3
e-ifnad 59

F
fā → fā(n)
fāch 37
fād 37, 204
fadera 59
falla 73, 137, falt 78.2*th*
famne → fēmne
fā(n) 31R, 55, 136.a, 137.b, 155,
    fenzen 136.a, 137b
fara 130, 136, 152, farande 150,
    farane 150
fat 37
fax 40
feder 40, 63, 64, 110
feithe → fēthe
feld 23, 73, 109, 208.5, fēld 75,
    208.5, field, fiēld 76.2, 208.5,
    211, fiuld 211
fella 73
felo 205.10
fēmne 37, 204.d, famne 37,
    99, 204.d
fenzen → fā
fēr → fir
ferde → ferthe
fere 40, 204.b
ferra → fir 118 or fora 121
ferst, first 66
ferthe, ferde 66
fet 204.a
fethansunu 99R.2

fēthe, feithe 76.2, 206.2
fethere 78.2*th*
fiā 99
fīand 76.2, 111
fiārda 124
fiārdandēl 99R.2
fidiransunu 99R.2
field, fiēld ⟶ feld
fīf 31, 75, 124
finda 133.a, fonden 208.12
finger 100
fiower 124
fīr, fēr 118, 204.b, ferra/firra 118, fīror 118R, fīr(e)st 118
fīre 75
firor ⟶ fīr
firra ⟶ fīr or fora
fisk 66, 73, 204.a
fiuchta 49, 133.b
fiuld ⟶ feld
Fīvel 31
flarde 40
flask 37
fleil 76.2, fleil/flail76.2R
fliā 132
fliāta 132
fliucht(h) 73
-flōka 137.a
flucht 73
fōged 78.1*g*
folghia 207
folgia 78.1*g*, 141
folle ⟶ fule
fon 29
fonden ⟶ finda
fora 121, ferra/firra 121
fordera 133R.3
forieta 135
forma 66, 124
forsmāia 78.1*g*, forsmage 78.1*g*
forth 121, forther/further 121
fōt 113, fēt 113
fōtwirst 66
frāna 99
frāse 37
frede ⟶ frethe
fremma 46
Frēsa 75, Frīsa 75, 205.7
Frēsisk 42
frethe, frede 66
frī 75
friōnd/friūnd 76.2, 111
Frīsa ⟶ Frēsa

fr(i)ūdelf 75R
frōwe 81, 99
fruchte, furchte 66
frūdelf ⟶ fr(i)ūdelf
fule, -a, folle 205.11, 209
furchte ⟶ fruchte
further ⟶ forth

G
gād 37, 44R.1
galga 99
gān 69, 137.a, 149.c, 149R, 150, 210.2
gāra 44R.1
garda 40
gāst 37, 44R.1, gēst 37
gē 78.1*g*
gēia 44R.1
gelden 73, 78.1*g*
genzen 78.1*ng*, 137, 149.c
(-)gēr 'spear' 44R.1, 100
gēr 'year' 78.1*g*
gerne ⟶ ierne
gers 66, 67, 103
gerstel, grestel 66
gēs 31, 113R
gēst ⟶ gāst
gī ⟶ ī
glīda 131
God 78.1*g*, Godi 205.1
gōd 119, goet 208.10, gued 207
goet ⟶ gōd
gold, gōld 75
grāt 115, 116, marra/māra 119, 204.a, māst/mēst 37.b, 119, 121
grava,greva, grouwa 136.a, growt 136.a, bigrowen 136.a
gravia, grāvia 75
grēne 115
grestel ⟶ gerstel
grēte 107
grētene 212
grētman 212
grētwird 212
grēva 99
*grinda 212
grīpa 131
grōia 137.c
grouwa ⟶ grava/greva
growt ⟶ grava
gued ⟶ gōd

gunga 62, 69, 137.a, 149, 149R, 206.5, 210, unga 137.a, 149R, 206.5

H
habba, hebba 141, 153, 208.13, hebbande 205.12
hāch, hāga *adj.* 78.2*ch*, 114, hāgosta 205.14
hāch, hāga *vb.*143R.2, 205.8 ⟶ āga
halda 137.a
half 40, ōther ~, thredda ~ 125
halt 40
hām, hēm 37
hand ⟶ hond
hār 37
harra ⟶ hiā
hat/haet ⟶ hwet
hāud ⟶ hāved
hāved, -w- 76.4, 103, 208.2, hāud 76.4, 208.2
hava, -w-, hāwa, hauwa 76.4
hāwa *vb.* 137.a
hebba ⟶ habba
heer ⟶ here 210.6
heffa 136.b
hei 43.b, 76.2, 101, 101R.1
heia 139.1
heila ⟶ hēla 206.2
heilich ⟶ hēlich
heinde ⟶ hende
hec ⟶ ek
hēl 37
hēla *sb.* 31, 76.2
hēla *vb.* 37.b, 46
hela 134.b
held, hild 208.4
helde 107
hēlich 37, heilich 206.2
helle 106
helpa 73, 130, 133.b, helpe 73
hēm ⟶ hām
hemma(n) ⟶ hia
hemmerke, hemmertse 43.b
henda 139.b
hende, hēnde, heinde 76.2
hengst 204.d
hēr[1] *sb.* 210.6
hēr[2] *sb.* 105
hēr[3] *sb.* 34
hēra 37.b, 46.b
here 73.1, 102, 210.6, hēr(e), heer 210.6, hiri 73.1, 102, 205.4

hēroch 205.2
herte 99, hirte 205.3
hēta 137, hēt 75, hīt 75, 137, 205.7
hī 90
hia 90, 204.c, 221, h(i)ara 90,
     harra 90R.4, him 90, 205.15,
     hiam 90R.2, 205.15,
     hemman, hemmen, himman
     90, 90R.2, hiarem, -em
     90R.2
hi(a)re → hiu
hiaram → hia
hild → held
him → hia
himman → hia
hīr 75, 204.a
hiri → here
hirte → herte
hīt → hēta
hiu 81, 90
hlī 75
hlēd(e)re, hledder/hladder- 66
(h)lāpa 78.2h, 137.a
hlērde → hlēd(e)re
hnekka 78.2h
hnīga 131
hoder → hwether
hof 23, 78.2v, hoves 78.2v, hove,
     howe 208.2
hōf 23, hōwes 78.3w
hok → hwelik
holt 73
hona 29, 69, 99, hoyne 207
hond 29, 109, hand 208.1
hopia 77
horn, hōrn 75, 103
hot → hwet
hove, hoves, howe → hof
hoyne → hona
hrene 78.2h
hrīther 31
hrōpa 137.a
hrūta 132.b
huk, hulk → hwelik
hund(red), hunderd 62, 124
hunige 205.2
hūs 76.11, 78.2z, hūses 78.2z
-hūsera, -hūrsa 66
hwarf 125
hweder 73, 94, 96
hwelik, hwelk, hwek 94, 96,
     208.7, hok 94, 94R, 208.7,
     huk 94

hwet 73, 93, 95, 208.7, hwete
     93R.4, haet, hat, hot 73,
     93R.3, 208.7
hwether 94, 208.7, hweder 73, 94
     hwedder 94, hoder 73, 94,
     94R, hōr 94, 94R
hwona 69
hws 'us' 78.2h, 'house' 207
hwā pron. 78.2h, 93, 93R.4,
     95.3, 96
hwā(n) vb. 31R, 55, 136.a, 137.b
hwāsā 96

I
ī, jī, gī 88
iāhweder, aider 96
iāhwelik 96
iā(n) 135.c
iāta 43.a
ield 23, 43.a, 78.3i, 211, iold 211
ielda 133.b
ieldera 208.5
ielkers 208.5
ielne 208.5
ielren 66, 208.5
iemma(n), iemmen 88, 210.3
iena 86, thī-iena 86
iēr 78.3i
ierne 78.1g, 78.3i, gerne 78.1g
*iersen 66
iest 43.a, 78.3, 108
ieva 76.2, 78.2v, 78.3, 135.c,
     iewa 76.2, 78.2v, io(u)wa
     76.2, 135.a
ieve 105, iouwe 208.3
ifestnad 79
ik 87
ing → ēnich
inna, in(ne)ra, inrest 120
ioun → ēvend
io(u)wa → ieva
iouwe 'law' → ēwe
iouwe 'gift' → ieve
iouwelīk → ēwelīk
irthe → erthe
īsern, īrsen 66
Israheleska, Irsa- 66
ita 131, 131R.2
*iugel 52
*iukel 52
*iunk(er) 52
iung 73, 78.3i
*Iunga, Jonga 52

iunger 116
iungosta 205.14
iūwe 92

J
jāmer(lik) 75
'Jorwert breaking' 76.2, 131, 135.c,
     136.a, 208.3

K
kairs(like), kaiser 66
kald 40
kanna → kenna
kāp 37, 44R.1, 75
kēi 44R.1, 76.2, 204.d, 222
keisere 76.2
kemen 204.b
kempa 73, 98, 99
kempth → kuma
ken 27, 104, kennes 104
keni(n)g 44, 47, 78.1ng, 100,
     kini(n)g 73, 78.1ng, 205.4
kenna 73
kera → kerva
kere 46, 64, 108, kerre 209
kersoma → krisma
Kerst → Crist
kerva 133.b, kera 133R.3
kessa 46
kest 73, 108
kētha 31, 46.b, 75, 139.a–c,
     kette 139.b–c
kēthere 212
kette → kētha
kī → kū
kiāsa 64, 132.1, tziāsa 132.a
kind 112
kini(n)g → keni(n)g
klage 105, 105R
klāth 37, 75, 112, klēth 37, 112
klinna 133.a
knī 75
kniucht 49
koma → kuma
kōmen → kuma
komp 29, 73
konna → kunna
kriāpa, krūpa 132R.1
criōce, criūce 76.2
krisma, kersoma 66
Crist, cristen, Kerst,
     kersten 66
kū 113, 113R.2, kī (PL.) 113,
     kūna 113R.2

kŭde → kunna
kuith → kŭth
kuma 73, 134.a, 134R.1, 205.5,
    koma 73, 134R.1, 205.5,
    kempth 78.1 p kōmen 29,
    kemen 204.b
kŭna → kŭ
kunna 145, 188, konna 188,
    kŭde 31
kŭth 31, 75, 139.a, kuith 207
kwinka 133.1

L
lāf 37
lam → lom
lamelsa 66
land → lond
lāre 37
lāsta → lēsta
lāva (PL.) 37
lēda 37.b, 139.b
ledza 139.d
leeg → lidza
leith → lēth adj.
leith → lidza
lēn 108
len(d)ze 43.b, 107
leng 121, langest 120, lengest
    120, 121
lēs 121
lēsa 37
les(se)ra → lītik
lēst/lērest → lītik
lēsta, lāsta 37
lēta 137.a, līt 73, 137.a, 205.7
lēth adj. 76.2, leith 76.2
letha → lith
lētsa 44R.2
letsen → lŭka
lēven, liouwen 76.2
līa → lītha
liā 132R.3
liâcht 37.c
liāf 37.c, 208.8
liāga 132.a
-liāsa 132.a
libba 76.2, 141, livath 76.2, liu-
    wath 76.2
lidza 135.b, 135R.1, leith 135R.1,
    205.6, līth 75, 135R.1, 205.6,
    leeg 135R.1
līf 207, lyf 207, liuwes 76.2
liōde → liŭde

liouwen → lēven
līt → lēta
lith 73, 205.5 letha 73, 205.5,
    letha 73
līth → lidza
lītha 76R.1, 131, 131R.4, līa
    76R.1, 131R.4
lītik, min(ne)ra, min(ne)st;
    les(se)ra, lēst/lērest 119
lītsa 44R.2
liŭde, liōde 37.c, 46.c, 75, 76.2,
    205.2, lŭde 75
liuwath → libba
liuwes → līf
livath → libba
lom 29, lam 208.1
lond 40, 75, lōnd 75, land 208.1
long 29, 73, 118
longe 121
lŭde → liŭde
luīte → wlīte
lŭka 44R.2, 132.b, letsen
    44R.2, 132.b
lungern 206.3
lyf → līf

M
ma 96
makia 41, 154, 221, makiande 150,
    makiane 150
*mala 212
man → mon
mā(r)/mēr → grāt
māra 204.a
marra/māra → grāt
māst/mēst → grāt
măster(e) 37.b
mēde¹ 76.4, meide 76.4, 206.2
mēde² 106
mele 104
mēn, mein 76.4, 206.2
mendza 43.b, 78.1ng
merch 40
merk 49R.4
meta 135.a, mete 209
mēta 139.b, mēte 209, mette
    139.b, 209
mete 108
mette → mēta
mīa → mītha
miâ 137.c
mīn 92
min, min(n)era, min(ne)st 121

mītha 76R.2, 131, mīa
    76R.1, 131R.4
*miuchs/*miux 49, 76
mōder 63, 110
mōdiransunu 99R.2
molne, monle 66
mon 73, 81, 113, man 88, 113, 208.1
mōna 29, 75
mōnandei 99R.2
mōnath 29, 100
monle → molne
morder 102R
muga 147, mugun 205.11
mund 100
mŭth 31, 75

N
nacht 40, 73
nā(h)wet, nāut 76.4
nān → nēn
nas 40
nāt 58, 59
nāut → nā(h)wet
nēdle, nēlde 66
nēi 76.4, 118, 121, nī 121, niār 118,
    121, nēst 118, 121
nēlde → nēdle
nema → nima
nēn, nān 37
nera 27R, 131.a
nēst → nēi
nētha 31
nēthe 105
neva 99
nī 75, 78.1g, nīge 78.1g
niār → nēi
niāta 132
nīge → nī
ni(u)gentich, (t)ni(u)gentich
    124, 124
nima 73, 130, 134.a, nimpth 78.1p,
    nema 73, 134R.1, nōmen 29
niugen 52, 76.3, 124, 204.a
nōch 59
noma 99
nōmen → nima
north 75, 120, nōrth 75
nose 109
*nōth 31

O
ōftne → āfte
olcnum 78.3w

ōlle → al(l)
ōlsā → alsā
on 29
onderd → ondward
onderk 78.3*w*
ondlete 78.3*w*
Ondreus 29R.2
ondser 78.3*w*
ondward, onderd 78.3*w*
ōne 29, 75
ongost 29
on- 209.12 → un-
opa → upa
opgrouwa 208.3
ōr → ōther
orda, ōrda 75
*ōs(e) 31
ōther 31, 78.2*th*, 96, 124, 124R.5,
    125, ōr 78.2*th*, 96

P
panni(n)g 78.1*ng*, penning 100
pāl 34, 75, pēl 34, 75
paus, pāgus, pāwes 78.1*g*
pīne 75
plicht 49R.2
*pliucht 49
prōgia, prōvia 78.1*g*
progost, provest 78.1*g*

Q
quetha 135.a, quān 135.c

R
rād 37, 62, 204.a
rāp 37, 204.a
rēda 137.a
rēdieva 99, 212
reid 76.4
reka 135.a, ritsen 135.a
rēka → rētsa
renna 133.a, runna 133.a
resta 139.b
resten(e) 210.6
rētsa, rītsia, rēka 139.a, 140
riāka 132
rīda 69, 75, 128R.1, 130, 131R.4
ridder 102R
rīke, rītse 44R.2
ritsen → reka
riucht 49, 76.3, 103, 204.a
riuchter(e) 102R
ruald, rwald → wrald
ruēka → wrēka

ruist → wrist
runna → renna
ruōgia → wrōgia
Rüstring *a*-mutation 134R.1,
    143.1, 205.5
Rüstring vowel balance 23, 100R.8,
    103R, 130R, 205.1–2

S
sā 78.3*w*
sā hwāsā 96
salla → sella
salt 40
sān 29
sang → song
satta → setta
sāver, sēver 37
sawen, sawn, saun, sowen 124,
    205.9, sogen 78.1*g*, 124,
    si(u)gun 52, 53R.2, 78.1*g*,
    124, 205.9
sawentich, saun-, tsawentich,
    tsaun- 124R.5
sax 40
schela → skela
schetten → skiāta
secht 49R.2, 50R.2
secht → sēka
sedza 43.b, 139.a, 139.d, 141
sēft(e) 31, 46.b, 75
sege 105
seil 43.c
seinda → senda
sēka 78.1*k*, 139.a, 140, sētsa 140,
    secht 78.1*k*
seke 105
sēkense, sēknisse 66
sela → skela
self 78.3*w*, selwis 78.3*w*
sella 46.a, 73, 139.a, 139.b, 211,
    salla 211, solla 211
senda 139.b, sente/sante 139.b,
    seinda 208.6
sendza, sandza 139.a, senka 139.a
serk 40, 49R.4
sētsa → sēka
setta 27, 46, 139.a, 139.b, 204.a,
    210.5, 211, satta 211, sette
    210.5, setton 205.11, sotta 211
sēver → sāver
sex 49R.3, 124, sexta 49R.3, 124
sexasum 125
sextich 49R.3, 124
*sīa 131, sīth 131, esīn 131

siā(n) 50R.1, 55.1, 69, 76.1, 135.c,
    150, 210, siuch, siuchst,
    siucht 49, 50, 50R.1, 56, 135.c
siātha 132
sibbe *adj.* 115, 117
sibbe *sb.* 106
sīe → wesa
sigun → sawen
sīn 90
sine 106
sinuwerdene 106
siochte → siuchte
sīth 31, 75
sīth → *sīa
sitta 73, 135.b
siuch, siuchst, siucht → siā(n)
siuchte, siochte 49, 50R.2
si(u)gun- → sawen
*siuka 52
siunga, sionga 52, 76.3, 133R.1
skecht → skeka
skeka 78.1*k*, skecht 78.1*k*
skela, skila, schela, sela 146,
    skilun 205.1
skeld, schild 208.4, skild 73,
    skelta(ta) 37.a, 99
skenza 43.b
skēp 34, 103
skeppa 136.b, eskepen 59
skera 134.b
skīa(n) 135.c
skiāta 132.a, schetten 207, 209
skild → skeld
Skilinge 78.1*ng*
skilun → skela
skīna 131R.3
skip 42, 103, skipu 205.1
skīta 131
skouwa → skūva
skrīva 76.2, 78.2*v*, 131, 208.3,
    skrīwa 76.2, 208.3, skriouwa
    76.2, 131, skrēf 78.2*v*, escri-
    uen 59
skrīver(e) 104
skūva 76.4, 132.b, skouwa 76.4
slā(n) 40, 40R, 75, 136.c,
    slōgon 205.11
slēpa 137.a
slīta 131
sliucht 49
slōgon → slā(n)
slūta 132.b
smel 40
smere 104

snethe 78.2*th*, 128R.2 snede
  208.11, snē 78.2*th*, 208.11,
  snei 208.11
snītha 76R.1, 128R.2, 131,
  131R.1, 131R.4, 208.11, snīa
  76R.1, 131R.4, 208.11
sochte 73
sogen ⟶ sawen
soldīe 77R.1
solle ⟶ sella
sompnia 78.1*p*
sond 208.12
sōne 75, 105
song 40, sang 208.1
sonne ⟶ sunne
sōth 31
sotta ⟶ setta
spada 99
-spǎtze, -spētze 37, 44R.2
spere 108
spīa137.c
spindel 78.1*d*R
*spiucht 49
*spōn 29n
spreka 135.a, spritzen 135.a
sprūta 132.b
sprētse 33.b
stā(n) 69, 135.c, 135R.2, 136.a,
  149, 149R, 150, 210, stēn
  136.a, 149.c
standa 136.a, stonda 136.a,
  149, 149R
stavia, stāwia, stouwia 76.4
stede 108, 210.6, stēd, steed 210.6
stef 40, 73, 204.a
steka 135.a, stetsen, stitzen 135.a
stela 130, 134.b
stēn *sb.* 37, 75, 100, 204.a
stēn *vb.* ⟶ stā(n)
steppa 136.b
stera ⟶ sterva
stereke ⟶ tser(e)ke
sterk 40, 49R.4
stert, stirt 73
sterva 78.2*v*, 133.b, 133R.3, stera
  78.2*v*, 133R.3
stēta 137.a, stet 155.6
stetsen/stitzen ⟶ steka
sthereke ⟶ tserke
stirt ⟶ stert
stīth 31
*stiunka 52
stiurke ⟶ tserke
stonda ⟶ standa

stonde 208.12
stoppia 77.b
stouwia ⟶ stavia
strēte 34, 75
strīda 139.b
strīka, stritsen 131R.5
sum 96
sune 109, sunu 205.1
sunne 73, 99, sonne 73,
  sunnan- 69, 99R.2
suster 110, swester 110
sūth 31, 120, sūther, sūthrost 120
swart 40
swera 27R, 136.b
swester ⟶ suster
swerd, swērd 75
swēte 115
swīthe 31
szurke, tsyureke, tszurke
  ⟶ tser(e)ke

T

tachtich, achtich 124R.5
tāker 37
tāne 37, 99
tār 40, 55.3
tefle, tiōle 78.2*v*
tegotha 31R, 124R.2
*tēi 31
tein 132, 204.b
tele 40, 105, 204.b
tēth ⟶ tōth
teyken ⟶ tēken 207
thā 37, 84, 221
thā(m) 37, 84, thām 84R.4
thē *rel.* 95.4
thēr *rel.* 95.2, 204.c
thek 40
thendza, thantsa, thinka 73,
  139.a, 140, thōchte 31
thet 78.2*th*, 84, 95
thetsa 140
thī, thiu, thet 84
thiāf 37.c, 208.8, tiēf 208.8
thiānia, tyennya 78.2*th*, 208.8,
  tiēne 208.8
thigia 131R.3
thī-iena ⟶ iena
thīn 88
thin(d)ze ⟶ thing100R.2
thindz(i)a 140, thuchte 73
thing 100R.2, 103, thin(d)ze,
  thinge 100R.2
thinka ⟶ thendsa

this 85
thiuchsel 52
thiukke 52, 204.a
thōchte ⟶ thendza
thoe 207 ⟶ tō
thorp 62
thredda half 125
threft 66
*thretsa, thritsa 44R.2, 140
threttīne, -ēn(e) 124
thria 124, 125
thrim(m)ine 125
thrimdēl 125
thrimenath 125
thrina 69, 204.a
thrirasum 125
thritich 124, triuchtich 50R.2
thriu 122
thriuch ⟶ thruch
thruch 66, 67, thriuch 49R.1
thrē 122, 124
thrīfald 125
thū 88, 88R.3
thūchte ⟶ thindz(i)a 73
thunder, thuner 78.1*d*R
thur(v)a 66, 145
thūsend 124
thweres 57
thwinga 133.a
thwong 29
tiēf ⟶ thiāf
tiā(n) 132.a, 150
tiān '10' 50R.1, 55, 69, 76.1, 124
tiānspatse 44R.2
tiēne ⟶ thiāna
til 84R.5
tiōle ⟶ tefle
tīt 208.10
tiūch 108
tiuche 49, 78.2*ch*, 204.a
tni(o)gentich 124
tolef ⟶ twelef
tontich ⟶ twentich
tōskeldeia 66
tōth 31, 113, tēth 31, 113
trǎst 37
treda 135.a
triuchtich ⟶ thritich
triūwe, trē(u)w- 76.1
tser(e)ke 44R.1, 49R.4, ts(i)erke
  206.4, stereke 78.2/ts/,
  sthereke 49, 206.4,
  tsiurke 49R.3, 76.1,
  173, 206.4, tsyureke

78.2, tszurke 78.2/ts/,
  szurke 78.2/ts/
tserl 43.a, tsirl 73
*tsēse, tsīse 44
tsiāk 43.a
ts(i)erke → tserke
ts(i)etel 44
tsin 43.a
tsirl → tserl
(t)si(u)gentich 124
tsiurke → tser(e)ke
tsīve 43.a
turve, ture 78.2v
tusk 204.d
twā 37, 122, 124
twādēl 125
twēde 125
twēdnath 125
twelef 73, 124, tolef 73,
  124R.6, 208.7
twelvasum 96
twēn(e), twēr 122
twentich, twintich 124,
  124R.6
twintich → twentich
twīa 125
twīdubel 125
twīfald(-ich) 125
twīna 125
twiska 69
tyennya → thiānia
twīrasum 125
tziāsa → kiāsa

U

ulle 78.3w
undad 78.3w
unebern 59
unefoch 59
unewaxen 59
unewis 59
unidelt, unedeld 59
unga → gunga
unwald 59
unwis 59
upa 73, opa 73
upwretsa 44R.2
urde 78.3w

urderva 133.b
ūs 31
ūse 92
ūser 66, 87, ūrse 66
ūte, ūt(e)ra, ūt(e)rost 120

V

vaxet → waxa
vinna → winna

W

wāch 37, 204.a
wada 136.a
wald, wāld, wōld(sket) 109, 206.6
walda 137.a
walla 136.a
warm 40
was → wesa
wasa → wesa
wāsande 37
wax 40
waxa 136.a, vaxet 78.2v
wega 135.a
wei 43.c, 76.4, 101, 101R.2, wī 75,
  101, 205.6, wīe 76R.1, 101R.2
wein 40, 43.c, 44
weisa → wesa
wel 121
weld, wild 208.4
wella, willa 149
wēna 46.b
wēpa 137.a
wēpen 103, wēpern 206.3
wēpenia, wēpen(a/e)d,
  wēpena/e 210.4
werand 111
wēren → wesa
werk 49R.4
werka 66, 140, wir(t)za 140, 208.4
werpa 133.b
wērs, wārs 66, 204.d
wertha 62, 64, 78.2th, 133.b,
  wirda 208.4, wurden 62
wesa 149.b, wasa 211, weisa 207,
  wessa 209, was, nas 40,
  wēren 64, sīe 76R.1
wēsa 37

west 120
wēt 204.d
weta, wetande → wita
weter 40, 103
Wetsens, Wetsinge 100R.2
wī pron. 87
wī → wei
wīa 137.c
wicht 49R.2
wid(w)e 99
wīe → wei
wīf 81, 207, wiif 207
wīgand 111
wike, wikun 205.11
wild → weld
willa 99R.1
willa vb. → wella
winna 133.a, vinna 78.2v
wird → word
wirda → wertha
wirra/werra → evel
wīrst/wērst → evel
wirtle 208.4
wir(t)za → werka
wita 142, 143, witane 73, 205.2,
  weta 143R.1, wetande 73,
  143R.1, 205.2
with 84R.5
witsing 100
wlīte 78.3w
wlīte, luīte 66
wōld(sket) → wald
word 103, wird 208.4
wrāk 37
wrald, ruald, rwald 66
wreka 135.a
wrēka, ruēka 66
wretsa 140
wrichta 66
wrist, ruist 66
wrīta 131
wrocht 66
wrōgia, ruōgia 66
wulf, wolf 73
wunde, wund 105
wurden → wertha

MODERN FRISIAN FORMS

Modern East Frisian
aller [Saterl.] 78.1*d*R
brom [Saterl.] 29
djunk [Wang.] 52
fiir [Wang.] 204.b
gäärs [Saterl.] 67
jäärsene [Saterl.] 66
(iis-)juukel [Wang.] 52
juugel [Wang.] 52
mjux [Saterl.] 49
niuugn [Wang.] 52
schiräck [Wurst.] 49R.4
serk [Saterl.] 49R.4
siuugn [Wang.] 52
sjiriik [Wang.] 49R.4
spilne [Saterl.] 78.1*d*R
stjúnk [Wang.] 52
thiuksel [Wang.] 49
thuuner [Wang.] 78.1*d*R
ton'yhr [Wurst.]
truch [Saterl.] 67
zierck [Emsingo] 49R.4

Modern Low German
(Frisian substratum)
bûs-dör 31, 75R.3
sjoekzaand 52
spōn(e) 29

Mainland North Frisian
bousem [Ock.] 31
gaeis [Ock.] 31

geers [Hall.] 67
goasem [Ock.] 37
goasen [Ock.] 37
goos [Wied.] 31
grüne [Mor.] 212
jöögel [Mor.] 52
jonk [Ock.] 52
(an-)jörsene [Mor.] 66
junk [Mor.] 52
ous [Ock.] 31
schörk [Wied.] 49R.3
sjoksand [Ock.] 52
spoon [Wied.] 29
toi [Ock.] 31
tjuksele [Mor.] 49

Island North Frisian
fiir [Amr.] 204.b
jonk [Föhr] 52
jügel [Sylt] 52
njoks [Föhr] 49
sark [Föhr-Amr.] 49R.4
seerk [Sylt] 49R.4
sjocht [Amr.] 49, 50R.2
sjok [Amr.] 52
sjong [Föhr-Amr.] 52
sjucht [Sylt] 50R.2
spuun [Sylt] 29
troch [Amr.] 52
tuner [Mor.] 78.1*d*R

Modern West Frisian
boas-doar 31, 75R.3
Br(j)ucht 49

died 34
fier 204.b
fiif 31
gers 67
gies 31
goes 31, 208.1
hier 34
hof 23
hôf 23
jûkel 52
mealle 212
mjoks 49
moal 104R.2
njoggen 52
noed 31
oes 31
pjocht 49
rier 31
sjocht(e) 49, 49R.2
Sjonge 52
skiep 34
skowe 76.4
Skylge 78.1*ng*
smoar 104R.2
spjucht 49
spoan 29, 75R.3
spoen 29, 75R.3
stjonke 52
taai 31
tonger 78.1*d*R
troch 67
tsjerke 49R.3
tsjok 52
tsjoksel 49